The Anime Machine

The Anime Machine

A Media Theory of Animation

THOMAS LAMARRE

University of Minnesota Press
Minneapolis
London

Part I reworks material previously published in "From Animation to Anime: Drawing Movements and Moving Drawings," in *Between Cinema and Anime*, special issue of *Japan Forum* 14, no. 2 (2002): 329–67, and "The Multiplanar Image," *Mechademia 1: Emerging Worlds of Anime and Manga* (Minneapolis: University of Minnesota Press, 2006), 120–44. Part II includes sections based on "Otaku Movement," in *Japan after Japan: Rethinking the Nation in an Age of Recession*, ed. Tomiko Yoda and H. D. Harootunian (Durham, N.C.: Duke University Press, 2006), 358–94. Part III reworks an argument initially presented in "Platonic Sex," *animation: an interdisciplinary journal* 1, no. 1 (2006): 45–60 and 2, no. 1 (2007): 9–25.

Published by the University of Minnesota Press
111 Third Avenue South, Suite 290
Minneapolis, MN 55401-2520
http://www.upress.umn.edu

Library of Congress Cataloging-in-Publication Data

Lamarre, Thomas
    The anime machine : a media theory of animation / Thomas Lamarre.
      p.   cm.
    Includes bibliographical references and index.
    ISBN 978-0-8166-5154-2 (hc : alk. paper) — ISBN 978-0-8166-5155-9 (pb : alk. paper)
    1. Animated films—Japan—History and criticism.   I. Title.   II. Title: Media theory of animation.
    NC1766.J3L36 2009
    791.43'340952—dc22

                                          2009026475

Printed in the United States of America on acid-free paper

The University of Minnesota is an equal-opportunity educator and employer.

16 15 14 13 12 11 10   10 9 8 7 6 5 4 3

The damming of the stream of real life,
the moment when its flow comes to a standstill, makes itself felt as reflux:
this reflux is astonishment.

—Walter Benjamin, *What Is Epic Theater?*

CONTENTS

PREFACE

THIS BOOK PRESENTS A THEORY OF ANIMATION, unabashedly centered on Japanese animations, which are commonly particularized and grouped under the loose heading "anime" or even "Japanimation." At the same time, this book is about "how to read anime." In fact, it was the difficulties that I confronted trying to read anime that led me in the direction of animation theory.

When I began teaching courses on Japanese mass culture in the early 1990s, not only were there few Japanese animation titles available on video with subtitles but also research on animation and anime was relatively rare. In the course of the 1990s, the situation changed dramatically. Animation surged on a number of fronts with the rise of digital animation; the increasing use of computer imagery in films; tie-ins and overlaps between video games, film, and animation; and, needless to say, the global boom in popularity of Japanese animations, launched in part through the exchange of VHS copies among fans internationally and then spurred with the rise of the Internet and file sharing. Research on anime has appeared in the wake of this surge in the popularity of Japanese animations, coeval with a new awareness of the ubiquity and centrality of animation. It is not surprising, of course, that research and scholarship follow cultural booms. It is the nature of criticism to follow, and the question of criticism is how to follow and where to intervene in the flow.

What has surprised me about research on Japanese animations and anime is the general lack of interest in animation as such, in animation as *moving images*. The bulk of anime commentary ignores that its "object" consists of moving images, as if animations were just another text. Such a treatment of anime as a textual object has tended in two directions. On the one hand, even when anime is treated largely as text, some commentators will call on the novelty and popularity of anime to bypass the tough questions that usually arise around the analysis of texts. Anime is, in effect, treated as a textual object that does not or cannot pose any difficult textual questions. Analysis is relegated to re-presenting anime narratives, almost in the manner of book reports or movie reviews. On the other hand, some commentators treat anime as text in order to pose "high textual" speculative questions (such as the nature of reality, or the relation of mind and body), again ignoring the moving image altogether but for different reasons. In this kind of textual treatment, the anime stories serve as the point of departure for philosophical speculation, without any consideration of the materiality of animation. A third common approach bypasses textual questions and the materiality of animation in favor of sociological and anthropological readings: anime is a source of information about Japan, especially about Japanese youth.

Even though I think all these approaches have their place and their merits, it is nevertheless in response to the tendency to bypass questions about animation and the moving image in favor of textual description, metatextual speculation, or sociological analysis that I wish to focus greater attention on "how to read anime." Yet I do not want to present a list of elements for formal analysis in the manner of David Bordwell and Kristin Thompson's *Film Art*, with sections and chapters devoted to lighting, sound, narrative, color, shots, takes, and editing. While such a presentation is useful, it tends to eliminate a sense of what is at stake in approaching the moving image at the level of form to begin with. Rather than rely on formal analysis as a point of departure, I thus begin with the materiality of the moving image itself. Building on the philosophy of technology, film theory, and art history, I gravitate toward questions that initially arose in film studies in the context of apparatus theory and the specificity thesis. While film studies has largely abandoned apparatus theory and the specificity thesis due to their implications of technological determinism and historical teleology, I feel that underlying questions about materiality and material or technical determination remain urgent. Ultimately, in my efforts to look at the material and technical specificity of animation while avoiding the determinism implicit in apparatus theory and specificity thesis of film theory, I have adopted the stance of experimental science and technology studies, which encouraged me to look at technologies of the moving image from the angle of their force.

In sum, the question of "how to read anime" led me to questions about the material and technical specificity of animation that lie prior to any elaboration of animation form. I found it necessary to ground my reading of animations in a theory of animation based on its materiality, that is, on the material essence or force within its technical determinations. As a consequence, rather than provide a list or catalog of formal features of animation or anime, I look at animations from the angle of how they work and how they work on the world. I give priority to function and value over form.

Because my emphasis is on animation as such, I look at anime primarily with an eye to technical determination and technical value, rather than beginning with socioeconomic determinations and values. I focus on what animation is, how it works, and how it brings value into the world. Of course, it is impossible and not at all desirable to dispense with economic or social considerations, and indeed, throughout the book, I consider some of the implications of the "anime machine" for reception or interaction, distribution, and production, which are summarized in the Conclusion in the spirit of offering thought for further research. Yet I insistently place the emphasis on the materiality and specificity of animation in this book because it seems to me that if there is nothing there, nothing to animation, then there would be no way for power to work there and no way for us to consider what happens between, for instance, the "anime machine" and the "production machine" or any other determinants. The result is a book with an emphasis on "how anime thinks technology" rather than on how anime thinks Japan, or how studios make anime, or how fans interact with anime. Such an emphasis is intended as much as a critical intervention into animation studies and Japan studies as a contribution to knowledge about Japanese animation.

As with any book, this one has benefited greatly from discussions with friends, colleagues, and students. Conversations with colleagues in Montreal especially have had a profound impact, and I thank Brian Bergstrom, Peter Button, Ken Dean, Hajime Nakatani, Tom Looser, Erin Manning, Brian Massumi, Anne McKnight, Xin Wei Sha, and especially Livia Monnet, as well as those students whose interests and ideas frequently sparked mine: Lawrence Bird, Inhye Kang, Gyewon Kim, Heather Mills, Harumi Osaki, and Marc Steinberg.

This project also benefited from discussions with friends and colleagues in Japan, and I owe thanks to Kotani Mari, Nakagawa Shigemi, Tatsumi Takayuki, and Ueno Toshiya, as well as my friends Tsuzura Junji and Narita Makoto. In the course of translating essays by Kotani Mari and Ōtsuka Eiji and supervising a translation of Azuma Hiroki for *Mechademia*, I found myself drawn deeper into their way of looking at manga, anime, and fans, and I am indebted to them for their patience and generosity in matters of translation. I am particularly indebted to Ueno Toshiya, not only as a constant source of theoretical inspiration but also for his efforts in arranging encounters with Ōtsuka Eiji and Oshii Mamoru.

The Anime Machine: A Media Theory of Animation builds on previously published essays (which were initially conceived as chapters for a book), so I would like to acknowledge the readers of those essays, as well as Anne Allison, Christopher Bolton, Markus Nornes, and Tomiko Yoda, who offered advice on the initial draft for this book. As I began to unpack the essays into the chapters of this book as originally planned, I found that, to address the underlying questions about the specificity of animation and technology, I had to excise half the material and thoroughly restructure and rewrite the other material. This led to delays in revision, and above all I owe thanks to my editor, Jason Weidemann, for patience and unrelenting support. I am also grateful for research support from the Social Sciences and Humanities Research Council of Canada and the William Dawson Scholarship at McGill University.

Finally, because this book would have come to nothing without Christine and Alex, I dedicate it to them.

THE ANIME MACHINE

AS THE EXPRESS TRAIN TO NARITA AIRPORT speeds through a tunnel, a series of images flashes by outside the train, silhouettes of a human figure sketched in neon lights on the dark wall of the tunnel. The speed of the train allows travelers to see an animation—a figure in light dancing outside their window. The speeding train produces animation in the same way that the speed of frames of celluloid film produces movement as they spool through a projector. But in this instance it is the movement of the viewer not the movement of the film that transforms the series of static images into a moving picture.

So much has been written about the profound connections between trains and cinema that it might seem odd to begin a book on anime with this example of "animation by train." The train–cinema interface is almost paradigmatic of the modern, and discussions of it usually focus on the late nineteenth and early twentieth century, with an emphasis on early cinema and silent cinema.[1] In an earlier historical context, train–cinema interfaces were decidedly novel, but they may feel old-fashioned and somewhat inappropriate in the context of Japanese animations or anime. There is a tendency to think of anime as belonging to a newer world of technology.

Much of anime is, however, unabashedly low tech. Its novelty does not derive from its use of cutting-edge technologies of imaging per se (such as computer-generated imagery and digital animation). Rather it is the dynamism of interactions that arise between viewers and animations that makes for the novelty of anime. In fact, what happens between anime and its viewers is so dynamic that *viewers* seems a somewhat outdated and passive term to describe a situation in which "viewing" may cross into conventions, fanzines, amateur manga production (*dōjinshi*), cosplay (costume play), and fansubbing. There is also the dynamism of a culture industry that entails crossover or tie-in productions in the form of manga, light novels, character franchises, toys, music, video games, and other merchandise. An anime series or film might thus be thought of as the nodal point in a *transmedial network* that entails proliferating series of narrative and nonnarrative forms across media interfaces and platforms, such as the computer, television, movie theater, and cell phone. So dynamic and diverse are the worlds that unfold around anime that we do better to think always in the plural, in terms of *animations*.

The Japanese animations that are loosely grouped under the term *anime* entail an exceedingly vast range of media platforms, aesthetic conventions, and fan activities; they are today distributed or circulated transnationally and, with increasing frequency, are also produced transnationally. Although some anime foreground the use of new technologies of animation production (they look high tech), the appeal of anime lies not primarily in high-tech or high-budget production. Many anime are decidedly low tech in their execution, in their look and feel. This low-tech feel does not, however, imply a lack of technical sophistication. Nor does low-tech production prevent high-tech interfaces—on the contrary. The novelty of anime comes in part from their ability to cross between ostensibly low-tech and high-tech situations, to the point that it becomes impossible to draw firm distinctions between low and high tech. Similarly, it is difficult in the context of anime to draw a line between high culture and low culture, or between avant-garde experimentation and mass culture industries. Anime tend to unfurl anime worlds or anime cultures that blur the boundary between production and reception, with fans participating enthusiastically in the dissemination of products and in the transformation of media and narrative worlds.

If I open with the scenario of animation by train, it is partly because I wish to establish a dialogue between the contemporary "postmodern" world of anime and the "modern" world of train/cinema—a dialogue that will take place at the level of *thinking technology*. In the course of this book, I will gradually begin to use the term *postmodern* and will even apply the prefix *post-* to a number of other phenomena, as variedly abstract as post-Heideggerian thinking, post-Lacanian viewing, or the post-action-image. Yet at the outset it is crucial to point out that I do not think of the postmodern in terms of a break with the modern, as what comes after the modern. Rather I propose that we think the postmodern as a situation in which the modern appears at once intractable yet indefensible, neither easy to dismiss nor available for redemption. It is rather like the steady expansion and intensification of commuter train lines in Tokyo: through continued privatization, informatization, and acceleration, the contemporary train is no longer what it was, and yet it does not, for all that, present a resolute break with the past. Like the commuter train, the technical sophistication of Japanese animations—especially apparent in their manner of thinking technology—does not rely on or shore up a familiar series of dubious oppositions or ruptures between low and high, between old and new, or between modern and postmodern. And so I begin with trains not merely because they are ubiquitous in contemporary Japan, crisscrossing and stitching together the metropolitan areas, or because they frequently crop up in Japanese animations.[2] I begin with trains to argue (by analogy) that animations can be thoroughly postmodern technically (digitalized, localized, privatized, accelerated) yet not present an opposition to or a break with the modern. I begin with trains also because they have become such an important focus for analysis of the impact of technology on perception, which provides a good point of departure for my discussion of how anime thinks technology.

The impact of speed on perception is especially prevalent in discussions of modernity and trains. In his classic study *The Railway Journey*, Wolfgang Schivelbusch stresses how the "train was experienced as a projectile, and traveling on it, as being shot through the landscape—thus losing control of one's senses."[3] He discovers that, initially, velocity made perception impossible, unimaginable. There were too many visual impressions coming too rapidly. Schivelbusch then finds, however, that travelers rapidly learned to accommodate themselves to looking at things at high speeds. On the one hand, another kind of perception developed— panoramic perception. Because velocity blurred the foreground, travelers began to take a broader view of the landscape, gaining a sense of separation from it, looking at the countryside as if upon a distant and exotic land, no matter how ordinary its features. Schivelbusch concludes that "panoramic perception, in contrast to traditional perception, no longer belonged to the same space as the perceived objects: the traveler saw the objects, landscapes, etc. *through* the apparatus which moved him through the world."[4]

On the other hand, Schivelbusch notes, "the dissolution of reality and its resurrection as panorama thus became agents for the total emancipation from the traversed landscape: the traveler's gaze could then move into an imaginary surrogate landscape, that of the book."[5] Finding it difficult to perceive things at high speed, travelers turned their eyes away from the window and onto books. Or, more precisely, they learned to shift their attention freely back and forth between the train window and book, between the distanced landscape beyond the train and the pages of their books with descriptions and depictions of other times and places. "Reading while traveling became almost obligatory."[6] Booksellers started to establish stalls in railway stations. Schivelbusch's account suggests that new modes of consumption follow directly from traveling at speed: there is an attempt to fill in, or compensate for, the perceptual rupture that rose between the modern traveler and the world.

If we jump from the modern world of Schivelbusch's trains to the world of contemporary Tokyo, so often purported to be postmodern, to consider the proliferation of kiosks in train stations with manga, newspapers, magazines as well as snacks, drinks, gadgets, incidentals, etc., such items make sense in a new way, as does the interconnection of department stores and train lines in Japan. It has become common to think of new communications technologies—ranging from technological devices such as computers and mobile phones, to infrastructures of the Internet and satellite communications, and to entertainments and software (video games, Microsoft Windows, etc.)—in terms of the speed and ubiquity of connection and transmission. And indeed today's traveler or commuter is as likely to devote her attention to a Game Boy, manga, or mobile phone with Internet connection as to a novel, newspaper, or magazine. Yet in light of Schivelbusch's account of how the proliferation of goods around trains comes in part from the impact of new technologies on perception, as a massive compensation for the perceptual uneasiness induced by speed, the postmodern world of information technologies and media mix does not feel like a break with the modern. The postmodern feels like an intensification of potentials incipient in the modern, with Japanese animations making an appearance where these different interfaces intersect and diverge again. Anime appear as a nodal point in information-rich wired environments with multiple media interfaces, as if somehow filling in the gaps generated by the layers of acceleration, of speeding up and slowing down, which make up the rhythms of everyday life as a perpetual commuter.

It might seem more appropriate in the context of anime to begin with computers, with questions about computer screens with multiple windows, and in fact I do look at the interconnection between anime and information technologies later in this book. Yet I open with the train because the questions about speed and perception raised in Schivelbusch's account of modernity strike me as the crucial ones for thinking about anime. Schivelbusch encourages us to situate reading, viewing, or gaming (the reader/text, viewer/anime, or user/game interfaces) within a world of circulation based on technologies of speed. Actually, he goes a step further, positing *ballistics* or *projectile motion* as the basic condition for modern modes of perception. The traveler is first and foremost a projectile. Ballistics—typified in the *bullet*—is the basic technological condition that emerges in Schivelbusch's account of the train. It is also captured nicely in the English nickname for Japan's high-speed Shinkansen train: the bullet train. For Schivelbusch the traveler is like a bullet.

In contrast to Schivelbusch's emphasis on a world of speed, on an accelerated world, there is a tendency to think of Japanese animations in terms of solitary and stationary reception. The term *otaku*, for instance, is today widely used to refer to "cult fans," that is, to those fans who are totally into manga, anime, video games, and a range of related merchandise and events. The term *otaku* derives from a formalistic way of addressing people that is calculated for its implications of distance between addresser and addressee—"your residence"—and so it is probably not a coincidence that we have come to think of otaku as people who prefer isolation, who remain at home in front of TV or computer screens, venturing out only in pursuit of collectibles or to attend fan-related events. Anime and game otaku are frequently associated with social withdrawal syndrome, sometimes with pathological overtones, and the overall emphasis is on their personal collections, on their mania to take items out of general circulation and into the safety of their rooms. We tend to think of the prototypical anime viewing experience in terms of the eternal child at home alone in front of the television.

We would do better to look at anime in terms of a nodal point in a world of circulation, a point whose mobility is today becoming increasingly evident. Television screens appear today throughout the city, most dramatically in the form of giant screens mounted on buildings. There are also television screens in commuter trains, and if we take into account handheld electronic devices with their smaller screens, it is clear that television and computer screens, and thus anime, are potentially everywhere. Nonetheless, even if we opt to stick with the prototypical viewing experience in which the fan withdraws from the world of school, work, commuting, and so on, into the world of television animations, we can nonetheless see how such withdrawal happens within an accelerated world of general circulation. By way of example, we might think about the circulation of manga and anime, with an emphasis on mobility.

One of the prototypical manga experiences is that of picking up at a kiosk one of the thick inexpensive weekly volumes that are full of new installments of a number of continuing series, and reading it on the commuter train. Some commentators even claim that the length of episodes in weeklies roughly matches the time between train stations. This is apocryphal, no doubt. Yet the appeal of the idea reinforces a sense of connection between manga and commuting, and other popular venues for reading manga include manga coffee shops (usually located near train stations), convenience stores en route, and more recently, with the introduction of plastic wrapping around manga to discourage "free" reading, used book stores. This is not to say that people don't read manga at home. But I wish to stress the association of manga with commuting.

In contrast, television anime series, commonly based on popular manga, are associated with home television. Here, too, rather than think of such viewing in terms of isolation and stasis, I think that we should think of watching TV at home in terms of a *slowing of movement,* in terms of a centripetal force that pulls things inward around it. Using the literal definition of *acceleration* in physics, which refers both to gaining and losing speed, we see that the withdrawal into anime at home is still acceleration, still a matter of speed differentials. Translation from manga to anime, and vice versa, is thus translation in the broader sense of *trans-lation* that comprises movement. The interaction of manga and anime is a matter of *difference in motion.*

The same might be said of the increased convergence of different kinds of anime-related media, television anime, animated films (screened in theaters or rented), and "original animation videos" or OAVs (sometimes written OVA) that are released directly to video or DVD. The increased linkage and convergence of these different circuits of production, distribution, and reception—manga, anime, film, and OAV, as well as toys, accessories, fanzines, etc.—serves to reinforce a sense that the underlying condition for Japanese animations is general circulation and acceleration.

Because it entails a spectator in motion, the train-animation scenario encourages us to think in terms of movement as a basic condition for animation, not only for the production of animation but also for its reception. In fact, as you watch the neon figure on the tunnel wall come to life, you may suddenly lose all sensation of forward or backward motion. Rather than feel the train racing forward and the figure rushing backward, you have the sensation that both you and the animated figure are standing still. In this instance, animation viewing produces the sense of a still point in a moving world, an eddy in the currents of accelerated circulation.

Much as Schivelbusch's account asks us to consider the impact of modern technologies of speed on perception, the train-animation encourages us to think about the impact of motion and effects of acceleration—slowing and gaining speed, stopping and starting. This is one of the reasons that I begin with such an example. I wish to highlight that the force of the moving image, which results from the mechanical succession of images, is the basic technological condition for animation. It is surely for this reason that many theories of animation gravitate toward philosophies that give ontological priority to movement over stillness, to process over structure, to becoming over being, and even to life over death.

The train-animation scenario is important for yet another reason. It calls our attention to the possibility of a specific apparatus for the generation and per-

ception of movement, one that differs in crucial ways from cinema. It pushes us to think more specifically about difference in motion within the moving image itself, and to consider how animation diverges from cinema.

The Specificity Thesis

If the relation between trains and cinema has become an important paradigm for analyses of modern perception, it is because many commentators have drawn an analogy between the mobile eye of the movie camera and the eyes of the traveler gazing from the speeding train. Both kinds of mobile vision force a confrontation with a sort of projectile vision. The mobile camera of cinema tended toward a bullet's-eye view, much like the train. In both instances, movement entailed a sensation of speeding into, and even cutting into, the world, which introduced a sense of a separation between viewer and viewed, while distracting attention from the technologies that allowed for this "surgical strike" on reality.

This way of looking at cameras and trains bears some resemblance to what is commonly called apparatus theory in film studies. With the intention of debunking the alleged scientific neutrality of film techniques and thus of challenging histories that naturalized the emergence of cinematic conventions (the classical film style), a series of film critics developed a devastating yet one-sided critique of the technological impact of the movie camera. Jean Baudry, for instance, called attention to the monocular lens, which he felt condemned the apparatus to impose the conventions of geometric or one-point perspective onto reality. As Comolli remarks of Baudry's theory,

> The notion of "the basic apparatus" (Baudry) is thus put forward: the camera is what produces the "visible" in accordance with the system of "monocular" perspective governing the representation of space: it is therefore in the area of the camera that we should seek, for the materials of cinema as a whole, the perpetuation of this code of representation and the ideology it sustains or reasserts.[7]

Comolli tempers Baudry's account, pointing to economic demands and to scientific developments that questioned the reliability of the human eye, concluding that "it was under the impact of an economic demand and as an ideological instrument that the cinema was conceived, made, and bought from start to finish."[8]

For the most part, film studies have abandoned apparatus theory, because of its tendency to deal with the movie camera deterministically. Apparatus theory looks like a theory dependent on technological determinism. It assumes that a technological device can somehow determine or structure the entire trajectory of cinematic innovations and conventions. But isn't Schivelbusch's account of

trains also a sort of apparatus theory? After all, he claims that the train traveler "saw the objects, landscapes, etc. *through* the apparatus which moved him through the world." Yet there is an important difference. Although discussed as an apparatus, the train for Schivelbusch becomes indicative of a more general technological condition, and thus invites an exploration of the impact of trains on perception more generally, as a key player in a new sociohistorical formation (modernity). The question of technological determinism associated with apparatus theory is at once expanded and muted in his study. The technical device (train) becomes a critical point for assessing the formation of a technological condition—the modern technological condition.

Film studies has gradually shied from anything that smacks of apparatus theory, and by extension, from theories based on the specificity of cinema—what is usually called the specificity thesis. Historically, as filmmakers strived to establish film as art, and as critics strove to convince the world of the importance of studying cinema, they insisted on its specificity. Their bid to establish the distinctiveness of cinema inevitably called on the distinctiveness of its technologies, claiming that such technologies made for forms of expression distinctive from those of other arts, especially from theatre.[9] The specificity thesis proved crucial not only in establishing and enforcing filmic conventions (whence the classical Hollywood style, for instance) but also in establishing the seriousness of cinema and thus its worthiness as an object of critical commentary. As Noel Carrol, in his critique of the specificity thesis, sums it up, "The assumption is that what a medium does best will coincide with what differentiates it."[10] Carroll objects above all to the implication of exclusivity, by which "each art form should explore only those avenues of development in which it exclusively excels above all other arts."[11] Underlying Carroll's objections to the specificity for cinema is a sense of technological determinism. He writes that the specificity thesis "appears to envision each art form on the model of a highly specialized tool with a range of determinate functions. A film, play, poem, or painting is thought of, it seems, analogous to something like a Phillips screwdriver."[12]

To avoid the teleological implications of technological determinism, early film studies has gravitated toward situating cinema within larger sociohistorical conditions or sociotechnical ensembles. One line of inquiry has hinged on the use of moving images in the late nineteenth and early twentieth centuries, a time before cinema had become cinema as such. The idea is that the film conventions that emerged in the 1910s and became dominant in the 1920s transformed diverse practices associated with moving pictures into a largely unitary world of cinema production. To counter this deterministic view of cinema, early film studies proposed to reposition moving pictures as one set of media practices

among others in a broader field of media interactions. Such a gesture avoids the technological determinism associated with apparatus theory and undermines the evolutionary conceits associated with the emergence of classical film styles, by dispersing the impact of moving pictures into a general mediatic or technological condition—that of Western modernity. David Bordwell and Ben Singer dub this approach the "modernity thesis" for cinema, for it stands in stark contrast to the "specificity thesis" that previously proved so important in film studies.[13]

In sum, early film studies brackets the specificity of cinema in order to challenge the teleological assumptions associated with the specificity thesis, which derived from its tacit reliance on the technological distinctiveness of cinema. The study of film then expands to comprise the study of the moving image in general (magic lanterns, slide shows, flipbooks, etc.), of visual culture (panorama, sideshows, etc.), or of media and technology (trains, typewriters, etc.). Film studies thus comes face to face with broad historical questions about the formation of modernity, in a manner reminiscent of Schivelbusch's discussion of trains. While this expansion of film studies is mostly a positive development, the risk is that the teleological tendency once associated with the *specificity thesis* is simply displaced onto the *modernity thesis*. Early film studies, for instance, often falls back on the linear teleological conceits of modernization theory, ignoring the condensations of different processes within Western and non-Western formations of modernity, relying on diffusion theory and generally ignoring the questions posed in Marxist, subaltern, and postcolonial theory about the relation between center and periphery in formations of modernity.[14]

Analogous questions arise around the study of animation and anime. What is at stake in developing a specificity thesis for animation or anime? What is at stake in avoiding a specificity thesis and developing a modernity or postmodernity thesis?

Animation has been around a long time. One might well argue that animation predates cinema, and that animation—in the sense of making images move—has always been the primary concern of cinema. Nonetheless cinema has dominated histories and theories of the moving image, generally subsuming animation while defining it as the lesser form. Only in the late 1980s and 1990s did animation start to emerge from the shadow of cinema. The astonishing surge in popularity of animated forms in mass-targeted and globally disseminated entertainments of the late 1980s and early 1990s, such as video games, television series, music videos, and special effects films, made animation impossible to ignore. Such changes had a profound impact on film studies. On the one hand, as early film studies expanded the discussion of cinema to the broader domain of the moving image (which comprised materials and practices often associated with animation), other film commentators spoke of expanded cinema and future cinemas or, more dramatically, of the end of cinema. On the other hand, outside film studies, other scholars began to call for animation studies. There had previously been books dealing with animation, and very good ones, usually focused on major studios or famous animators.[15] In the course of the 1990s, however, fans and scholars began to speak earnestly about animation as a distinct field of study. Conferences devoted to animation today are booming, and new journals have emerged dedicated to animation studies. This raises the questions of the specificity of animation, whether animation is best situated within expanded film studies or studies of the moving image, or whether animation is best seen as a distinctive art form.

Questions about the specificity of Japanese animations also arise. Awkwardly clumped under the rubric "anime," Japanese animations gained new visibility around the world with the meteoric rise of animation within global media in the 1990s. Given that Japan is the world's largest producer of animation, one might well argue that anime did not simply ride the wave of animation's new visibility and popularity but played a central role in it. Japanese animations were central to the tectonic shift in modes of image production and reception that generated the wave of interest in animation and animated media. In fact, the centrality, ubiquity, and popularity of Japanese animations raise the question of why we should not structure animation studies around the study of Japanese animation. Why do Japanese animations still need to be particularized and culturalized under the rubric of anime when clearly their history is as long and their scope as broad as any other national formation of animation production?[16]

The study of animation (and anime) is currently oscillating between specificity theses and modernity (or postmodernity) theses.[17] On the one hand, many commentators strive to determine what is specific about animation, and not surprisingly in light of the contemporary dominance of film studies, attention typically falls on what makes animation different from cinema. Or studies dwell on the interaction of cinema and animation, presuming some fundamental difference between them. On the other hand, questions about animation—especially in the context of digital animation, special effects (SFX), and computer-generated imagery (CGI)—frequently serve as a point of entry into analyses of postmodern media conditions (simulation, media mix, information theory, and intermediality, for instance).

In this book I begin with a specificity thesis for animation, unabashedly centered on Japanese animations. Yet my approach to the specificity of animation does not imply technological determinism, historical teleology, or formal exclusivity. In contrast with the emphasis on specificity that Carroll dismisses for its determinism (a film is like a screwdriver), my approach to the specificity of animation starts with a reconsideration of how we think about technology. I will propose two shifts: (1) thinking in terms of *determination* rather than *determinism*, and (2) thinking in terms of *machine* rather than *structure*.

The animation-by-train scenario proves useful here because it evokes, in condensed form, both the specificity thesis and the modernity thesis, reminding us that at some level it is impossible to separate questions about material specificity (of cinema or animation) from questions about material conditions or historical formations (modernity or postmodernity). In the course of this book, I will gradually take up discussions of postmodernity in the context of Japanese animations. Initially, however, rather than begin with a modernity or postmodernity thesis, I will stress the specificity of the animated moving image because I wish to avoid establishing a *massive* modernity or postmodernity thesis. Bracketing the specificity of cinema or animation runs the risk of displacing the question of material specificity onto modernity, where the question becomes so massive that almost anything or everything enters into the analysis. Ultimately, of course, as some of the newer approaches to early film attest, the specificity thesis and the modernity thesis are not in strict opposition. Rather a dialogue can unfold *between* the material and perceptual specificity of film or anime (microaesthetic analysis) and macrohistorical paradigms such as modernity and postmodernity.

In this study it is "technicity" (the "quality" or qualitative experience of technology) related to a technological condition that provides a way to move between material specificity and macrohistorical questions. What interests me in looking at the specificity of animation is the possibility for thinking the modern or postmodern technological condition with greater specificity. For I wish to ask, what exactly is it about the anime image that allows it to function as a nodal point in transnational multimedia flows?

From Apparatus to Machine

Central to this inquiry into the material and perceptual specificity of anime is the animation stand, a fairly simple apparatus for stacking celluloid sheets, which allows animators to introduce layers into the image. This apparatus became of central importance in the production of cel animation by the 1930s. Cel animation uses sheets of transparent celluloid, on which images are drawn and painted. The animation stand allows you to stack images in layers, producing, for instance, background, foreground, and middle ground layers. The result is a *multiplanar image,* an image composed of multiple layers or planes. The animation stand permits animators to regulate and play with the relations between layers of the image, and as such it shunts the force inherent in the moving image (as the mechanical succession of images) into techniques for the editing of elements within the image. The animation necessitates an internal editing of image, which is commonly called *compositing*.

The animation stand provides a number of ways to deal with the gaps between layers of the image. It allows for techniques of compositing that help to suppress the sense of a gap between layers, because movement within the image might undermine the sense of the stability of the image or of the continuity of movement across images. I will refer to this suppression of the perception of movement between layers as closed compositing. But there are other uses of the animation stand. It is also possible to composite layers of the image very loosely (open compositing), which imparts the sense of a truly multiplanar image. There is also "flat compositing," in which the play of layers remains palpable but comes to the surface of the image, which I will later call the superplanar image.

Considered as an apparatus, regardless of whether it results in closed, open, or flat compositing, or some combination thereof, the animation stand presents a contrast with the mobile camera of cinema. In the basic animation stand, the camera does not move the way it does in cinema. Generally, with the animation, the camera is fixed on a rostrum and moves very little. When there is camera movement, or something analogous to camera movement, it tends to be along two axes, horizontal or vertical slides, as with slow pans over the image. The pan over an image, however, can be as easily produced by sliding the drawing under the camera, rather than moving the camera. Because of the relative immobility of the camera, the emphasis in animation often falls on drawing the successive movements from frame to frame. One of the masters of animation, Norman McLaren offers this seminal definition:

> Animation is not the art of drawings that move but the art of movements that are drawn; what happens between each frame is much more important than what exists on each frame; animation is therefore the art of manipulating the invisible interstices that lie between frames.[18]

When you look at animation in this way, attention tends to fall on the animation of bodies[19]—in classic animation, this amounts to an emphasis on drawing bodies in motion, on character animation.

But, as I will discuss at many junctures in this book, animation is as much an art of compositing (invisible interstices between layers of the image) as it is of animating bodies (invisible interstices between frames). In fact, as I aim to make clear in this book, in the analysis of animation, priority should fall on compositing (the space *within* images that becomes spread across frames) over character animation (movement across frames). The animation stand makes this priority clear. With the animation stand, if you are not very careful with how you do character animation in conjunction, you will call attention to the layers of the image; it will seem that that you are moving the drawings (sliding them up and down, back and forth) rather than drawing the movement. You cannot address the interstices between frames without first dealing with the interstices between layers.

The animation stand makes it easy to simulate camera movement, not only by moving the camera but also by sliding the drawing. The relative fixity of the camera makes primarily for movement in two dimensions, and pans across images are common. This simulation of camera movement gives cel animation a certain affinity with digital or computer-generated animation, in which the camera movement is necessarily simulated. As I will discuss later, the problem of compositing is integral both to cel animation and to digital animation.

Due to the animation stand, cel animation has difficulty with movement into depth. The animation stand makes it difficult to do precisely what many consider the hallmark of the cinema: a sense of movement into the world of the image, into its depth. Walt Disney is credited with inventing an apparatus that allowed for the production of a sense of movement into depth in animated films—the multiplane camera system or multiplane photography. This device allowed for the simulation of depth of field and imparted a sense of the mobile, cinema-like camera within animation. Disney's innovation allowed animators to regulate the play between layers of the image, minimizing the sense of movement between layers and thus making the image feel stable and solid enough to permit a sense of movement into it. In other words, the multiplane camera system leads in the direction of an animated simulation of the mobile camera of cinema, of movement into depth.

In subsequent chapters, I will discuss innovations with the animation stand, but at this juncture, I wish to consider some of the questions that use of the animation stand raises about the status of the apparatus. As I mentioned above, film studies today shies away from apparatus theory because it smacks of technological determinism, because the apparatus appears to determine or structure the whole of cinema. When I turn to the animation stand as a basis for understanding animation, do I not then run the risk of making this "basic apparatus" (to borrow Comolli's turn of phrase cited above) appear to produce the "mobile" in accordance with a system of "multiplanarity" that governs the representation of space? Do I not make the animation stand somehow central to the perpetuation of a certain code of representation and thus potentially central to the maintenance of an ideology of and about animation?

While I deliberately do not use many of the concepts that Comolli favors (such as "representation" and "code"), his comments on apparatus theory are very much to the point. Thinking in terms of a basic apparatus of animation runs the risk of assuming technological determinism and thus of producing a teleological history of animation. To counter this tendency of apparatus theory, I propose a very different way of thinking about the apparatus. Rather than thinking of animation (or cinema) in terms of a technical device that actively and totally determines each and every outcome (determinism), I propose thinking in terms of passive determination, or more precisely, "underdetermination."[20] Rather than as an apparatus, I propose looking at the animation stand in terms of what Félix Guattari calls the *machine* or the *abstract machine*.[21]

When Guattari inverts the relation between machine and technology, asking us to consider "technology as dependent on machines, not the inverse," he also significantly expands the limits of the machine "to the functional ensemble which associates it with man."[22] It is in this way that Guattari strips the term *machine* of its mechanistic connotations. The machine is not an apparatus. The challenge is to find the machine on which the apparatus depends.

The animation stand, for instance, is an apparatus that sets up layers of transparent celluloid with drawings to be photographed. As such, it gathers into an ensemble a series of other technical devices and schema that do not in themselves belong together or naturally come together: a rack, a fixed camera, lights to provide sufficient illumination on the layers and through the layers, manual techniques of applying ink and color, abstract techniques of composing images in accordance with various conventions (as such linear or orthogonal perspective), and the industrially produced celluloid sheets and celluloid film in the camera. In sum, prior to the actual technology or technological device is an abstract machine—a *multiplanar machine*—that is at once technical/material and abstract/immaterial. Needless to say, because animation entails technologies of the moving image, the multiplanar machine might more accurately be called an *animetic machine* or a *multiplanar animetic machine*. The stacking of sheets or planes of the image (and thus compositing) happens in concert with the mechanical succession of images. Such a machine is not, then, a structure that totalizes or totally determines every outcome. It not only comprises the humans who make it and work with it, but also on other virtual and actual machines. It thus unfolds in divergent series as it folds other machines into it.

Apparatus theory in film studies came closest to this way of thinking about machines when it confronted the mobility of the camera. Baudry, for instance, insisted that the monocular lens of camera constrained it to reproduce one-point perspective, which in turn resulted in the imposition of a seemingly rational and scientifically accurate grid upon reality, enacting the ascendancy of technologized optics over human perception and generating a world in which human actions were necessarily reduced to cause-and-effect relations. Thus the singular apparatus determines the whole of cinema. Yet even Jean Baudry entertained, however briefly, the possibility that, because films consist of a series of images in motion, the result is not fixity and unity but mobility and multiplicity: "This might permit the supposition, especially since the camera moves, of a multiplicity of points of view which would neutralize the fixed position of the eye-subject and even nullify it."[23]

Baudry concluded, however, that the movement of the camera does not really make for mobility and multiplicity. In effect, he denied the ability of the camera to make any difference in relation to the mechanical succession of images. He saw the mobility of the camera producing a disembodied eye, an eye unfettered by a body, shoring up the illusion of a transcendent subject who stands over and above the world, separate from it. He concluded that film invariably produces an illusion of continuity despite underlying discontinuities, which condemns cinema to negate differences. For him, film lives on the denial of difference.[24] His view is indeed close to technological determinism.

In comparison to Baudry, Schivelbusch's discussion of the impact of trains on perception, although it too implies a fairly high degree of technological determination, has greater affinity with Guattari's ideas about the machine. Traveling at speed introduces a new kind of gap or interval into human perception of the world, and that specific interval, that manner of "spacing," does not serve to totalize the whole of perception or of experience related to train travel. Rather the new interval or spacing folds humans into its operation and starts to rely on other machines such as printing presses, department stores, and carriages or cars. Schivelbusch shows how the spacing or interval associated with accelerated perception creates connections with other activities, gradually extending train experience into a general modern techno-economic condition. For him, seeing through the mobile apparatus becomes indicative of an entire modern condition in which new modes of perception ground new modes of distribution and consumption.

In this book, because I focus analysis on movement in animation and thus on the animetic machine, I adopt something of the attitude of experimental science and technology studies in my approach to animation. I tend to approach technologies and technical determinations from the perspective of their force rather than their capture or submission. I tend to look at divergent series of animation. I look at how different series configure or transfigure questions about technological value. Simply put, I try to stick to the facts of animation. Thus, even when I take on decidedly social or cultural issues such as gender and sexuality, I look at the spin that the animetic machine puts on them. I look at how the animation thinks such questions. Consequently, I give priority to technical determination over social, cultural, historical, and economic determination. This is not to say that I do not think such determinations important. Economic determinations are especially crucial, since animations are, after all, mass-produced commodities. Studios and distributors want returns, and if we cast even a cursory glance at global animation production, we see that it mobilizes and hierarchizes labor across continents, with American, French, and Japanese production companies outsourcing labor-intensive tasks to Korean or Chinese shops.

If I do not give such economic determinations priority over technical determinations, it is not to dispense with them but to lay the ground for thinking about how animation matters, for thinking about what happens where the "production machine" meets the "anime machine." For similar reasons, in contrast with studies that begin and end with questions about Japanese values, I give priority to the essence or materiality of animation—its material essence, so to speak—over cultural determinations. In fact, as I will discuss later, studies that center on cultural determination usually wind up with cultural determinism, endlessly pointing and proclaiming, "This is Japan, this is Japanese."

Here I am interested in what animation brings to the world. I am interested in what animation is, how it works, how it thinks—how it brings value into the world. Pragmatically speaking, this means an emphasis on technical determination, both material and immaterial, in order to broach questions about how the "spacing" of animation matters.

The animations that are loosely dubbed "anime" are for the most part varieties of cel animation. It is first and foremost in cel animation that the force implicit in the moving image becomes shunted into the interval between planes of the image, placing emphasis on techniques of compositing or internal editing. This is where animation starts for me. This is where I detect its technical existence, its material essence. Such a point of departure puts me at odds with other studies of animation, in which the emphasis tends to fall on artwork, that is, on the work of the hand, on sketchers or painters for instance. The association of animation with the work of hand is so profound that, when Lev Manovich, for instance, speaks of animation today subsuming cinema, he refers to the primacy of the manual in animation. In accounts of the art of animation generally, the emphasis is on the work of animators; priority is usually given to the animation of characters and objects, followed by the artwork put into backgrounds. In contrast, because of my emphasis on technologies of the moving image, I begin with compositing, and throughout the book, situate character animation and background art in relation to compositing. To clarify my approach and to introduce Deleuze's study of cinema, which will play an important role in later chapters, let me turn to a provocative essay on animation by William Schaffer, "Animation I: Control Image."

Schaffer wishes to build a theory of animation from Deleuze's two-volume *Cinema*, and yet, remarking the importance of the mobility of the camera in Deleuze's discussion, he confronts the fixity of the camera in animation. In animation, he proposes, the analog to the mobile camera of cinema is the moving hand, because the hand that sketches the characters in series of poses is the source of their movement. Schaffer thus stresses the operations of the "invisible hand" in animation. Yet, if we look at a fuller range of the work of the invisible hand, we see that sketching, keying, inking, and coloring, for instance, must take into account the use of that work in layers, either laid one upon another or more instrumentally stacked and regulated in the animation stand. In other words, if we follow the lead of Norman MacLaren and look at the invisible interstices of the moving image, it is not the invisible hand that is primary, nor the interstices between frames, but the invisible interstices between layers. The work of the hand is folded into the multiplanar machine. This is why there are so many manual tasks associated with cel animation beyond the work of the hand that sketches the movement of characters, for instance. The key animator sketches the rough template for the overall movement with key frames, in-between animators fill in the intermediate movements, and then those sketches must be cleaned-up, carefully inked and colored, always with an eye to their use in layers. The multiplanar machine folds all manner of expressive machines into it, many related to the work of the hand, such as sketching, drawing, and painting, which are machines in that such art is often organized (a) compositionally in accordance with one-point perspective or some other structure, (b) tonally in accordance with conventions of shading and coloring, and (c) corporeally in accordance with techniques for modeling bodies, such as the Disney techniques of squashing and stretching, or angular mechanics, or muscular realism, to give some obvious examples.

Generally, accounts that stress character animation tend to ignore compositing and the planes of the image, thus neglecting the force of the moving image in favor of artwork. It is true that, in 1917 when animation started in Japan, it was three *artists* who entered the fray.[25] Shimokawa Ōten was a caricature and cartoon artist until Tenkatsu Studio hired him to make animation in the style of then popular Émile Cohl. Kōuchi Jun'ichi also drew newspaper cartoons, which led to a job making animated films with Kobayashi Shōkai Studios. The third to launch into the world of animation in 1917 was Kitayama Seitarō, whose experience with Western painting helped him receive funding from Nikkatsu for making animated films. Not surprisingly, as Tsugata Nobuyuki indicates in his study of Kitayama Seitarō, there was a variety of terms for animation in circulation, from *manga* and *senga* to *dekobō shin gachō* and *majutsu* (magic), which connected animation to diverse kinds of art and spectacle.[26] The variety of terms suggests that, even though animation had yet to be defined as an entertainment distinct from other sorts of shows or exhibitions, it had begun to gather into it a broad range of arts. What characterized animation even at this stage, however, was the relative fixity of the camera. As the subsequent history of animation attests, the analog to the mobile camera of cinema would not be the invisible hand but rather compositing. Much as the force implicit in the mechanical succession of images in cinema is shunted into the mobility of the camera, where it is at once prolonged and harnessed, so in animation, compositing prolongs and manages the gaps or interstices within the image, the animetic interval. Character animation plays a role analogous to montage, as I will discuss later in greater detail.

In any event, if I insist on starting with technical determination and its underlying machine, it not simply because it allows for a more accurate and comprehensive account of animation, but because it allows me to address the force of the moving image as it simultaneously in-folds or implicates expressive machines (perspective, composition, modeling, for instance) and out-folds or explicates divergent series of animation. I will consider, for instance, how divergent series arise when, under conditions of the relatively fixed camera within the animation stand, animators prefer to slide the drawing rather than draw the movement. Most importantly, looking at animation in terms of the multiplanar animetic machine will allow us to see how technical values can be configured and transfigured across divergent series of animation. This "out-folding" of animation extends well beyond traditional cel animation, beyond full animation and limited animation, into digital animation and CGI and SFX films and other media such as video games where compositing takes on as much importance as simulating camera movement, and the character function takes priority over montage.

Thinking Technology

Saying that "anime (or animation) thinks technology" may seem merely to be a provocative yet awkward way of saying "how anime thinks *about* technology." With this strange phrasing, however, I wish to indicate that animation at once *works with* technology and *thinks about* technology—and the two processes are inseparable. In anime, thinking about technology is inseparable from thinking through technology (not only using technology but also aligning thought with its operations). In this context, I refer to technical *determination*, which is not determinism but a sort of underdetermination. The implication is that determination is at once material and immaterial. Or, put another way, there is indeterminacy to determination, which generates an interval or spacing in which thinking might arise. I might have also said "anime thinks through technology." But I favor the expression "thinking technology" to avoid implying that technologies are neutral mediators whose work is done when the concept appears, or whose operations vanish from the scene of thought and are therefore negligible.

Looking at animation from the angle of how it thinks technology is a call to move beyond the book report or film review model that currently holds sway in studies of anime, which tend to rely on a summary of the anime narrative in conjunction with a consideration of major themes. In this vein, a number of commentators have written about the giant robots, machines, cyborgs, and techno-apocalyptic scenarios that appear in some Japanese animations. Such commentary is frequently insightful. Yet, when analysis is limited to story and themes, the result is rather like comparing conclusions without addressing arguments. Thematic analysis tends to consider what anime say about technology or how anime represent technology without any consideration of how anime arrive at such conclusions. There is no account of the process of argumentation, the operative logic, or the manner of thinking. In addition, because of its emphasis on representation, such a style of analysis often misunderstands the conclusions because it does not attend to what is in play and what is at stake. In effect, such an approach sees the problems and questions addressed in anime as external to anime. Problems and questions appear to come to anime from outside, and anime re-presents them. At its worst, this kind of analysis sees anime as a direct reflection or representation of the social problems of, say, postmodern Japan. At its best, it sees in anime an encrypted response and national allegory: Japanese animations appear as cryptic symptoms of postmodern Japan.

In contrast, to look at how anime think technology is to call attention to the material limits of anime, which at once constrain their "thinking" and make it possible. The animetic machine is, in this sense, an internal limit within the materiality of animation that allows for a distinctively animetic manner of doing, feeling, and thinking, of working on the world. While this approach grants a certain degree of autonomy to animation in a manner reminiscent of the specificity thesis for cinema, the goal is not to present anime as an enclosed, self-sufficient, autopoietic entity. On the contrary, Guattari's notion of *machine* implies heterogenesis, encouraging us to push beyond the reading of animation as symptomatic of the modern or postmodern technological condition, encouraging us to treat the putative "symptom" as a material process in its own right, a process that defies neat divisions and hierarchies between inside and outside, or between technology and value. In this way, rather than take anime as a symptom of social conditions or national culture, one sees divergent series of anime worlds working on and thinking through technical value. It is in this way that we can begin to understand how anime come to operate as nodal points in transnational and transmedial networks, which comprise crossover and tie-in productions or franchises, and spur fan activities that bring together a range of events and media platforms.

Looking at anime from the angle of the force of the moving image offers a way to avoid the technological determinism implicit in apparatus theory (namely, the animation stand somehow determines all of anime and anime-related franchises and fan activities), and to go beyond the reflection model or representation theory that remains prevalent in anime commentary (to wit, anime is a reflection, however distorted, of national culture and its socioeconomic discontents). Still, it would be an overstatement to say that the "machine theory" of animation moves beyond all that. In effect, the machine theory charts a course between these two ways of looking at Japanese animations. What then is machine theory?

When Félix Guattari proposes a theory based on machines rather than structures, he relies implicitly on Henri Bergson and explicitly on Gilbert Simondon. Bergson turned toward a philosophy of the image in a bid to resolve the paradoxes inherent in idealism and realism. Simply put, he wanted to navigate a middle course between the stance that reality is all in our heads (idealism) and the assumption that we have direct access to things out there, just as they are (realism or positivism). Bergson worried that idealism gave us a world composed only of representations, while realism imagined a world composed exclusively of things. He turned to the image, because the image is something more than a representation and something less than an object or thing.[27] Imagine, he proposed, that the world is made entirely of images, all of them bumping around and knocking into one another. In a completely deterministic world, you would expect that every action would produce an equal and opposite reaction: when one image strikes another, the reaction of the other would be an instantaneous cause-and-effect response. In Bergson's world of images, however, there arise specific kinds of images that do not react instantly when something acts on them. There is a delay between action and reaction. Such images have a "center of indetermination." They are living beings, according to Bergson. As Ronald Bogue explains, such images "introduce a gap in the universal interplay of mechanical causes and effects, a delay in reaction and frequently a shift in direction that exhibit what we may call choice."[28] The center of indetermination is where delay or duration arises, and with it thoughts, emotions, and affective responses.

Building on Bergson's deduction of consciousness from a universal flow of images or a vibrational whole, Gilbert Simondon proposes to look at technical objects in a similar way. Although Simondon looks at technical objects from the standpoint of Bergson's biology-centered philosophy, he does not propose that technical objects are the same as natural objects (organisms).[29] His aim is not to suggest that machines are alive or identical to living beings. Rather his thesis is that there are technical objects with centers of indetermination. Such technical objects introduce a delay between cause and effect. Consequently, as with natural objects or organisms, one might look at how they "evolve" and how they come to "feel" and "think." If I put scare quotes around the words *evolve*, *feel*, and *think*, it is because Simondon does not intend for us to look at technical objects as independent and self-sufficient life-forms (autopoiesis). The evolution and thought of technical objects happen in relation to humans. It is thus impossible to treat the technical object in isolation from what Simondon calls a technical ensemble. Still, even if machines are not self-sufficient closed systems, Simondon does accord them a certain degree of autonomy due to their force (to use a generic term). Or we might say that they generate zones of autonomy. Much as organisms co-evolve with their environment, so technical objects co-evolve with their technical ensembles, which include humans. This way of looking at technical objects and technical ensembles is the inspiration for Guattari's theory of "machinic heterogenesis"—and by extension it is the basis for my contrast between the apparatus (animation stand) and machine (multiplanar machine or animetic machine).

Thus, while I will start with the animation stand as *the* apparatus of animation that to some extent accounts for the specificity of cel animation, I also see at the heart of this technical object a center of indetermination. The center of indetermination introduces a gap or delay in the process, and thus makes for a machine that is at once material and immaterial, which can "evolve" into divergent series and can "feel" and "think." While looking at the apparatus is a good point of departure for understanding animation, the animetic machine is truly the "life" of the animation, what makes it act, feel, and think. The machine tends to fold out into an ensemble that comprises humans, but this does not mean that animators can fully master or easily control the machine. They must learn to work with this center of indetermination, to think with it, by giving it space to think. In other words, even when animators strive to become *auteurs* and stamp a singular vision or style onto their animations, they are making visible and palpable the force of the moving image as channeled and orientated via the animetic machine. They are working something out of anime by working within it. It is here that the specificity of animation truly matters.

Japanese Experiences of Technology

Because of my interest in what animation is, how it works, and how it brings value into the world, my account of anime tends to move between the philosophy of technology and the history of thought. My emphasis is not on cultural uses of a technology or technologies, or on the history of a technology. Rather it is on how technologies affect thought. It is on the positive and productive constraints that a machine places on thought, producing a positive unconscious, so to speak. As such, my emphasis is less on the unity of Japan and more on questions of modernity. In fact, I deliberately avoid the sort of history that takes a geopolitical divide between Japan and the West as the ground for analysis, which sets up a story of influence and reaction, a story of the arrival of technologies from foreign lands and of Japanese reactions to those technologies. This manner of structuring the history of technology invariably presumes and reinforces the unity of the West, and of national culture and geopolitical identities.[30]

Part of the interest of looking at how anime thinks technology lies in the challenge such an approach presents to those who insist on the unity of Japan, on the unity of national culture, to ground their discussions of anime. The emphasis falls not on unitary cultural (Japanese) uses of technology (animation) but on how the animetic machine generates divergent series that effectively work to disperse the putative unity of national culture or mass culture into subcultures or micromasses.[31] Such effects are not good or bad in and of themselves. My aim is not to sing the praises of machinic heterogenesis in order to celebrate animation as an inherently redemptive modality. My point is that, if we do not look at animation from the angle of its force and thus machinic divergence, we have no way of assessing its impact. We simply substitute the study of Japan and national culture for the study of animation and technologies. This is already a powerful current in histories of technologies in Japan.

Histories of technology in Japan typically hinge on modernization, beginning with the massive importation of Western technologies into Japan in the mid- to late nineteenth century, which was met first with great enthusiasm and then profound anxiety and uncertainty. Ultimately, the classic pro-modernization histories emphasize how Japan successfully adopted and domesticated foreign technologies, building an economically and technologically powerful modern nation. In one history of Japan's developmental trial and triumph, we learn that, when Commodore Matthew Perry arrived with two "black ships," steam frigates, at the entrance to Tokyo Bay in 1853 to open Japan to trade, he brought with him, as a gift, a scaled-down working steam engine; by 1872, an imported full-size train ran between Tokyo and Yokohama; and by 1895, a steam locomotive had been built in Japan.[32] The emphasis here is on how science and technology led to "civilization and enlightenment" (bunmei kaika), which was an important slogan of the early decades of the Meiji era (1868–1912). When such histories of technological modernization lean toward culturalism (as they commonly do), they imply that the Japanese gravitate toward science and technology, as if by their very nature and culture they took to engineering, instrumentalism, and rationalism, however Japanese in style.

Other takes on the modernization of Japan suggest that modern sciences and technologies were the agent of a profound split in the Japanese subject, a split that another popular nineteenth-century slogan "Japanese spirit and Western technologies" (wakon yōsai) at once acknowledges and disavows. It is as if a classic Cartesian dualism—body/soul or machine/spirit—had been displaced onto a geopolitical imaginary, Japan versus the West. "Japanese spirit and Western technologies" implies not only a divide but also a hierarchy, which reprises the problem of Cartesian rationalism: Japanese spirit, because distinct from the material world (Western materialism), stands above and beyond it and thus can act on it.

Subsequently, in the Taishō era (1912–26) and especially in the early Shōwa era (1926–89), scientific and technological materialism, now clearly as Japanese as Western, appeared so pervasive and intractable that the ascendancy of the Japanese spirit over the material world of technologies and commodities no longer seemed guaranteed, yet for precisely that reason, its ascendancy seemed all the more desirable. What is more, as philosophy entered directly into the fray, with new ways of thinking about technology inspired by Kant, Bergson, Nietzsche, and Heidegger, it became clear that the very separation of spirit and matter (or soul and body) was the problem not the solution. Particularly as Japanese industries boomed and expanded into extensive colonial networks, it seemed possible and even desirable to imagine a Japanese materialism, in the form of nonmetaphysical spirit–matter continuity beyond or prior to the metaphysical spirit/matter divide implicit in Western materialism.[33] It is not surprising that Heidegger and the critique of metaphysics became at this juncture a source of inspiration among Japanese philosophers who were gradually heading in wartime years toward a conceptualization of Japan "overcoming the modern" (kindai no chōkoku).[34] By this point, however, what it meant to overcome the modern depended on how one defined the modern, and there were many ways of thinking the question of modernity. Still, there was a powerful tendency to imagine modernity in terms of a Cartesian rationalism that abetted materialism, and in response, Heideggerian and phenomenological inquiry proved important.[35]

In the wake of World War II, particularly with the American destruction of two Japanese cities with nuclear weapons, the Japanese, like many other nations around the world, truly felt "overcome by modernity" (to use Harootunian's turn of phrase).[36] With alarming swiftness, however, with the economic successes born of American wars in East Asia, modernization was reborn in Japan, and the reconstruction of Japan promised to erase its wartime destruction. Not surprisingly, in light of the recentness of war experiences and the clear evidence that Japan's economic miracle was fueled by the American wars in Korea and Vietnam, this "second modernization" of Japan became (and remains) as fraught with anxieties and questions about modernity and technology as the prewar era, and maybe more so. Naturally, the questions about technology shift with postwar transformations in technology; with the identification of Japan with miniaturization, electronics, robotics, communications, and other information technologies; in conjunction with massive contracts for the production of American military equipment; and with the transformations in the dream of Japanese economic, political, or technological autonomy. Nonetheless, as the anime explored in this book attest, Cartesianism remains a central point of reference for characterizing modernity, and the Heideggerian critique of modernity remains an important point of departure, even as these philosophies too are effectively subjected to regimes of miniaturization and informatization.

In this book, to assess how anime thinks technology, I will draw connections between (a) Miyazaki Hayao's animations and Martin Heidegger's philosophy; (b) Anno Hideaki's animations and post-Heideggerian thinkers such as Azuma Hiroki, Michel Foucault, and Jacques Derrida; and (c) CLAMP's manga and its anime adaptation alongside Lacanian thinkers such as Saitō Tamaki and Slavoj Žižek as well as their feminist critics. Yet, in drawing such connections, I do not mean to imply that Miyazaki affords an animated version of Heidegger, or Anno Hideaki an animated version of Azuma Hiroki, or CLAMP a manga-anime version of Lacan. On the contrary, as attested in my tendency to use such terms as *post-Cartesian*, *post-Heideggerian*, or *post-Lacanian* when speaking of these animations, I find that, when animation takes on questions of technology, the force implicit in the animetic interval is a force to be reckoned with. The use of various rubrics such as *Cartesianism* or *post-Heideggerian* is not intended as a definitive characterization of an animation or animator. Such rubrics are more like the soulful bodies of anime characters: philosophical values are brought to the surface and reworked in anime, in accordance with the way in which the animetic machine acts, thinks, and feels.

There are, then, Japanese experiences of technology and of the modern technological condition, and commentary on anime sometimes evokes them. We might read, for instance, that the giant robot of anime reprises the Japanese awe vis-à-vis the technological power of Perry's black ships, or that the otaku fascination with space operas about global annihilation reflects the Japanese experience of the atomic bomb.[37] Yet, if we do not wish to posit a unitary Japanese experience of modernity behind every animation, we need to think in the plural, in terms of the diversity of Japanese *experiences* of technology and the diversity of Japanese animations. And we need also to reckon with the technologization of thought itself, to consider how it is still possible to think under such conditions. The challenge is beautifully posed as the train runs through a tunnel, bringing figures to life on the dark wall, and in that moment in which the force of the moving image makes it seem that you have stopped in your tracks, it is difficult to say whether the train will continue to move you through the world, or whether the world has suddenly arrived.

PART I. MULTIPLANAR IMAGE

CHAPTER 1

CINEMATISM AND ANIMETISM

IN ONE OF THE EARLY SEQUENCES in Ōtomo Katsuhirō's *Steamboy* (2004), as the young hero James Ray Steam travels by train to London, the English countryside streams past the window, and the landscape—a series of rolling hills, clumps of trees, and small houses—looks like a diorama (Figure 1). This is not, however, the kind of diorama that uses three-dimensional figures and scale models. It recalls the ones that children make in school with a shoebox and cardboard cutouts. Each house and hill and tree is decidedly flat, as if cut out and pasted in place. It is as if the speed of the train had separated the landscape into distinct layers or planes, and as you speed along looking out the window, you actually feel the gap between layers. This sense of a gap between layers of landscape is hard to convey with a series of screen grabs, so you'll have to imagine the movement between the images or watch the sequence from the film, preferably on a large screen because it accentuates the effect.

This sequence from *Steamboy* brings to mind Wolfgang Schivelbusch's observations on the effects of train travel on perception, discussed in the Introduction. Schivelbusch argues that traveling by train gave rise to a particular kind of panoramic perception in which the passenger "no longer belongs to the same space as the perceived objects; the traveler sees the objects, the landscapes, etc., *through* the apparatus which moves him through the world."[1] If scenes of travel by rail feel like the mobile camera of cinema, it is because one sees through a mobile apparatus (the train). It is in this way that commentators have linked trains and cinema at the level of modern perception. The link between trains and cinema makes sense in light of the emergence of the movie camera in the heyday of the steam train, which contributed to the prevalence of trains in films. Trains and

Figure 1. *In this sequence from* Steamboy, *as the landscape streams past the train window it appears composed of distinct layers; movement makes the houses, shrubs, and trees, even if these show some degree of volumetric modeling, look like flat cut-outs, as in a pasteboard diorama.*

movies just seem to go together. The history of film is full of examples of trains, from the train chases and train crashes that enlivened silent films, to the apocryphal stories of audiences fleeing in terror from the moving image of a train pulling into a station. Yet it is as *mobile apparatuses of perception* that trains and movies have become paradigmatically modern examples of the impact of speed on our experience of the world. Lynne Kirby underscores such a connection when she writes of the emergence of a "spectator-passenger" at the intersection of cinema and train.[2] Paul Virilio gives one of the boldest accounts of the effects of speed on perception. He insists that the landscape seen from the train window is art, just as much as the works of Picasso or Klee. He calls it an "art of the engine."[3]

Such commentators offer a sort of apparatus theory of perception. Seeing through the apparatus changes the way in which we see the world. The apparatus structures, organizes, and even determines how we experience things. Unlike the apparatus theory of cinema, however, which insisted on the monocular lens of the movie camera and downplayed its mobility, this train-inspired apparatus theory stresses speed and movement. Of the three commentators cited above, Virilio offers the boldest and broadest mobile apparatus theory, claiming, "What happens in the train window, in the car windshield, in the television screen, is the same kind of cinematism."[4]

Cinematism is a useful term because it builds on the sense of an overlap between movies and engines but does not limit such effects to films or to trains. In fact, Virilio is determined to address the *technological condition* in general. He writes about specific apparatuses but sees them as instances of the broader problems posed by modern technology. His vision is largely dystopian: even though he speaks of an *art* of the engine, this is for him a deadly and inhuman art. The spectator becomes an apparatus-subject, whose eyes and other senses are aligned with the apparatus, with the speeding train. As speed introduces a sense of separation between the world and the subject, the eye becomes a kine-eye, desirous of greater velocity and mobility, bent on its own destruction.

For Virilio, cinematism is part of a more general optical logistics that ultimately serves to align our eyes with weapons of mass destruction, with the bomb's-eye view. The eye becomes one with the bomb, and everywhere in the world becomes a target.[5] The essence of cinematism lies in the use of mobile apparatuses of perception, which serve (1) to give the viewer a sense of standing over and above the world and thus of controlling it, and (2) to collapse the distance between viewer and target, in the manner of the ballistic logic of instant strike or instant hit. In effect, Virilio presents us with a massive modernity thesis, which, as I will discuss later, might be defined as accelerated or hyper-Cartesianism, articulated at the level of technology. It is as if the monocular lens of the camera, raised to a new power through its acceleration into the world, had gained the capacity to order all of existence in accordance with Cartesian coordinate geometry. Virilio's approach to ballistic vision thus recalls those accounts of geometric or one-point perspective that show how the use of scalar proportions and a vanishing point create the impression of a rational subject who stands over and above the world, somehow separate from it. The logistics of ballistic perception adds speed to the imposition of a rational grid on the world, which in Virilio's vision results in an inescapable yet uninhabitable technological condition that at once expands the scope of application of Cartesian rationality and techno-scientific rationality and forces it deeper into the world and human bodies, leading inevitably to the destruction of all that is human. Cinematism is one instance of this process.

In contrast, even though it conjures up a mobile apparatus of perception, the train sequence in Ōtomo's *Steamboy* presents something very different from Virilio's cinematism or hyper-Cartesianism. It does introduce the sense of a gap between the space of the traveling viewer and perceived landscape, and yet, rather than evoke the ballistic logic of the bullet's-eye view that so disturbs Virilio, Ōtomo's sequence also highlights the separation of the landscape into layers, into distinct multiple planes. This is not to say that *Steamboy* does away with ballistic vision altogether. It does include a number of scenes in which our viewing position becomes that of the speeding train or speeding bullet. Nevertheless the train sequence with its diorama effects introduces another perceptual logic that apparently arises alongside cinematism. It is a perceptual logic in which our eyes do not turn from the window in order to align themselves with, or to identity with, the speeding locomotive. Rather the eyes remain intent on looking at the effects of speed laterally, sideways or crossways, rather than racing along the trajectory of motion. This is what I will call "animetism." Characteristic of animetism is the separation of the image into multiple planes. The result is a multiplanar image.

Insofar as animetism arises in the same world as mobile apparatuses (the world that, in Virilio's view, gives rise exclusively to cinematism), animetism not only implies a different way of *perceiving* things in an accelerated world but also promises a different way of *thinking* about technology and of *inhabiting* a technology-saturated world. Put another way, animetism does not take us out of the modern technological condition but hints at other ways of dwelling in it. Fault lines appear in the apparently unified and totalized modern technological condition, in high-speed hyper-Cartesianism denounced in Virilio.

The use of the multiplanar image in *Steamboy* can also be seen as part of its historical steampunk conceit. The film takes place in a world in which steam was widely used (1860s London), but steam technologies are here as the basis for high-tech weaponry. Water of exceptional purity allows scientists to produce a "steam ball" with incredible power, which results in a race among nations and other factions to seize this new military power. In other words, the steam ball recalls the atomic bomb (and its use of heavy water), and the steam technologies of the 1860s produce another version of the Cold War arms race. In narrative terms, the results are not especially interesting, because the storylines and characters associated with the Cold War imaginary today feel anachronistic (as anachronistic as steam power). What is interesting, however, is how the steampunk conceit allows Ōtomo to explore late nineteenth-century visual technologies, such as the diorama. The sequence of traveling by rail to London emphasizes the period optical effect by slowly pulling away from the diorama-like landscape to frame it with the train window—a classically modern dioramic moment.

Ōtomo has added movement and speed to the mix, which brings the nineteenth-century diorama into the world of the moving image. In other words, this is not just a multiplanar image but a multiplanar image under conditions of cinematic motion, which entails a mechanical succession of images. *Steamboy* thus asks us to consider the effects of technologies of the moving image on our perception of the world. Where Virilio stresses how mobile viewing, in trains and movies, introduces a hyper-Cartesianism or high-speed rationalized perspective, Ōtomo gives us a multiplanar image, couched as a diorama, which is experienced in motion. Exploring the emergence of modern technologies in the nineteenth century, Ōtomo discovers animetism rather than cinematism. He discovers a different potential of the moving image, one that arises from the same technologies but presents a different way of experiencing the world technologically, under conditions of speed.

The multiplanar image appears constantly in animation and especially in Japanese animations. In *Spriggan* (1998), for instance, in the sequence in which the young hero drives through Istanbul, the landscape appears as a collection of flat, superimposed layers of buildings (Figure 2). Again you feel the openness between the flattened planes of the image, which imparts a distinctive sense of movement. Rather than move into the landscape, you seem to move across it. This is one of the crucial differences between animetism and cinematism. Cinematism tends to put your eye on the point of a speeding bullet, on the tip of the plummeting bomb, or looking directly ahead from the locomotive—or conversely, you are the target, and the train or bullet or bomb is speeding toward you. It is a voyage *into* the landscape, which entails a push for greater mobility and velocity, for the ability to turn on a penny or to stop on a dime. Animetism is different, however. While it too is a modern art of the engine grounded in a speed-riddled instrumentalized perception of the world, animetism is not about movement *into depth* but movement *on and between surfaces*. This movement between planes of the image is I will call the *animetic interval*.

Since Ōtomo Katsuhiro worked on *Spriggan* (he is credited as general supervisor, although his input is said to have been minor), you might think that these multiplanar effects are part of his distinctive style. Or you might think multiplanar effects are characteristic of Studio 4°C, the production company for *Steamboy* and *Spriggan*, which also produced such experimental animated fare as Ōtomo's omnibus *Memories* (1995), the series *Eternal Family* (*Eikyū kazoku*, 1997–98), and the recent films *Mind Game* (*Mindo geemu*, 2004) and *Tekkon Kinkreet* (*Tekkon kinkuriito*, 2007). Multiplanar effects are not limited to Ōtomo or to Studio 4°C, however. They appear all the time, in animation *and* in cinema. Think of those car sequences in B movies where you can tell that the car

Figure 2. *The cityscape of Istanbul in this sequence from Spriggan separates into distinct layers, which appear very loosely composited under conditions of motion.*

is not really moving, but scenery is moving past the window. You can tell that it is fake, for you feel the gap between world of the car and the world of the land-scape. If such moments in cinema seem cheap, funny, or fake, it is because our conventions of cinema lead us to expect something different—say, a sequence filmed with an actually moving car driving down an actual road. We expect the film to give us a sense of moving *into* the world of landscape rather than having the surfaces of that world slide by the car windows.

Animation brings with it a different set of possibilities and conventions vis-à-vis movement and perception. Opening a gap between layers of the image has a distinctive feel in animation. Where in cinema such a gap tends to be perceived as an artifact of low-budget or unskilled film making, in animation we are more likely to accept it as art rather than artifact. Animation thus allows for the exploration of a different potential of the moving image. The multiplanar sequences that I pulled from *Steamboy* and *Spriggan*, for example, touch on a fundamental potential of the moving image, which becomes pronounced in certain kinds of animation, particularly in cel animation that works with layers of celluloid sheets, with at least two layers (background and foreground) and sometimes three or more. Characters and other entities are animated by drawing various phases of movements on sheets and then photographing them successively with an eye to projection. The subsequent projection of images produces a character in motion, animated. Yet, as I mentioned in the Introduction, for reasons that will become clearer in subsequent chapters, the layering of sheets or planes is more fundamental than character animation for understanding animation as a moving image. The various art tasks associated with animating characters—key frames, in-between animation, clean-up, and so on—are done with an eye to the animation of the character in a multiplanar world.

Very early in the history of animation production, animators began to stack images, and gradually there emerged animation stands, which are basically racks that allow animators to hold different layers of the image in place and to fix the distance between them while photographing through the layers from above. Putting the image layers in a rack or stand allowed animators to illuminate the images more evenly, and allowed for greater consistency and stability because it made it easier to hold key elements in place while introducing small changes as they photographed a sequence snapshot by snapshot. This setup also introduced a gap or separation between layers of the image, and thus made it possible to introduce a greater degree of rationalization into the movement of one layer of the image relative to other layers. The animetic interval (already implicit in the layering of images prior to the animation stand) became the site of a rationalization, instrumentalization, or technologization of the multiplanar image, allowing animators to harness or channel the force of the moving image in distinctly animetic ways.

Due to the stacking of celluloid layers, animation tended to put an emphasis on compositing (editing of image layers) over camera movement (the camera became relatively fixed), and yet there is no rule that animation must thus result in animetism. Animation does not have to open a sense of movement between layers. It can equally strive to suppress animetism. In fact, a great deal of animation leans toward cinematism, striving to produce the illusion of movement into depth, of travel into a world. Such animation deliberately uses techniques of compositing to suppress the sense of movement between layers of the image. For this reason, it is more accurate to say that cinematism and animetism are potential tendencies of the moving image rather than fixed media categories (cinema versus animation). What is more, animetism can have a profound impact on narrative structures, as we will see. Nonetheless cinematism and animetism are not genres. Which is to say, while I see a strong tendency toward animetism in Japanese animations, especially those that are often loosely called anime, I do not see anime as a genre or style or media that can be defined on the basis of animetism. Cinematism and animetism are different *tendencies* of the moving image, and as I will show in great detail in subsequent chapters, so-called anime is far from unitary in its relation to the animetic interval.

Anime comprises a range of techniques, styles, and modes of address, as well as genres and story lines. Much of what we think of as anime derives from variations on techniques associated with limited animation, that is, animation in which the number of frames used to construct motion is limited. Yet limited animation is not unitary. It too breaks into a number of different lineages, impulses, and combinations. There are divergent series. One aim of this book is to provide some sense of the complexity of animation, of Japanese animations, and of so-called anime. The difference between cinematism and animetism is a good point of departure, because it does not entail categories that will encourage us to begin with a simple classification of animation types, such as full animation versus limited animation, or Disney animation versus Japanese anime. Cinematism and animetism harness different potentials of the moving image in specific ways. Precisely because animetism is a *tendency*, a manner of harnessing a specific potential of the moving image, there is no such thing as *pure* animetism, any more than there is pure anime.

In a single film, and even within a single moving image (frame or shot), we might find various mixtures of cinematism and animetism. Frequently, tension and even conflict arises between them. As potentials of the moving image, cinematism and animetism imply different tendencies and orientations, and by extension, different ways of imagining a technologically accelerated world, and different ways of inhabiting that world. Thinking in terms of animetism thus allows us to look at how animation itself tends to conceptualize and even to cultivate a specific set of relations vis-à-vis technology, vis-à-vis what is sometimes called techno-scientific modernity or the modern technological condition. At this level, too, I see complex mixtures, tensions, and conflicts arising within any animation. Even though certain kinds of Japanese animation lean toward animetism, it should be clear that to lean or to tend in a specific direction entails some manner of negotiation with and maybe even struggle against other potentials of the moving image, such as cinematism.

At the very heart of animation technique, then, we can see the stirrings of highly specific orientations toward technology and toward our technologized world. Anime in this sense entails a way of thinking technology. This is one of the most compelling features of anime, and something that draws so many fans to it. Japanese animations are compelling not because they are exceedingly conceptual in their presentation of technologies (some are, some are not), but because their animation techniques imply a way of thinking about technology. Anime thus promises to open new ways of thinking about how we inhabit a technologized world.

To understand anime, then, it is not sufficient to discuss themes or to rehash stories. Because anime operates (and thinks) at the level of the moving image, we need to understand how its themes and stories operate from the level of the moving image. It is here that we can begin to understand how anime might enable an *animetic critique* of the modern technological condition through its negotiation with and struggle against the ballistic logistics of perception (cinematism or hyper-Cartesianism). At the outset, however, it is crucial to stress not only the *variety* of Japanese animations but also, and more importantly, the *diversity of thinking* about technology evidenced in anime. In light of this aim, the films of Miyazaki Hayao and Studio Ghibli provide an excellent point of departure, since these films frequently evoke multiplanar effects not only to challenge a technological relation to the world but also to imagine a critical relation to modern technologies.

CHAPTER 2

ANIMATION STAND

AS A TECHNOLOGY, cel animation appears relatively simple. It consists of taking photographs of images that have been inked and painted upon layers of celluloid. The photographs are then projected at twenty-four frames per second to produce a moving image. Initially we might think of animation as a combination of cinema (moving image) and art (drawing/painting). For a number of reasons, however, I feel it important to emphasize the cinema side of the equation. In fact, in keeping with the general tendency to rethink the project of film theory in terms of a broader field analysis of moving images, I will stress that the "material essence" of animation lies in the moving image, not in the art. Still, because there is so much artwork folded into animation, various styles and modes of designing, sketching, erasing, inking, painting, and composing images, it is tempting to look at animation entirely in stylistic, compositional, or art historical terms. In the course of this book, I will talk a lot about perspective, composition, and other ways of composing images, in a rather art historical manner. Nonetheless, to anticipate later discussion, I wish to signal some of the problems that arise when the emphasis falls primarily on the art side of animation at the expense of an analysis of the moving image.

First, there is a tendency to introduce a divide between low tech and high tech, between technique and technology, between art and techno-science, or between poiesis and technē. Even when done with computers, the art side of cel animation—designing, sketching, erasing, inking, painting—feels so low tech, so manual, especially in comparison to cinema, that we do not tend to think of it as technological at all. We think of art or craft. What is more, there are many different traditions and lineages of art and craft, and it is those that usually organize our knowledge about animation rather than discussions of tools, apparatuses, technological devices, or technical ensembles. Consciously or not, when we stress the importance of artwork in animation, we tend to introduce a fairly strict divide between technique and technology, which rides on a questionable division between poesis and technē.[1] To acknowledge the impossibility of separating art or technique from technology, I will occasionally employ the term *technics*.

Commentators who focus exclusively on the art side of cel animation take great liberty in their discussions of the history of animation, seeing art lineages that stretch back to antiquity or prehistory. Animation is sometimes deemed to be as old as prehistoric cave paintings, because such paintings imply a sequence of images. Similar arguments have been made about cinema and comics. There is, for instance, Siegfried Zielinski's evocation of a prehistory of cinema stretching back to antiquity, which he dubs the "deep time."[2] In his guidelines for understanding comics, Scott McCloud traces its sequential art back to cave paintings and ancient Egyptian hieroglyphics.[3] In the case of Japanese animation, it is not surprising, then, that some commentators would seek its origins in the illustrated handscrolls *(emaki)* of classical or early medieval Japan, that is, the late Heian and early Kamakura eras. This idea has been popularized and promoted by one of Studio Ghibli's renowned directors, Takahata Isao.

In a book entitled *Jūni seki no animeeshon* (Twelfth-century animation), for instance, Takahata discovers both "cinematic" *(eigateki)* and "animetic" *(animeteki)* features in medieval handscrolls, particularly in the famous comic animal scrolls, *Chōjū jinbutsu giga emaki*. The idea that the origins of anime lie in classical or medieval art is an appealing one, for it works not only to monumentalize anime but also produces a "shock of the old" or a "shock of deep time" in which dated, outmoded, and largely forgotten cultural forms suddenly reappear and feel somehow contemporary, even postmodern. There is a sense of time out of joint. But then, at another level, it turns out that nothing is out of joint at all. On the contrary, everything fits neatly within a Japanese art tradition. It is surely for this reason that the new Suntory Museum of Art, housed in a decidedly postmodern, high-end consumer complex, chose to open its doors with an exhibit of *Chōjū jinbutsu giga emaki* and cited Takahata's idea of "twelfth-century animation" in its advertisements.[4] Art journals had already prepared the way.[5]

Other commentators have outlined different art historical lineages for Japanese animation. Typically, it is the art of early modern Japan—of the Tokugawa or Edo period—that provides a point of reference. Edo Japan is frequently evoked as the origin not only for styles of composition in anime and manga, but also for anime fan cultures. This is especially true of superflat theory, which I will discuss in Part II. I should also point out that art critics in Japan such as Sawaragi

Noi have challenged such histories, showing how the construction of art historical lineages for anime and manga have tended to eliminate any consideration of the impact of American mass culture and Japanese pop art.[6] In sum, looking exclusively at the art side of anime tends to encourage an acceptance of received lineages for traditional art, and consequently the emphasis on Japanese art traditions easily turns into an insistence on the unity, antiquity, and continuity of Japan and Japanese traditions. There is a pronounced tendency to fall back on discourses on Japaneseness *(Nihonjinron)* rather than to consider the specificity of animation.

Looking at the cinema side of animation invites greater localization in historical terms. Because histories of Japanese cinema often rely on a variation of apparatus theory in which the movie camera is construed as an irrevocably Western technology, they frequently reinforce the sense of a strict opposition between Japan and the West. Nonetheless, in my opinion, because we can open the history of cinema into histories of the moving image, cinema studies presents a better point of departure for understanding animation than do art historical paradigms. Let me introduce some of the basic contours of Japanese film history.

Japanese film histories typically stress the foreign origins of the movie camera. This emphasis encourages a variation on apparatus theory in which Japanese filmmakers struggle to adopt Western technologies and to transform Western film conventions. Commonly, the film conventions are seen to derive directly from the movie camera, deterministically. At the same time, to counter the deterministic nature of Western technologies, histories call attention to what appear to be distinctively Japanese uses of the foreign apparatus. This strategy (of assuming technological determinism, giving it a Western origin, and then looking for Japanese resistance to the West) has the unfortunate effect of encouraging film historians to organize analysis around the differences between Japanese and Western cinemas. Interestingly enough, Japanese film histories construe as distinctively Japanese many of the practices highlighted in recent histories of early cinema in the West: other technologies of the moving image (magic lanterns) and exhibition practices *(benshi)* reminiscent of Tom Gunning's discussions of the "cinema of attractions."[7] Yet, where such practices and technologies in early film histories are taken as evidence of a new medium is still in flux, in Japanese film histories, they are construed as signs of the persistence of Japanese traditions or even a resistance to Western (cinematic) modernity. In effect, Japanese film history continues to struggle with the specificity thesis for cinema, and with the apparatus theory that grounds it. The result is a sense of incommensurability between Japanese traditions and Western modernity (cinema), rather than a sense of the radical otherness or historicity of the moving image itself. It is as if the radical otherness of the moving image could not be addressed directly but only displaced onto cultural otherness. The specificity thesis for cinema is shunted into a specificity thesis for *Japanese* cinema and by extension into a thesis about the uniqueness of Japan. Instead of an analysis of technical determination (moving image), the result is an insistence on cultural determinism (Japaneseness).

We should note then that, in Japan, at roughly the same time as in other countries (from the mid-1910s), a specificity thesis for cinema emerged, under the rubric of the "pure film movement" *(junsui eiga geki undō)*. The pure film movement basically argued that film conventions should ideally follow from the materials of cinema, often with an emphasis on the apparatus, calling for reforms to realize the essence of cinema.[8] Noel Carroll's critique of the specificity thesis is perfectly apt here: the pure film movement tended to envision cinema on the model of a highly specialized tool with a range of determinate functions. And anything that did not square with those determinate functions was construed as a sign of Japaneseness, whether negatively (as signs of the persistence of outdated, unenlightened traditions) or positively (as evidence of the persistence of Japanese values). But there is another way of looking at such developments, against the grain of this tendency to insist on national boundaries and cultural values. We might equally well read Japanese cinema in terms of divergent series rather than national boundaries, which is a call not to dispense with questions about the nation and formation of national cinema but to locate the sites where cinema troubles the imposition of national values, policies, or boundaries.

When I speak of the material essence or specificity of animation, I am not calling for animation to follow specific conventions in keeping with its apparatus, or its materials and technologies, and proposing to evaluate animations on that basis. When I speak of the essence or specificity of animation, my point of reference is the moving image not the apparatus. Which to say, I situate the "force" of the moving image (mechanical succession of images) prior to the apparatus, such as the movie camera or animation stand. The force of the moving image implies a radical otherness, historicity (an explosion of the new), and hetereity that makes for a *machine* prior to the apparatus or the technical ensemble.

The advantage of film history and film theory, then, is that it calls attention to questions about technology, modernity, power, and historicity. It presents a sharp contrast with art-based commentary on animation, which focuses on technique in order to bypass or rule out such questions. I will now turn to the animation stand, looking at it as an apparatus, but with the understanding that my ultimate aim is to comprehend the underlying machine without losing all sense of historical and technical specificity.

The animation stand effectively combines art "techniques" (drawing, painting, compositional techniques, and so forth) *and* film "apparatuses" (movie camera and film projector). The animation stand is a simple device for stacking sheets of painted celluloid in a rack, with the movie camera fixed above to photograph down through the layers. As a technical arrangement, it allows animators to draw on a range of techniques, tools, and devices. It is significant that it is difficult to ascribe a definitive historical origin for the animation stand, as one can with the movie camera.[9] The animation stand feels rather ad hoc, a combination of devices and techniques designed to rationalize and perfect an arrangement that already existed in "paper animation."

Before John Bray in 1914 introduced the use of celluloid into animation, animators drew a sketch on paper, photographed the sketch, erased elements and added new ones, and photographed the new sketch. When projected, the sequence of sketched images appeared to move. This is what I will call paper animation, by which I mean animation drawn on paper instead of celluloid, not animation made by cutting and assembling figures and backgrounds from paper (often called *kirigami* or cut-paper animation in Japanese). Paper animation did not vanish with the introduction of celluloid sheets. Even today it remains a cheap and accessible way of producing animation, particularly for amateurs who cannot afford celluloid.[10] Furthermore, cel animation incorporated the techniques of paper animation, making them one of the crucial stages in animation production. In the first stages of traditional cel animation, an animator or key animator usually draws sketches onto the pages of what is essentially a large flipbook. In the course of production, other artists add in-between images, clean up the sketches, trace them onto celluloid, paint them, and so forth.

Nonetheless, even though cel animation may begin with sketches on paper, this does not mean that the art techniques take precedence over the dynamics of the moving image. Even in paper animation, there is a sense of the multi-planar machine, which becomes tangible in projection. Historically, as animators produced animation through the process of drawing, photographing, erasing, and redrawing the character on paper, they quickly discovered that introducing a gap between layers made the process much easier. Either they could cut out the character or pieces of the character and recombine them on top of the background layer, or they could use tracing paper and continually retrace backgrounds and character elements with minor changes. The transparency of celluloid sheets makes this process easier and more efficient. Different layers of the image could be produced separately and recombined in various ways. Moreover, the transparency of the material (which holds ink and paint well) allows you to photograph through a number of sheets. There is, of course, a limit to how many layers you can stack and photograph—not only because of time and expense but also because the layers do absorb light. As you stack more and more cels, you begin to get silhouette effects, and a host of other problems arise. For instance, the colors of the lower cels, when seen through the upper layers, tend to change, and lighting becomes more difficult. Building on the transparency of the celluloid, the animation stand presents an additional rationalization and instrumentalization of the process. When you separate the sheets, for instance, you can introduce lighting between layers. Where early animators often relied on natural light when photographing their sketches (working close to a window), the animation stand, together with celluloid, allows you to introduce illumination between layers, which increases luminosity and clarity through layers, in addition to allowing the recombination of layers and the transformation of relations between layers.

The animation stand also has the advantage of permitting animators to reuse images. Backgrounds in particular can be used again and again. The transparency of celluloid also allows you to trace the same character again and again but with slight variations. Character sheets and characters elements can be used repeatedly. Of course, tracking the different sheets then becomes a demanding task.

This technical arrangement has an unintended side effect, an effect that becomes especially apparent under conditions of movement, which will in many ways define cel animation and will later enter into digital animation and special effects. The animation stand with its layers of celluloid sheets introduces effects of depth. Take the very simple scenario in which you draw the outline of a character in dark ink on a transparent sheet of celluloid, and carefully apply colors. You then place the character cel on top of a background (also painted on celluloid or on glass or some other support). These two layers alone can produce effects of depth. With the animation stand you are able to introduce more layers, and at the same time, you create a gap between the layers—an invisible yet palpable interval, a tangible effect of depth.

The effect of depth generated by the animation stand is very different from the depth of field associated with photography. It is not at all like the "monocular perspective" associated with the movie camera in the apparatus theory of cinema. Nor does it accord with the compositional techniques of what is variously called geometric, one-point, or linear perspective. Considered from the angle of art, such a use of layers feels more compatible with the layering techniques associated with Japanese wood block prints (ukiyo-e) of the Edo period, in which printers stamped various layers of color onto paper, which added effects of depth to a sketch boldly delineated in black (composed with such effects of depth in mind). This is surely one of the reasons why many commentators turn to Edo prints as a predecessor for anime. Unlike *ukiyo-e*, however, animation must address and somehow manage the relation between layers under conditions of movement, due to the mechanical succession of images.

In making this distinction, I do not mean to imply that *ukiyo-e* do not impart any sense of movement. I wish to stress how different animated movement is from that of wood block prints. Again, to highlight the problem of movement, we might think of the effects of depth arising from the animation stand as generating an *animetic interval*—an interval that is experienced in a state of movement. It makes for a depth that becomes palpable in motion. The animetic interval is at the heart of an *animation technics of the moving image*. The multiplanar machine, then, is not simply a matter of stacking or layering within the image. It is what arises when the multilayered image, under conditions of movement, opens an interval that effectively channels and directs the force of the moving image, making it central to the viewing experience. The multiplanar machine is also an animetic machine.

Animators initially confront the animetic interval at the basic level of relations between foreground and background. For instance, if you draw and color the background somewhat lighter than the character, the boldly drawn character will appear to be closer to the viewer—which is usually the desired effect. Even with simple forms of paper animation in which characters are drawn, erased, and redrawn on the same page with the backgrounds, it is common practice to draw characters more boldly than the background. With the introduction of a gap between the foreground character and the background layer, effects of depth become more palpable, which introduces new possibilities for playing with the relation between layers. Silhouette animation, in which cut-out figures appear as dark silhouettes against brilliant backgrounds, are interesting for the way in which they highlight depth yet disturb the sense of the background as being deeper than the foreground, because the brightness of the background pushes it forward, and the darkness of the figures makes them appear to recede or to be behind the background, as behind a screen.

But above all it is movement that makes the animetic interval apparent and important. It is movement that makes the gaps between layers integral to the viewer experience—which, as we will see, can be treated as a boon or a curse, depending on what your goals are. In any event, the interval must be addressed. The animation stand makes it relatively easy to impart a sense of movement of a layer *across* or *over* another layer. One common instance is that of a character moving across or over a background. You might, for instance, hold the character sheet in place while, shot by shot, sliding the background celluloid sheet slightly to the left or right. Of course you can also hold the background in place and slide the character sheet. When filmed and projected, the sensation is not that of the background moving but of the character moving. Of course, if you do not also animate the character shot by shot as well, you might unwittingly produce the sensation of the background moving rather than the character. If the character's legs and arms are pumping, we are more likely to feel it walking or running forward. In fact, producing characters whose movements are fluid, graceful, and continuous helps to mask the gap between celluloid sheets. Attention falls on the movement of characters, which serves not only to draw attention away from the sliding of layers but also to assure that the sliding of layers matches the actions of the character.

In later chapters I will talk about full animation versus limited animation. Full animation, often associated with the heyday of Disney feature-length animated films, strives to make the animation of characters appear as continuous or "full" as the movement of actors in live-action cinema. Limited animation, associated with television animation and thus with anime, dramatically decreases the number of drawings used for character movements, relying on other effects to impart a sense of movement. Both full and limited animations tend to rely on the animation stand, and so similar problems with movement and effects of depth arise. Simply put, both confront and must manage the animetic interval.

The real difficulties of the animation stand appear when you want to create a sense of depth of field and of movement *into* depth, as Walt Disney did in the early 1930s.[11] Say you want to create the sensation of moving into or out of a background—for instance, if you wish to adopt the viewing position of a character moving toward something in the background. Say that you want to create the sensation of a person walking toward a barn under the full moon. You begin with a background sheet with the barn and moon drawn on it. You might try changing the focus of the camera (zooming in or out), or try moving the camera closer or farther away from the picture. The problem is that, as the barn gets bigger, so does everything around it in the picture. The moon, for instance, also grows larger—rather than remaining the same size, as our conventional sense of the world dictates. Piling on additional layers doesn't help with this problem. You might try drawing the moon on a separate sheet. But the same problem will arise. The problem does not lie in the number of layers but in the relation between layers.

A long history of conventions received in art, science, and everyday practices leads us to assume that a relation of scale between layers is the best way to do things. We assume that scalar proportion is the most accurate way of viewing the world. Such expectations, needless to say, rely on geometric perspective and thus tend to echo Cartesianism to some degree. We expect things to remain in scale as we move around in the world. Not only does the barn look bigger as you walk toward it but also it starts to block out some of the other things in the field of vision around it, say, fences, bushes, trees, cows. If you draw a picture of a barn with fences and things around it, zooming in on the picture will not give the sensation of moving into depth. Everything becomes bigger, and the things in the background do not disappear behind the barn; the barn does not gradually block things. The challenge of movement into depth is that of keeping everything in the image in scale as your viewing position changes. One solution is to change the background sheet with each successive shot, changing the relative size of different entities from image to image, making the barn somewhat larger while the moon stays the same, and fences and trees disappear behind the looming barn. Clearly, however, this is very costly and time consuming, particularly if you want backgrounds with lots of painterly detail.

You might reduce the number of background drawings with editing techniques. For instance, you might cut back and forth between images of the person's eyes and images of the background (with relative proportions dramatically altered). Such techniques make it easy enough to depict movement away from the camera's viewing position: draw the character smaller and smaller (or bigger and bigger); successive exposures make the character appear to move and vanish into the landscape. Miyazaki Hayao's *Castle in the Sky* (*Tenkū no shiro Rapyuta*, 1986) provides a good example: as Sheeta falls from the airship toward the ground, she gets smaller and smaller (Figure 3). Thus she appears to move away from us. At the same time, to give us the sense of Sheeta falling rather than shrinking, the sequence intersperses images of the pirates looking down from the airship from above). Each time we cut back to them, they also look smaller and smaller. This setup lets us know that Sheeta is falling rapidly down and away from the airship. While this is a perfectly serviceable rendition of falling, such a sequence really doesn't give a sensation of movement *into* depth but rather of movement away from our viewing position.

In animation, the problem of movement into depth is not one of creating an illusion of depth by using techniques of composition, as is commonly supposed. It is not enough to draw a background in accordance with the principles of one-point perspective. Nor is the problem one of depicting movement toward or away from the camera's viewing position. It is matter of seeing from Sheeta's eyes, feeling the ground rush upward and the clouds race by, as you plummet through the clouds. Movement into depth is a matter of viewing from the position of the speeding object. It is a ballistic point of view, the bullet's-eye view, so to speak. The greater the velocity, however, the greater is challenge of managing the changes of proportion and scale that impart the sensation of moving into the world of the image. But the problem also arises at lesser speeds.

Figure 3. *After her initial plunge from the airship in* Castle in the Sky, *Sheeta loses consciousness, and her "flying stone" begins to control her fall. As she floats earthward, her movement into depth is rendered via a gradual diminution in the size of her figure.*

Apparently, conveying a sense of movement into the image became an obsession for Walt Disney. As the story goes, he felt that he could not make his feature-length animated film *(Snow White)* without the ability to produce the sensation of movement in depth—the sensation of a changing point of view at somewhat greater speed. Prior work on animated shorts had introduced a range of techniques of drawing backgrounds, animating characters, layering sheets of celluloid, and lighting them. Animators could produce a range of sensations of movement, of depth, and of weight in their animation. Disney, however, took up a challenge issued from cinema, that of imparting a sense of voyage into the screen world. As Noel Burch notes in his study of early cinema, the voyage into the screen would ultimately depend on breaking the flatness or tableau-effect of the screen by adopting a monocular perspective (that of camera) with a network of eye-line matches that allowed viewers the sensation of moving into a three-dimensional space.[12] Simply put, the eye of the viewer was aligned with the viewing position of the camera as it moved. Emphasis fell on the mobility of the camera's moving position, and all manner of practices and conventions arose to abet the production of the sensation of movement into depth, of a voyage into the cinema screen.

It may be that the financial failure of his work to date made Disney in the early 1930s feel that producing movement into depth in a full-length animated film would be a profitable direction to take, but in any event, he aimed for something analogous to cinema's voyage into the screen world. In cel animation, however, because you shoot a series of still pictures rather than stroll around with a camera (or use dollies, cranes, and other devices to introduce camera movement without introducing too much wobble), you can't use the camera as readily to impart a sense of movement into depth. Animation begins with relatively small inked-and-colored worlds that dramatically limit the range for camera movement and thus threaten to prevent any sense of movement inside those worlds. In fact, the camera in animation tends toward fixity rather than mobility.

Disney's solution relied on a rationalization of the animation stand. Drawing inspiration from the creation of depth on the stage with its layers of scenery, he designed an apparatus, the multiplane camera, which allowed him to regulate the distances between layers, which he could then calibrate in accordance with shifts in camera focus and position. Simply put, he rationalized the movement of celluloid layers in three directions relative to the camera's eye (right–left, up–down, forward–backward) where previously the emphasis fell on two directions (right–left, up–down). To return to the above example of the viewing position of a person walking toward a barn under the moon, the solution is to paint moon, trees, and fences on one layer, and barn on another. You then move the barn layer slightly up toward the camera (or the moon-trees-fences layer downward) shot by shot. Thus the moon stays the same size, while the barn grows and the trees and fences disappear behind the barn. What is more, with the ability to move layers in the three directions, you can produce a sensation of movement into depth at an angle, say, walking toward and past the barn on an angle.

In 1940, Disney received a patent on the multiplane camera, which he had already put to use in a *Silly Symphonies* segment called "The Old Mill" (1937). But it was in *Snow White* (1937) that the multiplane camera came into its own, remaining the dominant means of conveying depth of field and a sensation of motion in depth well into the 1990s. The basic problem addressed by the multiplane camera—the animetic interval—did not simply disappear with the ascendency of digital animation in the 1990s, however. Even today digital animation software packages emphasize their ability to produce multiplane camera effects. The basic idea is the same: the scalar relations between different layers of the image are constantly readjusted to assure that, at each point along its trajectory, the monocular viewing position presents a world that remains in scale, in proportion.

While I do not wish to suggest that Disney does not deserve credit for the multiplane camera, I wish nonetheless to stress that the problem of using sheets of celluloid had appeared earlier in the history of animation, and animators had already begun to use the animation stand. In fact, Ub Iwerks might also be credited for the multiplane camera, which he began to use as early as 1933. In the context of Japan, Seo Mitsuyo's *Ari-chan* (*Little Ant*, 1941) is usually cited as the first Japanese animated film to use the multiplane camera, photographing four layers. Here, however, I stress the importance of the animation stand rather than multiplane photography. This is because it is through the use of the animation stand that the basic set-up for the multiplane camera emerged. As soon as transparent sheets of celluloid were introduced, animation began to generate and cope with a specifically animetic interval within the moving image, with distinctive effects of depth, which animators might play with or attempt to mask. It is the animetic interval that makes multiplane photography at once desirable and possible.

As early as 1933, you see the Japanese animator Kimura Hakusan working with a rather sophisticated animation stand.[13] Even though he may not be using the same *apparatus* as Ub Iwerks was in that year, Kimura is working with the same basic *machine*, which channels the force of the moving image into an animetic interval, thus encouraging animators to think of animation (drawing, coloring, layering) in terms of the movement that would arise between layers. A recent exhibit on Japanese film heritage displayed the animation stand and camera of Ōfuji Noburō (Figure 4), one of the pioneers of Japanese animation, whose works met with international acclaim in the late 1920s. In fact, Ōfuji, renowned for his work with cut-paper animation, from the early 1930s gradually started to play with the movement between different layers of the film, sometimes using semitransparent paper elements that raised the play of movement between layers to a new level of intensity. This animation, too, results in a kind of multiplane animetic machine, even if it does not use the multiplane camera per se. It makes sense, then, to think of the animation stand and the multiplane camera in terms of a contrast between *invention* and *innovation*, somewhat in the manner of James Utterbeck: *invention* as ideas or concepts for new products or processes, and *innovation* as the reduction of an idea to the first use or sale.[14]

The stacking of celluloid sheets in an animation stand (or some variation on it) is the invention, while the multiplane camera system is an innovation

Figure 4. *The poster for a special exhibit on Japan's film heritage at the National Film Center in Tokyo includes this image of an animation stand that Ōfuji Noburō constructed to produce his cut-paper and silhouette animations.*

(even if patented as an invention). This is an important distinction in the context of Japanese animation, because it allows us to consider animation in an international context without attributing all innovation and invention in animation art to the West, or more specifically to America and the American master, Disney. This distinction allows us to avoid repeating the history of influence (apparatus) and reaction (Japaneseness) that plagues Japanese film history. It is sufficient to say that, by the 1930s, Japanese animators, like those in other countries, had begun to use celluloid sheets and to experiment with stacking and layering them in stands, and thus to work with something akin to multiplane photography. This explains why the multiplane camera quickly proved amenable to Japanese animators after its introduction to Japan. In their history of Japanese animation, Yamaguchi Katsunori and Watanabe Yasushi mention that an essay on the use of the multiplane camera appeared as early as 1938 in Japan, and prototypes were soon in use in the world of Japanese animation.[15] The rapidity of its adoption suggests that the multiplane camera can be seen more as innovation than invention.

Surely some historians might feel compelled to pinpoint the origin of the animation stand, as an invention, in order to establish an order of priority between countries, and maybe between the West and the Rest. The West often receives priority when one insists on Disney as the standard for animation, as the inventor of the apparatus. Apparatus theory is frequently in collusion with an emphasis on Western origins. As I remarked above, film histories that stress the introduction of the movie camera from the West into Japan tend also to stress the foreignness of the apparatus and to set up a divide between Western technology and Japanese practices. There is a consequent tendency to insist on Japaneseness, to shore up Japanese identity on the basis of its difference from and reaction to the West. Even with the movie camera, however, it may be argued that many of the basic principles and conventions underlying the *cinematic machine* had long been understood and practiced in Japan. But that is another story. What is interesting about the animation stand is that it does not demand a history of origins. To some extent, it defies origins. Its historical appearance is more of a threshold effect. It is a material limit for a force, which makes for a field of possibilities, and thus for varieties of animation that present divergent paths. This is why I prefer the terms *multiplanar machine* or *animetic machine*, which is a machine condensed and localized into a quasi-apparatus (the animation stand), which generates a field of material orientations by channeling the force of the moving image in specific ways.

At issue too is the extent to which one innovation—Disney's multiplane camera system for producing movement into depth—should be considered *the* dream of animation and its dominant visual attraction. Japanese innovations in animation were not so intent on the production of movement into depth. This was not due to a technological lag or lack. Nor was it necessarily a form of resistance to specifically Western technologies and conventions. Rather the animation stand, as a multiplanar machine, invites different ways of negotiating the animetic interval, which also imply different ways of thinking about and inhabiting the technologized world. As such, for better or worse, it addresses the modern technological condition. To consider how animation opens a diverse series of critiques of modern technology, however, I need to return to the tendency of the multiplane camera toward cinematism, and to explore some specific ways of dealing with the animetic interval, with an emphasis on Miyazaki Hayao's strategy of "open compositing."

CHAPTER 3

COMPOSITING

WHAT VIRILIO CALLS CINEMATISM can be seen as an intensification of one-point perspective and what is commonly called Cartesian perspectivalism. One-point perspective (also called geometric or linear perspective) makes the objects in a drawing look like they recede into the distance, appearing smaller the farther they are away from you. To produce geometric or one-point perspective, you have to use perspective lines, straight lines drawn at an angle to converge at one point, the vanishing point, on the horizon line (an imaginary line at eye level in the drawing). In his seminal account, Martin Jay describes it thus: "The three-dimensional, rationalized space of perspectival vision could be rendered on a two-dimensional surface by following all of the transformational rules spelled out in Alberti's *De Pittura* and later treatises by Viator, Dürer, and others."[1] As Jay reminds us, it is the combination of these "Renaissance notions of perspective in the visual arts" with "Cartesian ideas of subjective rationality in philosophy" that is commonly thought to produce "the dominant, and even totally hegemonic, visual model of the modern era."[2]

The notion of the modern hegemony of Cartesian perspectivalism had a powerful impact on film studies. Apparatus theory in particular, with its emphasis on the monocular lens of the movie camera, saw cinema imposing the same structures of one-point perspective (and thus the hegemony of Cartesian perspectivalism) onto the visual field of the moving image. Moreover, much as art historians gradually came to the conclusion that it was not techniques of geometric perspective alone that produced the hegemonic visual regime of modernity but their tricky combination with philosophies of subjective rationality, so apparatus theory backed away from the technological determinism implicit in the initial insistence on the monocular lens to place greater emphasis on ideological forces, economic demands, and modes of representation. But there persisted an insistence on the hegemonic structuration of the visual field of moving pictures in accordance with Cartesian perspectivalism, with a consequent search for "modernist" forms of cinema that disrupted the modern hegemonic regime of cinematic representation.

Virilio's cinematism can be read as a variation on the hegemonic visual regime of perspectivalism, one that puts the emphasis on speed and movement into depth—ballistic perception in which you see from the point of view of the speeding projective, the bullet's-eye view. Movement into depth in cinema depends on keeping things within the image in "proper" scale even as your viewing position changes. It is a matter of sustaining Cartesian perspectivalism in conjunction with camera movement or with the mobility of viewing position.

The Japanese animated shorts that survive from the early 1930s show an awareness of the relation between linear perspective and ballistic perception. Not surprisingly given the times, such animations are often linked to Japan's war of imperial expansion. In *Norakuro nitōhei* (Stray Black, second class, 1933), for instance, there is a scene that aligns the bumbling dog soldier Norakuro with the art of the engine (Figure 5). We see Norakuro racing at us down the road

Figure 5. *An animated short from 1933 based on the* Norakuro *series shows the bumbling "stray black" soldier dog driving down the road. While the scene is compositionally in keeping with geometric or one-point perspective, it does not generate a sense of movement into depth.*

in a car, with the road drawn neatly in perspective lines to the vanishing point. The viewing position has only to be reversed (the car looking ahead down the road) to achieve the vantage of apparatus-subject. A later feature-length animation from 1945, *Momotarō umi no shinpei* (Momotaro, divine soldiers of the seas) provides precisely that viewing position: we see from an armored tank as it fires down the road (Figure 6). Elsewhere in Japanese animation of the early 1930s, animators include scenes in which we adopt the viewing position of telescopes or binoculars looking from airplanes on military missions, as in *Sora no Momotarō* (Momotaro of the skies, 1931). In one sequence in this film, our viewing position approximates that of the airplane as it tracks the enemy (Figure 7). A later animation, *Momotarō no umiwashi* (Momotaro's sea eagles, 1942), which recreates the Japanese attack on Pearl Harbor, briefly offers a bomb's-eye view: from within the plane we see the bombs drop away from us toward the fleet below, or we see through the apparatus that constructs the world as a target (Figure 8).

Such examples, however, fall short of cinematism because they do not sustain an alignment of our viewing position with the movement of the projectile. The sequence from *Momotarō umi no shinpei* is somewhat exceptional: for a while it sustains a view down the road from the point of view of the American

Figure 6. *The famous feature-length Momotarō film of 1945 includes a scene in which we look from within the tank as it fires down the road, which encourages an association of geometric perspective with ballistic optics.*

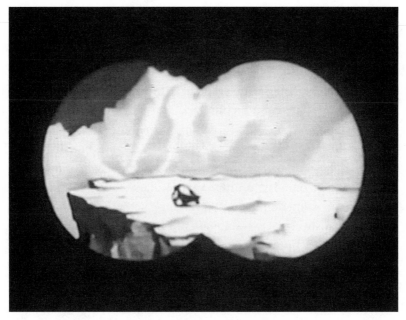

Figure 7. *An earlier Momotarō film from 1931 uses iris effects to simulate looking through binoculars at the enemy, in this case an eagle.*

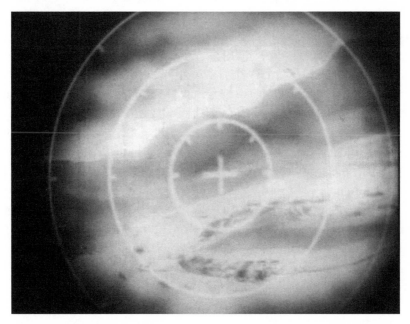

Figure 8. *A Momotarō film from 1942 that re-creates the attack on Pearl Harbor frequently adopts the viewing position of various apparatuses to emphasize the targeting capabilities of the aerial force.*

tank, using a vanishing point and providing a sense of the landscape moving past the vehicle. Significantly, the drawings for this sequence are very rudimentary compared with the detailed landscapes that characterize the film as whole, and the point of view is that of the feckless and undisciplined American soldiers. It would be rash, however, to conclude that ballistic perception is being evoked and dismissed as an American technology.[3] Rather, what is important is that, although these animations evoke one-point perspective at the level of *composition*, they do not use the movement in depth characteristic of ballistic modes of perception, which would demand specific procedures of *compositing*.

Disney's innovation, the multiplane camera system, was the first step toward producing movement into depth and thus the ballistic perception associated with cinematism. It allows animators to shift the viewing position of the camera shot by shot while adjusting the distances between celluloid sheets in such a way that everything remains in the scalar proportions that the principles of geometric perspective have established as accurate. The difficulty of the multiplane camera comes of the fact that you have to fuss with every shot, which makes it exceedingly time-consuming—and cel animation costs are above all labor costs. Each time you wish to move a bit farther into the image, you have to readjust the vertical distances between layers. And if the camera moves inward at an angle, the various layers have to be adjusted horizontally as well. To assure that things shift in accordance with scale, you must finesse the relations among layers shot by shot, vertically and horizontally. Otherwise, the viewer will feel the gaps between layers. You won't feel that you are moving into a solidly and accurately proportioned world.

This is surely why even Disney's use of the multiplane camera falls short of cinematism. In the opening sequence of *The Old Mill*, for instance, multiplane photography allows our viewing position to approach the old mill without things going out of proportion, a sort of slow tracking shot into depth. Multilayer photography also allows for a sense of depth of field akin to that of deep focus with the movie camera: foreground and background layers appear slightly blurred when the focus is on the figure in the middle layer. This is how the multiplane camera is used in *Ari-chan* (Little ant, 1941), reputedly the first animated film in Japan to use multilayer photography, and in *Kumo to Chūrippu* (The spider and tulip, 1943), which bears some resemblance to "The Old Mill." The emphasis is on photographic depth of field rather than on movement into depth. In fact, although there are moments in *Ari-chan* and *Kumo to Chūrippu* of things rushing out of the screen at you (raindrops especially), in the scenes emphasizing depth with multilayer photography, the movement of figures is primarily across the screen.

Cinematism in Virilio's sense demands a sustained sensation of movement into depth. It is not enough to draw an image of an island seen from a biplane through a telescope. It is a matter of rendering the plane's-eye view as it swoops down to the island, into the trees, and past dwellings. Here all kinds of technical difficulties arise, because the animation "apparatus"—the animation stand—works against the production of movement into depth. Although the use of multiple sheets of celluloid produces effects of depth, those effects are at odds with the production of movement into depth in accordance with Cartesian perspectivalism.

The same problem crops up in digital filmmaking. In the supplementary disk with commentaries on *Star Wars: Episode 1—The Phantom Menace* (1999), for example, techies talk about problems of movement within the digital image. After they had introduced layer upon layer of architectures into the image, they had to pay close attention when moving the (simulated) camera around because things did not remain in scale. You would see the slippage; or, if you could not exactly see it, you could feel it. One would think that computers could correct for every possible "deformation" of scalar relations automatically. But you would have to introduce calculations for every one of the many layers and for their relations, which is not such an easy matter. And if you then decide to add another layer or to alter one (as often happens during production or postproduction), everything changes. As a result, the camera doesn't move around very much in many of these sequences from *The Phantom Menace* that combine live-action footage of actors with CGI worlds. Some sequences feel more like tableaux than worlds that you can move around in, as if the use of digital technologies had unwittingly re-created the theatrical stances of early cinema. This is rather surprising, given that the first *Star Wars* movie (1977) gained renown for its use of the motion camera, which made for a film exploding with high-speed ballistic effects, precisely the sort of hyper-Cartesianism that Virilio denounces as a suicidal hyperinstrumentalization of the human lifeworld.

The problem is basically one of compositing. Compositing is a matter of assuring that the gaps between different elements within the image are not noticeable. It is a matter of rationalizing the relations between different layers of the image, and thus of harnessing the force of the moving image in certain ways, to specific ends. As live-action cinema draws increasingly on digital effects and CGI, it encounters the same problem that arises in cel animation—that of compositing layers of the image. The question is whether compositing will happen in accordance with Cartesianism or whether other manners of compositing can be envisaged.

Because cel animation uses two or more layers to compose an image, it forces a confrontation with effects of depth that are at odds with Cartesian perspectivalism. If you wish to produce the sensation of movement into depth in accordance with the Cartesian model (which is still received as *the* accurate representation of depth, despite evidence to the contrary), you need a specific kind of compositing within each image and between images: each image in the sequence must adjust the relation between elements in accordance with geometric perspective. The result is an illusion of moving within a volumetric 3-D world. In effect, it is a mobile version of Cartesian coordinate space. Movement into depth deploys geometric perspective to impart the sense that this image world is consistent, stable, and solid. A specific manner of rationalizing of space and time precedes the mobility of viewing position. We can think of this kind of compositing as "volumetric compositing" or "closed compositing" because the idea is to close the gaps within the image and between images even as the viewing position changes, which produces an apparently consistent world (consistent geometrically and volumetrically). If we think in terms of Alberti's famous metaphor of the "open window," which he first used as a rubric for painting with geometric perspective in 1495, it is as if you could step through the window and walk around in the world outside—and eventually fly and zip.[4]

In other words, producing movement into depth within cel animation is not merely a matter of drawing images in accordance with one-point perspective. It is not a matter of composition but of compositing. Nor can you rely on moving the camera or changing its focus, for the world into which you wish to move is full of interstices. There are gaps between the layers or planes of the image. This is why I see the animation stand as so fundamental to cel animation. In cel animation, the animation stand promises different ways of rationalizing the relation between planes of the image and, by extension, of controlling the relation between the camera and orientation in space. Where cinema tends to shunt the force of the moving image through the lens and into camera movement in three dimensions, animation tends to shunt the force of the moving image through the animetic interval into compositing. The animation stand might thus be seen as the apparatus of animation, but it does not for all that totally determine or structure the visual field.

The animation stand is an apparatus that sets up layers of transparent celluloid bearing drawings to be photographed. It gathers together a series of other technical devices and schema that do not automatically belong together or come together: a rack, a fixed camera, lights to provide sufficient illumination on the layers and through the layers, manual techniques of applying ink and color, abstract techniques of composing images in accordance with various conventions (such as one-point perspective), and the industrially produced celluloid sheets and the celluloid film in the camera. When I refer to the animation stand as an apparatus, I do so to stress its technical and material properties. But, as the discussion of compositing indicates, there is an abstract and immaterial dimension to this technical ensemble that does not reside exclusively in the technical and material devices. This is the *multiplanar* or *animetic machine*. As with Guattari's example of the lock and key, there are two types of form at work in this encounter of the movie camera with a multiplanar image. There are what Guattari calls "materialized, contingent, concrete, and discrete forms," namely, the ink, celluloid sheets, camera lens, lights, film, and other materials.[5] And there are "formal" or diagrammatic forms, which here is the multiplanarity that appears as a continuum across a range of profiles of concrete and discrete forms. But that multiplanarity happens under conditions of movement. As such, the animation stand is but the site of localization and condensation of a multiplanar machine or animetic machine, which works with the interval between planes of the moving image.

Guattari remarks, "One quickly notices that the machinic effect, the passage to the possible act, is entirely concerned with the second type of form."[6] He concludes that these diagrammatic forms appear infinite in number because they are an integral of the discrete materialized forms. Put another way, the animation stand allows for an assemblage or ensemble of very different and even incompatible kinds of materials. To put these materials to work together, it must somehow integrate across their differences. That integration is not in the materials. It is an abstract and immaterial diagram—a machinic effect. This explains how the same problem of compositing that appears in cel animation can arise in the context of using digital animation and CGI in live-action cinema. The multiplanar machine can appear in a context using very different material forms—just as the diagram of the lock and key appears in many different assemblages of concrete materials. I wish especially to stress this point because, even though almost no one today makes cel animation in the "traditional" way, the multiplanar machine—the diagram that first coalesces around the production of cel animation in the 1930s—appears in all manner of films and animations today. This is why many digitally produced animations still look like cel animation. It is not simply a matter of the persistence of forms and conventions but of continued innovation with the animation diagram that rationalizes the force of the moving image in a specific manner. This is the essence, or rather the material essence and underdetermination, of the multiplanar animetic machine.

A machine in this sense, then, is not a structure. It does not totalize or totally determine every outcome. Apparatus theory in film studies implied a structuralist bias whereby the structure of the movie camera (monocular lens) determined the whole of cinema, resulting in a convergence of cinematic modes of representation, sometimes dubbed the classical style, classical film form, or the classical Hollywood style. Not surprisingly it drew inspiration and support for this way of looking at cinema from accounts of Cartesian perspectivalism, which also tended to think in terms of structures and structuration of the perceptual field. As I will discuss in the conclusion, such moments of convergence (in film history, for instance, the convergence into a unitary set of conventions known as classical style) are predicated on divergent series; convergence addresses divergent series from the angle of their structural capture or technological submission. But convergence is not in the apparatus.

If a machine is not a structure, it is nonetheless a *determination*, at once material and immaterial, concrete and abstract. Guattari submits that the diagrammatic forms of a machine appear infinite in number, because it is an integral or integration, which generates an infinitesimal. But his evocation of the infinite doesn't mean that anything whatsoever can happen. It is more a matter of an internal limit, at once in the materials and in the relation between material forms. Thus the machine allows an unfolding of different forms. It does not force convergence when it rationalizes the force of the moving image. Rather it unfurls divergent series.

Cinematism, then, is a tendency that appears across divergent series of cinema and animation. It may become a site for convergence of divergent series, but it is not a force of convergence in itself. As with any tendency, it implies a way of harnessing a technical force. In other words, animation is not fated to strive for a sensation of movement into depth. Even in cinema, with the mobile camera, cinematism is not the easiest of effects to sustain. In animation, cinematism demands a great deal of technical attention, time, and money. When everything works, however, the results are astonishing, precisely because the viewer has the impression of being able to move around inside the image, as if the image had become a world. Moreover, the viewer can move around more rapidly and freely than in daily life. You zip around. As the term *cinematism* implies, we tend to associate this kind of movement into depth with cinema and the mobile viewing position of the camera.

Cinematism is not an exclusive property of cinema, even if it is the mobile camera of cinema that initially proposes this manner of rendering movement into depth. Variations on cinematism are as common in digital animation and video games (the avatar often entails a mobile viewing position that simulates movement into depth) as in cinema. Cinematism today is commonly associated with action films. It is especially associated with the use of digital animation and

CGI in action cinema. The tendency toward cinematism frequently arises at the point of intersection across or confluence of media platforms, where cinematics enter video games, and video games enter cinema. It is common where digital animation meets cinema, where it is less a matter of a voyage into the screen world than a flight through it. Think of the sequences in which Dash zips through forests and around rocks during the island chase scenes in *The Incredibles* (2004), or the digital scenes of Spiderman web-slinging his way through Manhattan. Such animation does not merely replicate or simulate the mobile viewing position of cinema. It strives to raise it to a new power, to multiply and intensify it. The cinematism of digital animation frequently appears to push the limits of live-action camerawork. If, as Nam June Paik says, "cinema isn't to see, it's to fly,"[7] then such animation has the potential to fly faster, deeper, and farther. This might be thought of as *hypercinematism* and hyper-Cartesianism.

The popularity and centrality of digital animation has significantly changed how we see animation. On the one hand, everything seems to be turning into animation. The popularity of digital animation and the increased use of digital effects in filmmaking has contributed to a situation in which it is possible to argue, as new media theorist Lev Manovich does, that animation, once subsumed by cinema, has now succeeded in subsuming cinema. He writes, "Born from animation, cinema pushed animation to its periphery, only in the end to become one particular case of animation."[8] Japanese animation director Oshii Mamoru expresses a similar sentiment, announcing that all cinema is becoming animation.

Oshii is renowned for his use of digital technologies to experiment with and challenge the boundary between cinema and animation in such animated films as *The Ghost in the Shell* (Kōkaku kidōtai, 1995), *Avalon* (2001), *Innocence* (2004), and *Tachiguishi retsuden* (The amazing lives of fast-food grifters, 2006). A recent collection of his essays and interviews under the title *Subete no eiga wa anime ni naru* (All film is becoming animation) begins with an account of Miyazaki's manga films written in 1984. As I will discuss subsequently, Miyazaki and Studio Ghibli insist on styling their animated films as *manga eiga* or "manga films," in contrast to anime. Miyazaki generally strives to approximate his work to cinema rather than anime. Oshii, however, is dubious about Miyazaki's insistence on the cinematic quality of his animations. He remarks, "The manga film, in fact, because of its methodological limitations, points to a transitional form that cannot ripen into 'cinema.'"[9]

In Oshii's account, as in Manovich's, the contemporary transformation of cinema into animation hinges on overcoming cinema as a recording of reality or indexicality. Oshii uses the term *jissha* or "recording reality," suggesting that the digital overcomes the limit between "live action" (*jissha*) and "animation" (*dōga*).[10] The loss of a cinematic recording of the actual reverses the trend of animation following cinema, making for a situation in which cinema becomes animation.

Even those who wish to hang on to cinema speak of "expanded cinema." In sum, the rise of digital animation and new media technologies make it easy to think that animation is taking over cinema, or at least radically transforming it.

On the other hand, some argue that traditional cel animation has disappeared. In the course of the 1990s, digitally animated features, especially those of Pixar, consistently defeated cel animation at the box office, leading many observers to conclude that cel animation was a thing of past. Yet the 1990s also saw a global boom in Japanese animations, loosely gathered under the rubric *anime*, many of which were series made for television. While in the course of the 1990s the production of Japanese animated television series gradually shifted from the older cel animation materials to computer production, a large number of these animations still look like cel animation. This is because, even if they are produced digitally, their manner of compositing is not that commonly associated with digital animation. It is not closed or volumetric compositing. Such animations entail what I will call open compositing, which plays with the layering of elements within the image and with the movement between layers. When we feel there is something anime-like, something animetic, about some American animations (for instance, *Powerpuff Girls* [1998–2004] or *Star Wars: Clone Wars* [2003–5] or *Avatar: The Last Airbender* [2005–8]), it is partly due to those moments when you feel the gap between planes of the image. This is where cinematism gives way to animetism, which implies very different procedures of compositing.

In sum, it is common today to speak of animation becoming the dominant logic of the moving image. Yet rather than find an underlying unity that would account for the ubiquity and popularity of animation, I would like to stress the multiplicity of animation. In my opinion, it is the coexistence of so many different varieties of animation based on divergent series of animation that makes for the overwhelming sense of the centrality and ubiquity of animation today. In other words, even in the realm of digitally produced animation, even in an era in which animation appears to have radically transformed cinema and even to have displaced it, I think it important to point out that there is more to animation than an expansion of cinema or a subsuming of cinema. In focusing attention on the importance of compositing to animation, I wish to signal a divergence at the heart of the moving image, which enables a bifurcation of its force into camera movement and into moving planes. It is not a matter of a simple division of the world of moving images into cinema versus animation.

Rather there are two tendencies, cinematism and animetism, which traverse cinema and animation, allowing us to think in terms of divergent series of animation and cinema.

Animetism begins when you allow some degree of play or openness to appear between the layers of the image, or when you flatten the layers to make them look and feel like a single layer. Animetism puts less emphasis on compositing the image tightly, on hiding the gaps between the different layers of the image as the camera (or viewing position) moves. Still, animetism is not the opposite of compositing. It favors an "open compositing" in which layers of the image are allowed to move more independently of one another. While open compositing tends to work against sensations of movement in depth, it makes possible other sensations of movement. Open compositing does not have you look from the tip of a bullet speeding toward its target, or from the train engine rushing down the rails, or the camera eye moving into a world. As mentioned in the first chapter, the idea is to look at the effects of speed on perception sideways. This gives a very different sense of motion and a different sense of orientation in the world.

Animetism begins with an image composed of two or more layers, separated in the animation stand. But, unlike the multiplane camera system, you don't try to produce effects of deep focus. Nor do you produce sensations for movement of the viewing position into depth in accordance with the scalar proportions of one-point perspective. With the animation stand, because the camera is fixed on a rostrum (the rostrum camera), camera movements are largely limited to tracking in and tracking out. If you don't adjust the distances between layers to keep things perfectly in scale when you move the camera, the elements in different layers will appear to pull apart or to draw closer together as they become smaller or larger, as you track in or out. The effect is like that of curtains opening and closing. When the camera tracks in or out, you see different planes of the image slide. Camera movement produces a sensation of sliding layers, and as movement into depth, the effect is decidedly different from the movement of a camera in cinema.

Historically we have come to associate the production of movement into depth with high production values, and as a result, for many viewers closed compositing looks good, while opening compositing may look cheap. The sliding layers feel like an undesirable artifact of layering rather than an art of animation. Many viewers consider it unnatural if trees or rocks appear to slide apart as the hero enters the forest or cave. But there is an art to working with the movement between layers of the image. Open compositing is not just a matter of being cheap. It has its art, its techniques, and its reasons.

In addition, with the animation stand and rostrum camera, you can move the layers of the image. Holding the camera in place, you can slide the drawings relative to one another. The result is lateral movement of a layer or layers relative to other layers. For instance, if you want a character to move left, you can slowly, shot by shot, slide the background layer to the right. If you also animate the character (say, move her arms and legs), the effect is not of the background sliding past the character but of the character walking forward. Here, too, as with the tracking movement of the rostrum camera, the resulting movement is not a movement into depth but a sliding or gliding movement. Such movement may also seem unsatisfactory to some viewers, because it sometimes feels as if the character were not moving forward. Rather, as is actually the case, the world seems to move by the character, a situation some might find unrealistic, although such a sense of the world is as natural as geometric perspective.

In sum, with the animation stand, the tendency is toward an open compositing and thus animetism—an "animetic" rather than cinematic sense of depth and movement. The film apparatus (the camera) is fixed or restricted in its movement and thus loses its privilege in constructing a sense of movement and depth. The camera becomes just another layer of the image. The animation stand, and the layering of the image, takes precedence over the camera and over the depth as rendered in drawing. But, to repeat, this animetism is not merely the product of an apparatus (of the concrete and discrete materials) but of an abstract and immaterial diagram, the multiplanar or animetic machine.

Let me draw an example from Miyazaki Hayao, who as we will see is one of the Japanese animators most committed to avoiding cinematism and working with animetism. His animations are marvels of open compositing. Take for instance a scene from his *Castle in the Sky*, in which the girl Sheeta and the boy Pazu begin to explore their surroundings after crash-landing on the island in the sky. As the children walk to the edge of a cliff, the foreground layer and the background layer slide apart to reveal the depths below (Figure 9). This is difficult to render with a series of screen grabs, but if you look closely at the images, you will note that, rather than movement into depth, this sequence involves a sliding of the planes of the image. While the view is supremely panoramic, the sequence is not constructed to impart a sense of moving into the image world. There is a sense of a world opening up, a world with various layers that invite exploration . . . and awe. Such a technique of sliding the planes makes the children's viewing position (and ours as well) feel less instrumental. This way of looking does not encourage us to seize this place instrumentally, that is, to poke into its every corner, to plunder its treasures, to dominate and exploit it (as the bad guys are prone to do). Rather this is a world that opens to us even as it remains apart from us. As it opens, you see depth, but these depths are not calculable by

Figure 9. *This sequence from* Castle in the Sky *does not alter scalar proportions to impart a sense of movement into depth but slides various layers of the image in conjunction with a shift in viewing position, which gives a sense of depth opening before the children rather than the children moving into depth.*

Cartesian geometry. This manner of viewing thus invites awe and reverence. We are witnesses not raiders.

Likewise with the subsequent views of the castle in the sky: they consist of layers of clouds that are slowly pulled across and between layers of architectures (Figure 10). Again, if you look closely at the screen grabs, you will see that the architectures remain in place, while layers of clouds are pulled through them, shot by shot. Such a panoramic perception does not make for movement into depth, and yet you definitely have the sensation of movement, a slightly giddy sensation that increases the sense of the wonder of this place.

Often when people talk about the art of Miyazaki Hayao, they present still images of his landscapes (which are truly impressive in their vibrancy and detail) or trot out his character designs or speak of his wacky machines or, predictably and almost tediously, bang on about how popular his films are. Miyazaki indeed has a range of skills. In his earlier work on classic animation series such

Figure 10. *In this sequence from* Castle in the Sky, *a sense of depth and motion—of a "movementful" world—is achieved by sliding the layer of clouds past the architectures.*

as the television series *Arupusu no shōjo Haiji* (Heidi, girl of the Alps, 1974) he became adept at producing landscapes, vistas, and panaromic views. He is exceedingly inventive in constructing frantic action sequences, especially in his subsequent series such as *Mirai shōnen Konan* (Future boy Conan, 1978) and *Rupan sansei* (*Lupin the Third*, 1971–72) and the film *Castle in the Sky*. He also has a knack for producing iconic yet expressive and memorable character types, and there is a sort of lexicon of instantly recognizable Miyazaki characters. Yet I would argue that the art of Miyazaki's animation *as animation*, that is, as an art of movement, lies in his finesse with the sliding planes of the animated image. Sequences of flying, gliding, floating, often in conjunction with panoramic viewing, so prevalent in Miyazaki's films, strike me as the key to his animation. And it is in his techniques of movement that the stakes of his art of animation are clearest.

Miyazaki almost studiously avoids the closed compositing and sensations of movement into volumetric depth. This is not simply a matter of budget. Although he now has access to large budgets and computer technologies that would allow him to lessen the sensation of movement between layers, he tends nonetheless to emphasize it. In the production of *Princess Mononoke* (*Mononoke-hime*, 1997), he began, reluctantly, to use some digital technologies, but he initially restricted their use largely to coloring or painting. His resistance to computer techniques is not simply a defense of traditional cel animation but also part of a general resistance to the sort of compositing that has almost come to define digital or computer animation—movement in accordance with Cartesian perspectivalism, which computers have made accessible. Indeed, when he does resort to computer animation, the sequences tend to stand out, as with the scenes in *Princess Mononoke* in which a wild boar charges after the hero (Figure 11). The scene stands out because, even though digital compositing would make it possible to produce effects of motion in depth, Miyazaki emphasizes lateral movement

Figure 11. *While the use of digital technologies would allow for a sense of movement into depth, the dynamism of this sequence from* Princess Mononoke *comes instead from lateral movement in combination with techniques of angling character motion (discussed in chapter 6), which work with open compositing.*

in ways that undercut the sensations of depth.[11] Almost as a rule, his films avoid or undermine sensations of movement into depth.

There is strong affinity between Virilio and Miyazaki in this respect: both are resolutely opposed to cinematism. But, where Virilio writes brilliant analyses of the technological closure and destruction of our world, Miyazaki strives to produce worlds without technological closure, by suppressing cinematism in his art while developing other ways of working with the potential of the moving image. Virilio thinks that it will not be easy—and it probably is no longer even possible—to strip away the effects of modern technologies, to get back to a slower, nonballistic world friendly to the human body and senses. There is an aura of technological determinism in Virilio: hyper-Cartesian hyperinstrumentalism will not go away. In contrast, even as he denounces a technology-centered worldview, Miyazaki strives to produce nonballistic worlds, other worldviews. This is the case with many of his films, especially the earlier action animations like *Conan, Lupin, Castle in the Sky*, and *Nausicaä of the Valley of the Wind* (*Kaze no tani no Naushika*, 1984). *Nausicaä* and *Castle in the Sky* in particular present an exceedingly pessimistic view of modern technology, in which the triumph of the ballistic worldview and the drive toward global destruction seem inevitable, totally determined in advance, in a manner reminiscent of Virilio. Yet Miyazaki is intent on fashioning another kind of world by using technologies differently. Indeed his animation is designed to produce an experience of another relation to technology.

Miyazaki clearly prefers animetism over cinematism. He favors the sliding sensation of speed. Only rarely in his works do you see from the perspective of a speeding vehicle, and even then the vehicle is likely to be a bicycle or glider or flying broomstick. Usually, you glide alongside the glider, as if gliding yourself, rather than zeroing in on a destination or target. Compositionally as well, he often turns to the slippery staircase, the canted deck, the tilting plane, and then gives you a sideways impression of falling, slipping, careening. At the level of narrative, too, Miyazaki avoids reaching a destination or conclusion or coming full circle. He avoids both linear progressive movement and cyclical regressive movement. Even his stories tend to move laterally, sideways, diagonally. At every level he strives to produce animetism not cinematism.

Interestingly enough, Miyazaki also differentiates his work and that of his studio (Studio Ghibli) from anime, insisting that his works are *manga-eiga* or manga films. Manga films are not adaptations of manga but feature-length animated films, largely geared to children or general audiences, such as those produced by Tōei Studios in the 1950s and 1960s, often referred to as Tōei *dōga* (literally "moving pictures" or "moving drawings"). Miyazaki places himself and Ghibli in the lineage of Tōei animated films, on which he worked from the 1960s. In contrast to manga films, anime for Miyazaki signals something like *telebi anime* or television animation. Miyazaki himself worked on animated series for television, but even in that work he now claims that he strove to produce something like manga films, trying to sustain the tradition of Tōei *dōga*. In chapters 6 and 15, I will talk more about how the contrast between manga film and anime works for Miyazaki and Studio Ghibli. Suffice it to say at this point, Miyazaki associates anime with war and violence. He and his longtime friend and partner, Ghibli cofounder and director Takahata Isao, also express their dislike of Hollywood action films. In sum, what I have presented as a contrast between animetism and cinematism, Miyazaki poses as a contrast between the manga film versus the action film/anime. In effect, Miyazaki sees in both anime and action films a ballistic optics of cinematism, and his manga-film techniques of animetism are designed to challenge and to offer alternatives to that cinematism.[12]

In the next chapter I will explore Miyazaki's use of animetism in the context of *Castle in the Sky*. In anticipation of that analysis, I would like to make a couple more points about animetism versus cinematism in the context of Miyazaki's preference to work with sliding planes of the image in an attempt to produce a different relation to speed and technology. First, because cinematism is often associated with technophilia, there is the temptation to construe cinematism as technology in contrast to cinematism as art or technique, and to posit an opposition between art and technology or, if you will, between *poiesis* (poetics) versus technē (tools), between creating and crafting.[13] Miyazaki is much sharper than that, however. He knows that the art of animation is not separable from its tools; it is "techno-art" or "techno-poetics." Indeed the very challenge of his work lies in its attempt to rethink technology without rejecting it.

Second, it is tempting to posit a divide between cinematism as high tech versus animetism as low tech. While Miyazaki's films do seem to favor something like low tech in the form of limited technology or minimal technology (bicycles, windmills, gliders), the challenge of his work again lies in its refusal to posit a strict opposition between something like low tech and high tech, or between technique and technology.

Naturally, as Thomas Hughes points out, there is a risk in defining technology so broadly that one loses all sense of focus by speaking, for instance, of the technology of cooking or coaching. Thus he limits technology to the creative activities, individual and collective, of craftsmen, mechanics, inventors, engineers, designers, and scientists.[14] Similarly, with regard to the creative activities of animators, individual and collective, even though some of those activities would fall outside Hughes's definition, I think it justified to speak of technology, without positing a divide between low tech and high tech, precisely because it is technologies of the moving image that underlie animation production, which fold so-called low-tech or nontechnological activities into it. This is the essence of the anime machine. In other words, my sense of what technology is agrees with Hughes's, and yet, precisely because I am dealing with a technical ensemble that blurs the distinction between the technological and the nontechnological by folding machines into the animetic machine, my definition has fuzzier edges.

Because animation tends to gather nontechnological modalities in a technical ensemble, it makes sense that Miyazaki's animations are able to avoid a divide between low tech and high tech per se. And their critique of technology becomes more a question of shifting our relation to technology than of refusing it or standing outside it.

Third, some commentators distinguish between science (as noninstrumental observing and knowing) and technology (as instrumental seizing and remaking). In Miyazaki's films, scientific observation sometimes appears to afford a superior knowledge of the world. His heroine Nausicaä, for instance, through scientific observation of and experimentation with fungi from the poisonous sea of growth sweeping over the earth, discovers the truth: the organisms are not poison; they are purifying the earth of its toxins, releasing them as gas. Nonetheless, Miyazaki does not resolutely separate science from technology. Scientific observation has the potential to open our thinking about technology, however. In this respect, like the German philosopher Martin Heidegger, Miyazaki inverts the traditional relation between science and technology: technology is not applied science; rather, modern technology demands physical science (practices come before their formalization), but the situation retroactively creates the illusion that science comes first.

In sum, although we see in Miyazaki's thinking about technology traces of traditional and often questionable distinctions (art versus tool, low tech versus high tech, technique versus technology, science versus technology), his films *as animation* do not allow us to embrace simplistic oppositions. Rather his animation encourages us to open a different relation to technology from within technology, much as animetism harnesses a different potential of the moving image than cinematism does. As such, Miyazaki's preference for open compositing challenges the technological determinism implicit in apparatus theory and in structuralist theories of perspectivalism. His animations invite us to ask, as Martin Jay does, "is there one unified 'scopic regime' of the modern or are there several, perhaps competing ones?"[15] But as we will see, in Miyazaki, it is not so much a question of *competing* with cinematism as a hegemonic modern regime of the moving image as it is a matter of returning to a moment prior to cinematism in order to imagine how things might turn out differently.

CHAPTER 4

MERELY TECHNOLOGICAL BEHAVIOR

CASTLE IN THE SKY TELLS THE STORY OF A BOY AND A GIRL, Pazu and Sheeta, who must save the world from destruction. But this is a postapocalyptic world. Weapons of mass destruction (WMDs) have already led to global destruction in the distant past. Although people have largely forgotten those events, the WMDs remain. No one knows how to locate and deploy them, and yet the danger remains that someone will rediscover and use them. This is precisely what happens in *Castle in the Sky*: knowledge of the WMDs and the ability to activate them has fallen into the hands of a power-hungry, unscrupulous man, Muska, who leads a group of men named for their "darkglasses" *(kuromegane)*.

The film opens with pirates launching an attack on a large, stately, dirigible-like "flying ship" *(hikōsen)* below them in the clouds. As the pirates on their "flaptors" race past the windows of the luxury skyliner, the female chief of the pirates, Dora, spots the treasure that they wish to seize: the girl Sheeta gazing out the window. The pirates storm the ship, and a battle ensues between them and the darkglasses. As it turns out, these factions are battling not simply for the girl but for her pendant. At the end of this opening sequence, Sheeta will escape both the pirates and the darkglasses by falling from the flying ship (see chapter 2, Figure 3).

After the title sequence (which I will discuss below), the film returns to the unconscious Sheeta as she falls through the evening skies toward the lights of a human settlement far below, with the clouds parting slightly to convey depth. Suddenly, magically, radiance bursts from the jewel in the pendant around her neck, and the jewel brakes her fall. She no longer plummets headlong but, stretched horizontally as if asleep in bed, floats gently earthward. The film thus introduces its magical object, a jewel with mysterious powers, around which all the conflicts in the film will revolve.

As Sheeta floats earthward, the film introduces Pazu, a boy who works in the mining village. He spots the light in the sky, realizes that it is a person, and runs to catch the unconscious Sheeta. Pazu takes her into his dwelling, and as the two become acquainted, pirates come in search of Sheeta. Pazu disguises her, and together they flee. Thus begin their adventures together, with first the pirates and then the darkglasses in pursuit of them. At the end of a fast-paced madcap sequence in which the pirates chase them through the village and onto mining rails stretched high over shafts and gorges (which plays brilliantly with the sliding layers of the image to produce effects of speed and depth with a minimum of ballistic vision), the darkglasses arrive in armored tanks. Caught between the pirates and the darkglasses, as the rails collapse, Pazu and Sheeta plummet into the depths. This time the jewel saves them both, and they float radiantly down into a mineshaft. In the mines, the children learn from an old-timer about the "flying stone" (*hikōseki*), a luminous mineral that exerts an anti-gravitational force. The walls of the mine glow with this magical, largely forgotten energy source, and it is a pure crystal of this mineral that forms the jewel in Sheeta's pendant.

When the children exit the mines, the darkglasses capture them, taking them to a towering fortress. Their leader Muska attempts to force from Sheeta the secret of her flying stone. Sheeta agrees to cooperate in exchange for releasing Pazu. As it turns out, however, Sheeta's jewel awakens a giant robot, which then opens attack on everything in its perimeter, as if to defend Sheeta. Apparently, the jewel is somehow keyed to Sheeta's body, activating its powers, and thus the robot's, to protect her. In the meantime, Pazu, who has joined with the pirates, returns in the nick of time to rescue Sheeta as the robot lays waste to the fortress and the countryside. The pirate boys, under the leadership of their mother Dora, prove more pragmatic and good-natured than they initially appeared. With the light from Sheeta's jewel pointing the way, the pirates, Pazu, and Sheeta together head for the castle in the sky, with the darkglasses not far behind.

In the midst of a battle in which the darkglasses pursue and capture the pirates, Sheeta and Pazu escape in a glider and fly through an electrical storm. At the heart of the vortex of clouds and lightning appears Raputa, a seemingly halcyon world of gardens, flowing waters, graceful arcades, and domed architectures. Plants have taken over the long uninhabited flying castle, and a large tree grows at its center, while robots tend to the gardens and squirrels. The aura of paradise found, however, is quickly broken by the arrival of the darkglasses whose leader Muska aims to power up the flying castle, which is also (as the term *shiro* implies) a military fortress. Muska can deploy the flying fortress's WMDs, but only with the assistance of Sheeta; it is her jewel that is the key to activating the command system. Rather than assist Muska, Sheeta (with Pazu) speaks the words of destruction, and the castle begins to self-destruct. Fortunately, Pazu and Sheeta (and the pirates) escape in the nick of time, and the final scenes of the movie are of the two children soaring in Pazu's glider, gazing on the tree, formerly imprisoned in the flying fortress, as it now floats freely and serenely up into the clouds.

This postapocalyptic set-up offers humans a second chance to get their relation to technology right. While in the past humankind proved unable to control its ability to destroy the world, an opportunity arises for humans to break the cycle of technological destruction of the planet. Significantly, *Castle in the Sky* takes place in a world that recalls our nineteenth century, which is frequently considered the heyday of confidence in techno-scientific modernity.

The opening sequence presents a world with a period look. As is generally true of Miyazaki's films, it is difficult to say exactly what period this is,[1] but dress (the ballroom attire on the luxury liner and the frock coats of the darkglasses) and technologies (telegraph and Morse code) suggest that it is, or is like, the nineteenth century. But it is the nineteenth century again, a second moment of technological modernization. The technological frame of reference, however, is almost exclusively militarization rather than industrialization. In sum, in *Castle in the Sky*, the opportunity to develop a better, nondestructive relation to technology is predicated on returning to and rethinking the nineteenth century, and in particular the modern commitment to technological progress, techno-scientific modernity.[2] The rise of techno-scientific modernity is presented in the title sequence, as a backstory for the film, in the form of a brief history of the technological rise and fall of humanity.

Using hard etched lines and pastel tones reminiscent of antique prints, the title sequence opens with a bucolic image of the wind personified: a cloud with a women's face blowing the wind (Figure 12) and a person standing alongside a human-sized windmill. Subsequent images show the progress of humanity in harnessing the power of the wind. Humans harness wind to power machines that dig deep into the earth. Then humans—or rather, men—conquer the skies with ever grander and more elaborate flying machines, what Helen McCarthy nicely describes as "a panoply of magnificently dotty eighteenth- and nineteenth-century flying machines rendered in a graphic style and gentle color scheme reminiscent of antique prints."[3]

Next come vast flying cities, castles in the sky. But disaster follows this

Figure 12. *The title sequence from* Castle in the Sky *provides, in condensed form, the technological backstory for the film, running full circle from images of the wind to windmills, windmill-derived industries, and finally military fortresses in the sky, which culminate in mass destruction and a return to the "goddess" blowing the wind.*

technological triumph. A great storm arises, and in the wake of dark clouds and lightning a flying city lies in ruins on the ground, with streams of people pouring forth. Finally, as if coming full circle, the title sequence returns to the shepherd girl, who resembles Sheeta, next to the windmill designed to pump water.

The title sequence does not specify the source of power for the flying machines and flying castles. Subsequently in the film we learn that, to power their conquest of earth and skies, men mined pure crystals of flying stone and ultimately constructed flying fortresses, that is, military installations in the sky. Although the title sequence hints at these possibilities, its history remains deliberately sketchy, incomplete. The result is something like a natural history of technological rise and fall, so broad that it verges on epic or myth. The antique look of this sequence only appears in two other moments in the film: a photograph of Raputa taken by Pazu's father before his disappearance (it hangs in his workshop where Pazu builds flying machines, determined to find Raputa and prove his father was not crazy) and in the sequence in which Muska tells Sheeta about how the robot fell from the sky. In other words, the old-fashioned look allows us to see the past as it appears from the present time of the film—antiquated, hazy, almost mythic. We see the past with their eyes, through their technologies. Our view of the past is literally marked and colored by visual technologies. Visual technologies at once enable and obscure our ability to reckon with our technological history. The title sequence thus gives us a clue to what troubles Miyazaki: the technological rise and fall of humanity seems predestined, and modern technology seems by its very nature destructive.

The situation presented in the film is dire: technologies appear by their very nature to generate social unevenness and to lead to global destruction. So overwhelming is this sense of the destructive force of technology that Miyazaki's film makes it difficult to know if destruction is inherent in technology or in humans. Are humans destructive by nature? Or are technologies destructive by nature? Insofar as technologies appear to determine the course of history and society, Miyazaki's stance toward nineteenth-century-style technological modernity verges on technological determinism; modern technologies of destruction appear irresistible and inevitable: even if we defeat them, even if they self-destruct, they will reappear, as if part of human nature. Consequently, we might conclude that the only alternative would be the complete elimination of technology, a total rebellion against technology that would culminate in a "return" to a nontechnological world or nature. At the end of the title sequence, for instance, the world returns to its apparently natural state after the collapse of advanced technologies.

Miyazaki's response, however, is not so pat as an elimination or rejection of all technologies, or of technology in general. First, at the end of the title sequence with its apparent return to a more natural state of affairs, a girl stands alongside a windmill, and windmills are, after all, technology. Second, machines are often a source of wonder and awe in Miyazaki's films, and not simply for their destructive power. Of the dotty flying machines in the title sequence, McCarthy aptly remarks, "All were designed by Miyazaki himself, and despite their extravagant appearance, all are workable according to the technology on which they are based."[4] Similarly Pazu's delight in watching the flight of birds and constructing flying machines is not merely an impulse toward technological destructiveness. There is something marvelous about technologies of flight, something beautiful about human ingenuity and innovativeness that Miyazaki does not wish to fore-close. Third, while *Castle in the Sky* casts technology in a deterministic and teleological light (technologies determine our condition and push us invariably toward the same end, mass destruction), the film also puts linear, progressive time out of joint: the nineteenth century has returned, yet because it is difficult to imagine a perfect and exact repetition of history, we are already prepared for this new line of historical development to swerve. Finally, and most importantly, Miyazaki is aware that animation entails technology, even if it be as simple as the animation stand and rostrum camera. Here we catch a glimmer of how Miyazaki will respond to the problem he poses about technological determin-ism: animation should be more like the windmill and less like the WMD. In sum, Miyazaki's animation does not entail a wholesale rejection of technology. It strives to develop a different relation to technology.

Miyazaki's stance toward technology recalls that of the German philoso-pher Martin Heidegger whose thoughts on technology remain a point of depar-ture for much of contemporary thinking about such questions. Like Heidegger, Miyazaki is often taken for a technophobe who would have us return to a pre-technological world, in which human activities will no longer contribute to the devastation of nature. It is fairly easy to tease out moments of antitechnological sentiment in Heidegger and Miyazaki, but as I have already indicated, a whole-sale rejection of technology not only proves difficult but also does not say much about technology other than "it is evil." This is not the stance of Miyazaki's animation or Heidegger's philosophy.

In his seminal essay on Heidegger and technology, Hubert Dreyfus points out that Heidegger "comes to the surprising and provocative conclusion that focus-ing on [technology as] loss and destruction is still technological."[5] In Heidegger's thinking, "All attempts to reckon existing reality . . . in terms of decline and loss, in terms of fate, catastrophe, and destruction, are merely technological behavior."[6]

Heidegger wants to direct our thinking about technology away from a cer-tain manner of humanistic thought that always places human actions and thus human loss and gain at the center. Such a way of placing humans at the center is not merely humanism but High Humanism. Needless to say, to challenge the tenets of High Humanism is not to submit that humans are nothing or un-important. Nor is it to deny human agency. Rather, in Heidegger's view, when we think only in terms of how technology makes for human loss and gain, we do not arrive at an understanding of what technology is and how it works—what Heidegger calls the *essence* of technology. In his opinion, if we don't under-stand the essence of technology, we will either push on blindly with it, or, what amounts to the same thing, rebel helplessly against it. Or we might mistakenly suppose that there is an easy way to get technology under control so that it can serve our rational purposes.

Much like Heidegger, Miyazaki's *Castle in the Sky* remains suspicious of easy answers to the questions posed by modern technology, especially those that assume that we can measure and control the effects of technology solely on the basis of human loss and gain. Moreover, even though Miyazaki's works are full of antitechnological and apocalyptic statements (as are Heidegger's), Miyazaki does not present instrumental solutions to the problems of technology (nor does Heidegger). Their view is both darker and more hopeful, because, to quote Dreyfus's apt formulation, "The threat is not a *problem* for which there can be a *solution* but an ontological *condition* from which we can be *saved*."[7] This is precisely what Sheeta and Pazu offer when they intone the words of destruction and thus destroy the castle in the sky: they offer not a solution to a problem but salvation from a technological condition.[8]

Still, as an adventure or action-centered film, *Castle in the Sky* runs the risk of posing the threat of technological destruction as a problem with a solution. The bad guys (darkglasses) are, in effect, a problem because they want to find the lost WMDs and reactivate them to rule over the world from the skies, while the good kids (Pazu and Sheeta) with their wacky friends (the pirates) must stop them. Thus the easy solution to the technological problem would appear be stopping the bad guys from using WMDs. Yet, if it is not already clear from the film itself that technology is not a matter of problems and solutions, Miyazaki says as much in an interview with novelist and critic Murakami Ryū. Murakami praises Miyazaki's *Castle in Sky* for offering a happy ending without humanism.[9] In other words, Murakami astutely notices that Miyazaki does not present us with a resolution in which a human-centered instrumental relation to technology saves the day. Such a solution might entail, for instance, the hero seizing the weapons of mass destruction and placing them under the direction of other, apparently trustworthy authorities. Such an outcome would be not merely humanism but High Humanism, and as Murakami notes, Miyazaki is wise to the instrumentalist assumption inherent in High Humanism. The assumption is that there are human individuals or human collectives that can properly and adequately brake or direct WMDs. This manner of thinking is at the heart of the Cold War arms race: the assumption is that the good guys will use the weapons properly and humanely, whereas the bad guys will not. For Miyazaki, however, there is no humanist solution in the sense of more or better human regulation or control of technologies. The problem is not merely one of human reason.

In the interview, Miyazaki does not respond directly to Murakami's observations about humanism; instead he expresses his discontent with boys'-adventure stories, because they usually entail a simple resolution in which the defeat of the villain solves all the problems.[10] The boys'-adventure story, in effect, operates by presenting a technological problem and finding a technological solution. Miyazaki's aim is to hollow out the boy's adventure genre from within, to transform it. In *Castle in the Sky*, as in his other adventure films, he strives to alter a film genre that tends to frame technological threats in terms of problems and solutions—which genre entails, as Murakami Ryū notes, a sort of humanism, or to be more precise, High Humanism. Miyazaki knows that defeating the villains and seizing the weapon is not an appropriate answer to the problems posed by modern technology. Such an answer leaves you within "merely technological behavior."

To counter merely technological behavior, *Castle in the Sky* poses the question of technology in the form of a riddle or mystery—that of the flying stone. In Miyazaki's early plans for the movie, he suggests such titles for the film as "Young Pazu and the riddle of the flying stone," "Captive of the castle in the sky," "Treasure island in the sky," or "The flying empire."[11] In other words, this is a boys'-adventure story, with echoes of nineteenth-century adventure tales (such as *Treasure Island* and also Jules Verne), and yet the treasure poses a riddle. The riddle is not simply how or where to find the technological treasure. The riddle asks what this precious technology is *in essence*. The questions and problems that arise around the flying stone thus imply a *technological condition* rather than a *technological problem*. The almost hermeneutic circling of the film around the flying stone contributes to the transformation of a problem into a condition. Once technology is posed as a condition rather than a problem, it is possible to envisage salvation from it. This is what Sheeta and Pazu offer, salvation from a technological condition, rather than the solution to a technological problem. Since we know, and Miyazaki knows, that there may well be more flying stones, giant robots, and flying fortresses out there (and if not they can be invented again), and so it isn't enough to read for us the film in terms of putting an end to a technological problem (that is, the WMDs). Rather our relation to technology must change. Here, too, Miyazaki is very much like Heidegger. Both wish to move us from a *correct* understanding of technology (as problem/solution) to a *true* understanding of it (as a condition).

In Heidegger's view, the scientifically informed technology that increasingly dominates the world is not something fundamentally new or even modern.[12] Nonetheless, the "essence of modern technology is to seek more and more flexibility and efficiency *simply for its own sake*."[13] The only goal becomes optimization. Everything—nonhuman and human—is seen in terms of how its usefulness might be technologically optimized. Such is the modern technological condition: an understanding of existence in terms of optimization. As such, the problem of technology is not only its destruction of nature and culture but also (and more importantly) its restriction of our thinking. Still, this realization about the technological condition does not lead to a dead end. If technological solutions will not suffice, we can nevertheless save ourselves from this condition by opening a new relation to it. In Dreyfus's opinion, Heidegger seeks to show how we can recognize and overcome our modern technology-restricted thinking by recognizing our essential receptivity to technology. We can break out of the technological understanding of the world whenever we find ourselves "gathered by things rather than controlling them."[14] When engaged in practices that draw you in, you experience a focusing and nearness that resists technological ordering. This can even happen in our relation to modern technology. Heidegger's example is the highway bridge, and he focuses on it in such a way as to bring out how it works to produce technological ordering and its continuity with pretechnological or nontechnological things. This is what Heidegger calls gaining a free relation to technology. This is exactly what happens in *Castle in the Sky*.

As Sheeta and Pazu open themselves to the flying stone and experience the wonder of its apparently magical powers, it gathers and focuses their attention on technologies in such a way that they come to understand the connections between the flying stone and the nontechnological world. They come to see how the flying stone functions to produce a technological ordering of the world. Insofar as we are caught up in their adventures, we too are invited to transform our relation to modern technological order, by recognizing how it gathers us and conditions our thinking, which encourages a historical understanding of it. As Dreyfus puts it, "The danger, when grasped as the danger, becomes that which saves us."[15]

Although Miyazaki's manner of thinking modern technology in *Castle in the Sky* is eerily close to Heidegger's, it should be noted that Miyazaki, as a creator of animated films produced for general audiences, faces the challenge of modern technology in a very different register from Heidegger. It may be possible for him to show how Sheeta and Pazu, by grasping the danger as the danger, save themselves from the modern technological condition. But how does this work for viewers? Miyazaki has to work with the ways in which viewers open themselves to the film, and this kind of viewer receptivity may not necessarily help to open a free relation to technology. It may simply encourage passivity, an unthinking consumption of panoramic spectacle. Miyazaki is well aware of this impasse. He is aware of how animation can catch and focus attention in specific ways. Even though he labors to produce films that will not result in something like "merely technological behavior" among children (such as sitting in front of the television all day destroying their imaginations and openness to the broader world), he knows that it is exceedingly difficult to produce via animation on the screen the kind of receptivity essential to gaining a free relation to technology.[16]

This is where harnessing a different potential of the moving image—the animetism that comes of an open compositing of the multiplanar image—promises a way of interacting with animated worlds, one that gathers and focuses the viewer's attention in such a way as to encourage a recognition of the technological ordering of the image, which would help viewers to understand it and move beyond it. In this respect, Miyazaki's use of open compositing has to be understood less in terms of a solution to the problems posed by the technological ordering (that is, the ballistic vision of cinematism that he attributes to anime and action films) and more in terms of a way to recognize and understand what cinematism truly is. Only thus will animation break out of its modern technological condition.

In *Castle in the Sky*, and in much of Miyazaki's work in general, technologies of flight are the key to gaining a free relation to technology, at once thematically (everything revolves around different ways of taking to the skies) and technically (how to render flight in animation). The question of "how animation thinks" becomes a matter of "how animation flies." It is in animated flight that Miyazaki proposes to gather and focus our practices of perceiving speed. We thus need to take a historical look at Miyazaki's animations, with attention to bodies that fly, before we can consider how his animations try to generate a free relation to technology.

CHAPTER 5

FLYING MACHINES

MIYAZAKI LOVES TO DESIGN VEHICLES, and all sorts of cars, boats, and planes figure prominently in his films. He is obviously not a mere technophobe. *Castle in the Sky* marks a turning point in his animation, however. After *Castle in the Sky*, Miyazaki would make two films geared largely to younger children (in contrast to *Nausicaä* and *Castle in the Sky*, whose worlds, in his thinking, appealed more to older children and adolescents): *My Neighbor Totoro* (*Tonari no Totoro*, 1988) and *Kiki's Delivery Service* (*Majo no takkyūbin*, 1989). These two films move away from the large epic and adventure worlds that had brought him into the limelight. Although these two films also center on bodies that fly and the joys of flight, they move resolutely away from an overt engagement with the modern technological condition that characterizes *Nausicaä* and *Castle in the Sky*, almost as if Miyazaki had gained his free relation to technology in *Castle* and began to inhabit it. Later, in his third film after *Castle in the Sky*, *Porco Rosso* (*Kurenai no buta*, 1992), Miyazaki self-consciously plays for laughs his prior engagement with adventures centered on technologies of flight—in fact, when you finally glimpse the face of the pig pilot, he looks like Alexander Key, the novelist whose book inspired *Conan* as well as *Nausicaä* and *Castle in the Sky*. It proved difficult for audiences to share the joke in its entirety, however.

Miyazaki's three subsequent films—*Princess Mononoke* (*Mononoke hime*, 1997), *Spirited Away* (*Sen to chihiro no kamikakushi*, 2001), and *Howl's Moving Castle* (*Hauru no ugoku shiro*, 2004)—brought him unparalleled box office success in Japan and won a long-overdue broad-based theater release of his films in North America as well as greater acclaim internationally. Yet, as many commentators have pointed out, Miyazaki's vision of technologies and the technological condition in these films seems more deterministic and less nuanced than in his earlier films.[1] In terms of Miyazaki's thinking technology in animation, *Castle in the Sky* is truly a turning point. It was also Miyazaki's first film with Studio Ghibli, which he established in 1985 with his longtime friend and collaborator Takahata Isao, also a director of animated films. Takahata first served as Miyazaki's producer on *Castle in the Sky* and ever since has produced Miyazaki's films. The history of Miyazaki's collaborations with Takahata prior to *Castle in the Sky* and the foundation of Ghibli is crucial to understanding Miyazaki's changing relation to bodies that fly.

Takahata Isao was born in 1935, and Miyazaki Hayao in 1941, which meant that, in 1959 when Takahata was graduating from Tokyo University, Miyazaki was graduating from high school.[2] Takahata began working at Tōei Studios in 1961, working as an assistant director on their fourth feature-length animated film, *Anzu to Zushiomaru* (Anzu and Zushiomaru). Tōei Studios referred to its animated films as *dōga*, literally "moving pictures" or "animated drawings," and the animation studio is known as Tōei Dōga.[3] Tōei's first three *dōga* enjoyed international success, gaining prizes at film festivals and appearing in English dubs (usually re-edited). *Hakujaden* (Legend of the white serpent, 1958) became in English *Panda and the Magic Serpent*. *Shōnen Sarutobi Sasuke* (The youth Sarutobi Sasuke, 1959) was dubbed in English as *Magic Boy*. *Saiyūki* (Journey to the West, 1960) was distributed as *Alakazaam the Great*. Yabushita Taiji directed these films (and subsequently a number of others), and it was under Yabushita's direction on *Anzu and Zushiomaru* that Takahata learned the trade.

Miyazaki began as a temp at Tōei Dōga in 1963, at a time when the studio's success with feature films was allowing them to expand into television animation. Takahata (direction) and Miyazaki (in-between animation) both contributed to a television series called *Ookami shōnen Ken* (Wolf Boy Ken, 1963), but the *dōga* that has become legendary in the Studio Ghibli annals for bringing together the dream team is *Taiyō no ōji Horusu no daibōken* (Prince of the Sun: Hols's great adventure, 1968; released in English as *Little Norse Prince*). This film combined the talents of Takahata as director, Miyazaki as key animator and scene designer, and Ōtsuka Yasuo as animation director. Understanding Ōtsuka Yasuo's style of animation is especially important to understanding Miyazaki's. In fact, in 2004, in conjunction with its traveling exhibition on the manga film, Studio Ghibli produced a documentary on Ōtsuka Yasuo entitled *Ōtsuka Yasuo no ugokasu yorokobi* (Ōtsuka Yasuo and the joy of making movement). In this documentary Takahata and Miyazaki highlight the impact of Ōtsuka on Japanese animation in general and on their own animation in particular. Later I will write more about Studio Ghibli's insistence on referring to their animations as manga films, a term that does not mean that these animations are adapted from or even inspired by manga. The term *manga film* indicates something like feature-length animated films for children or general audiences, often (as in this instance) stands in contrast to anime or animated television series.

Miyazaki worked closely with Ōtsuka in 1964 on the film *Garibaa no ūchū ryokō* (Gulliver's space travels, 1965), and impressed with his work, Ōtsuka used Miyazaki's ideas for the last part of the film. When asked to make *Prince of the Sun* in 1965, Ōtsuka made his only condition the appointment of Takahata as director. Miyazaki began voluntarily to participate in the project at that time, only to be pulled away on another project. But then, with the key animator suddenly hospitalized, Miyazaki returned to *Prince of the Sun*.

Loosely borrowing elements from Norse myths and tales, *Prince of the Sun* tells of a young boy, Hols (often called Horus because of the Japanese pronunciation of Hols), who must defeat the ice demon Grunwald who is intent on destroying the human settlements. In the opening sequence, Grunwald's pack of wolves attacks Hols, and he defends himself with only an axe. When the wolves appear about to win, Hols unknowingly awakens a stone giant. Hols pulls a blade from the shoulder of the giant and learns that, once forged anew, the sword will transform him into the Prince of the Sun. Soon thereafter, upon the death of his father and after an encounter with Grunwald, Hols takes up residence in a fishing village. Hols discovers and kills the giant fish responsible for the disappearance of their fish, earning the gratitude of the villagers. The gray wolf, a minion of Grunwald, continually appears outside the village, seen only by Hols, who frequently leaves in pursuit of the wolf. On one chase, Hols encounters the young girl Hilda in an unpopulated village. Hilda's beautiful voice endears her to Hols and the villagers, but gradually we learn that Grunwald controls her actions via the jeweled pendant around her neck. Hilda spurs the villagers to grow suspicious of and to expel Hols, which clears the way for Grunwald's full attack. Subsequently, however, inspired by Hols's kindness and the love of an orphaned child, Hilda chooses to sacrifice herself to save the child. Hols returns to the village, forges the sword with the villagers, and defeats Grunwald in a final battle. Hilda, too, returns to the village, with the return of sun and spring.

Miyazaki apparently contributed to *Prince of the Sun* some of its most moving scenes (the villagers listening to Hilda's song) and innovative devices (the ice boats and ice mammoth). What is more, in the documentary on Ōtsuka, Miyazaki cites Hilda's magical pendant in *Prince of the Sun* as the inspiration for the flying stone pendant in *Castle in the Sky*. There is indeed an affinity between Sheeta and Hilda, as girls who suffer under the burden of a pendant that controls their relation to the world, from which they must free themselves.[4]

The 1960s were a tremendously productive time for Tōei Dōga and also a time of labor strife. Miyazaki, Takahata, and Ōtsuka also sealed their friendship through their participation in the animators' union (Miyazaki as chair and Takahata as cochair), and the three stuck closely together through a series of projects and studios. In 1971, Takahata and Miyazaki left Tōei to join Ōtsuka at A Pro, in order to make an animated series based on *Pippi Longstocking*. Among numerous other projects, the three adapted Monkey Punch's manga into an animated television series also called *Rupun sansei* (*Lupin III*, 1971–72). Received poorly when it first aired, *Lupin* went on to become one of the most touted and influential television series in Japan. Soon after (in 1973), Ōtsuka, Miyazaki, and Takahata moved on to Nippon Animation, where Miyazaki worked especially on the *World Masterpiece Theater* television animation series, contributing as key animator and director for animated adaptations of such children's classics as *Anne of Green Gables* and *Heidi*. At Nippon Animation, Miyazaki also created an animated adaptation of Alexander Key's novel, *The Incredible Tide*, under the title *Mirai shōnen Konan* (Future boy Conan, 1978). Takahata directed some episodes, Ōtsuka served as animation director, and Miyazaki directed and worked as key animator. Even though Takahata's and Ōtsuka's contributions are evident, you also see in *Conan* the emergence of something decidedly Miyazaki.

Conan takes place in a postapocalyptic world and deals with the aftermath of weapons of mass destruction, for, even though technologically advanced industrial society has come to an end, the weapons linger on. The adventure begins when a preternaturally strong youth, Konan (or Conan) meets a young girl Rana (or Lana). The girl, who possesses psychic powers, becomes caught up in a struggle to regain the secrets of solar energy that powered the "old" WMDs. Lepka, the villainous head of Industria, knows that Lana's grandfather possesses the secret and pursues her in an attempt to wrest the secret from him. Conan and Lana together flee and do battle with the bad guys. As even such a brief summary suggests, there is more than a passing resemblance between *Conan* and *Castle in the Sky*.[5]

In 1982 in *Animage*, a magazine devoted to anime published by Tokuma shoten, Miyazaki began to serialize a manga, *Kaze no tani no Naushika* (*Nausicaä of the Valley of the Wind*, 1982–94), which also draws some of its inspiration from *The Incredible Tide* and *Conan*, spinning a tale of the young girl Nausicaä, who struggles to save the world from its technological condition, and who, like Key's heroine, has the power to communicate with animals. Nausicaä, too, lives in a postapocalyptic world in which industrial civilization as such has vanished after devastating the earth with WMDs. Yet the WMDs linger, inviting men and women hungry for power to recover and reactivate them. The film adaptation, which Miyazaki reluctantly agreed to make when the publisher Tokuma shoten insisted that it would only fund a film based on his manga, consists of material largely reworked from first quarter of the manga. (It would take Miyazaki thirteen years to complete the manga, working on it in starts and stops between films.)[6] Significantly, although the *Nausicaä* manga has a mysterious stone that is the key to activating the giant robots who once destroyed the world, the film version of *Nausicaä* eliminates the mysterious stone, but Miyazaki would use this segment of the *Nausicaä* story in *Castle in the Sky*. In sum, there is a great deal of overlap thematically from *Conan* and *Nausicaä* to *Castle in the Sky*, as if Miyazaki were consistently, even obsessively working through his concerns about modern technology in animation. Even his *Lupin III* film, *Lupin the Third: The Castle of Cagliostro* (*Rupan sansei: Kariosutoro no shiro*, 1979) works with similar themes and devices, albeit in a more playful manner.

In light of Miyazaki's prior projects, then, *Castle in the Sky* appears as a summation. The nineteenth-century look of the film recalls the period feel of Miyazaki's television animation adaptations of *Anne of Green Gables* and *Heidi*, which Miyazaki renders in *Castle in the Sky* with generic ease. The story, especially its magical flourishes, recalls both Tōei feature-length *dōga* (especially *Prince of the Sun*) and Miyazaki's previous postapocalyptic epics (*Conan* and *Nausicaä*). I don't wish to imply that Miyazaki's prior work merely served as preparation or apprenticeship for *Castle in the Sky* or for his subsequent films with Ghibli. It is not a question of straightforward continuity or direct influence. From his Tōei Dōga animations to his television animation to *Castle in the Sky*, we see a dazzling array of animated worlds. Nonetheless, in *Castle in the Sky*, Miyazaki gathers those worlds into one epic world with a distinctively Miyazaki look and story arc. *Castle in the Sky* marks the emergence of a distinctive Miyazaki-Ghibli world and worldview, and in a stable and marketable form.

Significantly, however, that world and its worldview are in crisis even as they emerge. In effect, the crisis comes of the conflicting stances toward technology that appear in Miyazaki's animation.[7] By the time of *Castle in the Sky*, the delight in speeding vehicles and action sequences—so carefree and playful in *Lupin* and *Conan*—is proving awkward for Miyazaki to sustain alongside his critical take on techno-scientific modernity. It is difficult to play with speeding vehicles and launch a critique of the modern technological condition. In my opinion, *Castle in the Sky* succeeds precisely because Miyazaki launches his critique of technology even while playing with speed and machinery. *Castle in the Sky* succeeds precisely because it manages to gather and focus our manner of interacting with technology, not by rejecting technologies but by bringing them into focus differently. In his interviews about the film, however, he expresses discomfort about *Castle in the Sky*, speaking of his general discontent with boys'-adventure films, as we have seen. Maybe Miyazaki sensed that he had, in fact, summated or finished the genre—"finished" in both senses of the word, at once polishing it (giving it a beautiful finish) and closing or completing it. In any event, he turns away from it after *Castle in the Sky*.

Miyazaki's take on the boy's-adventure genre was always unusual in its sensibility, showing a tendency to question and even undermine goal-oriented actions. Working with Takahata, who seems equally intent on hollowing out adventurism, albeit in different ways, encouraged Miyazaki's tendency toward a sort of antiadventure adventure film that asks viewers to question their delight in treasures, magical powers, or thrills and to transfer that interest onto other broader technological concerns. We have seen how *Castle in the Sky* presents a stance toward technology that is close to that of Heidegger. If the goal is not to accept or reject technology but to change your relation to it, the central issue becomes that of *how* you get caught up in the film, how the film gathers and focuses your practices of perception in relation to technology. This is where Miyazaki draws on his experience making Tōei *dōga*. This is where Miyazaki's insistence that his animations are manga films not anime comes into play. At stake is developing in animation a different perception of technology.

Miyazaki's films strive to shift our perception of technology at three different but interrelated levels. First is his use of open compositing of the multiplanar image, that is, his manner of rendering movement, speed, and depth by emphasizing the sliding of layers within the image. He avoids and deemphasizes the ballistic optics of cinematism because, for him, these constitute a "bad"—that is, merely correct or accurate—relation to the modern technological condition, one that tends toward optimization for its own sake. This is not to say that he never uses ballistic modes of perception. In *Castle in the Sky*, for instance, the chase sequence on the train tracks over the gorge is full of images of things rushing out of the screen at you, and while Miyazaki mostly generates thrills with lateral views of motion, there are nonetheless many views down the rails that exploit perceptual ballistics. Yet Miyazaki undercuts such effects with humor: Sheeta decks two burly pirates with a shovel in the face, they grimace and slowly collapse. The timing and the interactions are almost slapstick, slightly loony, and always harmless, and jolts and slams are rendered theatrically, in the scale of human bodies (a fist in the face) and at the level of bodily knowledge.[8] In addition, as in the fistfight between village men and pirates, Miyazaki not only brings ballistic optics back to the level of the human body but also associates them with a preening yet harmless machismo. Just as this film is still able to play with technologies even as it critiques them, it is also able to play with masculinity even as it questions it. Nonetheless this film largely marks the end of Miyazaki's willingness to render overtly masculine behavior with humor or affection.

Second, Miyazaki's films abound in whimsical, implausible-looking contraptions that nonetheless fly through the skies or move over the earth. Usually such vehicles appear too voluminous and weighty to move at all. In *Castle in the Sky*, especially in the title sequence, there are the aircraft that seem to combine dirigibles, bicycles, and propellers, and one has to wonder how they could get off the ground; like the castles in the sky, they appear to hover or float rather than fly in the sense of speeding through the skies. While the gunships of *Nausicaä* seem not entirely unlike our airplanes, the flying jars and large airships defy our sense of aviation. Miyazaki seems to like bulbous entities with lots of spindly legs or propellers; vehicles as different as the catbus in *Totoro* and the mobile castle in *Howl's Moving Castle* are such entities. Miyazaki's giant insects in *Nausicaä* and insect-inspired planes in other films (like the flaptors in *Castle in the Sky*) also seem at once preposterous yet oddly coherent; they are large and many-limbed, yet swift. Sometimes familiar vehicles occur in anachronistic combinations: in *Kiki's Delivery Service*, the dirigible appears in conjunction with televisions, together with the boy Tombo's transformation of a bike into a plane. All in all, such funny and eccentric vehicles, often with lots of flapping legs or spinning arms that make them whimsically accessible to the human body, seem calculated to avoid streamlined ballistic-designed craft. Miyazaki studiously avoids jets and rockets, and when he cites such designs, they are closely associated with the evils of war (in *Howl's Moving Castle* in particular).[9] Miyazaki uses humorous and eccentric designs to open the technological ordering of our modern world to other possibilities, by generating vehicles that look implausible yet somehow accurate, thus refocusing our perception of technologies of flight and movement.

At the same time, the paragons of flight are those that stay aloft with the minimum of technology: Nausicaä's seagull-like glider Meeve (or Mehve or Möwe), Pazu's glider, Kiki's broomstick, or Totoro as a gust of wind. Such vehicles are closely linked with animetism, because it is in sequences of gliding, floating, or soaring that the sliding layers of the image can be emphasized to their best effect. These minimal flying technologies are thus associated with a third register of animation—the animation of human bodies, that is, the animation of the characters who inhabit these worlds.

Miyazaki's animations highlight youthful bodies and children's energies, too. Generally the characters on whom Miyazaki lavishes his attention tend to be children, old men or women, with an occasional adult woman, often in a role characterized as masculine. With the exception of *Lupin*, his animation generally does not devote much attention to adult men, and even his version of the character Lupin the Third is more youthful and sweet-hearted than usual. Interestingly enough, in Studio Ghibli's documentary on Ōtsuka's animation, Ōtsuka and Miyazaki stress the importance of the youthful energies that young animators can impart to movement as in-between animators. They see the energies of young animators translated directly into vigorous and vital animation. Harnessing youthful energies plays an important role in Miyazaki's attempt to produce a free relation to technology in animation.

In sum, Miyazaki's thinking of a free relation to technology in animation relies on a gathering and focusing of attention on bodies that fly—at once vehicles and human bodies. He does this at three different levels: (1) emphasizing animetism and avoiding (or comically deflating) cinematism by stressing the movement between multiple layers of the image; (2) designing whimsical vehicles and/or minimizing flight technologies while avoiding streamlined ballistic structures; and (3) harnessing or channeling the energies of young bodies. These three impulses already come together beautifully in the scenes of the young Nausicaä on her glider in *Nausicaä* and appear again with Kiki soaring on her broomstick. But it is in *Castle in the Sky,* which from the outset until the end is a film that dreams a world of clouds and winds, that Miyazaki's animetism reaches its fullest expression in sensations of flying, soaring, gliding, or wheeling through the clouds or along the earth. In contrast to the scenes that humorously deflate ballistics or ridicule the streamlined biases in flight design, the scenes that open the sliding of layers of the image evoke sensations of awe and wonder, sensations of a world whose vastness and depth is somehow ungraspable. Miyazaki's animetism is, to some extent, an experience of the sublime, an aesthetic experience of the world in which the world exceeds our ability to grasp it rationally or to order it hierarchically. Yet, insofar as flying and animating do not deny recourse to technology, however minimal, Miyazaki does not embrace the Romantic sublime that tends to repudiate the technological. Nor does he produce a technological sublime.

The sensation of sliding layers is entirely different from speeding into depth. Rather it is a sensation of *induced movement* or *relative movement*, such as that you feel when you are on a train stopped in a station, and the train next to yours begins to move forward or backward. You feel that you are moving, your train is moving. Or when your car creeps forward at a stoplight but you are not aware of lifting your foot from the pedal, you feel that the car ahead is backing up or even that the *world is moving*. This is how Miyazaki begins to imagine a free relation to technology: when movement is rendered with sliding planes, the world is not static, inert, lying in wait passively for us to use it, in the form of a standing reserve, to evoke Heidegger's term. The world is not "enframed" or made into a picture.[10] On the contrary, Miyazaki assures that when we move, the world moves, and vice versa. Opening a relation through animation technology to the dynamism of the world promises a way for us to gain a free relation to our modern technological condition, to save ourselves from it. Yet for all that it seems rather simple to formulate, such an experience is difficult to render. After all, Miyazaki doesn't want to embrace the art of the engine. He thus takes the "big" or "high tech" vehicles of flight and transportation (planes, cars, trains) and deflates or deforms them, and at the same time he gravitates toward "small" or "low tech" vehicles (gliders, bikes, broomsticks). The result is vehicles that fit perfectly into a world of sliding layers. Vehicles associated with ballistic perception are defanged, while other wind-powered vehicles feel ideally suited to move in a multiplanar, movement-full world. Yet the question remains of what kind of human bodies are suited to these flying machines, to these gliding, wheeling, soaring, and sliding machines. I have indicated that Miyazaki, following Ōtsuka, stresses youthful energies in his animators and in his animated characters. This is where another art of animation comes into play, the art of animating characters, which has a profound impact on the imagination of a free relation to technology.

CHAPTER 6

FULL ANIMATION

FULL ANIMATION refers primarily to the number of drawings used to animate the movement of characters. The projection rate for film is twenty-four frames per second, and so, technically, if you really wanted to produce a figure with as much movement as an actor in cinema, you would have to draw twenty-four images for each second of animation. But no one would ever want to spend that much time and money when most of character movement in animation can be rendered with twelve drawings per second, which is sometimes called "on twos." Faster movements may require "on ones," that is, the full twenty-four drawings per second. The Disney average, which created the norms for full animation, is said to be about eighteen drawings per second. Of course, this number refers largely to the movements of characters. If you start to change the background or the different layers of background, you could potentially end up with a lot more than twenty-four drawings. Normally, however, background layers change at a much slower rate than the characters move.

From the early days of animation, rotoscoping became an important technique for achieving full animation. With rotoscoping, you first film your sequence (with actors). You then use the film footage to draw as many of the twenty-four frames per second as you think you need. You might draw twelve frames per second or even less. Still, the appeal of rotoscoping is that it potentially allows you to produce animation with an aura of cinematic fullness at the level of character movement without having to guess about how to draw all the intermediate movements. After all, it isn't necessarily easy to figure out how to draw all the intermediate movements of, say, a man picking up a sledgehammer, raising it over his head, and letting it strike. Nor it is easy to render dancing, skating, jumping, or any number of other activities. Copying film footage eliminates the guesswork and promises greater accuracy—accuracy in accordance with live-action cinema, that is.

Naturally, you can use rotoscoping against cinematic fullness. You might have characters whose limbs move like those of human actors in films but whose facial expressions are exaggerated. You might draw fantastical backgrounds or introduce figures and characters not in the filmed sequence. Even though rotoscoping is a technique that relies on drawing what is first filmed, it doesn't have to adhere to cinematic conventions. In *The Ghost in the Shell* (1995), director Oshii Mamoru shot long video sequences of the streets and waterways of Hong Kong, rotoscoping the footage while introducing colors and designs that tweaked the scenes into his vision of a futuristic global city. The result was breathtaking, a strangely cinematically real yet fantastical world, a world not cinema and not *not* cinema.

Rotoscoping is still big today, in a variety of guises. The motion capture used for digital actors, for instance, is a variation on rotoscoping, but you "film" the movements of the actors by capturing the data from sensor points placed strategically on their bodies, and then feed the data into the computer, where you begin to "draw" the animated character onto the digital film data. There is, needless to say, a lot more computer drawing than filming in this instance. In contrast with digital motion capture, which is often geared toward producing cinematically realistic worlds and character movements, Richard Linklater in his films *Waking Life* (2001) and *A Scanner Darkly* (2006), and Oshii Mamoru in *Amazing Lives of Fast Food Grifters* (2006) digitally paint onto digital footage, which results in multiple layers of color and movement in the cinematic image.[1] In *Waking Life* in particular, you truly feel the movement between layers of the image. This is because, as the artists painted outlines and colors onto the digital footage, the film footage turned into a multiplanar image. Where the movie camera tends to produce the sense of a solidly composited world, the digital interventions resulted in open compositing. The film makes some viewers dizzy not only because of the open compositing but also because your senses remain somehow aware of the underlying "closed" compositing of the film footage even as the image separates into layers of movement and color. Your senses are torn between closed and open compositing. What is more, while the use of film footage should allow for full animation of characters, the artists who did different sequences of *Waking Life* for various reasons do not strive for full animation of characters. The movement of the digitally painted actors is halting and sketchy, as if seen obscurely through some peculiar filter, or as if coming from another dimension, weirdly illuminated. In addition, the backgrounds seem to move as much as the characters, and the gap between character and background layers becomes palpable.

The digital rotoscope experiments of *Waking Life* serve as a reminder of how the full animation of characters is usually imagined to operate. Usually, the background is relatively static, against which the movements of the characters appears all the more dynamic. The art of animation is usually imagined in terms of lavishly painted backgrounds upon which characters move fluidly, gracefully, that is, *fully*. Of course, in animated worlds, elements of the landscape and inanimate objects frequently come to life—a car, a spoon, a fence, a tool, truly any object can be imagined to speak and move, to be animated. This is why animation is frequently associated with animism, with a world and worldview in which everything is endowed with a vital spirit. Yet, as Ueno Toshiya reminds us, such animism occurs in an age of technology.[2] In other words, the animism of animation is not that of an ancient era; it arises where the force implicit in the succession of mechanical images is stunted into the animation of characters and objects. Typically, the ideal is one in which the animated figure, whether animate or inanimate, organic or inorganic, moves fully. Its movement usually happens against a background, which may have moving luminous elements (streams, clouds, vehicles, and other entities), but which is nevertheless relatively stable and solid. In full animation, you are not supposed to produce a sense of movement by pulling the background while the character (or whatever figure) remains motionless and immobile. You are supposed to draw the movement of the character or animated entity, not simply move the layers of the drawing.

This is precisely what happens in limited animation: you move layers rather than animate characters. I will first discuss full animation, however, not only because animators as profoundly different as Walt Disney and Norman McLaren agree on the primacy of drawing movement instead of moving drawings, but also because this is the tradition into which Miyazaki entered during his apprenticeship at Tōei Dōga. Many commentators and viewers still consider full animation to be *the* art of animation, and Miyazaki and Ghibli are frequently presented as the last true practitioners of full animation in Japan today.[3] The history of Tōei *dōga* and the animation of Ōtsuka are crucial to understanding the spin that Miyazaki puts on full animation. So let us turn to the animated film that is touted as the first full-length color animated film in Japan (and in Asia, the Studio Ghibli documentary adds), Tōei Dōga's *Hakujaden* (Legend of the white serpent, 1958), which relied extensively on techniques of rotoscoping.

Ōkawa Hiroshi, the first president of Tōei Studies, founded Tōei Dōga in 1956, with the ambition of creating animated films to rival those of Disney and with an eye to exporting Japanese culture to the world. *Hakujaden* was the first-large scale work, but as Yamaguchi Katsunori and Watanabe Yasushi explain in their history of Japanese animation, there were at that time few experienced animators among the many new staff members hired for the newly created animation studio.[4] As a consequence of the general lack of experience as well as the ambition to rival Disney's full animation, Tōei Dōga resorted to a variation on rotoscoping, common in Disney's animation, in which sequences were filmed with actors and then a selection of stills from the developed film served as the basis for the drawings.[5] The cleaned-up sketches of actress Sakuma Yoshiko and actor Ishikawa Yoshiaki (later to be voiced by Miyaji Mariko and Morishige Hisaya) served beautifully for key animation.[6] Yet, needless to say, filming the sequences before drawing them takes time and money. Large-scale action sequences such as the storm at sea were re-created and filmed in the studio to produce footage for the animation staff, a process that required a month to complete.[7] It was like producing two films, even if it is only the second film, the animated film, which is actually released. The animated film adds art to the film footage as well. *Hakujaden* required an astonishing attention to detail, not only for the animation of characters but also for the Chinese-style landscapes and architectures, to be sustained across innumerable images (in this case a total of 214,154 drawings).

Among the many interesting features of *Hakujaden* is the palpable difference between the animation of the humans and that of the animals, especially the cute little panda. Because the film was produced before the panda craze that brought so many of them from China into zoos around the world, the panda was quite a rarity in Japan, and it took over a year for the filmmakers to get their hands on a photograph of a panda, to serve as a model for animator Mori Yasuji's sketches.[8] There was no way to do anything close to rotoscoping a panda. As a result, the energies of the panda, and that of many of the other prominently featured animals in the film, are notably different from those of the human characters with their cinema-inspired movements. Where human hero and heroine appear almost part of the landscape with their beautifully detailed clothes, idealized expressions, and gestures attuned to live-action cinema, the animals bounce, roll, stretch, and bend. They fairly burst with life. The animals also feel closer in style and movement to the kind of animated expression globalized through Disney—the so-called squash-and-stretch technique.[9] Nevertheless, if they fit with the rotoscoped action at all, it is because they feel like an enhanced rotoscoping that builds on the animators' sensation of their body.

With the animal characters, you can also feel the signature style and energy of different animators. In the Ghibli documentary, for instance, Ōtsuka Yasuo notes how the scene of the giant pig battling with the little panda in *Hakujaden* (Figure 13) builds on the characteristic styles of two animators, Daikubara Akira (pig) and Mori Yasuji (panda). Daikubara was especially adept with large-shouldered hulking figures with powerful yet mistimed movements, and Ōtsuka traces Daikubara's signature style from the giant pig in *Hakujaden* through other Tōei *dōga* films and into some of Ōtsuka's own characterizations, such as Captain Dyce in *Conan*.

Figure 13. *In the battle between the hulking pig and the diminutive panda in* Hakujaden, *we see the characteristic styles of two Tōei animators, Daikubara Akira and Mori Yasuji. The pig uses a mallet in a manner that anticipates Ōtsuka Yasuo's exercise in full animation based on a boy lifting and pounding with a sledgehammer.*

In any event, what is important is that, within full animation, even though the general aim is usually to produce a sensation of movement as fluid as that in cinema, movements with very different energies emerge, even when the same number of drawings per second is used. Watching the Ghibli documentary on Ōtsuka (or reading about Disney's animators), it is clear that producing energetic movements like those of the little panda in *Hakujaden* is not simply a matter of using lots of drawings per second or a matter of copying cinema literally. Rather the animators work through the movements with their own bodies, twisting and turning, squashing and stretching, exaggerating the gestures and expressions, getting a feel for the movements. In effect, they are doing something like motion capture on their own bodies. They translate the movements of their bodies into drawings, which they have already conceptualized cinematically in the sense that they understand their own movements in terms of frames. Ōtsuka Yasuo, for instance, works in the classic way: on a flip pad atop a light table, he sketches, with breathtaking rapidity, the movements in a sequence, often drawing with the first movement first and the last movement immediately after, and then filling in two additional movements (Figure 14). He thus decomposes one movement into about four sketches.

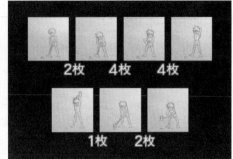

Figure 14. *In the first three panels, Ōtsuka Yasuo demonstrates with his flipbook how to produce character animation with key frames, and in the fourth panel we see clean versions of the sequence.*

One of Ōtsuka's favorite exercises in teaching animation, for instance, is a sequence in which a boy pounds something with a heavy sledge hammer; the boy picks up the hammer, raises it high, and finally lets it strike home. This movement can be easily decomposed into about four sketches. In effect, these are key frames, the work of a key animator. Key frames are the drawings of the starting and ending points that define a movement. In the instance of the boy with the hammer, the start and end of the movement are not enough to characterize the movement: you need (at least) a sketch of the boy as he first starts to lift the hammer, a sketch of the hammer held as high as he can raise it, and the hammer as it strikes. Once Ōtsuka has drawn the key frames on his flip pad, flipping through the pages gives a rough sense of how the movement will look when animated. All of this can, of course, be done on computers today, and Ōtsuka is not averse to using computers to activate sketches. Yet even when computers are used, the fundamental principles are those of hand-drawn full animation. The same is true of Miyazaki and company. After years of resistance to computer techniques, Studio Ghibli has gradually adopted digital technologies of animation, but the idea—or more precisely, the *abstract diagram*—is that of classic full cel animation.

What Ōtsuka likes about the hammer exercise is that it forces animators to address the energies and forces of the body. After all, the hammer is heavy, and as the boy tries to pick it up, his shoulders will raise dramatically as he labors to lift it, and the weight of the hammer will skew his body weight to one side. If the hammer proves almost too heavy for him to lift, he might only bring it as high as his chest. As he wields it overhead, the weight of the hammer will surely make his knees buckle or sag. In other words, what interests Ōtsuka is the way in which we see something of the material character of the body, its dynamics or its signature energies. In Ōtsuka's opinion, if the boy were simply to pick up the hammer without any of these adjustments, he would look like an automaton or robot. His body would not appear to have any internal character, life force, or, if you will, a soul.

If we look at this animation exercise another way, it would seem that what Ōtsuka likes is the way in which the tool opens the body, and the body opens to the tool. Insofar as we see the body open to the tool, our perception is potentially gathered and focused on the technological relation. It would seem that such animation techniques almost automatically create conditions conducive to a freer relation to technology. Yet a number of obstacles arise that threaten to spoil the potential to use animation in this way. Miyazaki, for instance, worries about how these sequences become generic. In his opinion, we're so accustomed to seeing boys wield heavy tools, brandish swords, and tote guns, that it becomes impossible to gather and focus perception. Such scenarios evoke the now familiar and even hackneyed ideals about young men who are full of energy and pure of heart, ideals that were worked and reworked incessantly in Japan's wartime animated films and Tōei's animated films. This is one of reasons Miyazaki shifts the burden of bearing weapons and tools onto women and girls. In his interviews, he mentions that he resorts to female heroes because girls, as principal characters in action stories, disrupt certain narrative conventions and expectations, especially when it is a woman or girl who picks up the gun.[10]

In addition to the problem of viewers' habituation to certain kinds of animated movement (that is, generic forms of action), full animation presents two other problems with respect to conveying the dynamics of the body: in-between animation and clean-up.

Typically, in the workflow of traditional cel animation, the key animator hands over his rough and loose key frame sketches to assistants who work on cleaning up the roughness and filling in additional frames between the key frames to make for smoother motion. Miyazaki, for instance, worked as an in-between animator under Ōtsuka at Tōei. Clean-up is important for pragmatic reasons: when striving to line up the contours of a body across images, it is easier to match up a single clean contour line. If you leave a lot of sketch lines, not only do the boundaries of the body appear porous and irresolute, but also the movement is blurrier. In-betweens and clean-up make for cleaner, smoother movement, and yet a problem arises, because clean-up in particular tends to lessen the dynamics or energies of the body. With the erasure of the blizzard of sketch lines, with the production of a single clean contour line, comes a diminishment in our sense of the weight of things. The sense of implied mass tends to disappear with clean-up.[11]

This is one reason that Ōtsuka, like his mentors Daikubara Akira and Mori Yasuji, seems to exaggerate the weight of things, their burden on the body, and the strength of the body in response. Exaggeration promises to compensate for the diminishment of our sense of implied mass that results from clean-up, and to sustain a sense that the character has its signature energies, its individuality, its life or soul. This is also why Ōtsuka and Miyazaki insist that young in-between animators are crucial to producing vigorous lively animation. They prefer to hire in-between animators in their late teens or twenties. As you age, they claim, you lose the feeling for producing energetic movement. We'll have to take their word on this point, but it is worthwhile to point out that this emphasis on the energies of animation makes a certain set of labor relations appear not only desirable but also natural. Key animators are experienced old pros who set up the frames for movement, while the in-between animators are young, less experienced workers whose energies are harnessed to make the animation come to life.

Highlighting the dynamism of movement at the level of key animation and in-between animation promises to compensate for the loss of implied mass via clean-up. Implied mass tends to anchor a body in the world. It implies a sense of gravity. It gives a sense that a body responds to the forces in the world around it. This is especially important in animation because everything conspires to lessen a sense of natural physical laws, of rootedness. Ōtsuka doesn't emphasize just any movements; he stresses gravity-marked movements. Such movements promise to produce the sensation of a character rooted in its world and responsive to it. It is here that we begin to see how full animation constitutes a response to the multiplanar machine, to the abstract diagram that generates an animated world composed of sliding planes.

Because animated worlds are composed of planes or layers, they easily defy conventions that we deem natural based on the world of cinema, and even the physical laws of nature. In the stock scenario with the animation stand and rostrum camera, there is a tendency for the gap between layers to become palpable. In fact, even if you use only two celluloid sheets, say, a background landscape and a foreground character, without an animation stand but simply placing one atop the other, you can easily generate a sense of a character not anchored in its world in accordance with cinematic conventions and natural laws. Move either layer up or down from shot to shot, and the character appears weightless. The character appears to defy gravity, to float, to glide, to fly, without even moving its limbs. This is part of the magic of animation, which derives from the multiplanar machine, from the shunting of the force of the moving image into the interval between planes of the image.

Of course, similar effects can occur in cinema, and early cinema is full of such tricks. Gradually, however, cinema tended to move the force of the moving image into camera movement (particularly movement into depth) and to displace that force into the gaps between shots or takes (montage). Because cel animation entails a different relation to camera movement, it tends to shunt the force of the moving image into compositing, to displace it into the animation of characters, or both. If I have thus insisted on the priority of compositing over character animation (or object animation), it is for two reasons: first, to call attention to the force of the mechanical succession of images, and second, to avoid the assumption that animation is primarily about artwork in the sense of the drawing and composition of images, and consequently that animation is more about art or technique than technology. Now, however, it is clear that compositing and character animation present a bifurcation of the force of the animated moving image into two streams or channels. Thus we need to explore the relation between compositing and character animation. Let me return to the point of departure, the effects of rotoscoping.

In *Waking Life*, for instance, digital rotoscoping—that is, digitally painting on film footage—tends to separate the moving image into multiple planes, which heightens the sense of the main character being somehow out of touch with the world, as if searching for another dimension of experience beyond the world defined by natural laws. As the example of *Hakujaden* attests, when rotoscoping is used in the service of full animation of character movement, the idea is to call upon the tendency of live-action cinema to generate bodies that appear to have mass, to respond to gravity, that buckle under weight; bodies that are somehow responsive to the world. Yet rotoscoping is not enough, because the multiplanar machine of animation makes compositing so important.

Because it enables the production of bodies that appear more in tune with natural laws and cinema conventions, full animation can serve to mask the animetic interval, the gap between planes of the image. If you put the emphasis on drawing the movement and not on moving the drawings, our attention becomes focused on character movement rather than on the gap between planes of the image. We still feel the animetic interval but it is now shunted into or embodied in the movement of character. Disney was the master of this kind of movement. In the scenes of animals skating in *Bambi* (1942) or of the fairies coloring autumn leaves and frosting ponds in *Fantasia* (1940), the "natural" movement of the characters' bodies, rendered with full animation, imparts a sense of heightened movement or response, because a simple movement of the limbs allows the characters to cover so much distance so rapidly. The result is a sense of fully realistic and fully realized magic. The animetic interval is at once masked by and embodied in character movement. Full animation promises to fold the animetic interval back on itself, making for a substantial body with a substantial relation to the world.

Cinematism tends to demand full animation of characters. There is a tendency toward closed compositing to sustain the illusion of a substantial world, which provides a stable and solid space in which the movements of the character appear equally substantial. If we move forward many years to the time when digital animation began to make inroads into cel animation, the ballroom scene in Disney Studios' *Beauty and the Beast* (1991) manifests this tendency of cinematism. The scene became famous for its seamless combination of volumetric depth (the ballroom) and gracefully waltzing animated characters, with the viewing position of a simulated camera rotating around them. In the wake of this digital magic, it seemed that everyone wanted to introduce volumetric depths and closed compositing into animated features, to impart a sensation of movement into depth, of moving around inside animated worlds. Ironically, however, the increased use of volumetric depth alongside cel animation techniques (*Treasure Planet* [2002] is a prime example) failed at the box office in comparison with fully digital animations. Some commentators wrote of the decline and even impeding death of cel animation.[12] In fact the situation has proved more complex because digitally animated films, such as those of Pixar and Blue Sky Studios, started to favor cartoonish characters in conjunction with volumetric depth (in contrast with the photoreal characters of *Final Fantasy: The Spirits Within* [2001]). At the same time, other kinds of digitally produced animation, especially for television, tended to stress the flattened and layered images reminiscent of cel animation, and actual cel animation—such as *Les Triplettes de Belleville* and Miyazaki's films—garnered critical and box office attention.

In any event, for all that Ōtsuka's and Miyazaki's animations are in the

lineage of full animation (and insist on their difference from the limited animation of anime), they are not as full as the classic Disney standard of eighteen frames
per second. This is in part because Ōtsuka and Miyazaki did a lot of television
animation, which demands some reckoning with limited animation techniques
in order to make budget, and in part because limited animation also allowed for
a broader palette of artistic expression. I will further discuss the implications of
limited animation within Tōei *dōga* in chapter 15. At this juncture, however, I
wish to explore how Ōtsuka's and Miyazaki's animations imply a relation to the
animetic interval different than those of Disney's classic full animations.

As Ōtsuka's example of the boy with a sledgehammer suggests, he highlights the dynamics of the body as it *shifts its weight or center of gravity into different planes*. Later, in his work in television, Ōtsuka found a way to sustain this
kind of dynamism in a more limited way, that is, with fewer frames per second.
In the Ghibli documentary, Ōtsuka shows his solution in the context of his work
on Miyazaki's television series *Conan*. When he animates the figure of Conan
running at us out of the background (a typical limited-animation move because
it requires fewer frames per second), Ōtsuka introduces a slight tilt into each
successive image. The axis of Conan's body is vertical in the first image, tilted
slightly to the left in the next, and slightly more to the left in the one after that
(Figure 15). In Ōtsuka's opinion, putting the axis of each image of Conan off kil-
ter introduces roughness and energy into animation. This is, in effect, a limited
version of his boy-with-hammer scenario. Basically, instead of having the body
shift its weight into different planes, the animator shifts the body into different
planes. This technique imparts the same kind of energy as fuller animation, yet,
unlike an animated dynamics that relies on something like implied mass (which
might be cleaned out of the smooth animation), this technique of *angling the
image* retains its energies even after clean-up.[13]

Ōtsuka's animation provides the clue to how Miyazaki finesses the problem
of humans that fly in *Castle in the Sky* (and in his animation more generally). On
the one hand, Miyazaki embraces the weightlessness of the body enabled by the
multiplanar machine. In *Castle in the Sky*, Miyazaki even builds an excuse for
weightlessness in the story: antigravitational stones. He favors open compositing,
a sense of the sliding of layers of the image. Using sliding planes in conjunction
with cleaned up characters, however, he risks producing a world in which nothing
appears grounded or responsive. Everything potentially floats and slides away, ungrounded. His goal, however, is not weightlessness or complete openness. Rather
the goal is to articulate a new relation between body (character animation) and
world (open multiplanarity), which is grounded and rooted, related to earthly
and earthy existence. The cleaned-up movement of full animation works against

Figure 15. *This sequence from* Conan *is presented as a prime example of Ōtsuka Yasuo's "peg hole technique" for angling the action of characters, which imparts dynamism to animation even in more limited animation. Images have been slightly cropped to highlight the movement of the character.*

him, however, by generating idealized weightless versions of rough, dynamic, individualized movements.

On the other hand, to counter this tendency toward an ungrounded relation to the world, in the manner of Ōtsuka, Miyazaki tries to reintroduce a relation to the earth by constantly angling the axis of those bodies in flight. Thus you feel the pull of the earth, the lift of the wind, and the buoyant energies of youth. Such forces and energies, highly condensed in flight sequences, run consistently throughout the film. In this way, Miyazaki's animations strive to find a site where open compositing and his limited full animation work perfectly together. Simply put, his animations find a way to make weightlessness work effectively, work responsively with open compositing. That happens primarily in scenes of floating, flying, and gliding.

The result of Miyazaki's use of Ōtsuka-like techniques is indeed a new relation between body and world, in which the body is suspended between earth and sky, yet angled earthward, as if to point to a new relation to the earth. Because his animations place less emphasis on using full animation to mask the animetic interval, they do not tend to generate characters who appear to transcend their world, magically. Rather his characters, suspended between earth and sky as between planes of the moving image, remain somehow responsive to the world. This is also how Miyazaki strives to open a freer relation to technology: opening character animation to the animetic interval in a differently dynamic way. The multiplanar animetic machine thus promises a way to free thought and save bodies from their technological predicament.

CHAPTER 7

ONLY A GIRL CAN SAVE US NOW

THUS FAR I HAVE EXPLORED how Miyazaki's animation strives to transform our relation to technology in three registers: open compositing, flying machines, and character animation. At the level of compositing, Miyazaki's animation works with the play between layers of the image (animetism) in order to avoid ballistic movement into depth (cinematism). It tends toward opening compositing. At the level of flying machines, Miyazaki's designs for large vehicles are frequently whimsical and eccentric, and it is smaller, human-powered or wind-powered machines (glider, bicycle, windmill, broomstick) that are designed to capture our sense of wonder and awe. Such human-scaled flying machines not only counter forms of technophilia but also mesh perfectly with the lateral view of speed and movement that comes of open compositing. At the level of character animation, Miyazaki builds on and transforms the Tōei *dōga* lineage of full animation techniques. He uses techniques of angling the axis of movement of human bodies in order to impart a sense of dynamism to them. With such a combination of open compositing, vehicle design, and character animation, Miyazaki's animation produces not only an open, movement-full world but also characters who appear dynamically angled toward that world, somehow responsive to it, even in their unmoored state. Significantly, such openness or responsiveness to the movement-full world does not entail an elimination of technology. Instead of rejecting technology, Miyazaki's animation strives to transform our relation to the modern technological condition.

As we have seen, much like Heidegger, Miyazaki's animation strives to gather and focus our perceptual practices differently, in order to gain a freer or truer relation to technology. Technology then appears not as a problem with a solution (better control or complete rejection) but as a condition from which we might learn to free ourselves by understanding the essence of technology. In Miyazaki's animation it is above all technologies of flight that hold forth the promise of a freer relation to technology. Quite literally, his animation proposes to have us take to the skies differently, to fly differently. Indeed, in his essays and interviews, Miyazaki frequently develops such a contrast: on the one hand, there is the jumbo jet, the Landsat image, and anime, and on the other hand, there are the early days of flight when flying felt wonderful, which experience is associated with clouds and light, the manga film, and even ancient animism.[1] Clearly, his animations strive to afford an experience of the latter. Interestingly enough, gender and genre also enter the mix.

Throughout Miyazaki's work, boys and girls have very different relations to flight, and in terms of character animation, girl energies are consistently distinguished from boy energies. Sheeta and Pazu are prime examples. Not only do they take to the skies differently but also they are animated differently. This suggests that gender is somehow central to Miyazaki's efforts to gain a free relation to technology.

From the outset, Pazu is all exertion and effort. He clambers, climbs, leaps; he takes charge, fights, and forms alliances. He yearns to build a plane in order to fly to the castle in the sky, and his goal is to clear his father's name. (Apparently, his father's claims to have seen Raputa met with scorn and ridicule, and he disappeared in search of it.) Pazu's dreams and desires are concrete and goal oriented. What is more, Pazu has a passion for machines, mechanics, and engineering; technologies of flight especially capture his imagination. This is a general trait of Miyazaki's boys. Think of the boy next door (Kanta) in *Totoro* playing intently with a model airplane, or the boy Tombo in *Kiki* hard at work transforming his bicycle into a flying machine. In later films like *Spirited Away* and *Howl's Moving Castle*, the boy actually becomes a flying entity (a dragon and a bird of war).

In terms of animation, Pazu directly recalls the hero of Miyazaki's 1978 television series *Conan* as well as Hols (or Horus) in *Prince of the Sun*. Ōtsuka worked as animation director on both, and these energetic boys are deemed the hallmark of his masculine dynamic style.[2] They recall Ōtsuka's exercise based on the boy with a hammer. The idea is to put the boy in a situation of exaggerated strength and exertion: Hols pulling the sword from the shoulder of the stone giant, Conan with his preternatural strength lifting just about anything. Although Ōtsuka did not design or animate him, Miyazaki's Pazu definitely follows from Ōtsuka's Hols and Conan. The scene in which Pazu catches Sheeta as she floats serenely down from the sky is a prime instance. No sooner has Pazu

Figure 16. *The scenes in which Pazu catches Sheeta as she descends from the skies succinctly establish the different energies of the two characters: Pazu is all exertion, and Sheeta buoyant and pliant.*

placed his arms under her than the flying stone ceases to work, and the full weight of Sheeta nearly topples Pazu from the platform. Squatting low, grunting and straining, Pazu rights himself (Figure 16). It is always in relation to *physical exertion with things* that the boy's body opens to the world and reveals its energies in animation.[3] As such, it affords one possible way to focus our attention on technological practices. We sense the body opening to tools, to weight, to physical entities—as with Pazu scaling the wall of his prison or clambering on the side of the flying castle.

To return to the interview with Murakami Ryū cited previously, Miyzaki explains that, generically, boys'-adventure stories tend to deal with a boy who has a great deal of energy but initially does not know how or where to direct it.[4] As we have seen, in Miyazaki's opinion, the problem with the boys'-adventure genre is that it all too easily directs the boy's energies into defeating the villain in battle, resulting in a pat resolution and, in effect, a closed human-centered relation to technology. Consequently, Miyazaki introduces girls and women into his adventures, to disrupt genre conventions and expectations. Women with guns or a resolute stride, for instance, create a sense of something unusual in his opinion.[5] This is certainly true of the women warriors Nausicaä and Kushana in *Nausicaä* and the analogous figures of San and Eboshi Gozen in *Princess Mononoke*. Such female figures imply a shifting of our perceptual weight in relation to technology. Their way of holding a gun or striding into battle potentially focuses our attention differently. In *Nausicaä* and *Princess Mononoke* it is above all female heroes in the midst of war that promises to shift our perception of and relation to war technology.

In *Castle in the Sky*, however, Miyazaki seems less interested in shifting women into men's roles (or girls into boy's roles) than in minimizing the boy's role, largely by eliminating men and highlighting the girl's role as such.[6] Subsequently, in his next two films after *Castle in the Sky* (*Totoro* and *Kiki*), he concentrates on girls and their magical relation to flight. We have Mei and Satsuki with the "wind god" Totoro, and Kiki with wind under her broomstick. Such a shift in emphasis away from boy energies toward girl energies also allowed Miyazaki to imagine stories that comprised a series of minor adventures without grand design or teleology—a series of little adventures. Significantly, in such animations, he de-emphasizes the question of the modern technological condition. Such shifts in emphasis suggest that, in making *Castle in the Sky*, Miyazaki became aware of a basic impasse of the adventure film or action film: technology risks appearing as a problem with a solution, rather than a condition. In his many of girl-centered animations, the question of technology lingers in muted form: technological devices frequently confuse our sense of place and time, and the films defy our efforts to find any one sociohistorical frame of reference. Still, it is difficult to say whether Miyazaki's shift in emphasis to the open-ended "little" adventures of girls constitutes an attempt to place us beyond the question of technology altogether, or whether it is an attempt to dwell within the free relation to technology explored in his prior films.

In any event, the question of technology remains inextricably linked to girls in Miyazaki's animations, and we are invited to ask about the relation of girls to technology.[7] Simply put, we do not know if (a) girls are nontechnological (in the sense of the opposite or negation of technology) or (b) they are differently technological (enabling a different relation to technology). The question is fundamentally one of whether girls are disabled, disenabled, or differently "abled" vis-à-vis technology. Such questions about girls and technology come to a head in the relation between Sheeta and her flying stone. Her stone imparts a quasi-magical yet hypertechnological relation to flight. Sheeta is thus at once nontechnological (magical) and differently technological (hypertechnological in that the stone entails sophisticated forms of telecommunication and telecommand).

Unlike Pazu who must labor to take to the skies, Sheeta inherits the flying-stone pendant. Its powers initially appear to be a part of her being. She only activates the flying stone in a dream-like or unconscious state, and the stone is somehow keyed to her body. Apparently Sheeta is the descendant of an ancient bloodline that bears the historical burden of the (destructive) power of the flying stone. Sheeta knows nothing of this history, however, retaining only vague memories of words in a strange language spoken to her as a child. In this respect, the stone is more *condition* than *ability*.[8] As a condition, the stone seems to give Sheeta magical powers, yet these appear beyond her control. Sheeta's relation to the stone is simultaneously passive and active, which sets the tone for her unusual status. The action of the story hinges on Sheeta being kidnapped, rescued, whisked away, passed from group to group—as if she, like the stone, were a mere resource to be seized, an object with latent rather than manifest powers. Her agency, especially in relation to her inherited technological power, is thus exceedingly limited. While she decides to join Pazu in the glider to search for Raputa, she does not pilot it. She is buffeted by events, as if carried by wind. In short, Sheeta is at one level a damsel in distress. Although she is plucky and spunky (she bashes Muska on the head with a bottle to escape), she remains somehow helpless, not in control. What is more, as the film progresses, Sheeta's seemingly magical gift appears more and more to be a curse. It turns out that she was born into a condition that is a threat to her and to the entire world.

Sheeta is a direct descendent of Hilda in *Prince of the Sun*, and Miyazaki modeled Sheeta and her flying-stone pendant on Hilda and her pendant.[9] Hilda's pendant operates more obviously as a curse, forcing her to do harm despite her better impulses. The adventures of Hols are the focus of *Prince of the Sun*, pushing Hilda to the margins, but Miyazaki makes Sheeta's quest as important as Pazu's. While Hilda remains a somewhat distant and mysterious figure, Miyazaki brings the girl's plight to the fore in his depiction of Sheeta. *Castle in the Sky* can be read as a rewrite of *Prince of the Sun* in which the girl's adventure is given parity with the boy's adventure. There remains nonetheless a fundamental asymmetry between boys and girls in both films, which Miyazaki's animation reworks as a relation to technology. The "magical" pendant in both films implies a technological condition, specifically telecommunication and telecommand. The pendant controls Hilda's actions from a distance, making her akin to a robot. Likewise, Sheeta's pendant puts her in a situation in which she may do harm to others, despite her inclinations. Like Hilda, she must ultimately find a way to break free of the power of the pendant. In sum, in Hilda and Sheeta a technological interface (telecommand) appears synonymous with a gendered condition (women as instrument, as object of exchange, removed from power except by proxy).

Character animation repeats this coincidence of technological device (pendant) and gendered condition (woman as object or instrument). The bodies of Hilda and Sheeta have only the faintest trace of implied mass, with slack arms, willowy movements, and distant ethereal expressions. They appear barely of this world, ready to float away. Their movements are flexible, buoyant, and ethereal. In *Castle in the Sky*, in contrast with the dynamics of the Pazu's body revealed in physical exertion, the dynamics of Sheeta's body appears in moments when the stone takes control—as she floats serenely earthward in its radiance or as she throws up her arms when the flying stone emits a burst of radiance. At such moments the distinction between human body and flying machine almost vanishes. Her body approximates a technology of flight. This becomes common in Miyzaki: while boys (Pazu, Kanta, and Tombo) must build flying machines, girls (Sheeta, Mei, Satsuki, and Kiki) have natural access to a magic that allows them to fly.

With his distinction between boy energies and girl energies, Miyazaki develops two distinct relations to technology. Boys interact with the mechanical and industrial. They are all about leverage, forces exerted against objects, through machinery and machine labor. Boys deal with *direct actions on objects*. Girls, however, are associated with telepathy, telecommunication, and telecommand, with technologies that appear magical because they entail *action at a distance*. The effects of Sheeta's stone appear magical precisely because their technology is so advanced as to be beyond our comprehension: her stone entails biological interface (a stone keyed to her body only), voice-activated systems, telecommanded robots and weaponry. In effect, then, boys deal with technology in terms of problems and solutions, while girls experience technology as a condition. Consequently the burden of salvation from the technological condition falls on girls. At the end of *Castle in the Sky*, for instance, Sheeta teaches Pazu the words of destruction that make the flying stone destroy the castle. Both are willing to die to stop the killing, but the ultimate sacrifice (death) is the girl's initiative—sacrificial suicide to save humanity follows directly from her experience of technology as condition.

At the same time, insofar as the girl's experience of technology as a condition is inseparable from a gendered condition, salvation from the technological condition promises salvation from the gendered condition as well. In other words, in saving the world from destruction, it is as if the girl simultaneously overcomes her received female condition, literally breaking with a condition in which she is manipulated and controlled by telecommand via devices keyed to her body. The girl apparently transcends the received stereotypes of female condition as passivity and exchangeability. Here, however, Miyazaki's use of girl energies in animation reaches an impasse or rather confronts a paradox.

On the one hand, Miyazaki's animations appear to challenge conventional or received roles for girls and women. For instance, Miyazaki puts women into roles where their use of technologies coded as masculine such as guns, tools, and engines serves to focus our attention on those technologies in a different way—Kushana in *Nausicaä* or Eboshi Gozen in *Princess Mononoke*. With such types, as Susan Napier points out, "Miyazaki is clearly not only attempting to break down the conventional image of the feminine but also to break down the viewer's conventional notion of the world in general."[10] Similarly, in his depictions of girls and boys, Miyazaki generally avoids stories that end in marriage or even romantic alliance between the heroine and hero. His boys and girls appear first and foremost to be friends, partners, or allies. In this way he avoids scenarios in which girls figure as objects of exchange between men. In *Castle in the Sky*, for instance, he avoids the scenario typical of the boys'-adventure film and men's-action film in which the hero slays the villain and wins the girl, which inscribes a quasi-Oedipal transfer of male authority from symbolic father to the husband hero, reducing the girl to an object of exchange, a future wife. In this manner, Miyazaki strives to wrest women and girls from conventionally gendered scenarios.

A paradox appears, however, but not simply because Miyazaki has to evoke the very stereotypes and clichés that he wishes to trouble, and consequently his animations are exceedingly ambivalent vis-à-vis established roles for boys and girls. The problem runs deeper. The same problem appears in Heidegger as the need for a god.

Gaining a free relation to technology entails gathering and focusing our perception of technology differently, thus opening an understanding of its essence. In Heidegger's opinion, we have to experience the technological object—even the fortress in the sky, for instance—in terms of the way in which it gathers and focuses our practices. As Dreyfus puts it, "we experience our role as receivers, and the importance of receptivity, thereby freeing us from our compulsion to force all things into one efficient order."[11] This is precisely what Sheeta does: she experiences her reception of the "gift" of this technological order characterized by the fortress in the sky and flying stones. The danger, when grasped as the danger, becomes that which saves us. Thus Sheeta recalls the words of destruction that destroy technologies of destruction. Put another way, the receptivity or opening to technology affords salvation or *releasement* from the technological condition. Yet, as Dreyfus remarks of Heidegger, releasement "is only a stage, a kind of holding pattern, awaiting a new understanding of being, which would give some content to our openness—what Heidegger calls a new rootedness."[12] This is where the story of *Castle in the Sky* leaves us: releasement via openness to technology, which gives a vision of new rootedness, a vision of a new relation to the earth. But what would give that vision of rootedness content and constancy?

Heidegger thinks that some being, object, or entity must appear to impart constancy to openness or receptivity. Otherwise, the promise of a new way of dwelling in the world remains but a vision; the new way cannot take a stand, take root, or somehow persist. Dreyfus suggests we call such special objects cultural paradigms. But Heidegger calls the new object that will ground a new understanding of reality a god. This is why he says "only another god can save us." Heidegger sees the need for a new god.

Castle in the Sky makes a very similar move. While the story leaves us suspended at the moment of releasement with a vision of new rootedness, its animation offers a figure who brings content and constancy to its imagination of characters angled toward the earth: the girl. This is what makes the role of the girl so difficult to parse. She embodies the technological condition, affords salvation or releasement, and appears as the new god or new paradigm to give constancy to a new understanding, a new way of living with technology, a new rootedness. This places quite a burden on the young girl, who must become akin to a god or savior of animation technologies. An image in the title sequence—a young woman's face blowing the wind for the windmill—provides an important clue as to how Miyazaki strives to realize the promise of the girl-god in gaining a new rooted understanding of technology.

The film gradually undermines our delight in the flying stones and the flying castles. We learn that such an energy source inevitably results in technologies that encourage destruction of the earth, as if being able to live above the earth could only result in disregard for it. Yet the film sustains our delight in flying, and we discover an alternative way to take to the skies, using the wind as an energy source. Unlike oil, coal, gas, uranium, or flying stones, the wind is not only abundant but also ungraspable. The wind cannot be possessed or entirely territorialized, yet it sustains a relation to earth. We come back to the ground. Wind-powered technologies are the key to Miyazaki's attempt at a paradigm to give constancy to the vision of a new rootedness.

If we recall that the term animation derives from the Greek *animus* or wind, we come full circle. Animation is an art of wind, an art of opening spaces to channel the flow of the wind. Animation is an art of spacing, of producing intervals through which the wind may blow and turn the wheels, limbs, eyes, and ears of the animator's drawings. The wind of animation arises in gaps that appear between layers of image when you avoid closing the image world. The wind blows through the characters, in their tendency to become weightless and unmoored and in the dynamics of angling their weight through different planes. In Miyazaki's animation, the medium (animation) truly becomes the message (wind power). In sum, wind-powered animation is the paradigm for a new rootedness. Miyazaki's embrace of the animetic interval implies an openness to technology that at once releases us from its determinism, from the modern technological condition, and offers a paradigm for dwelling with a different relation to technology.

But why in the title sequence is it a young woman who generates the wind for the windmill? Apparently, Miyazaki's wind-powered animation needs a new god, in the form of a girl, who will impart some manner of constancy to the new understanding of technology—Nausicaä of the Valley of the Wind, Sheeta, Kiki, Princess Mononoke. The girl is the site of futurity in Miyazaki's animations. *Castle in the Sky* strives to produce an experience of receptivity to the animetic interval, an experience that is to serve as the paradigm for a future world organized around an energy source that is abundant, clean, and yet ungraspable, the wind. Without the figure of the girl, however, this future would simply appear as a return to the past, a return to old technologies and old forms of social organization, and thus as a repetition of older understandings of the world.[13] In Miyazaki's animation, openness to the animetic interval translates into the need for a new god, and it turns out that only a girl can save us now.

CHAPTER 8

GIVING UP THE GUN

PRODUCING AN ANIMATED FILM like *Nausicaä* or *Castle in the Sky* requires the labor of many people with different talents working together, often for months or years. To return to a simple example of labor division, the key animator produces the key frames and assistants do in-betweens and clean-up. Subsequently, if the combination of key and in-between animation passes muster, teams of artists do the inking and coloring on celluloid sheets, which is a painstaking and tedious but important task. Producing cel animation demands a number of other tasks and talents as well. Animation is, like cinema, a modern industrial art, with antecedents in craft guilds and cottage industries but nonetheless modern in its combination of wage labor, work divisions, and technologies. My goal in this chapter is not to give a detailed account of workflow and studio organization; if I underscore that traditional cel animation implies a division of labor and a hierarchy of talents, it is because I wish to make tentative and exploratory remarks about the relation between the animetic machine and the animation studio.

The workflow in large animation studios—Disney Studios in the heyday of cel animation production with its huge teams of artists comes to mind—is not unlike assembly-line work in some respects. Producing the big feature-length animated film requires a division of labor into specific tasks, with different teams of workers devoting their time almost exclusively to one task. But animation production can also be very small scale. In the 1920s and into the 1930s, animation was a sort of cottage industry. Anyone with a camera, paper or celluloid, and drawing skills could mobilize family or friends to make an animated film. With paper animation (because paper costs far less than celluloid), the major limitation on production was the number of hours you and your team could bear to work, alongside the costs of film stock, development, and drawing equipment. Interestingly enough, when the animators who would later form Gainax Studios launched into producing an animated short (*Daicon III Opening Animation*) for a science fiction convention in 1981, they had never used celluloid. To date they had imagined their animations on paper, flipbook-style, and for their first amateur production, they could not afford celluloid and used sheet vinyl instead.[1] In other words, even into the 1980s, alongside the big animation industry productions, the basics of animation production remained accessible. The same is true today, even as animation has largely come to be produced digitally. There are large high-budget productions that demand teams of workers (even as computer drawing and coloring eliminate many jobs and change the workflow), and smaller "amateur" productions, many of which begin only with paper, or scanning images into a computer, or drawing simple images on the computer. Of course, the dream of digital technologies is that one person might, on her own, make an animated film of a quality to rival the big studios.[2]

Commonly, however, for the vision of one artist to emerge (say, that of the director or producer) in the production of a feature-length animated film, the skills and operations of the other artists must somehow align with yet remain subordinate to the overall vision of the one artist. The world of production, the work of animators, must be organized or coordinated in a certain way if the animated film is to have a recognizable style or stylistic signature—what is called in film studies an *auteur*, which is an artist or author effect.

Miyazaki Hayao is an auteur in the sense that he puts his stamp on every aspect of production (writing, directing, animating); he is notorious for retouching or redoing images that do not meet his standard. As a result, there really is a Miyazaki style, a Miyazaki look and feel and treatment, and we recognize his films as Miyazaki films, we see in them his vision. Since the foundation of Studio Ghibli in 1985, with Takahata Isao, Miyazaki has also contributed to establishing a recognizable Ghibli style or brand. Ghibli films, too, are designed to have a Ghibli look and feel, and they address viewers in a certain way and present the world in a certain way. They thus imply a worldview that contributes to the constitution of a Ghibli world.

The dynamics of the Miyazaki auteur effect and the Ghibli-brand world have thus far made it easy for me to evoke Miyazaki's name as if he alone were responsible for a distinctive mode of animation and manner of thinking technology, when in fact the Miyazaki effect—Miyazaki as *auteur*—emerges within a theater of operations known as Studio Ghibli, as it strives to secure a perimeter for staging its animated worlds and worldview.[3] I will return to the animation studio as a theater of operations below. But first I think it time to summarize or clarify how I see the various levels of determination (agents, determinants, or actors) that have entered into my account thus far, sometimes explicitly, sometimes implicitly—such as technical determination, cultural determination, authorial determination. For instance, at the same time that I have evoked Miyazaki as the author or creator, I have insisted on the importance of looking at animation as a machine, specifically a multiplanar machine, which determines or limits what animation is and what it can do. This may raise questions about agency for some readers. Do I see Miyazaki producing animation or animation producing Miyazaki? Does Miyazaki determine animation or does animation determine Miyazaki?

The problem with such questions is that they entail a false opposition, which tends to force a choice, in which the options are presented so starkly as to be meaningless—human agency versus technological determinism. Clearly, Miyazaki determines his animations to some extent, and at the same time we must also acknowledge that Miyazaki the author is also an effect of labor organization; to recognize such effects does not amount to denial of the human or human actors. Miyazaki is definitely an actor. My point is, Miyazaki cannot determine his animations deterministically, any more than the multiplanar machine can deterministically control all possible outcomes for animation. To understand Miyazaki animations, we have to look at more than Miyazaki as a person or creator; we need to consider what animation is. To call attention to the multiplanar machine (a technical ensemble) does not rule out other determinants or actors, as among them human agents. Even though I give a sort of ontological priority to the multiplanar machine and speak of the specificity of animation or what animation is *in essence*, I am not embracing technological determinism or essentialism (essence here is a vague material essence) or erasing human agency—on the contrary.

Looking at the operations of the multiplanar machine situates human agents less deterministically than those analyses that focus exclusively on the artistry of the master creator. From the angle of the multiplanar machine, human actors now appear important as much for the indeterminacy they bring to the machine (how they open structural autopoieisis into machinic heterogenesis) as for their determining role (their mastery or control). Insofar as the multiplanar machine implies a specific kind of interval or spacing, which implies a specific set of material orientations resulting from a specific manner of channeling a technical force, the machine is at once a site or moment of determination *and* indetermination. Therein lies the difference with apparatus theory. Apparatus theory holds to determination to the point of determinism. In contrast, machine theory looks both at material forms and immaterial structures, at determination and indetermination. Otherwise, the machine would be just a feedback mechanism, a static loop, purely mechanistic, without relation to the human or to life.

By giving priority to the animetic machine, I am deliberately shifting attention away from cultural determination in the form of Japaneseness. A common way of looking at the relation between Miyazaki and his animation, for instance, is to situate both within Japan and to stress the cultural or sociohistorical determination of animation. Miyazaki then appears as a product of his culture, and his animated films, too, are seen largely as a product of Japanese culture, as an expression of Japaneseness. Such an approach easily slides into cultural determinism or culturalism, inviting a view in which animation produced in Japan directly and inevitably reproduces Japanese values. This has become an exceedingly popular way of looking at Japanese animations, and lumping them all into the category of anime encourages this tendency to construe all Japanese animations as expressions of Japanese values. The result is a simple reproduction of unitary, self-identical, and monolithic Japaneseness. There are so many critiques of such a manner of thinking about Japan that there is no need for me to reiterate them here.[4]

To avoid cultural determinism, some commentators on anime find in Japanese animations a critical response to the monolithic reproduction of Japanese values. In her account of *Princess Mononoke*, for instance, Susan Napier shows that Miyazaki's film can read as a critique of Japanese nationalism.[5] This is one way of dealing with cultural *determination* without falling into cultural *determinism*. Yet, if I shift from questions about cultural determination toward questions about technical or technological determination, it is because I think that the study of animation must acknowledge both (1) animation as such, its specificity; and (2) the global status of Japanese animations, their transnational flows. If one begins with cultural determination, the specificity of anime and its transnational flows tend to fall by the wayside, or such concerns are tacked onto the discussion, as if an afterthought. Ōtsuka Eiji, an editor, critic, and writer, poses the question bluntly: why do so many Americans see Miyazaki's films as distinctively Japanese, as receptacles of Japanese values, when they are so clearly globally targeted entertainments?[6] The answer is Orientalist habits of thought whereby the identity of the subject is formed by projecting unitary difference onto the Other, which Ueno Toshiya has referred to as techno-orientalism in the context of anime reception.[7]

This is not to say that Japanese animations do not or cannot express or critique Japanese values. Animation, like cinema, has a history of nationalization and cultural nationalism. In the late 1910s and early 1920s, animation in Japan was frequently seen through the lens of film reforms geared toward the production of an internationally intelligible yet recognizably Japanese style of film, commonly under the rubric of the Pure Film Movement. In the 1930s, animation in Japan came largely under the auspices of the wartime government, and animated shorts and films thus produced were designed to express national values, the virtues of the Japanese empire and the military. Later, when Ōkawa Hiroshi founded Tōei's animation studio in the 1950s to compete with Disney films, those animated films, while globally targeted, were nonetheless supposed to look Japanese, to manifest Japanness in some manner. Around the same time, however, in the 1960s, a number of Japanese animated television series found their way to audiences around the world, often with very little cultural adaptation other than dubbing, and for the most part audiences did not know them or see them as Japanese. In sum, on the one hand, animation production has often been associated with the production of national values and cultural nationalism, yet on the other hand, the Japaneseness of Japanese animation can sometimes go entirely unnoticed. Such seemingly contradictory modes of production and reception arise because such Japaneseness belongs to a history of producing films with an eye to export. It is as much an address to the world as to Japan. The Japan of animation is commonly Japan in the world, not Japan folded back on itself in self-absorbed isolation. The long history of international coproduction of Japan's animated films, whether official or unacknowledged coproduction, further complicates the idea of an isolated expression of Japaneseness. For instance, in addition to coproductions with studios in India, Europe, America, China, or Korea, Japanese animation studios have often farmed out the labor-intensive work to animators in Korea and (increasingly) China, which raises questions about whether such animation is actually produced in Japan.

In sum, if I do not give priority to national culture and Japanese values, it is because looking at Japanese animations primarily in terms of cultural determination tends to naturalize and reify national culture, to treat culture deterministically. Yet I should also point out that looking at technology and technical determination runs a similar risk. Such an approach can slide into determinism, especially when questions about culture enter the mix. As I mentioned previously, the history of Japanese cinema tends to adopt some of the assumptions of apparatus theory, almost by default. The basic historical scenario is one in which the movie camera comes from the West to Japan and, as a foreign technology, presents a dilemma for native culture or traditions. Historians of Japanese cinema have aptly contested the technological determinism implicit in the emphasis on the apparatus, by stressing the Japanese assimilation, adaptation, and domestication of the foreign apparatus and its associated conventions. Some scholars equate localized practices of film exhibition with native cultural resistance to foreign technologies. In their emphasis on cultural assimilation or adaptation of the apparatus, such histories of Japanese cinema seem to agree with historian of technology David Nye, who writes, "rather than assuming that technologies are deterministic, it appears more reasonable to assume that cultural choices shape their uses."[8] But is it so reasonable to assume the priority of cultural choices?

In his challenge to technological determinism, Nye throws the net wide, contesting the idea that technologies are inherently dangerous or out of control, that technologies dictate social change, or that there are laws of historical development linked to mechanization. He sees in a broad range of modern thinkers—Marx, McLuhan, Foucault, Toffler, Heidegger—the same reliance on technological determinism, which he also attributes to the left in general: "The left generally assumed that a society's technologies defined its economic system and social organization. Thus the primitive mill produced feudalism, while the steam engine produced capitalism."[9]

Miyazaki might well be added to Nye's list of leftist critics of modern technology.[10] *Castle in the Sky* and *Nausicaä* develop a scenario in which weapons of mass destruction appear out of control by their very nature, and technologies seem to dictate social organization, with the primitive mill associated with a quasi-feudal community affording a sharp contrast to the inherently dangerous world of big technologies. Much like Heidegger, Miyazaki's animations imply that modern technology is not just dangerous in its applications but in its effect on human perception and human thought. As such, Miyazaki's response to technological determinism presents a strong contrast with Nye's. Looking at this contrast will bring us back to the question of cultural or authorial determination in the context of the animation studio.

Nye explicitly adopts the stance of a specialist in the history of technology, whose historical knowledge (which he feel distinguishes him from leftist critics of technology) proves that cultural choices shape the uses of technologies. Interestingly enough, he opens with the example of Japan as evidence against technological determinism, as evidence of cultural choice. He uses the now cliché and largely contested example of Japan "giving up the gun." The passage is worth citing at length.

> However, history provides some interesting counterexamples to apparently inevitable technologies. The gun would appear to be the classic example of a weapon that no society could reject once it had been introduced. Yet the Japanese did just that. They adopted guns from Portuguese traders in 1543, learned how to make them, and gradually gave up the bow and sword. As early as 1575 guns proved decisive in a major battle (Nagoshino), but then the Japanese abandoned them, *for what can only be considered cultural reasons.*[11]

To prove that guns do not inevitably push society in a certain direction, Nye emphasizes the role of culture, specifically in the register of symbolism and values. He argues that government restriction alone cannot explain giving up the gun; instead, samurai warriors gave up guns because guns had little symbolic value for them. This situation, for Nye, proves that cultural values can determine the impact of a technology. But note how he slides from taking cultural uses into account to assuming cultural determinism. For instance, to shore up his point, Nye must let the numerically small samurai class stand in for all of Japan, thus conflating samurai values with Japanese values. The result is a retroactive projection of a unitary and homogeneous national culture (as constructed in the Meiji period) onto earlier periods of Japanese history—*Nihonjinron*. Nye sidesteps any account of the violence, coercion, and negotiations that were so crucial in the Tokugawa shogunate's push to give up the gun. In his account, Japan gives up guns because "they" (the samurai/Japanese) did not value them as symbols of authority. Nye thus erases the historical theater of operations, the efforts of the Tokugawa shogunate to secure its perimeters. He replaces such operations with ahistorical symbolic values, with cultural choices that are conflated with national values. Like many historians who evoke culture but who are not really interested in cultural specificity or material history, Nye falls back on national culture as if it constituted a self-evident point of departure for writing history. The result is a tendency to think about cultural difference solely at the level of national values, namely, German uses of technology, Japanese uses of technology, American uses of technology, and so on. Oddly, in Nye, national culture then appears *the* site of choice and even of rational choice. Cultural use becomes national choice, and national choice is confused with rational choice.

In stark contrast with Nye, in films such as *Castle in the Sky* and *Nausicaä*, Miyazaki strives to imagine and to offer an experience of giving up the gun, indeed of giving up the entire history of weaponry, from guns and bombs to weapons of mass destruction. Miyazaki obviously takes technological determination more seriously than Nye, and his vision flirts with technological determinism. Crucially, however, Miyazaki's animations shift the question of technology from that of problems with solutions (in the manner of Nye) to the question of a technological condition that affects perception and thought (like Heidegger), from which there might be salvation or releasement. As a result, Miyazaki's animations don't simply give up the gun. As we have seen, they don't simply give up ballistic perception or cinematism but try to open it animetically. Similarly, the moment of salvation or releasement, with its vision of a new rooted existence, does not appear as a cultural choice. Miyazaki's animations thus stand in stark contrast to Nye's equally fantastical story of cultural choice, in which the preference of samurai for swords appears as the crucial explanation for giving up the gun.

Of course, you can introduce cultural questions into a discussion of Miyazaki's animations. You can step outside the film and ask if Sheeta's actions reflect a Japanese experience of technology or a Japanese way of thinking about technology. Surely at some level it is specific to Japan. Yet the fact that Miyazaki's thinking about technology reads so well alongside Heidegger indicates the degree to which Miyazaki's animations address the modern world rather than dwell on the uniqueness of the Japanese experience of it. Naturally, one might trace the affinity between Miyazaki and Heidegger to the profound impact of Heidegger on Japanese thought, situating Miyazaki in a Japanese lineage of Heideggerian thought. But to begin and end with questions about culture, Japanese or otherwise, runs entirely counter to Miyazaki's animation. Therein lies its challenge.

Miyazaki's film consistently troubles the idea of a culturally determined choice. After all, even though Sheeta initiates the decision, Sheeta and Pazu intone the words of destruction together, and they come from markedly different cultures: Sheeta comes from a pastoral culture, and Pazu from a mining town. In addition, these cultures or economies are not in any way coded as Japanese. More importantly, Sheeta's decision derives from her bodily experience of the technological condition. As the descendant of those who previously devastated the earth, she has inherited a responsibility, which is not imaged culturally but technically and physically—a magical stone keyed to her body. Hers is a bodily disposition not a cultural disposition—or rather it is at once a technological condition *and* a cultural condition. Simply put, cultures in Miyazaki's film appear as techno-cultures. It is impossible to separate culture and technology, as Nye does.

Note that Nye introduces a separation between culture and technology by evoking the diffusion of Western technologies to a non-Western site—Japan in the mid- to late sixteenth century, that is, the late Muromachi period or "warring countries" *(sengoku)* period. To enforce the distinction between the technology (gun) and its cultural use, he imparts a unity to Japan that it did not actually have at that time, ignoring how the introduction of the gun and its rejection were part of a draconian imposition of unity onto largely autonomous domains. To downplay the historical violence associated both with technology and with culture, he projects the subsequent unity of Japan (the unification of domains under the Tokugawa shogunate) backward historically.

Miyazaki deals with the same historical events in *Princess Mononoke*, but because his emphasis is on the violent impact of technology rather than cultural choice, he makes it impossible to separate the gun from the "culture" that accepts or rejects it. While *Princess Mononoke* shows the effects of gun manufacture in

Japan in the late sixteenth century, the story is not framed as a problem of foreign technology denaturing the native. It is not a story predicated upon national culture, upon Japan confronting the West. *Princess Mononoke* is a story of the irrevocable changes spurred by gun manufacture, with an emphasis on the loss of a sense of the sanctity of nature and on the eradication of local difference as semi-autonomous techno-cultures come into contact in new ways due to the introduction of guns. Unlike Nye, then, *Princess Mononoke* does not retroactively project unity on Japan to lessen the impact of this particular technology. In fact, the film ends before the Tokugawa shogunate would impose its Neo-Confucian order and give up the gun. In other words, in *Princess Mononoke* the cultural choice of "giving up the gun" does not appear, precisely because such an emphasis poses the question of technology as one of a problem with a solution, in the manner of Nye. Rather than a technical problem that can be muted or even resolved through cultural choices, the gun in Miyazaki's animation constitutes a technological condition, which affects the way we perceive and think about the world. As such it appears deterministic, as a fate rather than a device, as much myth as history.

At the denouement of the film, Lady Eboshi fires on the *shishigami*, the god or spirit of the forest in the form of a giant stag with enormous antlers, shooting off his head. The headless body transforms into a dark oozing substance that gradually covers the land, killing all life. The boy Ashitaka and the girl San eventually return the stag's head to the forest, which restores the land. A great wind then sweeps through, gathering and whisking away the debris. In the end, then, while the gun has destroyed the sanctity of nature forever, the wind appears to offer something beyond the technological condition of the gun. The children watch the wind, transfixed. Rather than "giving up the gun," which is now impossible, we have once again a vision of the wind, or rather an experience of the wind—an experience of animetism, which is equally an experience of "technicity," of the qualities of a technology, and which in this instance summons the technicity of cel animation.

In sum, while it is always possible to step outside the animation and seek the message of the film in something like cultural uses and choices, Miyazaki's animations do not encourage such a gesture.[12] Miyazaki animations think the question of technology technically or animetically, not culturally. They focus our attention on technics, technicity, and techno-cultures. This is the virtue and challenge of Miyazaki's animations: they spur us to open a free relation to technology rather than fall back on cultural choice to mute the impact of technologies. Where Nye reinscribes human agency vis-à-vis technology *within* culture (turning national culture into rational culture or rational choice), Miyazaki's emphasis on technical determination does not confine human agency within culture. Nor does it erase the human. In sum, addressing technological determinism allows Miyazaki to avoid cultural determinism. This is what allows him to imagine salvation or releasement from the modern technological condition, with the vision of a new world, which is not that of a particular culture, ethnicity, or nation.

Yet, as we saw in the previous chapter, the question arises of what will give constancy to this newly envisioned world, what will enable us to prolong the vision and dwell in its world. Heidegger sees a need for a new god. In contrast, instead of *a* god, which in his opinion marks the totalitarian moment of Heidegger's thought, Dreyfus suggests new *gods*, special objects or *cultural paradigms*. Here the question of culture reappears. But what is the difference between cultural use/choice and cultural paradigm? An emphasis on cultural use/choice tends to give the impression of humans standing over and above technologies, able to accept or reject them, or to alter and assimilate them, as with the samurai giving up the gun and holding onto the sword. An emphasis on cultural paradigms tends to see humans and their cultures as more continuous with technologies. It is not so much a matter of choosing one technology over another as it is a matter of being caught up in a technological condition that affects or orientates potential actions and choices—not a deterministic structure but a field of potential actions.[13] A cultural paradigm is, in fact, a techno-cultural paradigm or, more precisely, a techno-cultural field of actions potentialized by a machine.

In such Miyazaki animations as *Nausicaä* and *Castle in the Sky*, a new techno-cultural paradigm emerges, one already implicit in *Conan* and *Lupin the Third: The Castle of Cagliostro*, which extends into subsequent films. The paradigm is of a wind-powered world, with the girl as the new god to guide us. The paradigm is animetism itself. It is a perceptual experience of the open interval of multiple planes of the image as rendered with open compositing, which attains its finest expression in scenes of gliding, soaring, flying, floating on the wind. Insofar as such an experience of the technicity of cel animation works to open technological ordering in an attempt to provisionally free us from it from within, the paradigm of animetism does not appear designed to ground a new order. It is a nonorder, and Miyazaki's animations are happiest when they deconstruct technological ordering. They deliberately do not offer a programmatic guide for a new techno-cultural order. Still, we can ask the question. Does animetism enable the formation of a new kind of community, or coalition, or cooperative? This question can be posed at three levels: that of Miyazaki's animations, that of Studio Ghibli's official image, and that of the organization of labor within the studio.

Miyazaki's animations typically scramble sociohistorical points of references. You can't tell exactly when and where the action takes place. Even in *Totoro* and

Princess Mononoke and *Spirited Away,* which offer historical points of reference (to 1950s Japan, sixteenth-century Japan, and 1990s recessionary Japan respectively), there is a tendency to undermine a unitary sense of sociohistorical reference and temporal ordering. The figure of Totoro gestures toward ancient Shintō wind spirits and toward trolls in contemporary illustrated children's books. A variety of techno-cultures coexist in *Princess Mononoke,* which serves to scramble the temporal priority usually imposed on these "communities" and to fragment the sense of a unitary Japan. While *Spirited Away* may be read as voyage into the past, that past is not firmly locatable.

When a vision of a better social organization emerges, especially in Miyazaki's early films, it appears as an eclectic mixture of pastoral, medieval, and feudal economies or techno-cultures. The Valley of the Wind in *Nausicaä* has its castle and fief, with lord, warriors, and peasants, gathered peaceably around their windmills cultivating the land. *Castle in the Sky* has a mining village based on an actual village in Wales whose community Miyazaki greatly admired, yet its utopian memories and projections are of a quasi-feudal pastoral windmill society. Nonetheless, the eclectic combination of sociohistorical and techno-cultural references creates uncertainty—is this truly a medieval or feudal order? Is there a disguised sympathy or nostalgia in Miyazaki's animations for such an order, for an order that might enforce giving up the gun? Or is it nostalgia for an imaginary pastoral existence? Because Miyazaki flirts with technological determinism, he verges on establishing the sort of one-to-one correspondence between technology and culture to which Nye rightly objected: windmill equals feudal-pastoral order. But this is surely why Miyazaki's animations tend to scramble sociohistorical or techno-cultural references, precisely to resist technological ordering. This is a quasi-deconstructive gesture vis-à-vis technological ordering, designed to explore openings or moments of freedom within ordering, rather than offering a new order.

As I will discuss in conclusion, a problem arises where commerce meets the animetic interval. I do not mean to imply that everything would be okay if the market and commercial concerns never entered the picture. That is clearly impossible. After all, animations are commodities. Miyazaki and Ghibli must figure out how to distribute films and make profits, and what is more, they must settle on a *pattern of serialization,* that is, on a specific manner of introducing, designing, or licensing products related to their animations. Where working with and experimenting with the animetic interval implies an encounter with the force of the moving image and thus divergent series that scramble technical ordering, patterns of serialization bring some degree of convergence to the experiment. They encourage looking at animation with an eye to unfolding and refolding it within a commercial ordering.

In response to such pressures, Ghibli's strategy is to downplay the feel of commercialism. The Ghibli Museum, for instance, presents quasi-domestic spaces in proximity to nature (within a park), deemphasizing commercialization and stressing fantasy, art, and education. It is antithetical to the theme park. There are whimsically designed playgrounds and passages for children and adults alike. Above all, the effect is one of eccentric elegance and tasteful play, and as is generally true of Ghibli's commodities, great care is taken to assure that Ghibli merchandise is restrained in scope and design, which gives the impression of products that are tasteful but not highbrow. This is the Ghibli-brand world. It combines childlike playfulness with commercial restraint. It appears as noncommercially driven commerce. Similarly, the Ghibli Museum presents its animation as nontechnologically-ordered technics. Iwai Toshio's stroboscope animation machines on the ground floor of the museum perfectly convey the Ghibli tendency to straddle high tech and low tech, new media and old media, technology and technique.[14] In Iwai's stroboscopes, models of famous Miyazaki characters, such as Mei and Satsuki from *Totoro*, meticulously carved and painted in various poses, begin to rotate and gather speed. When they reach a certain speed, under the stroboscopic light, the poses blur together to produce an animated figure before your eyes. Thus Iwai shows us how character animation works, echoing the Ghibli flair for producing accessible technical art that operates by gathering and focusing our attention on technological operations. Likewise, the museum exhibits on making Ghibli animated films run the gamut from presenting sketches and cels as art (framed in accordance with art conventions) to operating a film projector.

Ghibli's self-presentation entails a conflation of technological ordering with commercialism, consumerism, and even capitalism. Its strategy vis-à-vis consumerism is consonant with (and seems to derive from) the critique of the modern technological condition. In effect, Ghibli equates serialization and technologization, and as a consequence the goal is to minimize serialization, in keeping with the minimization of technologies in the animations. Ghibli does not serialize its animations across multiple media, spinning out sequels, prequels, or side stories. Although they produce some tie-in merchandise and occasionally make animated commercials, the Ghibli world is nothing like, say, the Pokémon world. You won't soon (if ever) see a *Nausicaä* RPG (roleplaying game) or *Princess Mononoke* duel cards in advanced generations. If the Ghibli film is truly going to gather and focus our perceptual practices, it must to some extent stand alone and allow us to take it in, to contemplate it, in its own techno-aesthetic terms.

As Miyazaki is well aware, such a strategy can fail.[15] There are no guarantees at the level of reception. If you obsess on *Totoro* sitting in front of the television night and day, chances are you are blocking rather than encouraging a free relation to technology. Studio Ghibli thus tries to draw lines and impart limits through its marketing and distribution, studiously cultivating its image, not only with its museum but also with its art exhibitions and publications. Above all, Ghibli wants to distinguish its manga films from television anime and to avoid association with "subculture" audiences (otaku) who become obsessed with them. As Ōtsuka Eiji and other commentators have noted, however, otaku fans gravitated toward Miyazaki, especially his earlier films like *Castle in the Sky*; such films are not so different from what is typically considered otaku fare: you have a cute little girl whose skirt flutters up to show her panties, and you have giant robots and flying machines.[16] What's not to like for the stereotypical male otaku? Ghibli thus comes to insist on its production of "general" films, that is, films for general audiences—in contrast to anime otaku fare.

A contradiction, then, haunts Ghibli's efforts to produce a good relation to the consumer or commercial order. Because Ghibli conflates serialization with technologization, the emphasis falls on minimizing serialization. This is supposed to make for a certain kind of distance between viewer and animation. On the one hand, the animation is to gather and focus viewer attention in order to afford an experience of animetism, which is to open viewer experience beyond technological ordering. On the other hand, the viewer is not supposed to become too wrapped up in the film, too close to it, obsessive. Ghibli walks a fine line, between mass or generic appeal and an insistence on animation that, in the manner of high art or pure art, affords aesthetic distance and allows for contemplation rather than thrills and obsession. Out of this oscillation between mass art and high art emerges the *brand*, the Ghibli brand. Ghibli comes to signal something like a high-minded, high-art brand of animation amenable to general mass audiences across the world. The openness associated with animetism becomes indistinguishable from the production of an animation brand for global audiences, and there is a conservatism or traditionalism implicit in this brand-conscious address to the world.

The Ghibli-brand world is not conservative or traditionalist in the sense of embracing Japanese traditions or promoting Japaneseness. In stylistic terms, it tends toward a sort of cozy European kitsch with environmentalist undertones, typified in the numerous technologically and culturally eclectic burgs in Miyazaki's films with their beatific openness to sea, sky, and greenery—pan-bourgeois neopastoralism. If there is a community implicit in the Ghibli-brand address to the world, it is one full of ambivalent fascination for traditions in general, for other worlds and other futures.

In sum, thinking serialization in the same terms as technologization fails.

Different forces and different material determinations are involved. Experimenting with the minimization of the force of the moving image, shunting that force into dynamically angled characters and open compositing, is not the same thing as minimizing serialization, which is an attempt to regulate the circulation of commodities. It is at this level, where commerce meets animation in patterns of serialization, that Ghibli's experimentation threatens to turn into regulation. This is also the level of the studio.

On the one hand, as mentioned previously, Miyazaki's animations might be said to involve an undisguised imposition of hierarchy, insofar as he is intent on controlling every aspect of each animated film, which results in the Miyazaki signature style, the Miyazaki author effect. On the other hand, because animetism derives from cel animation technics, it evokes a sense of craft production, of fine artistry, in contrast to mass production. What is more, Studio Ghibli is fairly small scale, and it projects an image of intimacy and cooperation among artists. This combination of artistic hierarchy and close cooperation is tricky. It is not simply exploitation in the sense of using a division of labor and hierarchy of talents to rationalize production and thus to maximize how much you extract from the worker per yen spent. But a distinctive asymmetry arises, reminiscent of guild associations. The director-animator-producer is not merely a master but a supreme artist, a charismatic figure, while those animators subordinate to him are potentially to become master crafters; they are future directors and producers, maybe. Studio Ghibli, however, has a noticeable problem with succession. No one has appeared to take the mantle from Miyazaki and Takahata. Despite some fairly solid films by other younger directors, these films have proved less popular, and the impression is that they do not compare favorably with Miyazaki's or Takahata's work.

Recall Miyazaki and Ōtsuka's preference for employing a large number of young people, between eighteen and twenty-five, because young workers, especially as in-between animators, are alleged to impart a sense of energy, vibrancy, and flexibility to the final product. The emphasis is not on labor hours or quantity but on quality, and the quality of youthful energy is especially hard to define. It is rather like the wind. It powers the mill but remains somehow ungraspable, immaterial, yet renewable. This vision of youthful animators may not bode well for upward mobility, however. And in fact, the Ghibli emphasis is not on promoting young directors intent on dramatic innovation. The goal seems to be to reproduce the Ghibli-brand world, which demands artistry in the service of someone else's vision. It is in this sense deeply conservative.

One of the rare critics of Studio Ghibli, Oshii Mamoru, sees in Miyazaki's and Takahata's work not only a potentially totalitarian and closed worldview but also a chain of command that actively discourages innovation, experimentation, and autonomy.[17] Indeed the Ghibli combination of artistic hierarchy and cooperation, with energetic youth under the guidance of charismatic leaders, in the service of preserving and sustaining a brand of animation and a worldview, calls to mind some of the quasi-feudal communities evoked in Miyazaki's animations, such as the Valley of Wind. It is as if Miyazaki and company, in their critique of the modern technological condition, unwittingly fell in step with draconian procedures like those of the Tokugawa shogunate for "giving up the gun." Which is to say, when the animetism that enables a critique of modernity at the level of perception becomes a paradigm, actualized in a pattern of serialization, it enters into a theater of operations, becoming caught up in securing the brand's perimeters.

PART II. EXPLODED VIEW

CHAPTER 9

RELATIVE MOVEMENT

S ITTING ON A STATIONARY TRAIN, not moving at all, you suddenly feel that your train is sliding forward or backward. This often happens if you are parked alongside another stationary train, and that train begins to move. As the other train slides past your window, you feel that your train, not the other, is moving. This sensation, as mentioned in the previous chapter, is one of induced movement or *relative movement*. Your sense of motion is relative to the motion of things in the world around you. A similar situation arises if you are on a train in motion, and a train passes on another track alongside yours. For a moment or two, you have the feeling that your train is not moving at all. It is as if you had come to a standstill.

With the sliding planes that compose the animated image, Miyazaki Hayao does something analogous to give viewers a sense that, even though they are apart from the world seen (enabling panoramic perception of it), their movement in this world is nonetheless relative to the motion of the world. Thus Miyazaki undercuts the sensation that the panoramic world is merely out there, inert, waiting for us to seize and exploit it (as a standing reserve, to employ Heidegger's turn of phrase). Rather, Miyazaki imparts a sense of a world full of movement, a "movementful" world and a dynamic Nature, toward which characters are dynamically angled. This way of animating is the basis for Miyazaki's way of thinking technology: his use of animation technology constitutes an attempt to inhabit the technological world differently.

There is, however, duplicity inherent in Miyazaki's approach. On the one hand, insofar as he sustains a sense of depth that allows for panoramic perception, Miyazaki gives the impression that viewers can stand over and above the world and see it in an encompassing way. On the other hand, his use sliding planes produces a sense of relative movement, which gives the impression that the world exceeds our grasp, our perception of it; the world is in motion, and our perception of the world follows from our movement relative to it. There is thus a tension in Miyazaki's animation between *panoramic depth*, which evokes a subject standing apart from the perceived world, and *relative movement*, which makes the subject's perception of the world relative to its movement. It is in scenes of soaring and flying that he strives to overcome this tension, artfully spreading the animetic interval across the depths of the multiplanar image, effectively channeling the force of the moving image into the sliding of a glider through the clouds.

Depth in Miyazaki's animations comes from stacking or layering the planes of the image, and he enhances this sense of depth with the painterly detail of his landscapes. The use of fairly simply drawn characters upon detailed and highly artful backgrounds assures that the world (of nature) appears deep and complex. Over the years, Miyazaki's background paintings have tended to become more and more elaborate and artful, building on a range of art historical traditions and techniques, to the point where painterly detail has for many critics come to define his art more than the use of movement. The forests in *Princess Mononoke*, the bathhouse architectures and seascapes in *Spirited Away*, and the alpine fields of *Howl's Moving Castle* are prime examples. Architect Fujimori Terunobu, referring primarily to the buildings in *Spirited Away*, writes, "With Miyazaki Hayao, depth into the screen is born."[1] Indeed, Fujimori equates Miyazaki's use of depth with the discovery of one-point or geometric perspective in the fifteenth century, which later became associated with Cartesian perspectivalism. Yet, not surprisingly, Fujimori then begins to hedge, acknowledging that, in Miyazaki, fifteenth-century realism happens together with twentieth-century surrealism. Although Fujimori's discussion does not take movement into account, it nonetheless points to an important problem in Miyazaki. Implicit in Miyazaki's use of open compositing is a resistance to hyper-Cartesianism. Yet, as Fujimori's comments suggest, a sort of Cartesianism lingers in Miyazaki's worlds, minimized and perplexed but not eliminated. It lingers in Miyazaki's commitment to conveying a sense of depth.

His commitment to depth is most evident in his painterly backdrops, which gradually come to define the feel of his films. The paintings in *Princess Mononoke* in particular created a sensation. Film critic Satō Tadao calls attention to technologies of lighting, remarking that the luminosity of the screen makes for a particular kind of glow, but no one could ever have imagined the sparkle of water as Miyazaki depicts it.[2] It is not only the attention to detail and composition but also color and luminosity that gradually come to characterize depth in Miyazaki's film. This imparts a sense of *preexisting depth*. In other words, movement may feel relative (via open compositing), but depth does not. Miyazaki thus produces an experience of Nature as absolute as anything envisioned in Disney.[3] In Miyazaki, however, it is the *dynamism* of Nature (rather than inert plentitude) that provides an absolute and abiding frame of reference. There are, however, other ways of working with the layers of the animated image.

If the different layers of the image were drawn with relatively equal emphasis on detail and were analogous in style, the result would be a flattening of the sense of difference between layers of the image. The world of the image would feel flattened. The background would not feel deeper than the other layers, and consequently there would be no sense of a preexisting depth and no recourse to an absolute frame of reference. The sense of a gap would arise only under conditions of movement, of the movement of the image layers relative to one another. This is a world of relative movement without a fixed or absolute point of reference. How are we to situate ourselves in such a world of relative movement?

Media artist Tabaimo evokes this problem of flatness and relative motion in a media installation entitled *Japanese Commuter Train (Nippon no tsūkin kaisoku)*, first presented at the Yokohama Triennale in 2001.[4] Along the walls of two adjoining rooms, Tabaimo reconstructed the interior of a commuter train. On the side walls of the rooms she painted, in flat manga-like style, the car interior (seats, handgrips, racks, windows). On the far wall of each room, she drew the interior of another train car, giving the impression that we are entering into two adjoining cars of a long commuter train. Significantly, even though Tabaimo draws the forward and backward cars in accordance with geometric perspective (the lines of the car interiors recede toward a vanishing point), the forward and backward views do not afford a ballistic perspective. We cannot see from the vantage of the speeding engine. There is no sense of movement into depth. Rather, in the manner of animetism, Tabaimo gives a lateral view of the effects of speed and a sideways experience of movement. The train windows in the installation are actually screens, and images of cityscapes pass by the window-screens (Figure 17). Our sense of movement is an induced or relative movement: we are in a stationary train car that appears to move only because things in the world outside the window move.

Because Tabaimo deliberately sticks with drawing flat images, using only the barest indication of modeled contours or volumetric depth, and because the images that move past the train windows are equally flat and drawn in a relatively uniform style, no sense of preexisting depth arises between train car and cityscape, and no sense of a preexisting divide between interior and exterior. We

Figure 17. *In this sequence of screen grabs from the DVD of Tabaimo's installations, note how the cityscape runs "flatly" past the train windows.*

still have a sense of relative motion, however. This means that we sense the gap between layers, but this is thoroughly *relative difference* imparted through *relative movement.* The result is a world in which it seems that nothing truly happens (it is utterly banal), and at the same time, just about anything might happen: if difference between layers and our sense of movement through the world is entirely relative, if the world does not preexist our experience of it in some absolute way, who can say what might emerge?

Tabaimo plays with this tension between banality and surprise. Incongruous images disrupt the smooth flow of the banal landscape past the window screen of the train installation. There is something nonsensical and absurd about the appearance of out-of-place images—a giant face passing by the train window— and we are pressed to make sense of these seemingly arbitrary happenings. In a world without interior or exterior in which incongruous images crop up in a seemingly random fashion, we are asked to construct our own set of relations, to detect correspondences, to draw connections and sometimes to make little stories from them.

Tabaimo's world differs greatly from Miyzaki's, in which the modern subject grapples to alter its relation to a technologized world, in a classically modernist manner. Tabaimo's train installation, with its child-like chic and aura of naïveté, situates us in what might tentatively be called a postmodern world. Instead of an unambiguously positioned subject who looks through the window onto the world, giving it order or discovering its inherent order, the window has become a screen on which images flow, eliciting affective responses but not imparting any sense of a deeper order. Depth comes to the surface, as affect. The subject becomes a process without end, a series of affective responses to a banal and superficial flow of images. Rather than *a* subject or *the* subject, the sense of relative movement in this installation implies a series of little subjective nodes. This is a quintessentially postmodern situation.

In her incisive analysis of movement and image in Tabaimo's installations, Livia Monnet argues persuasively that Tabaimo's art does not shock us into an encounter with the violence of contemporary Japan.[5] Its incongruous images are not all that disruptive. They do not produce a shock to thought. They are icons of violence at best. Consequently, Monnet suggests, Tabaimo's media art is more a symptom of popular manga and anime ways of looking at the world than it is a critical relation to them. This is because Tabaimo's media installation stops short of taking any risks or discovering any focal concerns in our technological condition, remaining content with a personalized twist on the distractions of everyday life.

Nonetheless, even if one deems Tabaimo's efforts a failure, I do not think that this tendency to flatten and "relativize" movement in the world (whether we call it postmodern or not) is destined to fail. The loss or refusal of an absolute frame of reference, or an inability to locate one, does not necessarily spell an end to values, or the end of any engagement with or commitment to the world "outside" our train windows. With the transformation of the window on the world into a screen without definitive boundaries between inside and outside, another challenge appears. As Monnet implies, when disruptions in the flow of images are as banal as the images, what can actually make us care about anything? Is there anything that can truly move us to tears or laughter or action? Is there any moment in the series of moments that would make us care enough to want to prolong it, whatever the risk to the sense of security or immunity that may come of dwelling in a world without inside or outside?

Naturally there is not an easy answer to such questions, but Tabaimo's *Japanese Commuter Train* provides a clue about how we situate ourselves in the world of relative movement. We tend to turn away from "big" or grand questions about techno-scientific modernity toward "little" questions and personalized relations to technological processes. Faced with a flow of images on the train window-screen, we are compelled to choose what suits us amid the flow. This is not exactly a choice, however. It may be an affective response that is grounded in a sort of training or conditioning, one that is necessary for us to navigate this world of flows to begin with. Amid flattened, dehierarchized, and relativized flows of images, we are summoned to make a personal selection, to personalize our relative movement, to find our focal concerns. In effect, the world of relative movement becomes a regime of relative focal concerns. We are asked to stylize ourselves as a generation of new humans *(shinjinrui)*; or as otaku boys obsessed with little-girl worlds (the *rorikon* or Lolita-complex otaku); or as "parasite singles," young women who prefer to live at home with their parents, devoting their earnings to their own pleasures rather than dreaming of marriage and children; or as female otaku or "rotten girls" *(fujoshi)* in love with idealized love between boys; or as misfits who suffer from social withdrawal syndrome *(hikikomori)*; or as Akihabara types *(Akiba-kei)* who organize their daily life around anime, manga, and electronics; or as multiple-personality-disorder or MPD types.

Fujoshi, rorikon otaku, *hikikomori, Akiba-kei*, parasite single, *shinjinrui*, MPD—these are but a few of the most notorious types in a seemingly ending series of permutations on hyper-personalized types that have made an appearance (largely to be pathologized) in the Japanese media from the 1980s, and which have spread with manga and anime to other information-rich environments around the world. The popular media delineate such types not to understand how we are living today in a regime of dehierarchized and relativized flows of images but to introduce new forms of *regulation* across flows. In the chapters of this section, I will deal especially with the male otaku, a boy or young man who is supposedly obsessed to the point of dysfunction with collecting, disseminating, commenting on, and retooling anime, manga, and games. The male otaku is a media type that has become so persistent as to be paradigmatic of the world of relative movement as articulated around anime and manga. Yet, as indicated in my use of the term "media type" to describe otaku, *fujoshi, hikikomori*, and other related types, I am suspicious about the ease with which such terms are generated and applied. I see the concentration of media discourses on otaku not as an attempt to describe and understand actually existing practices. Such discourses act primarily to regulate the buzzing proliferation of personalized media worlds. Thus, even though I use the term "otaku" and focus largely on discourses about male anime otaku, I see otaku less as an identifiable type of person (fanboy, or geek, or recluse) and more as a set of activities related to constructing personalized worlds amid the media flows exemplified in anime. Similarly, other commentators on otaku, such as Japanese critic Azuma Hiroki, have gravitated toward terms like "otaku-related" (*otaku-kankei*) or "otaku-type" (*otaku-kei*) culture.[6] Otaku, then, refers to a set of practices related to the reception of anime, games, manga, and related media. We may move into or out of intensified zones of otaku activity at different phases of our life, or even at different times of the year, week, or day. But to some extent all of us are engaged in otaku activities.

The question of anime otaku is clearly a question about technology. If I used Miyazaki Hayao as a point of departure, it is not only because he is notorious for distancing himself from the world of anime and anime otaku with his films for "general" audiences. I also evoked him because his resistance to anime and otaku takes the form of an impulse to ground the relative movement implicit in the multiplanar image via a universal or absolute frame of reference—Nature and humanity (especially the humanity of children). In fact, from the time Miyazaki begins to express his resistance to the world of anime otaku, roughly from *Castle in the Sky*, his animations become more painterly than "movementful." In effect, this subtle transformation in Miyazaki speaks to the risk inherent in using focal concerns to counter the modern technological condition. The risk is that focal concerns may not require us to address and remake *the* world; we are all invited to make our own little world, to stylize and personalize our technological existence. In response, Miyazaki's animations refer more insistently to the world and to the humanity of children. But the question of this section is that of what happens when focal concerns—the technologically enabled proliferation of personalized little worlds—do not readily find solace in Nature or Humanity or Children. How is it possible to construct new worlds of value within a regime of relative movement?

CHAPTER 10

STRUCTURES OF DEPTH

WHEN LAYERS OF THE ANIME IMAGE are dehierarchized, with no one layer appearing deeper or sharper than another, depth appears right on the surface. This has the odd effect of drawing greater attention to the composition of images. As we have seen with Miyazaki, even though his animations favor movement *over* depth rather than *into* depth, there is nonetheless a sense of depth and thus of the possibility of panoramic perception, and thus of a view of the world that entails some degree of transcendence of the world. In contrast, when backgrounds become more schematic than painterly, even when they are highly detailed, attention is drawn less to the fluidity of movement within the animated world and more to the structural interplay of elements within the image. We become more attentive to how elements are distributed. The dehierarchization of layers encourages a tendency toward what I will call a distributive perceptual field or simply a distributive field. Because all the sensory elements appear on the surface of the image (rather than arrayed and ordered in depth), the structuration of the perceptual field takes on new importance. This is not to say that the distributive field does away with movement. With the flattening of layers, the force of the moving image is spread across the surface of the image, as potential. The composition or structuration of elements then takes on greater importance in giving direction or orientation to the movement of surface depths (potentials).

As I will discuss in later chapters, the tendency toward the distributive image becomes especially pronounced in a specific lineage of limited cel animation, which is often called upon to characterize anime (and even Japanese animation generally). Because limited animation often flattens and dehierarchizes layers of the image, it invites us to perceive the structuration of elements rather than relations of movement. It is not surprising, then, that theories of limited cel animation tend to insist on static structures of the image rather than grapple with relational movement. This is also unfortunate because such an emphasis on static structures also encourages us to think technology in terms of structure (autopoiesis) rather than machine (heteropoiesis). To counter this tendency, I will continue to stress movement over structure, even as I take up questions of structure and composition. The goal of this section as a whole is to move toward a movement-centered theory of limited animation, to counter the bias toward describing it as static in contrast to the dynamism of full animation. Nonetheless, because flattening and dehierarchizing layers of image does encourage an emphasis on the composition and structuration of elements in the anime image, I feel it important to start with theories that deal with composition and to grapple with some of the problems that arise with such an emphasis. One of the more influential theories, and without a doubt the most commercially successful approach, is the artist Murakami Takashi's *superflat*, which is presented in the catalog to the *Super Flat* exhibit held in 2000.

In the catalog Murakami and other contributors strive to conceptualize a superflat lineage of art that includes postwar anime, media art, and photography, as well as paintings and woodblock prints of early modern Japan, of the Tokugawa or Edo era (1603–1868).[1] Murakami's point of departure is a study by art historian Tsuji Nobuo of Edo era art called *Kisō no keifu*, which in the catalog is translated as *The Lineage of Eccentricity*.[2] Tsuji uses the term *kisō* in the sense of an art that is conceptually *(sō)* weird, strange, or fantastical *(ki)* rather than in the more literal sense of eccentricity as an off-centered movement. The translation of *kisō* as eccentricity is nonetheless a good one insofar as Murakami teases out of Tsuji's lineage of Japanese art something like a noncentered movement. Murakami follows Tsuji's discussion of how Edo's eccentric artists structured the image in such a way as to bring everything to the surface. He writes of how the gaps or interstices *(sukima)* within the image are suppressed, or become invisible.[3] Murakami's account confirms what I have described as the flattening and dehierarchizing of the layers of the image. When the background does not look farther away than the foreground, your eyes cannot detach, isolate, and hierarchically order the elements in the image. Instead, your eyes follow the lines that zigzag across the surface. Such images are structured to encourage *lateral movement* of eyes. Eyes begin scuttling, meandering, scanning, as if restlessly oscillating around a center that remains nonlocalizable. This is superflat movement.

Murakami sees the same kind of structuration of the image *(gamen kōsei)* at work in anime, specifically in the lineage of anime that culminates in the work

Figure 18. *A prime example of super-flat in Murakami Takashi's exhibition and catalog depends on a juxtaposition of a famous view of Mount Fuji by Hokusai with images from a sequence from* Galaxy Express 999 *by animator Kaneda Yoshinori. Hokusai image used with permission of Brooklyn Museum.*

of animator Kanada (sometimes Kaneda) Yoshinori. In fact, as a first example of superflat, the catalog juxtaposes a series of stills of the explosion of a planet from *Ginga tetsudō 999* (*Galaxy Express 999,* 1979) with a famous woodblock print from Hokusai's *Sanjūrokukei* (*Thirty Six Views of Mt Fuji,* 1831?). The compositional similarities are striking (Figure 18). Both images flatten the relation between different planes (foreground, background, and middle grounds), with zigzagging, arcing, sweeping lines that encourage the eye to wander over the surface of the image, restlessly scanning it.

With the exception of these passing comments about the movement of the eyes, Murakami thinks entirely in terms of the structural composition of the image. He has little to say about animation as movement. His discourse includes general remarks about speed, information, and scanning, and there are some provocative remarks about the timing of weird movements in limited animation. Overall, however, the emphasis falls on the structuration of the image, which affects the movement of the eyes over the image. The emphasis falls on techniques of image composition rather than animation and the force implicit in the moving image as a mechanical succession. Needless to say, by eliminating the moving image, Murakami effectively eliminates questions about modernity and modern technologies, which makes it easy for him to sustain analogies between Edo art and otaku anime at the level of composition, as if above and beyond modernity.

Across the essays on superflat, the point of reference for thinking composition is the Renaissance tradition of geometric perspective, which becomes *the* example of modern Western structuration of the visual field. The very notion of superflat hinges on establishing a fundamental difference between Japanese traditions of flat or planar composition on the one hand and Western traditions of one-point, linear, or geometric perspective on the other. The presentation of one-point perspective within superflat theory largely agrees with the ideas put forth in Martin Jay's account of Renaissance notions of perspective, discussed in chapter 3, which outlined how the combination of perspective in the visual arts with Cartesian ideas of subjective rationality produced the dominant and even totally hegemonic visual model of the modern era.[4] The basic idea is that the scalar ordering of elements with respect to a vanishing point results in a fixed and stable viewing position that appears to stand outside and to rule over the hierarchically ordered world presented in the image. This is Cartesianism. In contrast to Cartesianism, superflat composition is said to disperse and distribute elements across the surface of the image, thus dispensing with the fixed viewing position of the subject as well. Because eyes are compelled to pursue restless lines across the flat image, the viewing position and thus the modern subject become dispersed across the visual field. Superflat theorists take the fragmentation and dispersion of the viewing position across the image as a quintessentially postmodern condition.

Superflat theory develops an opposition between Western modernity and Japanese postmodernity, which it posits at the level of the structuration of the visual field. It thus tends to reify an opposition between (a) modern compositional structures of depth with hierarchical ordering of elements versus (b) postmodern structures of superflatness with nonhierarchical distribution of elements. Everything boils down to a strict divide between Cartesianism and superflat, to shore up a structural divide between modern Western visuality and postmodern Japanese visuality.

Superflat theory forgets that the theory associating geometric perspective with modern Western subjectivity is but one theory of modernity. Even Martin Jay, who has consistently stressed the links between the modern rational instrumental subject and geometric perspective, acknowledges that there are other visual regimes of modernity. What is more, a number of scholars and theorists have thoroughly challenged the association of modernity with the transcendent subject who stands over and above the world. Michel Foucault, for instance, associates the

Cartesian subject with the classical era rather than the modern. Foucault argues that it is the breakdown of the universal grids of knowledge of the Renaissance era that defines the emergence of modern regimes of disciplinization.[5] Building on Foucault's approach in the domain of visual history, Jonathan Crary finds that visual theories of the nineteenth century abandoned the classical Cartesian subject associated with geometric perspective and the camera obscura. Instead of "structural and optical principles of the camera obscura,"[6] Crary submits that modern vision becomes "a question of a perceiver whose very empirical nature renders identities unstable and mobile, and for whom sensations are interchangeable."[7] Similarly, media theorist Friedrich Kittler argues that modern media networks are characterized not by an emphasis on the transcendence of the subject but by a sense of the fallibility of human perception in comparison to scientific instruments and technologies of recording and observation.[8] In sum, despite the differences among these theorists, they nonetheless agree that modern visual regimes and media networks do not operate through the production of a universal or transcendent subject (in the manner of the fixed viewing position of one-point perspective).

It is decidedly odd, then, that Murakami and other commentators on superflat are so insistent on an opposition between modern Western structures of hierarchical depth (geometric perspective) versus postmodern Japanese structures of nonhierarchical distribution (superflat). What drops out is the possibility of Japanese modernity, and questions about subjectivity, disciplinization, and power that come with it. Evidently, superflat theory wishes above all to avoid dealing with questions about Japanese modernity and its relation to Western modernity.[9] As such, superflat theory risks becoming yet another discourse on Japanese uniqueness (Nihonjinron), which celebrates Japan as always already postmodern.

As I discussed in chapter 2, looking at Japanese animations exclusively in terms of compositional features makes it easy to eliminate the impact of modern cinema and modern technologies, which in turn makes it easy to construct art historical lineages in which the sources of Japanese animations appear to lie in Edo Japan or even in the ancient Japanese past. This happens not only in histories or theories of animation but also in animation itself. There are, for instance, any number of anime that draw inspiration from Edo art, as different as Watanabe Shinichirō's *Samurai Champloo* (2004) and Takahata Isao's *My Neighbors the Yamadas* (*Hōhokekyo to tonari no Yamada-kun*, 1999). Anime with an Edo look or Edo theme have gone through booms of popularity in Japan.[10] But it is possible to make anime images using compositional techniques of any time or place, and there have been Japanese animated films that draw inspiration from Chinese art,

Persian art, European art, classical Greek art, and arts of other styles, places, and eras; and frequently one finds combinations of compositional styles. Anime is exceedingly eclectic and diverse in its stylistics.

My point is not simply that the emphasis on Edo art in superflat theory tends to ignore the stylistic diversity of Japanese animations. What concerns me is the tendency of superflat to eliminate questions about movement in animation, and with them questions about the moving image that inevitably force some consideration of modern technologies, Japanese modernity, and Japan in the world. This is not to say that composition is not important in animation. It definitely is, and I would not want to dispense with an analysis of composition or of the structuration of the visual field. Edo legacies are important. What demands attention, however, is the relation between structuration of the visual field and technologies of the moving image. Instead of reifying connections between Edo art and otaku anime,[11] for instance, we might consider what happens to the so-called eccentric image under conditions of mechanical movement.[12]

The inability of superflat theory to deal with animation movement comes in part from a deterministic view of structure, which is common in many discussions of geometric, linear, or one-point perspective. Clearly the idea of superflat is calculated to challenge a set of values associated with Western geometric perspective, such as the idea that one-point perspective is perceptually natural and scientifically accurate, and thus best suited to the needs of modern rational societies. Even today, it is not uncommon to find scholars who see geometric perspective as determining the course of modern science and by extension processes of social modernization. Samuel Edgerton's study of linear perspective is a prime example. He writes, "a fundamental difference arose after the Renaissance between the West and the rest of the world in respect to the way in which one not only looked at pictures but conceived of physical reality in the first place."[13] For Edgerton, geometric perspective signals a lag in development between the West and the rest (the non-West). Simply put, his is a modernization theory of geometric perspective.

Edgerton sees knowledge of geometric perspective as essential to scientific modernization, and thus when artists and scientists in the non-West do not understand its principles, they tend to stymie the progress of their society. He concludes, for instance, that "allowing Chinese artists, unprepared and unfamiliar with Renaissance chiaroscuro and perspective, to illustrate Western books on science and technology . . . hardly contributed to that great nation's difficult struggle for secular modernization"; their poor understanding of perspective was actually a great disservice.[14] Ultimately, Edgerton hedges on the question of whether geometric perspective will prove beneficial or dangerous to a particular society in the long run. Yet, in the meantime, he feels "every literate, educated person in the world who desires to succeed in technology and science, whatever his or her ethnic heritage, native language or economic status, must learn to read a modern working drawing to scale, and comprehend instantly those peculiar perspective conventions invented by western European artists during the Renaissance."[15] In sum, Edgerton expounds a modernization theory of geometric perspective yet remains ambivalent about the long-term impact of modernization (as instrumentalization and rationalization) on societies. Martin Jay expresses similar ambivalence about modern rationalization at the end of his essay when he concludes, "the radical dethroning of Cartesian perspectivalism may have gone a bit too far." He concludes, "However we may regret the excesses of scientism, the Western scientific tradition may have only been made possible by Cartesian perspectivalism or its complement, the Baconian art of describing."[16]

In its challenge to Western perspective and to the modern subject of science and reason, superflat theory makes two gestures. On the one hand, to overcome the sense of a temporal lag between the West and Japan, it projects Japan into the future; even early modern or Edo Japan becomes projected into postmodernity. On the other hand, it accepts the determinism implicit in modernization theories of geometric perspective. It displaces that determinism onto technologies of information and communication to shore up its postmodernization theory of the superflat image. In other words, even as it grinds away at a binary opposition between Western modernity and Japanese postmodernity, superflat theory reproduces modernization theory, repeating it in the form of postmodernization theory. Superflat theory thus proves highly ambivalent vis-à-vis technological modernization and the modern technological condition. It does not, in fact, wish to challenge the technological determinism implicit in the modernization theory of one-point perspective. Its primary aim is to challenge the idea of a temporal or developmental lag between Japan and the West, for which it overcompensates by projecting Japan into the future.

The futuristic projection of Japan is fraught with ambivalence with respect to technological modernization, precisely because superflat operates as a sort of futuristic technology of postmodernization. This ambivalence becomes very evident in the stance of Murakami's superflat theory vis-à-vis ballistic technologies and war. Commenting on the anime stills from *Galaxy Express 999* that are paired with Hokusai's view of Mount Fuji, for instance, Murakami writes of "the beauty of that climactic battle scene and the disintegration of the Planet Meteru scene!"[17]

Murakami's superflat thus presents a stark contrast with the worldviews of Miyazaki Hayao or of Paul Virilio. Where Miyazaki and Virilio see ballistic technologies and optical logistics as destructive of the lifeworld, Murakami remains ambivalent, as if loath to surrender the possibility of something productive at the heart of destruction. Thus superflat embraces artworks that run the gamut from bucolic landscapes to planetary destruction, from scenes of the everyday life of city dwellers to scenes of future war.

In the third installment in his trilogy of superflat art exhibitions entitled *Little Boy: The Arts of Japan's Exploding Subculture*, Murakami directly addresses this ambivalence, presenting it as a general condition of Japan's "little boys," that is, with the first generation of male otaku.[18] He evokes the feelings of impotence experienced by a generation of Japanese boys in response to Japan's war defeat, detecting in their responses to the atomic bombs dropped on Hiroshima and Nagasaki—code-named "Fat Man" and "Little Boy"—both fascination and identification with the atomic bomb. Styling male otaku as "little boys" is his way of signaling their ambivalent condition and their ambivalent response to military power. While constrained to remain boys under the security umbrella of "manly" American military-industrial power, little boy otaku found solace in a two-fold attachment, at once to childhood and the objects associated with it (toys, anime, manga, games, dolls) and to the power of military technology.

Oddly, however, Murakami blunts the fundamental question, which Rey Chow succinctly poses, the question of "the normativization of war and war technologies [that] takes place as well among—perhaps especially among—the defeated."[19] Instead of addressing the normativization of war technologies that follows from superflat's ambivalence vis-à-vis modernization theory, Murakami conjures up, in his discussion of Japan's little boys, the image of Japan as the victim of (Western) civilization. Japan is a monster born of Western civilization.[20] With such statements Murakami appears to resolve some of the ambivalence inherent in his conception of superflat. His stance suddenly seems to dovetail with what is commonly called *higaisha ishiki*, the victim consciousness or victim mentality wherein the Japanese nation appears in the role of the innocent victim within the global history of twentieth-century national and imperial wars.[21]

Murakami's stance toward the little boy monster-victim seems intent on sustaining ambivalence, however. He does not come out openly in favor of correcting and overcoming Japan's victim mentality through the remilitarization of Japan (as the Japanese right wing advises). Nor does he recommend embracing or celebrating this Japanese sense of impotence, monstrosity, and victimization. Murakami remains ambivalent about the ambivalence of the little boy. Yet the exhibit, by its nature, *promotes* the concept of the little boy and its ambivalence vis-à-vis military technologies. The superflat little boy exhibit thus implies not only a normativization of war technologies but also a spectacular inflation of ambivalence vis-à-vis technological determinism (modernization).

Superflat discourse will not decide if it is inside or outside modernization, for strategic reasons. It wants overtly to be outside Western modernity but seems covertly to want to remain inside modernization. War and technologies of military destruction thus become exceedingly important in superflat because they present a challenge to the idea that modernization is all about rationality, progress, and productivity. In fact, war technologies and military destruction may appear exceedingly irrational, as the opposite of progress and productivity. You can embrace military technologies without embracing modernization directly. Of course military technologies also imply developmental stories of progress and advancement. Yet there is always something irrational and empty in scenarios of progression toward destruction. In other words, if superflat theory in its ambivalence gravitates toward military technologies and future war, it is because such technologies can pose as a limit case for modernization wherein you both have and do not have rationalization and Cartesianism. It is in much the same way that you may have and may not have Cartesianism within hyper-Cartesianism. The ambivalence of *Super Flat* and *Little Boy* vis-à-vis war technologies is a strategy to situate Japan at once as an alternative nonrationalist mode of modernization (postmodernization) and as outside modernization (as Westernization) altogether. Superflat ambivalence tentatively introduces a divide between instrumentalization and technologization on the one hand, and rationalization and hierarchization (rational transcendent "modern" subject) on the other. The result is a fascination with techniques of flatness, which are taken as harbingers of a condition of *technologized dehierarchization* (informatization). Military destruction, as a leveler of hierarchies, not only becomes a source of fascination but also operates a limit case for instrumentalized flatness.

If I have lingered over superflat, it is not to debunk it but because the problems inherent in superflat theory can tell us something about anime, especially about lineages of limited cel animation in which techniques of flatness intertwine with an ambivalent fascination for the flattening effects of military technologies and for the instrumentalization of social relations, which I will discuss in subsequent chapters. Of interest in superflat art and theory is how their commitment to technological determinism, however glancing or halting it may seem, invites a critical examination of flattening effects in anime. Yet, instead of offering a critical examination, superflat art and theory turn to anime to reinforce their stance of ambivalence vis-à-vis the modern technological condition, and to sell it in a slightly altered and repackaged form. In my opinion, however, the "original" packaging (anime) remains more interesting and challenging in its thinking about technology than superflat's repackaging of it.

Still, superflat theory poses very clearly the problem of technological determination in the register of the composition of the image. It implies that *techniques* of flattening and dehierarchizing layers of the image are *structurally* inseparable from *technologies* of flattening and leveling, of informatization and distribution. What is more, it suggests that the field of the image (the distributive image) is inseparable from a psychological structuration, that is, a sense of impotence, monstrosity, victimization, and ultimately ambivalence vis-à-vis technologization, which gravitates toward military technologies and ballistic operations as a limit case for modernization. Unfortunately, by thinking structures deterministically, superflat theory also curtails the critical possibilities latent in the distributive image. It unwittingly repeats the technological determinism implicit in the modernization theory of geometric perspective that it opposes. The task then is not to abandon questions about structure but to open structure to movement, and to attend to indeterminacy as well as determinacy.

One way to avoid the determinism that frequently comes with structural analysis is to read structure as determining but not deterministically, as *a* determinant rather than *the* determinant. In his critique of superflat, for instance, Thomas Looser reminds us that many of the Edo artists evoked in Murakami's superflat understood Western geometric perspective perfectly well but used it in very different ways. He writes, "The single point perspectival space that hierarchizes a unitary modern subject position did not appear in Japan until far later than in the West, and even then, it was used simply as one among many modes of spatial organization that could be played with, and even layered over other kinds of space."[22] Some of Hiroshige's images, for instance, often play with two viewpoints within the same image, inviting us not so much to reject depth as to layer viewpoints. Thus Looser argues, in effect, that layering takes priority over positioning, which opens the viewpoint to multiplication and distortion, to play and divergence. What is more, he sees in the superflat fascination with Edo art and apocalyptic imagery, "a romantic desire for a real limit, a real ending, or a real horizon."[23] Put another way, there is a bid for determinism in such desire.

Determination, however, is not the same thing as *determinism*. Materiality is not teleology. Theories of determination acknowledge that a "machine" (in Guattari's sense) may produce an orientation in the world, a set of directional constraints (a field), and even a trajectory. Even David Nye, who misreads and thus dismisses structuralism and poststructuralism as thoroughly deterministic, must nevertheless reintroduce some sense of technological determination: he turns to the idea of technological momentum.[24] At issue is whether we read something like geometric perspective as determinism or determination (or, to underscore its difference from determinism, underdetermination). Or, put another way, it is a question of whether we read perspective as *structure* or as *machine*. The impasse of superflat theory comes in large part from its reading of geometric perspective as structure, deterministically. In contrast, Looser's reading of one-point perspective is closer to a machine (layering). Unlike a structure of perspective, a machine of layering is able to fold geometric perspective into it, which allows for divergent practices and divergent series. Looser argues that Edo society allowed for social layering or divergence, and this divergence or multiplicity is precisely what superflat theory finds appealing yet ultimately eradicates in its drive to structure it deterministically, even apocalyptically, via modernization theory.

In his semiotic study of perspective, Hubert Damisch notes that the perspective paradigm lends itself to two contradictory interpretations. He writes, "An affirmation of a perspectivism one might call 'classic,' and whose formal apparatus guarantees the possibility of disengaging, of switching from one point of view to another, but against which Nietzsche protested, in the name of a radically different perspectivism: one in which the different points of view are anything but complementary, each one manifesting a divergence which he embraced."[25] Superflat theory affirms classic perspectivism or Cartesianism, without considering the sort of protest in the name of divergence that appears in Nietzsche and Looser. As a result, superflat theory transforms the mode of spatial organization that promises divergence (that is, layering) into a deterministic structure. It transforms the layering machine into a superflat structure. To do so, it covertly systematizes another mode of spatial organization, *orthogonal perspective*.

Many of the examples of Edo art in superflat discourse employ some variation on orthogonal perspective in which diagonal lines serve to divide the image into various planes. In fact, the qualities that Murakami attributes to superflat art largely assume an underlying structure of orthogonal perspective. Although orthogonal perspective does not insist on scalar relations, as does geometric perspective, it does impart a sense of depth. It only appears flat if you take geometric perspective as the norm for depth. It is only in relation to Western geometric perspective that orthogonal perspective has been deemed unsystematic or disorderly. In addition, in contrast to the historical association of geometric perspective with Cartesianism, there is no theory or philosophy of the subject of modernity associated with orthogonal perspective. This is why orthogonal perspective so readily poses as the diametric opposite of modernization, that is, as the antithesis of rationalization, instrumentalization, and homogenization.

It may come as a surprise then that Samuel Edgerton, at the end of his book devoted to rehabilitating the modernization theory of geometric perspective, trots out an exploded view of the front wheel assembly of a Yamaha motorcycle (Figure 19). In the exploded view or exploded projection, which is com-

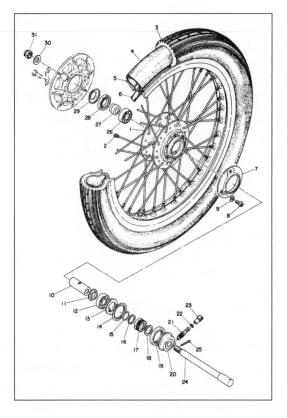

Figure 19. *Exploded view of the front wheel assembly of a Yamaha motorcycle, from the* XS650 Models 1974–77 Service Manual. *Courtesy of Yamaha Motor Corporation,* USA.

monly used in engineering diagrams and assembly instructions, we see all the elements pulled apart yet held in place, to show how the wheel is put together. Yet the pieces of the wheel more distant from us are not smaller in accordance with one-point perspective. There is no horizon line or vanishing point in the manner of one-point perspective. Nor does exploded projection maintain scalar relations as one-point perspective does. Rather elements are arrayed along the diagonal with the sizes of pieces unchanged, in the manner of orthogonal perspective. This is reasonable, even rational, since you would not want to think that the nuts or bolts on the backside of the motor are smaller than those in front when trying to assemble the wheel. You need some indication that these are the same nuts and bolts.

Because the diagram appears at the end of Edgerton's book without comment, we don't know how Edgerton sees this example. From the tone of the book, I suspect that his association of Japan with exploded projection is calculated to signal something about Japanese success in scientific modernization in contrast to what Edgerton construes as Chinese failure. It seems that we are to read the transformation of orthogonal perspective into a rational and instrumental mode of scientific diagramming as a sign of a Japanese predisposition toward scientific modernization.

For my part, I would like to read exploded projection or the exploded view against the determinism implicit in modernization theory. What should concern us is not whether a particular structure of depth or a particular system of perspective is inherently, teleologically, more rational or scientific than any other. What should concern us is the possibility that any structure of depth can be systematized or modernized, much as any language can be modernized. In other words, from a semiotic point of view, neither a mode of perspective nor a language affords any guaranteed dispensation toward or opposition to modernization. This is not to say semiotic structures do not have any potential for critical engagement, but they will not do the thinking for us.

In summary, I have lingered over superflat art and theory because superflat addresses a flattening and dehierarchizing of the visual field that is crucial to understanding lineages of anime that use multiple layers yet composite them flatly. Superflat calls attention to what I call the distributive field. The impasse of superflat comes of its unacknowledged commitment to the technological determinism implicit in the modernization theory of one-point perspective. The result is not only a very narrow theory of modernity but also an inability to address the instrumentality or rationality of superflat; superflat pretends to be structureless, even as it relies on structures to crush the divergence implicit in machines (both of layering and one-point perspective).

It is in order to address these problems clearly that I have sought the underlying structure of superflat, which superflat theory at once assumes and disavows. That structure is exploded projection or the exploded view. My aim, however, is not to establish exploded projection as Japanese tradition, as an alternative Japanese teleology of modernity, or as a structure of postmodernity in opposition to modernity. Ultimately, I will look at how the structure of exploded projection serves to capture the force of the moving image as flat compositing spreads it across the surface of the image. At the same time, I will look at how the moving image operates to open (or reopen) the structure of exploded projection, machinically, into a divergent series of animation.

Nonetheless, to avoid falling into a utopian vision in which divergence appears predestined, I should also add that my turn to looking at structures of exploded projection also provides a way to acknowledge the instrumentality and rationality implicit in the distributive image. The controlled quasi-orthogonal structural "explosion" of elements across the image surface forces a confrontation with the anime fascination for military technologies, which frequently accompanies the flattening and dehierarchizing of the image in limited animation. The important question is whether the relative movement that comes with the flattening and dehierarchizing of the image allows us to think technology differently or whether, like Murakami's superflat, it leaves us suspended in ambivalence, with projections of precocious impotence into the future.

CHAPTER 11

THE DISTRIBUTIVE FIELD

AN IMAGE COMPOSED OF MULTIPLE LAYERS is a basic feature of cel animation, and the question of how to "composite" the layers of the image is central to animation. We have seen how fixing the camera to the rostrum in the animation stand constrains camera movement along two axes, and so mobility along three axes (movement into depth) demands a great deal of effort and technical control, while it is very easy to produce a sense of movement by sliding the layers of the image. This situation places the burden of coherence in movement on techniques of compositing. Considered with respect to the force of the moving image, compositing in cel animation is analogous to camera movement in cinema. In cel animation, the force of the moving image cannot be shunted as readily into camera mobility; instead it is shunted into the movement of planes of the image. Compositing is what makes for a sense of the coherence of the image under conditions of movement in animation. It is a question of what kind of "body" will emerge or, more precisely, what sort of sensorimotor schema will serve to harness and channel the force of the moving image.

Even though I associate compositing with cel animation, and camera mobility with live-action cinema, these are two tendencies of the moving image. Cinema can use techniques of compositing. In fact, what other commentators describe in terms of cinema becoming animation, I see in terms of a new emphasis on compositing in cinema, spurred by the use of CGI and digital effects. Conversely, animation is often interested in producing a sense of movement in depth. Significantly, however, for cel animation to produce movement into depth, it must first address compositing. This suggests that, in animation, compositing takes priority over camera mobility. What is more, I would hazard to say, if cinema today is becoming animation, it is because compositing is taking priority over camera mobility in the production of moving images. This is not to say that films, animations, and video games don't often place an emphasis on camera mobility. They do, and frequently in the form of a highly mobile ballistic logistics of perception, a high-speed pumped-up Cartesianism. Yet there is an increasing emphasis on compositing as a basis for the generation of hyper-Cartesian movement. A sequence from Oshii Mamoru's *Avalon* depicts the situation perfectly: in this film-become-animation, in the midst of a military conflict full of ballistic angles and accelerated war technologies, the battle suddenly stops and shows itself to be composed of layers (Figure 20). It is in fact a video game, and the heroine, Ash, moves in and out of the gaps in the de-composited image.

If cinema is taken as a point of reference, compositing might also be described as "internal montage" or "editing within the image."[1] It is a matter of dealing with the gaps or interstices that arise between planes in a multiplanar image. Usually, compositing is used to lessen or suppress our perception of gaps between layers. In the world of cel animation, for instance, the multiplane camera system allowed animators to develop a particular kind of compositing that eventually closed the image into the scalar world, which let them play with the relation between image layers in such a way as to impart a sense of movement into depth that felt "natural" by reference to camera mobility in cinema. Initially, this depth compositing entailed fairly simple imitation of the depth effects of the camera lens. For instance, a background would appear out of focus, and the foreground layer in focus, or vice versa. You see such effects in the first Japanese animation to use the multiplane camera, *Ari-chan* (Little ant), where

Figure 20. *In this image from a sequence from* Avalon, *Oshii Mamoru uses digital animation to render explosions in stacked layers, making the world of the video game appear multiplanar.*

the multiplane photography generates a sense of "natural" depth, which serves to transform the gap between layers in such a way that we at once feel it (as depth) and ignore it (as natural, that is, cinematic).

Gradually, building further on cinematic conventions for camera mobility, the use of the multiplane camera gravitated toward producing motion into depth, even if that motion into depth was as rudimentary as changing the focus through the layers when the viewing position approached an object. Ultimately, the goal became sustaining a sense of scalar proportions (in accordance with geometric perspective) as the camera's viewing position moved. The multiplane camera system thus led to the production of images with a sense of volumetric depth, and the illusion of movement into depth, especially at high speed, has become a staple of American digital animation, exemplified in the action sequences of Pixar productions—which is where hyper-Cartesianism dovetails with hypercinematism.

There are other ways of suppressing the sense of gaps in the multiplanar image, as the prior chapter on superflat demonstrated. Superflat proposes to eliminate the sense of a gap between layers by flattening the multiple planes of the image into a single plane. In his art, for instance, Murakami carefully and systemically eliminates effects of depth. Particularly important is the flat application of color. While a very close look at his earlier paintings will reveal traces of brush strokes, these vanish with a single step away from the painting. In addition, background colors do not produce an effect of depth; figure and background are equally vibrant, equally present; all grounds appear on the surface. Solid black outlines around figures assure that contours take precedence over textures (which impart a different sense of surface depths), and the composition in accordance with diagonals brings to the surface the depths that might arise with orthogonal perspective. The result is a proliferation of flattened planes on a single plane. In this sense, flattening the relations between layers does not just result in a uniplanar image but in a superflat or "superplanar" image. As a procedure, the production of a superplanar image might be thought in terms of "flat compositing."

Something like flat compositing frequently happens in animation, especially in limited cel animation, wherein the sense of depth imparted with painterly backgrounds disappears in favor of more schematized and iconic styles for rendering locations and characters. Sometimes a minimal sense of depth is imparted by making the background layer or layers somewhat darker than characters in the foreground or middle ground. Yet such depth is largely iconic and schematic. Some limited animations do not even bother with such minimal indications of depth. The overall tendency is toward a dehierarchization of layers of the image, such that one layer does not become the frame of reference for the others. Or, if a layer does provide a frame of reference, it tends to be an arbitrary, temporary, or contingent frame of reference.

The question then arises about what happens under conditions of movement. Procedures of volumetric compositing in animation serve to shunt the force of the moving image into an accelerated mobility of the simulated camera, almost eradicating the sense of movement between layers (now reduced to simulated effects of motion blur). In contrast, as mentioned previously, procedures of flat compositing push the force of the moving image to the surface of the image, in the form of surface depths with potential energies or potential forces. What happens to these? How are these forces or potentialities harnessed or organized, when not shunted into mobility of viewing position?

To approach such questions, let me back up a few steps, returning to the distinction between superflat and one-point perspective from the previous chapter.

Recall that superflat theory insisted on a strict divide or opposition between modern Western depth and postmodern Japanese superflat, to the point that superflat appeared as technique without structure, and as technologization without rational systematization. To counter such a rigid manner of thinking, I proposed that techniques associated with superflat also have a structure, one equally open to systematization, as evidenced in the exploded view or exploded projection. In sum, rather than an opposition between modernity and postmodernity (or between the West and the rest) in the form of structuration versus destructuration, or rational systematization (Cartesianism) versus radical dehierchization (antirationalism), I posited another structure, that of exploded projection. My aim, of course, is not to establish and shore up a new binary opposition: one-point perspective versus exploded projection. My turn to structure had two motivations: on the one hand, I wished to address the rationalization and instrumentalization implicit in superflat theory, which superflat theory denied; on the other hand, I wished to consider how structures emerge to capture the machinic force of the moving image, even as that machinic force continually reopens structures.

When we add movement to the mix, structures appear as modalities for the differentiation/integration of forces. Much as structures of one-point perspective frequently appear to differentiate and integrate the mobility of the camera in cinema, so structures of exploded projection frequently appear to differentiate and integrate the mobility of layers (compositing) in cel animation, especially limited cel animation. With such an approach to movement in animation we can begin to pose certain questions about technology. Crucial is the question of what happens to ballistic perception with flat compositing.

On the one hand, because flat compositing brings different planes of the image to the surface, it seems designed to bring gaps to the surface as well. In this respect, flat compositing might be seen as a flat variation on the open compositing characteristic of Miyazaki Hayao—but with the openness brought to the surface. We might thus take the tendency of flat compositing to be toward hyperanimetism and an antiballistic mode of perception. On the other hand, flat compositing is, in its way, as "closed" as the volumetric compositing that has gained in intensity with digital animation. After all, both procedures of flat and volumetric compositing seem calculated to eliminate a sense of gaps between layers of the image. Flat compositing then is not simply the opposite of hypercinematism and ballistic modes of perception. It implies a different approach to them. (Miyazaki Hayao, in fact, complains about anime for its tendency toward ballistics and militarized action.) In sum, flat compositing seems to head in two directions at once.

Such uncertainty about how to situate the tendency of flat compositing vis-à-vis technologies of ballistic movement (hyper-Cartesianism) is at the heart of Murakami Takashi's ambivalent portrait of the "little boy" otaku. Murakami is uncertain about how to address the prevalence of military technologies and future-war space operas in the lineage of anime that he associates with otaku. If one reads him closely, he situates otaku in both tendencies, as the defeated people who identify with the technologies of victors (the bomb's-eye view) while nurturing an aura of powerless victimization and childlike innocence (ground zero). While it is possible to tease an interesting reading of anime out of Murakami's ambivalence, he does in fact remain ambivalent and hence cannot clearly delineate what is at stake in such ambivalence vis-à-vis ballistic technologies. For my part, to anticipate subsequent discussion, I see this "flattened" relation to technology as the flipside of what Heidegger called gaining a free relation to technology. Gathering and focusing attention on the essence of technology—as with the notorious otaku obsession with every detail of the image—does indeed open a different relation to the technological condition. But this "freeness" is not that of the classical modern subject, the rational and transcendent agent associated with one-point perspective, the camera obscura, and the Renaissance window on the world. This otaku "freeness" moves toward an articulation of thoughts and actions within media networks—as focal concerns—wherein lines of sight replace viewing positions, which makes for a "subjectile" that maneuvers within the exploded projection alongside projectiles, not a transcendent subject but a projected or projectile subject pursuing lines of sight.

To illustrate these points, let me turn to a group of amateur animators who later went on to form one of the most important animation studios in Japan, Gainax Studios. Murakami Takashi also gives a prominent position to them in his discussion of little boys.[2]

Takeda Yasuhiro, who together with Okada Toshio was integral to the formation of Gainax Studios, recalls in his memoirs that, when he and Okada secured permission to host the annual Japanese Sci-Fi Convention for 1981, they decided to produce an original film for the opening rather than rent or borrow footage.[3] Through a friend, Takeda met Yamaga Hiroyuki and Anno Hideaki, who were then freshman at Osaka University of Arts. He then brought Akai Takami to join them in producing the opening animated film for the 1981 Osaka Science Fiction Convention (also called Daicon, taking the first character of Osaka and the first syllable of convention). The animation short, known as *Daicon III Opening Animation*, made such an impact at the convention that the team would subsequently produce a second, even more elaborate animated short, *Daicon IV Opening Animation*. These two shorts are the stuff of legend for a number of reasons: because amateurs succeeded in producing animations that technically and artistically outshone the work of major animation studios; because their themes and materials highlighted the interests of a new generation of SF and animation fans, later to be dubbed otaku; and because producing these films brought together all the key figures who would go on to found Gainax Studios and to produce such highly popular and commercially successful animated films and series as *Royal Space Force: The Wings of Honneamise* (*Ôritsu uchûgun Oneamisu no tsubasa*, 1987), *Nadia: The Secret of Blue Water* (*Fushigi no umi no Nadia*, 1989–90), and *Neon Genesis Evangelion* (*Shin seiki Evangerion*, 1995–96).

In his memoirs, Takeda recalls that at that time Anno Hideaki had never worked with cel animation but only with paper animation. In fact, when he interviewed Anno, Anno pulled out a pad of paper and quickly produced a flip-book animation of a powered suit with great detail and complexity.[4] In other words, this is a kind of animation that places the emphasis on the design and animation of figures with little advance concern for the use of layers to produce backgrounds with depth of field or movement into depth. It is significant that, to demonstrate his abilities to Takeda, Anno chose to draw a powered suit. This choice is significant not so much because it shows Anno's allegiance to certain kinds of SF anime, but because the powered suit is truly an embodiment of the multiplanar image within a character form. The design of powered suits, tactical armor, mecha, and transformers follows from their use within the multiplanar world. The angular elements of powered suits lock into place, unlock, and re-lock like so many planes of an image, open to kaleidoscopic reconfigurations. Transforming mecha appear to embody the layers and the traversal forces of the multiplanar image in a single figure.

Nonetheless, to repeat my argument in the Introduction, even though animation relies heavily on the art of hand (as with Anno's sketches of a powered suit), such hand arts do not explain animation. Animation folds the art of the hand into a multiplanar machine, where their relation to the machinic force of the moving image thoroughly transforms them. Animation is not the art of sketching characters that will then be forced into movement. As Anno's flipbook sketches of a powered suit attest, such designs already embody the motion inherent in the multiplanar world of animation. The powered suit is multiplanar, already channeling the forces implicit in the multiplanar image on its surfaces. The art of character design anticipates its movement within the multiplanar machine, anticipating the dynamics of compositing.

With respect to compositing, the Daicon animation team apparently could not afford celluloid sheets and thus used vinyl sheets instead. Because it is difficult to make paint adhere properly to vinyl, using vinyl presented an obstacle to stacking layers.[5] In ad hoc fashion, the team managed nevertheless to produce an animated short in the manner of cel animation. When you watch the *Daicon III Opening Animation*, it is clear that, given the difficulties with using layers, the sense of movement is neither that of movement into depth or of movement over depth. The movement is all on the surface, superflattened. Interestingly enough, much of the movement is ballistic, of missiles and spacecraft. When figures or projectiles speed across a background, there is a sense of sliding planes, yet without a preexisting structure of depth. Yet this kind of movement is as exhilarating as hyper-Cartesianism, because the animators use movement to generate a sense of depth rather than the reverse. They pick up on something implicit in the mecha and space-opera animations that are their inspiration: without using scalar proportions in accordance with geometric perspective and without using painterly backgrounds to impact a sense of preexisting depth, you can produce an emergent sense of depth by arraying elements within the image (and across images) in the manner of an exploded view or exploded projection.

Daicon III Opening Animation begins with a pun on the word "daicon" referring at once to the Osaka SF Convention and to the Japanese radish daikon. In the film, a little girl receives a glass of water from a friendly spaceman with instructions to water a daikon. When aliens try to stop the little girl, space battles ensue, and in one sequence the girl fires missiles from the jet pack on her back. The missiles apparently have tracking devices, for they twist and turn through the sky, correcting their trajectory in pursuit and leaving white contrails in their wake (Figure 21). While the compositing of the projectiles against the sky is largely flat, their trajectories create a sense of depth. This is because the trajectories have a common source and a common target, which imparts a sense of an origin and end for their movement. Out of the blue (literally) a vanishing

Figure 21. *In these sequences from* Daicon III Opening Animation, *the first panel shows how missile contrails can generate a fleeting field organized around one-point perspective, but the next two panels demonstrate that this field is then "perverted" or distorted into other fields of force.*

point appears, because the trajectories of the missiles seem to converge. Then, the trajectories diverge, only to appear to converge again.

The rapid divergence, convergence, divergence, convergence of the missiles as they race from their source seeking their target produces a phantasm of one-point perspective in its ballistic form. Yet it is not exactly one-point perspective: even though there is a sense of an origin and destination for the movement that recalls the vanishing point of one-point perspective, nonetheless the relative sizes of projectiles do not follow from scalar projection. The emergent sense of depth is more that of the exploded view in which elements are arrayed in accordance with their initial positions, in the manner of an engineering diagram. This is, in fact, a diagram of projectile movement, almost like a blueprint for understanding ballistic movement. It is ballistic perception brought to the

Figure 22. *As the girl races toward us in* Daicon III Opening Animation, *the effect is not primarily one of movement into depth, for this movement brings depth to the surface, instantly shifting us to a lateral view of motion and to lines of sight.*

surface. Instead of movement into depth, you have movement that generates an exploded view of movement on the surface of the screen.

There are scenes set up in accordance with one-point perspective, for instance those of the little girl racing at us like a bullet with missiles hot on her trail (Figure 22). Even in such instances it is the exploded view that organizes the perceptual field, for speed brings depth to the surface of the image. The overall effect is one of superplanarity, which means that this world is also one of shifting planes. We see projectiles racing at us or away from us, and then suddenly we see the contrails of the missiles laterally, and it is as if we were gliding, wheeling, surfing alongside the projectiles, traversing the battlefield, and riding the shock waves of war as upon powerful currents. Bringing depth to the surface allows for sudden transitions from one plane of movement to another plane of movement. Rapid cuts underscore the abruptness of transition. But it is not editing or cuts that produce the sensation of shifting rapidly from plane to plane on the surface of the single plane of the screen; it is the play of layers within the image under conditions of flat compositing that allows us to wheel from plane to plane.

This world of movement is more unsettling and dazzling than that of multiplane photography or volumetric compositing. It is a world in which projectiles appear suddenly and generate a ballistic field of perception. There are moments that verge on panoramic perception, briefly imparting a sense that you are watching from some position beyond the action, but then the viewing position shifts abruptly from one plane to another, which induces a sense of shifting lines of sight across the projection rather than the sense of a stable viewing position. Instead of panoramic perception, the result is like an assembly diagram for perception in an accelerated world of projectiles.

Such techniques allow the Daicon animators to play between the open compositing characteristic of Miyazaki's worlds and the "closed" compositing characteristic of volumetric worlds. Put another way, the Daicon animation plays between cinematism and animetism, but as if to push the dynamics of animetism to the limit.

As with Miyazaki's animetism, we tend to see the effects of speed laterally. Yet, where Miyazaki's techniques at once deflate and "soften" the effects of speed, the lateral view in the Daicon animation enhances the effects of speed. This is because the use of flat backgrounds, together with lack of interest in opening the play between layers in depth, brings the depth of the multiplanar image to the surface, producing a superplanar image on which surface depths temporarily appear, full of potential energy. This is not to say that this kind of animation does not or cannot employ detailed backgrounds. Subsequently, with the formation of Gainax Studios, the same animators will have recourse to detailed backgrounds. Yet, unlike Miyazaki's luminous backdrops, their backgrounds do not provide a fixed frame of reference for movement or for action. In other words, backgrounds do not provide a sense of a preexisting world of depth that can structure movements and orientate actions. In the next chapter I will discuss how this way of structuring animated worlds tends toward multiple frames of reference, which has a profound impact on narrative. Here, however, since my emphasis is on the exploded view of ballistic movement, I would like to call attention to how such techniques allow the Daicon animators to play with the cinematism that comes of the closed compositing, which is more characteristic of animated worlds with volumetric depth or multiplane camera and lens-like depth of field.

Daicon animation frequently produces echoes, phantasms and fleeting moments of depth in the manner of geometric perspective, as with the trajectories of tracking missiles. Because planar and scalar relations are flattened, however, the evocation of such depths in Daicon animation is not only fleeting but also twisted. There is a deformation and perversion of scalar volumes. Consequently, the projectile distribution of elements in the image takes precedence over scalar ordering. This twisted variation on hyper-Cartesianism allows the Daicon animators to take animetism to its limits. In sum, the Daicon animators evoke ballistic movement in depth (cinematism), which emerges as potential depth upon flattened planar structures (exploded animetism). One result of these techniques will be a distributive field in which movement into depth is replaced by density of information.

Where in Miyazaki much of the force of the moving image is shunted into open compositing, in the Daicon animation, due to the flattening of compositing, the force of the moving image is distributed on the surface of the image. This gives the impression that any element in the image may serve to direct a line of sight; any element may generate a field of potential depth. Density of information, a sense of tightly packed elements with potential depth, begins to take precedence over movement within a world. At the same time, because this is a *moving* image, the sensation is one of information incessantly rising to the surface.

Styling themselves Daicon Studios, the same team of animators produced a second animated short for the 1983 Osaka SF Convention, *Daicon IV Opening Animation*. The second animation consciously rebuilds and intensifies the first animation. In the first sequence, the little girl who in the prior film successfully battled aliens and watered the daikon (which transformed into a spaceship that then regenerated the surface of the planet) transforms into a young girl/woman designed for sex appeal, dressed in a bunny costume vaguely reminiscent of a Playboy bunny. Her mission is fundamentally the same—to battle aliens and regenerate the planet, to make destruction into rebirth. But the animation has grown up as much as the little girl. The short film fairly explodes movement, not only with action sequences but also with citations and references. The cuts from action to action are so rapid that it becomes difficult to piece together the action in a directly causal sequence, but there is an overarching story: "Bunny" battles aliens, and the battle results in mass destruction that paradoxically generates a lush green postapocalyptic world.

Now, as even a cursory description suggests, there are a number of registers of analysis of *Daicon IV Opening Animation* that I have temporarily bracketed, namely, analysis of themes, narrative, and editing. This is in keeping with my general emphasis on the essence of animation, on the animetic machine. For reasons outlined previously, I am convinced that if analysis begins with narrative and themes or even patterns of editing, it will never arrive at an understanding of what anime is or of how it thinks. We will merely be reading anime as textual object. Hence I will continue to stress the animated moving image, looking at how relations of movement intersect with structures of depth. The Daicon animations themselves encourage such an approach. As they enhance speed and movement through the use of rapid cuts in conjunction with flattened and de-hierarchized fields of distributed information, structures of exploded projection emerge to place a material limit on dispersion and flatness, generating tempo-rary fields of potential depth associated with lines of sight.

In one sequence, for instance, Bunny speeds through the skies riding on a sword as on a surfboard, turning, spinning, and wheeling acrobatically. When she leaps from the sword, it splits into seven sword-missiles with contrails in the seven colors of the rainbow (Figure 23). The sword-missiles generate a sense of depth as they speed along their determined trajectories like so many smart bombs. The movement of each missile appears at once erratically realized and precisely directed, as if each missile had its own intelligence, a way of figuring

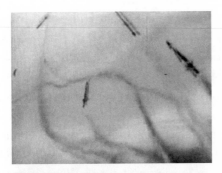

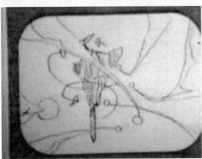

Figure 23. *As Bunny's sword in* Daicon IV Opening Animation *splits into seven missiles in the colors of the rainbow, we again see linear trajectories twisted along intelligent pathways, which makes less for a viewing position on a field of action than for lines of sight across shifting fields. The first panel shows the animation, and the second and third panels show Anno's sketches rendered as line test animations.*

out how to reach its target. Taken individually, each contrail "perverts" linear trajectory from origin to destination. This is perversion in the simple sense of twisting what would normally be straight by the conventions of geometric perspective. Simply put, the speed of these projectiles imparts a sense of one-point perspective and depth but in a perverse or twisted form, in a deviation from ballistic perception. It is not a pure divergence even though it continually diverts its course. Precisely because it has an aim and trajectory, it is a perversion of a linear course and, in a sense, of a viewing position. The result is a line of sight, with a subjectile tracking an objectile.

Taken collectively, the contrails of sword-missiles impart the sense of a horizon and a vanishing point where lines should converge, but then the contrails do not converge. They diverge again, perverting the evocation of one-point perspective, at once implying it and deviating from it. Depth momentarily comes to the surface in accordance with what Edgerton, for instance, presents as *the* rational scientific method, only to break into multiple trajectories, multiple targets, and multiple depths. But such depth is not structured to last here. Rather, what lingers in the wake of the missiles is a field of purely potential depth born of the distortion of scalar relations.

Such a take on ballistic movement tends to flatten the hierarchical ordering of the image. It is impossible to say whether any one element in the perceptual field is intrinsically more important than any other element. Where geometric perspective is designed to assure a scalar order of elements with a center and a periphery, here the sense of center and periphery gives way to a field in which elements are distributed. And, as "sighting" (line of sight) takes priority over positioning, any element in the image can potentially operate as a field. Any element is potentially a projectile, not an object to be contemplated or seized but an objectile with a field with potential depth. In sum, instead of a one-point structuration to produce depth with distinct positioning, the structure of exploded projection generates fields of potential depth traversed by lines of sight. Movement functions to generate emergent depths, potential depth. The result is very close to a logistics of information retrieval, and not only because viewers are asked to skim and scan fields, and to discern degrees of separation or connection in the manner of a network. It is also like information retrieval in that elements of the image do not function as inert, discrete data but as fields, that is, as potential depths that, if pursued, promise to generate links and connections. Here the subject must remain in motion (subjectile), and the movement of the subjectile along lines of sight becomes as integral as the projectiles in sustaining the exploded projection.

The tendency of the ballistic sequences toward information retrieval explains how, in *Daicon IV Opening Animation*, action sequences are readily followed by a series of rapid pans over crowds composed of iconic characters pulled from a dizzying number of animated television series, special effects films, and Hollywood science fiction films. There are far too many citations to even begin to enumerate them. It is possible to slow down the animation, to pause on frames and make a list of references, and for those interested, Murakami Takashi provides a long series of names and references.[6] More than identifying the characters, however, what interests me here is how the dizzying pans and rapid cuts across fields composed of iconic characters echo the logic of the projectiles. Flattened ballistic perception meshes with information explosion. There are no hierarchies among characters drawn from such radically different sources as *Doraemon*, Fritz Lang's silent film *Metropolis*, *Godzilla*, and *Star Trek* (to scratch the surface). The animation succeeds in bringing references, as potential depth of information, to the surface, inviting us to skim and to retrieve and recompose fields. Rather than discrete objects, we have distributive fields of information. Each iconic reference operates as a field of potential depth, inviting us to "click" on it, to retrieve and pursue its connections.

Daicon IV Opening Animation is information-surfing before the Net. The flattening of multiplanar images produces an effect akin to multiple windows on a computer screen. And the depth of those stacked computer windows is like that of exploded projection, with no window hierarchically deeper than any other, and each implying transversal links to others. It is interesting to note, in light of these analogies between anime layers and computer windows, that limited cel animation emerged and became dominant in Japan roughly at the same time as discourses on information society (mid-1960s to mid-1970s),[7] and anime came to global attention with the rise of information networks in the 1990s.

Such analogies raise questions about the relation between the distributive field and technology. Previously I discussed Murakami Takashi's ideas about the fascination of anime otaku for military technologies. Murakami suggested that the otaku delight in future war and military destruction comes of a sense of defeat, inferiority, and impotence vis-à-vis the American military-industrial complex, which results in an almost masochistic desire to undergo the experience of the bomb. But his account becomes very confused. He suggests that these impotent little boys identify with the destructive power of the bomb, that these victims perversely identify with the victor. Yet he never follows through with this line of thinking. Sometimes Murakami attempts to describe a condition that is between victim and victor, at once both and neither (a monster). At crucial junctures, however, his account establishes a clear temporal priority: first victimization, then fascination with victorious technologies. In other words, for all its ambivalence, Murakami's discussion of otaku as little boys gives precedence to the bomb and thus the defeat and victimization of Japan. Such a gesture tends to naturalize a unitary Japanese "victim mentality." At the same time, as I argued previously, there is an underlying commitment to modernization theory in discussions of superflat art. The superflat combination of modernization theory and victim mentality results not only in a normativization of war technologies but also in a spectacular inflation of ambivalence vis-à-vis technological determinism (modernization) in which military destruction promises to put an apocalyptically definitive limit on the apparently boundless flattening of superflat.

Murakami would like us to believe that the Daicon animations are prime examples of superflat otaku ambivalence. But we need to ask if this is true. Do such animations leave us suspended in ambivalence? Do they not afford a way to think technology animetically? Such questions can be approached from two directions: from the direction of technical optimization, and from that of unity and multiplicity.

Recall that Heidegger, Virilio, and Miyazaki, in their different ways, posed the question of technology as one of techno-scientific optimization, as an optimization of technologization for its own sake. Virilio in particular is the prophet of doom when it comes to technical optimization. Across a range of technologies—technologies of perception (cinema), of war (remote missile guidance), of information (the Web), and of biology (genetic engineering)—Virilio sees the optimization of a technological logistics that relentlessly produces greater speeds in an attempt to collapse distances and compress time, producing a world in which humans cannot live, at least not without such a thorough genetic remake that they would no longer be human. Everywhere he sees suicidally accelerated Cartesianism. Something analogous happens in Miyazaki, but unlike Virilio who despairs of ever returning to a longer, slower, human-scaled world, Miyazaki strives to create precisely such a world and an experience of it, which would run counter to the technical optimization of perception, namely, the ballistic logistics inherent in cinematism. The Daicon animations, however, approach optimization from a very different angle. They embrace technical optimization. The density of information, the dizzying rapidity of cuts, the explosion of projectiles across the screen, not to mention the attention to spaceships and powered suits, all are part of a technical optimization of the perceptual field.

As such, these animations are not about a sense of defeat, impotence, or ambivalence vis-à-vis technologies. In fact the Daicon team excels at such optimization, and the resounding success of their first opening animation surely gave them a feel for their technical acumen. Significantly, the Daicon team was working not only with less than optimum materials (from paper to vinyl) but also with techniques of animation that might easily be described as low tech. Or, to put it more precisely, they were using thoroughly modern and established techniques of the moving image that hark back to the early days of animation. This makes their bid for a new mode of technical optimization all the more interesting. For, while we are justified in thinking of their animation as somehow "new" or "postmodern" or "information-age," we also have to acknowledge that this newness is teased from decidedly modern techniques of the moving image.

When it comes to thinking technology, then, a great deal depends on whether one thinks that optimization is always just optimization, or whether one thinks that there can be different modes of technical optimization, some of them better than others, some of them potentially opening a critical relation to the technological condition. Can there be such a thing as a *critical optimization*, or does optimization invariably result in incessant crisis, in the destruction of the human life world?

The rise of information and new communication technologies is frequently construed in terms of the emergence of a new and better kind of technological condition, one that stands in contrast to the older modern technological condition. The Daicon animations seem to embrace such a shift. In *Daicon IV Opening Animation*, for instance, when the sexy bunny girl succeeds in her mission, the detonation of sword-missiles produces an explosion of green: waves of forest rapidly spread across the surface of the earth. There is an eerie transformation of world destruction into world renewal: even as we see urban architectures shattered and tossed on shock waves reminiscent of nuclear test films, petals of cherry blooms, not ashes, flutter serenely across the apocalyptic landscape.

Themes of destruction and rebirth are relatively common in anime, and so commentators frequently use them as handles to grasp anime generally. But it is important to note that, in *Daicon IV Opening Animation* specifically, the themes of destruction and regeneration imply an underlying shift in the technological condition: even when their explosions recall the mushroom clouds and ground zero of the atomic bombs, these bombs seem to belong to a different technology, one that promises a different relation to the world, a beautiful eco-friendly relation. There is a yearning for a new technological order. The final images of *Daicon IV Opening Animation* render this yearning succinctly: we see the world from a distance, and on the rim of the earth, a point of light swells and promises to burst in the manner of an atomic bomb, but as the light continues to swell, it becomes the sun rising past the horizon (Figure 24). It is as if the atomic bomb might return to what it always was: an expression of the power of the sun, and maybe a power source that promises a friendly relation to the world, solar power.

Nonetheless, as such utopian eco-images suggest, the Daicon animations do not quite know how to imagine their new postatomic, postballistic technological condition. If we consider how their use of the moving image generates a distributive field dense in information, we might, with a nod to Virilio, call this new kind of bomb the "information bomb."[8] In fact, we might consider the Daicon animations to be poised at a moment of technological transition, from the nation-centered military-industrial complex to transnational flows of information. We might conclude that the Daicon animations sit on the verge of the information age but are not yet able to see it clearly.

At the level of image, for instance, *Daicon IV Opening Animation* appears uncertain about an easy passage or complete transition from military-industrial complex to globalized information networks. The two techno-formations remain

Figure 24. *As the sun comes over the horizon of the Earth at the end of* Daicon IV Opening Animation, *it initially suggests an atomic explosion seen from space, which turns out to be the sun.*

distinct yet are clearly related and somehow coeval. There is not an easy passage from the one to the other, from old to new technologies, or from modern to postmodern. Still, the Daicon animations are not simply ambivalent about technology. The Daicon team's optimization of modern technologies of the moving image implies a dialectical image of technological optimization—an image in which two possible conditions coexist uneasily, as if oscillating between two futures. The Daicon animations thus invite us to ask, once again, where technical optimization can take us, if anywhere. It is here that questions about unity and multiplicity come into play.

Structurally, the exploded view does not posit a unified viewing position in the manner of one-point perspective; it does not imply a window on the world. It is a diagram that shows how something can be taken apart or put together.

As such, the viewer is a reader or interactor who intermittently situates herself at various points within the assemblage, adopting the angle of different components. These are not so much viewing positions as lines of sight. Exploded projection offers multiple lines of sight that constitute different trajectories across the assemblage. And, as its use of engineering diagrams attests, the exploded view clearly lends itself to optimization. One path of optimization is the distributive field and information network, as we have seen. As such, even though the exploded view does not imply a unified viewing position or the transcendent subject associated with classical Western modernity, it does raise questions about unity and multiplicity. Consider how the exploded view shows the whole taken apart. As a structure, it implies at once a dispersion of the one into the multiple, and a capture of multiplicity within unity. There is an inherent oscillation between multiplication and unification, between dispersion and capture, for dispersed elements remain tied to the whole, while the whole is relentlessly shattered anew.

Such an oscillation between the one and manifold runs throughout *Daicon IV Opening Animation*. There is, for instance, the breaking of the one sword into seven swords of the colors of the rainbow. This is a classic example of the breaking of the one into the manifold. It also happens with the movement of the missiles, whose paths converge and diverge, converge and diverge. Previously I described this convergence and divergence into terms of the temporary construction of a vanishing point, in a fleeting evocation of one-point depth. We might also think of these temporary depths as lines of sight across the perceptual field. In any event, even as we perceive the divergence and dispersion of elements across a distributive field, we retain a sense of the whole, of the underlying integration. Thus the question arises about whether the distributive field can allow for actual divergence and true multiplicity. With each moment of capture comes a new moment of dispersion, and vice versa. With the technological optimization of such a structure comes the promise of even vaster integration. Can there ever be elements or zones that truly diverge? Or does the exploded projection merely expand in scale without allowing for difference?

In space opera and future-war anime, the imaging of integration and dispersion tends to settle on images of planets exploding. Take, for instance, the scenes of the exploding planet from *Galaxy Express 999*. As a prime example of superflat, Murakami Takashi used a series of stills showing the surface of the planet on which arcs of lava-like light erupt, and bursts of energies zigzag like lightning. The film, however, alternates those images of the surface of the planet with images of the entire planet (Figure 25). Images of the whole round planet serve to underscore a prior and maybe underlying integration or wholeness, which lingers

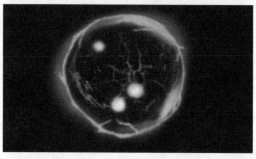

Figure 25. *In the sequences of the destruction of a planet in* Galaxy Express 999, *evoked in Murakami Takashi's discussion of superflat, images of planetary explosion alternate with images of the whole planet, evoking integration amid disintegration.*

through the explosion. It is very much like the exploded view of the Yamaha motorcycle wheel assembly: image by image we see the components of the planet in a state of disintegration that simultaneously shows us a reintegration. In the exploded view, taking something apart (destroying it) and putting it back together (remaking it) appear in the same image. In other words, destruction does not appear in opposition to creation. Technological optimization of destruction can thus appear simultaneously with prior integration or holism.

In light of the exploded view, the transition in *Daicon IV Opening Animation* from military destruction to eco-rejuvenation comes as less of a surprise. Recall the final images in which the sun coming over the horizon of the earth first recalls an atomic bomb and then transforms into the orb of the sun. Destruction has expanded the scope of integration to the planet and maybe to the sun and thus the solar system. We can also read this rising sun as a symbol of Japanese integration, of Japanese nationalism and empire, as on the Japanese flag, *Hi no maru*. In other words, even without a unified viewing position, the exploded view—this world of relative movement without any interest in absolute depth— can imply a yearning to experience and recover a sense of integration; such yearning courses through the distributive field associated with technologies of information and communication that are commonly characterized as "flat."[9] As a structure, the exploded view can impart a material limit to the in-folding of expressive machines and the out-folding of divergent series. The question of technical optimization of flatness or planarity in anime thus becomes one of whether structures of exploded projection completely capture or harness this other potentiality of the moving image, or whether there can be truly divergent series within anime and zones of autonomy in animation production.

The male otaku is the figure on which such questions have frequently settled, not only because the autonomy of the otaku seems genuine to some commentators and spurious to others, but also because the figure of the otaku inscribes an oscillation between the one and multiple, as a household of one, and one of a household.[10] And so, before returning to the transformation of Daicon Studios into Gainax Studios, and before exploring how questions of technology are thought animetically in Gainax's *Nadia*, I will turn to questions about "otaku imaging."

CHAPTER 12

OTAKU IMAGING

N HIS *OTAKUGAKU NYŪMON* (Introduction to otakuology), Okada Toshio, self-proclaimed "otakingu" or king of the otaku, begins with a tentative definition of otaku as "people with a [highly] evolved sense of sight" *(shinka shita shikaku o motsu ningen)*.[1] Put another way, otaku present an evolution in human perception.

Okada calls attention to the importance of the VCR in this transformation. With the advent of videocassettes and new recording technologies, fans were able to make copies of their favorite series, to collect them and watch them repeatedly. As fans replayed episodes, they began to notice differences in the drawing of characters. Okada uses the example of three versions of the character Ryō from the 1974–75 animated series *Gettaarobo (Getter Robo)*, one drawn by Komatsubara Kazuo, another by Nakamura Kazuo, and a third by Noda Takuo. Because fans could now pause on images or watch at reduced speeds, they began not only to make distinctions between different styles of drawing but also to attend to the work of key animators *(genga-man)* and in-between animators *(dōga-man)*.[2] Otaku then are people who began to look at anime with close attention to how it was put together.

What Okada describes as otaku perception is like the distributive perceptual field, insofar as he remarks how dedicated fans begin to break down the distinction between center and periphery in their viewing of anime. The work of an in-between animator, for instance, may become as noteworthy as that of a key animator. The work of a team of animators may impress viewers more than that of the director or writer. In other words, otaku perception entails a form of connoisseurship, which demands a new kind of literacy or competency in reading images. Above all, the new competency demands an attention to production details as so much "data" about the animation (what is often called *neta* in Japanese), which has the effect of flattening the image into a distributive field of elements.

An earlier fandom, without access to videos, tended to focus its activities almost exclusively on story synopses and chronologies, and thus novelizations were very important. Naturally these forms of interaction with anime persist. With the advent of the VCR, however, fans began to grapple with the anime image as a production with multiple layers, as a field dense in information. This way of looking at anime dehierarchizes the image along two axes. First, it flattens the hierarchy of production by which directors are supposed to be of primary importance, followed by producers or writers, followed by animation directors, key animators, and character designers. Second, it flattens the hierarchy of elements in the visual field—to give some simplistic examples, character design or mecha design may prove more important than story or character, or the key animation of battle scenes may garner as much attention as character development, especially with repeated viewing. Of course, the best animation could be said to combine the best talents in all these areas within one film or series. Nonetheless what is important is the ability to make these distinctions, to discern the interplay of different elements and "signature layers" with the anime image.

We might think of this otaku knowledge of the anime image in terms of an extension of the superplanar image discussed in the previous two chapters. Otaku knowledge entails a sense of the image as composed of multiple layers, yet there is no preestablished hierarchy among elements or layers. In this respect, Okada's description of otaku perception resonates with Murakami Takashi's superflat. In fact, Murakami clearly draws on Okada Toshio's description of otaku vision. His conceptualization of superflat involves an astute combination of Okada Toshio's *Introduction to Otakuology* with Tsuji Nobuo's *Kisō no keifu* (Lineage of eccentricity). Significantly, well in advance of Murakami, Okada had tentatively established, in exceedingly general terms, a direct line of descent from the world of Edo art to the world of contemporary Japanese anime, video games, and special effects films. In both Edo culture and otaku culture, Okada detects a mode of discernment that he contrasts with Western subcultures.[3] Okada's impact on Murakami is also evident in Murakami's lineage of Japanese limited animation. For instance, Murakami draws on Okada's broad contrast of Miyazaki Hayao and Tezuka Osamu from *Introduction to Otakuology*.

In contrast to Miyazaki who, as we have seen, situates himself in the lineage of manga film and Tōei *dōga*, Okada sees Tezuka Osamu as the pioneer of limited animation in Japan, beginning in 1962 with the adaptation of his manga *Tetsuwan*

Atomu (*Mighty Atom* aka *Astro Boy*) for the small screen.[4] Subsequently, in the late 1970s and early 1980s, with such television series as *Space Battleship Yamato* (*Uchū senkan Yamato*, 1974), *Galaxy Express 999* (*Ginga tetsudō 999*, 1979), *Mobile Suit Gundam* (*Kidō senshi Gandamu*, 1979), and *Macross* (aka *Superdimensional Fortress Macross*; *Chōjiku yōsai Macross*, 1982), various transformations of the limited animation style came to establish the distinctive look and feel of anime. The emergence of journals dedicated to anime such as *Animage* in the early 1970s spurred a new appreciation of this specific lineage of limited animation. Murakami Takashi follows Okada's basic sketch of this otaku anime lineage in his *Super Flat* exhibition.[5]

To some extent, such overlaps are not surprising. After all, Okada Toshio (b. 1958), Murakami Takashi (b. 1962), and Anno Hideaki (b. 1960) are of the same generation. This generation was frequently referred as the "new type" or "new human type" *(shinjinrui)*, which was retroactively construed as the first generation of otaku.[6] In *Introduction to Otakuology*, Okada refers to those born between 1955 and 1965 *(Shōwa 30 nendai)* as first generation of otaku, while those born between 1965 and 1975 are the second generation, and those born 1975 to 1985 constitute the third. In sum, Okada positions himself in the first generation of otaku, and he uses this position to authorize his expertise about otaku. Consequently, his "otakuology or "study of otaku" is the stuff of personal experience as much as study. The same is to some extent true of Murakami and Anno: when they speak about otaku, they speak as otaku.

With Anno and Okada, the overlap is more than generational, however. Recall that in the early 1980s, when hosting the Osaka Science Fiction Conventions, Okada Toshio and Takeda Yasuhiro selected Anno Hideaki and Yamaga Hiroyuki, then freshman art students at Osaka University, to make animated films for the opening of the 1981 and 1983 conventions. These efforts established an amateur animation studio called Daicon Film. Because the Daicon animations were amateur productions (but with a technical sophistication that rivaled and even surpassed that of major studios) and because they cited and celebrated a broad range of anime, SFX films, and science fiction, they created the sense of an otaku idiom created for and by otaku. The success of Daicon Film subsequently led to the formation in 1985 of one of Japan's most successful animation studios, Gainax Studios, with Okada Toshio as a founder and later its president. Even today Gainax has the buzz of being the otaku studio.

Anno Hideaki became Gainax's foremost director, working as animation director on Gainax's first feature film, *Royal Space Force: The Wings of Honneamise* (1987) and subsequently directing three very popular series: *Gunbuster* (*Toppu o nerae*, 1988), *Nadia* (1989–90), and the series that is commonly deemed the crowning achievement of Gainax animation, *Neon Genesis Evangelion* (1995–96). As an animator, Anno gained renown for his mecha design and ballistic sequences. The sequences of tracking missiles in the *Daicon* animations are his work, and before Gainax had firmly established itself, he lent his talents as an animator to Miyazaki's *Nausicaä* (1984), working particularly on the giant robot mecha sequences at the end of the film. Interesting enough, in the wake of his disenchantment with the otaku lineage of animation, he has made a short film for the Ghibli Museum entitled *Kusō no kikai-tachi no naka no hakai no hatsumei* (The invention of destruction within fantasy machines, 2002).

Anno worked on the 1982 *Macross* television series, and around the time of *Nausicaä*, he was also working as an animator on the film *Superdimensional Fortress Macross: Do You Remember Love?* (*Chōjiku yōsai Makurosu: Ai oboete imasu ka*, 1984). The final battle scenes in this film take superplanar ballistics to the limit; crackling lines of energy, planar explosions, and the luminous lines of force bring the depth of battle action and optics to the surface. At one point, the battle plays beautifully in all its multifield flatness across the visor of the hero's space helmet. War comes so close that violence turns to brilliance and awe, and you can feel war bringing you to the brink of an existential crisis: can you love anything but war? This type of question comes to the fore in the SF television series typically cited as constituting *the* otaku anime lineage (*Macross, Gundam*, and *Yamato*): how can you enjoy your war and rue it too? These animations produce a space in which war can be your thing without you necessarily embracing war. Flattened ballistics contribute to this effect, because, with their relative depth and relative movement, they produce the sense of a "personalizable" world: each line of sight can develop into a personal way of connecting the dots, so to speak. You make your world within the anime war. War becomes as much an occasion for world-generation as world-destruction. The exploded view makes it possible to sustain destruction and generation within the animated image.

Such techniques and themes were Anno's heritage and passion as he embarked on his career as animator and then writer and director. His is a lineage that stands in sharp contrast to Ghibli (founded, incidentally, in the same year as Gainax). At a festival of children's animation held in France in 1992, for instance, in an interview published with the French anime magazine *Animeland*, somewhat to the interviewer's surprise, Takahata Isao remarks that he doesn't much care for the Gainax film *Wings of Honneamise*. To distinguish his work from theirs, Takahata approximates his own work to that of art animation— Disney of the late 1930s and early 1940s, Paul Grimault, Frédéric Back, and Yuri Norstein.[7] Takahata does not speak in detail, yet, as we have seen in the context of Miyazaki, art techniques come to imply structures of depth and universal frames of reference in Ghibli films, which is in turn underscored in the emphasis on general audiences. In contrast, Gainax animations and their techniques were, for many years at least, associated with highly specific or localized audiences (male otaku).

The difference between Ghibli and Gainax, however, is not merely one of their targeted audiences or of generational communities of taste (that is, old type versus new type or *shinjinrui*). The difference also lies in superplanar relativity, which Gainax films highlight, but which Ghibli films strive to suppress. The works of the two studios thus imply fundamentally different relations to ballistic technologies and ballistic perception—and thus to the modern technological condition. The difference can also be thought of in terms of an emphasis on art animation and thus on painting and painterly techniques (Ghibli) in contrast to an emphasis on engineering and graphic design (Gainax). Okada Toshio's *Introduction to Otakuology* provides the perfect gloss for the Gainax otaku approach: for his table of contents, Okada uses a globe, a telescope, and a toggle—*in exploded view*—with the parts labeled as different topics. This is in keeping with the idea of the otaku world as one of assembly diagrams, and with the otaku "evolution in perception" as a matter of seeing how animation is put together in an exploded view—with all the bits at once apart and together—an explosion arrayed across multiple planes yet in a single plane.

To understand how anime thinks technology, we must also explore how anime strives to inhabit technology; we need to ask, "what inhabits this exploded view?" and "what can dwell in the superplanar world?" One answer comes via Okada: persons with a capacity for and interest in navigating distributive fields of perception. For him it is otaku (or new-type humans) who inhabit the superplanar world, by inventing new modalities of perception.

Okada also provides a very literal vision of what it means to inhabit this kind of anime image world. In *Introduction to Otakuology,* he includes sketches of typical rooms for each of the three generations of otaku.[8] A couple features are common to the three rooms. First, the otaku's room looks like an office or study, a place of work or study rather than rest or relaxation. The distinction between leisure and work breaks down in this space. Second, these rooms are equipped with imaging and recording technologies (there is generation shift from VCRs to computers) as well as filing and storing technologies (shelves, folders, and cases as well as cassettes, floppy disks, DVDs, and other storage media). The evolution in perception entails technological mediators ranging from the low tech (pens and labels) to high tech (the latest computer). The overall impression is of a studious and even compulsive *intervention* into the flow of media images: capturing, ordering, packaging, storing, routing, and rerouting (sharing) images. Here as elsewhere (as with his establishment of a university for otaku studies), Okada puts the emphasis on the productivity of otaku activities as a form of intellectual/ technical intervention into the world of the image. Needless to say, even though I am focusing largely on the visual, this is a multisensory image that comprises an array of modalities of seeing, hearing, touching as well as different registers linked to and across modalities (sound, voice, music, for instance).

Okada's presentation of otaku implies that the best way to live in the anime world is to contribute actively to its tendency toward flattening and dehierarchizing the image by intervening directly into the production and flow of images. As such, the otaku intervention into the image flow is not merely a different way of perceiving the image. It is a way of acting on images. Otaku perception is also otaku action. Otaku intensify the trend toward isolating perceptual elements (bits of sound and sight), dehierarchizing layers, and flattening the production hierarchies. Otaku then is a way of going with the flow of images *and* of intervening into that flow in order to enhance its tendency toward superplanarity. Otaku inhabit the exploded view by studiously extending and intensifying it.

But what is the value of this otaku intervention into the image flow? Are otaku merely going with the flow, maintaining and furthering a new technological status quo? Or are there critical possibilities in the otaku intervention?

Anno and Okada part company on this issue. Until very recently, when he announced the death of otaku, Okada has consistently celebrated and promoted otaku, presenting it not only as an "evolved" knowledge formation but also as a truly Japanese culture. The last chapter of *Introduction to Otakuology* contends that "otaku are the true heirs of Japanese culture."[9] Like Murakami Takashi (but without the hedging), Okada sees a perfect fit between the culture of Edo Japan and contemporary otakudom. More recently, Okada sees American otaku looking back at Japan establishing it as the site of authenticity. And the first chapter of *Otaku no mayoi-michi* (The labyrinth of otaku, 2003) is on "Americans who feel they 'want to become Japanese.'"[10] In sum, his aim is to sing the praises of otaku activities as an authentic expression of Japanese values. His celebration of otaku thus verges on the good old nationalism of *Nihonjinron* (discourses on Japaneseness), relying on the same familiar dialectics of Japanese identity: we only become Japanese by comparing ourselves with the West, and so we feel most ourselves when the American look is on us.

Anno, on the contrary, wants to present a critique of otaku-type activities and behavior, but from within that world, by pushing the limits of the otaku lineage of limited animation. *Evangelion* and *Introduction to Otakuology* are worlds apart in this respect. Not surprisingly perhaps, Okada Toshio expresses no interest in *Evangelion* (he claims not to have seen it). And he has broken ties with Gainax. Yet, between *Nadia* and *Evangelion*, Okada played a central role in writing and producing a two-part OAV series called *Otaku no video 1982 & 1985* (same titles in English), which Gainax released in 1992. This series presents otaku in a manner that anticipates crucial features of both *Evangelion* and *Introduction to Otakuology*. *Otaku no video* combines animated footage telling the triumphant rise of Gainax's otaku empire in a fantastical form, with black-and-white "mockumentary" interviews with otaku whose faces are obscured with mosaics and voices digitally masked to protect their privacy (but reputedly the otaku are staff members of Gainax).

Animated segments tell the story of two friends whose passion for anime leads them to found a studio. The story begins with an average and likeable first-year university student (Kubo Akira) whose chance encounter with a high school friend (Tanaka) transforms his life. Tanaka (reputedly a stand-in for Okada) is a serious otaku, obsessed with animated television series, manga, fan clubs, and amateur publications. Kubo is gradually drawn into Tanaka's world, abandoning his healthy normal life (and his girlfriend) in favor of Tanaka's nerdy, creepy otaku club. Together with Tanaka, Kubo becomes so impassioned about anime that the two of them form a garage model kit company—kits for assembling personalized models of figures from anime or manga series, typically of sexy women, as with Kubo and Tanaka's buxom creation "Misty May."[11] After hitting rock bottom with the commercial takeover of their first company, the two friends finally succeed with an animation company and begin to fantasize about "otakunizing" the entire world.

Because the animation tells an otaku success story, it is bursting with references to manga and anime series, which makes the triumph of the otaku feel like an intervention into a flow of images comprising not only anime and manga but also spin-offs, tie-ins, toys, clothes, novels, music, and other related merchandising. That the otaku boys in *Otaku no video* begin with garage kits and then expand into the animation business serves as a reminder of the importance of toys and figures as the point of departure for multimedia or transmedia industries. It was in the early 1980s with series like *Macross* that toys begin to provide the source for anime series rather than the reverse. Okada saw the importance of merchandise sales very early, and after brisk sales of mascot figures and garage kits at the 1981 Daicon, he formed General Products in 1982 to sell SF- and anime-related merchandise. In fact, the anime sequences in *Otaku no video* reprise the story of Okada Toshio and the foundation of General Products and then Gainax Studios, but in a triumphal form, as a grand narrative of trials and triumph that makes the otaku team resemble the heroes of SF anime epics.

Otaku no video also packs the animation sequences with otaku information, recalling the information-saturated multiple-field planarity of the Daicon animations and the explosion of the anime image into multiple frames. At the same time, it includes a series of mockumentary interviews with otaku that deflate and undercut the triumphal anime narrative. These interviews, called "A Portrait of an Otaku, " alternate with the animated story. In these portraits, *Otaku no video* presents a series of different interviews with otaku who became obsessed with otaku-related activities in different ways and at different times of their life. A respectably ordinary businessman tells of his passion in college for *dōjinshi* (fan-authored manga, sometimes translated as "fanzines," which introduce new stories involving established characters or entirely new characters and stories). The businessman sees his otaku days in retrospect as the best time of his life. Other otaku are obsessed with cosplay (costume play), pornography, with weapons, garage kits, games, collecting, or piracy. There is even an American fan obsessed with Japan as the land of anime.

Otaku no video anticipates certain aspects of Okada's apologia for otaku in *Introduction to Otaku*. In fact, *Otaku no video* is so funny that it makes me wonder how serious Okada really is in his apparently straightforward endorsement of otaku in *Introduction to Otaku*. Interestingly, because the animation sequences in *Otaku no video* draw on classic epic anime, their narrative arc recalls that of *Nadia* and *Evangelion*. What is more, like *Otaku no video*, *Nadia* and *Evangelion* alternate between straightforward heroic stories of trial and triumph (saving the world from invaders) and otaku-like "portraits" in which characters appear flawed, vulnerable, alone, and largely incapable of heroic action or communal life. In sum, despite the profound difference between Okada and Anno, and despite their subsequent split, we see, in *Otaku no video*, a moment of intersection wherein the otaku is at once celebrated and disavowed. This sense of crisis vis-à-vis otaku was due in no small part to the Miyazaki Tsutomu incident, which had a profound impact on *Nadia*, *Otaku no video*, and *Evangelion*.

Between 1988 and 1989, Miyazaki Tsutomu mutilated and killed four girls, ages four to seven, and he then sexually molested their corpses and ate portions of two victims.[12] Camera crews and reporters exploring his home stressed his collection of shojo manga and anime, and Miyazaki Tsutomu became known as the Otaku Murderer. This incident resulted in a general reaction against otaku with an emphasis on social pathologies such as *hikikomori* or "social withdrawal."[13] This panic over the pathological effects of otaku lifestyles apparently had a profound impact on Anno Hideaki during the making of *Nadia*, in serialization at the time, and it may have spurred disenchantment with the otaku world and his sense of shame at being a television anime director, which I will discuss in chapter 14. It was not until the mid- to late 1990s, partly through the astounding popularity of *Evangelion* (as a widespread otaku commercial success), that it became possible to affirm otaku. That is when Okada's *Introduction to Otakuology* appeared, celebrating otaku in a straightforward way that was not possible at the time of *Otaku no video*.

Otaku no video is interesting in the way that it at once addresses the growing sense of moral panic vis-à-vis otaku and deflects it. In response to the general panic about guys whose obsession with shojo-related anime and manga appeared to cut them off from the world, *Otaku no video* takes an odd tack. Its mockumentary sequences seem to confirm that male otaku are indeed cut off from the world—especially from the world of actual women. Yet *Otaku no video* acerbates this stance in an attempt to sever completely the connection between the world of otaku images and the actual world "out there." It is as if there is no connection between otaku and the real world. *Otaku no video* thus succeeds in playing the otaku's social withdrawal and obsessions for their pathos and comedy. The preference of the otaku for images appears as a largely harmless disposition, a mild sort of arrested development that places otaku outside reality. In some respects, the term *otaku* itself allows this take.

Within the term *otaku*, there is a certain degree of subtlety. Addressing someone as "otaku" is a formal way of saying "you" by referring to you as "your residence." Thus using the term *otaku* can have a double connotation. It can imply very formalistic social relations. The reference to otaku in the 1980s was often to boys and young men who played video games together without really interacting in ways traditionally deemed sociable—these guys weren't talking much to each other or roaming the streets together; they were interacting through the games. In these game contexts, boys called each other "otaku" as if sustaining cordial but distant (not sociable or intimate) relations with one another. At the same time, otaku can imply "housebound" due to its reference to the residence. This connotation of otaku became pronounced when linking fan behavior to social withdrawal syndrome.

While it flirts with the image of the otaku as a creepy and maybe dangerous type, *Otaku no video* also deflates the otaku threat by exposing otaku as comically pathetic homebodies whose pursuits separate them from the real world. *Otaku no video* remains noncommittal about the social status of the male otaku, exposing the pathologization of otaku without endorsing it. But the vision of otaku underwent a series of changes in the 1990s. Gradually, by the late 1990s, a new image appeared, that of the otaku as a fundamentally good and redeemable young man who had buried himself in anime and games. This became the basis for the social rehabilitation and recuperation of the otaku phenomenon. In many ways it was the phenomenal success of otaku-related commerce in the

1990s, as well as the transnational boom in anime, that served to diffuse the media panic about otaku as sociopaths that had reigned in the late 1980s and early 1990s. Gainax's *Evangelion* was pivotal in that it made the otaku market impossible to ignore. Otaku had to be affirmed, if only as a commercial force. By the late 1990s, not surprisingly in view of the commercial visibility and viability of otaku-related activities, the tendency was toward social redemption of the lonely male otaku. *Densha Otoko* or *Train Man*, a novel reputedly composed of Internet exchanges on the 2channel (*2channeru*) site, told the story of an otaku who overcomes his shy and awkward isolation and wins the girl, with the help of anonymous on-line advisors.[14] A sort of male Cinderella story in which the unlikely boy wins a princess with the assistance of Internet fairy godmothers and the magic of digital connectivity, *Train Man* became a multimedia phenomenon, spawning a series of manga, a television drama, and a movie. In fact, the redemption of the male otaku in the late 1990s was so complete that Okada Toshio himself announced the death of otaku, excoriating younger otaku that they were not truly otaku. New terms emerged in an attempt to put an edge back on anime/manga/game-related activities, such as *Akiba-kei* (Akihabara-type, that is, those who hang out in anime, manga, and game stores in the Akihabra area, perfecting their collections).

In the context of how anime thinks technology, the importance of Okada Toshio lies not only in his shrewdness about the interconnection of toys, games, and anime but also in his conceptualization of otaku activities, which situates otaku perception as an intervention into the image flow that remains entirely within the image flow. Okada sensed the formation of an image world without an outside. In effect, as attested in his canny use of exploded projection as the table of contents for his study of otaku, Okada discovered the exploded view, which situates the viewer-reader along lines of sight, as a "subjectile." The otaku is not a fixed subject who consumes anime objects or patronizes the anime world. The otaku is an interactor whose pursuit of the potential depths that traverse the anime/manga/game world make of him (or her) a cooperator in the production and promotion of the expanding world. The pivotal role of the garage kit, with which you assemble and personalize your anime character or vehicle, reinforces this sense of the fan as a producer, assembler, or fabricator, who engineers as much as navigates his or her path within the manga/anime/game world.

In sum, Okada's discussion of otaku signals a transformation of consumable objects into operable worlds; commodities might be likened to strategic salvoes and stockpiles of weapons in a military theater of operation. If I push the military associations here, it is because the anime series in question are frequently worlds of love and war. Or, to borrow the title of the Murakami Ryū novel that served as a source of inspiration for Anno's *Evangelion,* these are theaters of love and fascism.[15]

In contrast with Okada, Anno Hideaki is notable for his ambivalent oscillation between celebration and harsh criticism of otaku and anime. In the next chapter, I turn to Anno's pivotal anime series, which was also Gainax's first massively popular television anime *Nadia,* for it launched the Daicon-style, otaku-related, information-saturated, exploded view onto the small screen with great success.

CHAPTER 13

MULTIPLE FRAMES OF REFERENCE

THE TELEVISION SERIES *NADIA* tells the story of a girl of mysterious origin, Nadia, who wears a pendant with a jewel called the Blue Water, which has astonishing powers. At the 1889 Paris Universal Exposition, Nadia meets a boy, Jean Raltique. Jean helps her to escape from a woman (Grandis Granba) who, with her two henchmen (Hanson and Sanson), wishes to steal Nadia's mysterious Blue Water. The action is set in the late nineteenth century, which is presented as a time of great confidence in scientific advance and technological progress. As a budding young inventor, Jean in particular is brimming with enthusiasm for technology and scientific progress. Yet, in the course of the series, as Jean and Nadia learn that advanced technologies once brought mass destruction to the world, these nineteenth-century ideologies of technological development and progress begin to feel rather hollow. It turns out that the jewel itself, the Blue Water, is the key to reactivating weapons of mass destruction. What is more, Nadia turns out to be the descendent of an ancient people whose technologies still threaten to annihilate the world. There is also a secret society composed of descendants of that people. These Neo-Atlanteans pursue Nadia, intent on recovering the Blue Water to reactivate ancient weapons of mass destruction.

If the story and characters of *Nadia* closely resemble those of *Castle in the Sky*, it is because the series derives from a treatment written by Miyazaki Hayao in the 1970s, when he was developing classic stories for television for Tōhō animation, one of which was to be *Around the World in Eighty Days by Sea*. The series was to combine the classic Jules Verne stories *Twenty Thousand Leagues under the Sea* and *Around the World in Eighty Days*.[1] Miyazaki later used elements of this treatment in his adaptation of Alexander Key's *The Incredible Tide* into the series *Conan*. Subsequently, he reworked many of these elements into *Castle in the Sky*. When NHK and Tōhō approached Gainax in the late 1980s with the idea of a series based on this largely forgotten treatment, they wished to build on the success of Miyazaki's *Castle in the Sky*. Audiences could be expected to make the connections between *Castle in the Sky* and *Nadia*, or at least to respond favorably to a winning formula.

Both stories follow the adventures of two orphans—a boy whose passion is building flying machines, and a girl of unknown origins who possesses a jewel with incredible powers. A secret organization pursues them, intent on seizing the young girl and her jewel. A gang of bumbling crooks led by an intrepid woman is also in pursuit of the girl and her jewel, but this gang ultimately proves friendly and aids the children. Most importantly, in both stories the jewel turns out to be the key to reactivating ancient WMDs, and the girl's possession of the jewel makes her an unwitting accomplice in a history of global annihilation. As for the boy, he must also grapple with his implication in a history of global annihilation, but at the level of his confidence in science and his delight in engineering, that is, at the level of a modern faith in scientific advance. *Nadia* and *Castle in the Sky* are clearly designed to force us to think about the modern technological condition and its tendency to produce advanced ballistics that threaten to bring global annihilation. But Miyazaki Hayao and Anno Hideaki (the director of *Nadia*) have very different ways of telling this story about the modern technological condition. They have very different ways of thinking technology animetically.

Some of the differences between *Nadia* and *Castle in the Sky* are due to basic differences in the stories. For instance, because written as an adaptation of Jules Verne stories, especially *Twenty Thousand Leagues under the Sea*, *Nadia* introduces Captain Nemo and the crew of the *Nautilus*, and with them a range of narrative complications and character developments, suited for the extended serial treatment characteristic of television animation. Moreover, the story lingers on the transformations in Nadia's attitudes toward Nemo: initially she hates him and what he stands for, yet not only do his actions prove to be on her behalf but also he turns out to be her father, and so Nadia must abruptly reconsider her relation to this stern and rather inscrutable father. *Castle in the Sky* does not have time or place for a Nemo character, and so the story does not devote much attention to the familial backstory of its girl with a jewel, Sheeta.

In *Nadia*, as in the Verne novel, the attraction of Captain Nemo comes of his complex and ambivalent relation to advanced technologies. As the possessor and commander of futuristic machinery and weaponry, Nemo and the *Nautilus* are emblems of techno-science. This is how Nadia sees them, and why she loathes them. At another level, however, Nemo is a man whose life has been shattered by the destructive power inherent in advanced technologies; he wields them only to prevent further destruction. His mission is to prevent the secret organization, the Neo-Atlanteans, from taking possession of the Blue Water, for the jewel is the key to reactivating the weapons of mass destruction built ages ago in Atlantis.

A host of other narrative twists and turns distinguish *Nadia* from *Castle in the Sky*, and despite their common source and fundamentally analogous trajectories, the two animations truly diverge and pose different questions. Some of the narrative differences derive from the demands of television serialization in contrast with those of stand-alone feature-length films, and exploring such differences in the context of *Nadia* and *Castle in the Sky* could tell us a great deal about the dynamics of television animation versus animated films, and about Anno Hideaki and the Gainax world versus Miyazaki Hayao and the Ghibli world. Given the focus of this study, however, rather than dwell on a detailed synopsis of the two animations and their differences, or provide an encyclopedic list of characters attributes and other characteristics (fans have compiled and posted intricate summaries and guides to *Nadia* on the Web),[2] I propose to address character and story in terms of animation, looking at them *as animation*. Ultimately, of course, the goal is to explore how these animations think technology.

One salient difference between *Nadia* and *Castle in the Sky* lies in how they work with the multiple planes of the image and with backgrounds. Like *Castle in the Sky*, *Nadia* uses sliding planes to impart a sense of movement, as well as pans of the camera across the image. In the first episode, for instance, the sense of movement derives more from moving the planes of the image and panning the camera than from animating the characters. The episode opens with a shot through the clouds, which part to reveal a sailboat on a river. *Nadia* then shows the young male protagonist Jean piloting a boat up the Seine toward Paris to attend the 1889 Paris Universal Exposition, where he plans to enter his flying machine in a competition. Our sense of the boat moving arises from sliding the foreground layer of grass and of the background layer of scenery (Figure 26). These layers slide to the left, which makes the boat appear to be moving to the right, that is, forward. There is also a planar speed differential: the foreground grass moves faster than the background scenery. In fact, in many scenes in *Nadia*, the background layer scarcely appears to move at all (the middle layer or layers are of course still): our sense of movement derives primarily from the relatively fast sliding of the foreground.

The first episode introduces another common strategy for rendering movement: the camera pans down the image, from the top of the Eiffel Tower down to Jean standing at the base. Elsewhere the camera pans across the drawing of

Figure 26. *In one of the first sequences from* Nadia, *our sense of the movement of the boat along the river is produced by sliding the foreground layer of grasses and flowers to the left, while the middle ground and background remain almost entirely stationary.*

an array of odd-looking flying machines. In addition, the movement of characters tends toward dramatic poses and outsized repetitious gestures rather than toward fluidly cinematic action.

These are general tendencies of limited animation, and some critics and animators might argue that *Nadia* is scarcely animation at all. I have already mentioned the insistence that the art of animation lies in *drawing the movement* and not in *moving the drawing*. Such a stance also tends to shore up a divide between full animation and limited animation. Typically full animation is construed as *the* art of animation. In contrast, limited animation, with its pans across images and relatively static characters, is seen as the antithesis of art, as cheap animation eager to turn a quick buck. I will discuss limited animation in greater detail in chapter 15, but already it should be clear that I see moving the drawings as equally important to animation as drawing movements. Because of my emphasis on movement, on animation as an art of the moving image, I also tend to dethrone the art of the hand. Although integral to animation, the art of the hand in drawing movement (especially evident in character animation) is folded into the animetic machine, which is the site for harnessing and channeling the force of the moving image to generate orientations and directions. Animation is as much a matter of compositing under conditions of movement as it is about animating characters or objects. This is true both of full and limited animation.

Generally speaking, *Nadia* favors moving the drawing (or moving the camera or viewing position) rather than drawing the movement (which is more characteristic of full character animation). Its procedures for *moving the drawing*— sliding the layers of the image and sliding the viewing position (camera) across the image—entail an open compositing that is at the same time flattened. In other words, *Nadia* tends to flatten the multiplanar image into a superplanar image. The contrast between *Nadia* and *Castle in the Sky* makes this flattening clear. Immediately evident is the difference in how these two animations construct a relation between figure and background. The panoramic views in *Castle in the Sky* use deep backgrounds with luminous painterly detail. The panoramic views in *Nadia* are very different. Take, for instance, the views from the Eiffel Tower in the first episode.

After Jean arrives in Paris and meets his uncle (and we learn that an American warship has been sent in pursuit of sea monsters that are impeding flows of maritime commerce and that are also responsible for the disappearance and maybe death of Jean's father), Jean spies Nadia riding down the quay on a bicycle. Smitten, he follows her to the Eiffel Tower, where Nadia is taking in the view. Initially we might simply think that the backgrounds and animation in *Nadia* look cheap in comparison with *Castle in the Sky*. Needless to say, television animation like *Nadia* is lower in budget than Miyazaki's manga films, and *Nadia* is in some respects a low-rent *Castle in the Sky*. There is nonetheless as much artistry or technique in *Nadia*. In the first episode especially, because the goal is to wow viewers and draw them into the series, the aim is to establish a look and feel. As the camera pans across the Parisian cityscape to convey Nadia's view from the Eiffel Tower, we see backgrounds full of detail (Figure 27). Yet the schematization of line and the softened colors make for backgrounds that do not produce a sense of a preexisting depth. These look almost like illustrations for children's textbooks or schematic diagrams. Moreover, where in Miyazaki's films the simplified traits of characters (and their coloration) make them stand out from their backgrounds, *Nadia* flattens the relation between character and background in its use of line and color.

Consequently, as in Tabaimo's installation, the lack of interest in establishing a sense of preexisting depth in *Nadia* creates the sense that anything can happen out there. Anything might pop into view. Tabaimo plays this possibility whimsically, with glancing gestures at random violence: incongruous faces crop up in place of the cityscape outside the train window, and in other installations,

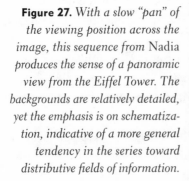

Figure 27. *With a slow "pan" of the viewing position across the image, this sequence from* Nadia *produces the sense of a panoramic view from the Eiffel Tower. The backgrounds are relatively detailed, yet the emphasis is on schematization, indicative of a more general tendency in the series toward distributive fields of information.*

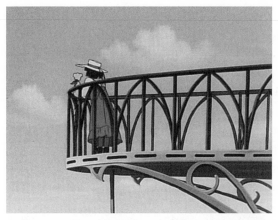

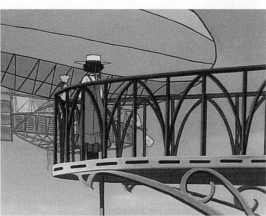

Figure 28. *A flattened world of dehierarchized elements is one in which new elements continually appear from zones off-screen, with a tendency toward a sense of the simultaneity of actions, as in the scene of the appearance of the blimp in* Nadia, *which is followed by the sudden appearance of the villains.*

knives, a murder, a murderer. In *Nadia* a blimp suddenly slides into view, obstructing the sky (Figure 28). Then, out of thin air appear the villains, Grandis and her two henchmen, Hanson and Sanson, intent on seizing the jewel. Astonishingly, it turns out that Nadia is an acrobat: she and her white lion cub leap, somersault through the air, and finally jump down a shaft onto the downward-bound elevator. Flatter compositing imparts the sense of a space and time structured around sudden appearances and disappearances. Many of these devices are not specific to *Nadia* but part of a general rhetoric of television anime in which figures pop abruptly on and off the screen, or heads poke into a scene, or screens suddenly split into two, three, four, or more planes. Usually the planes are articulated diagonally to emphasize a field of multiple actions, in contrast to horizontal and vertical splits that often stress simultaneity.

In fact, I would hazard to say that for many viewers these variations on relative movement within a flattened multiplanar image define the look and feel of anime. In contrast to the exaggerated fluidity of character movement that came to characterize Disney's full animation, there is angular slipping of planes of actions with sudden and sometimes incongruous apparitions.[3] This is about sliding sketches over one another, setting up rhythms and tempos of appearance and disappearance. Such diverse uses of multiple planes come from an innovation on the basic animation technology: the innovation lies in flattening the sense of gaps between stacked layers of celluloid while retaining the sense of multiple planes. The result is the sense of a space without a preestablished frame of reference. In effect, the enframing function of the frame (the boundary of the image) begins to feel less important than the rhythmic appearance and disappearance of different figures and planar fields. We begin to feel the animetic interval less in the invisible interstices *between* frames as in the invisible interstices *within* the frame (compositing), which explodes the frame itself, folding the animetic interval outward into crazy kinds of editing that seem to follow naturally from flat compositing.

There are material limits, of course, to what will pop onto the screen, and how. I will subsequently consider what happens when the figure or character rather than the frame tends to operate as the material limit of the image. At this point, however, I wish to stress how the flattening of the multiplanar image into a superplanar image tends to dispense with a single fixed frame of reference. It tends toward mobile, contingent, multiple frames of reference. Here Anno Hideaki, director of *Nadia*, is far more ambitious and effective than Tabaimo when it comes to thinking the impact of "superplanar relativity" on frames of reference. Where Tabaimo is content to extend an anime-like or manga-like rhetoric of the image to large media installations, Anno focuses attention on the breaking of the frame of reference to pose questions about the modern technological condition.

Nadia, as mentioned above, begins with a highly specific historical frame of reference: the 1889 Paris Universal Exposition. There is also an ideological frame of reference. The panoramic views from the Eiffel Tower ring an early note of disenchantment: as the camera pans over stately and orderly architectures, it slides into dark billows of smoke rising from factories (see Figure 29). Evidently, modern progress is not all colors and light. *Nadia* provides other indications that we are to see the dark side of late nineteenth-century European modernity: along with commercial prosperity comes pollution and destruction, and colonial empires accompany voyages of scientific discovery. There are references to racism and the grab for Africa. There are sidelong allusions to modern racism: Nadia's dark skin sometimes seems to place her in the company of the colonized of India or Africa,[4] and the motley crew of the *Nautilus* under the command of Nemo (who is reputedly Indian in Verne's story) provides something of a multi-

Figure 29. *Even within the beautiful panorama of Paris,* Nadia *inserts signs of the crisis of modernity, here in the form of industrial smokestacks, elsewhere with reference to the colonial grab and racism.*

cultural and multiethnic counterpoint to modern divisions based on racialized thinking, as if presenting an alternative formation.

Superplanar relativity, however, explodes these historical and ideological frames of reference. Such frames are established contingently and swiftly open into other frames of reference. Nadia, for instance, turns out to be Atlantean not human, a descendent of colonizers not the colonized; thus, even as her dark skin sustains a reference to the colonized others of the white West, her sparkling blue eyes open into a literally alien frame of reference that sits oddly with nineteenth-century colonialism, and that disturbingly tends to trump the framework of colonizer and colonized. Similarly, while the historical time line for the series remains the late nineteenth century, the imperial ventures and warfare of that era open smoothly and seamlessly into a radically different historical frame of reference, that of atomic bombs, nuclear holocaust, and late twentieth-century technologies. It is as if the techno-scientific politics of the post–World War II era were being played out in the late nineteenth century. Significantly, even though the nineteenth-century characters in *Nadia* express surprise and admiration over such marvels as rivetless hulls and electricity, such things are mundane for the contemporary viewer, whose response to their nineteenth-century awe is surely in part to marvel at the naïveté of that awe. For the contemporary viewer, the wonder is that techno-science could ever have inspired such naïve wonder. In addition, the postwar frame of reference is at the same time a distinctly SF frame of reference. Technologies characteristic of the postwar era—such as airplanes, submarines, electricity, computers, atomic bombs—open into futuristic technologies such as spaceships and mysterious energy sources. They also imply a quasi-mythological frame of reference. But let's first look at the vehicles by way of example.

The friendly villains' vehicle, the *Gratan* (the *Grandis Tank*), transforms from something like an armored tank, into hot air balloon, or into boat, all at the touch of the hands on organ keys, in a sly nod to the prehistory of computer command. On the one hand, the design of the *Gratan* extends technologies of the nineteenth century into more sophisticated configurations reminiscent of late twentieth-century vehicles—not unlike Miyazaki's wacky flying machines in *Castle in the Sky* (or the steam technologies imagined in Otomo Katsuhiro's *Steamboy* and other steampunk stories). On the other hand, the *Gratan* design feels decidedly 1960s or 1970s, a riff on the heyday of television anime. It does not look out of place alongside the futuristic vehicles based on the highly advanced Atlantis technologies, such as the *Nautilus* or the Neo-Atlanteans' *Garfish* or airship, which also have a 1960s or 1970s look.[5] The use of pop-jazz syncopations reminiscent of 1960s and 1970s action adventure and spy music furthers the retro-future feel of *Nadia*.

Nadia is not merely imprecise or anachronistic in its presentation of the late nineteenth century. It does not inadvertently confuse 1889 with 1989. While deliberately cartoonish, the series does not simply melt and amalgamate historical references into cartoonish lumps. Rather it strives to open the one set of historical and ideological references into other frames of reference. The result is a *multiplication of frames of reference* right on the surface. We see late nineteenth-century technologies alongside futuristic Atlantis technologies that strangely echo the postwar era, especially as seen in 1960s and 1970s anime series. In addition, along with the Atlantis frame of reference comes a range of biblical references and other historical and mythological points of reference. At the same time, in conjunction with its riffs on different Verne novels, *Nadia* compulsively cites an astonishing number of anime films and series, even as it echoes *Castle in the Sky*. As the series unfolds, the Atlanteans prove to be alien colonists from Nebula M-78, intent on transforming humans into servants, which introduces yet another frame of reference, while introducing questions about what sort of power formation is at issue. Apparently, Atlanteans engineered the human race to serve them. After failed attempts to upgrade and enslave cetaceans, the Atlanteans turned to primates, manipulating their DNA to produce humans. Atlantean intervention provides the missing link between ape and human, the intelligent design, so to speak. The Atlanteans split into two factions, however, on the question of human worth. While Captain Nemo and company wish to leave the planet to humans and live among them, the Neo-Atlanteans feel that the human race is too destructive and can only be held in check by forcing them to bow to the wishes of their creators, their gods, the Atlanteans.

In sum, as even this glancing overview of references attests, *Nadia* brings multiple frames to the surface: nineteenth-century science, 1960s and 1970s design, postwar nuclear politics, the Bible and ancient myths, human evolution, space travel, interplanetary and interracial conflict, to name a few. Anno Hideaki would intensify this multiplication of frames of reference in his next anime series, *Evangelion*, combining Kabbalistic thought with biotechnology and mecha combat in a postapocalyptic future world under attack by mysterious Angels (to name just a few of the salient frames, many of which are anticipated in *Nadia*). *Evangelion* multiplies frames of reference to the point where viewers no longer know exactly which frame of reference is *the* frame of reference, or if there is *a* frame of reference for the series. Likewise with *Nadia*: even though it is easier to impose a single frame or a unitary narrative structure on *Nadia* than to deal with the multiplication of frames, the challenge of *Nadia*, like *Evangelion*, lies in the multiplication. In effect, the superplanar image—which brings multiple planes to the surface—unfolds as a superplanar narrative structure with multiple frames of reference, each one equally salient, each promising a key to unravel the strands of narrative strewn across the series.

CHAPTER 14

INNER NATURES

AS WE HAVE SEEN, the flattening of the movement of multiple planes in *Nadia* goes hand in hand with a tendency to multiply frames of reference. While Miyazaki's animations also play with the sliding of planes, movement is relative to a preexisting depth in them, which comes to function as an absolute or universal Nature. Nature promises to afford a frame of reference, thereby grounding movement; the dynamic angling of characters serves to enframe the figure, tilting it earthward. *Nadia*, however, works with *relative depth* and *relative movement*. Consequently, in *Nadia*, as in Tabaimo's installations, our sense of what is inside and outside becomes thoroughly relative, too. A sense of inside and outside gives way to a positioning determined by the relative movement of planes. In effect, this is not exactly a positioning or a viewing position, at least not in the sense of a fixed subjective stance. Viewing or reading the anime world entails transversal lines of sight. Similarly, Nature no longer provides a frame of reference that is simply "out there." Nature might just as easily be "in here." Nature might just as readily be produced or manufactured, much as the Atlanteans in *Nadia* engineer humans, both their nature and their history, through the genetic manipulation of primates. Consequently, *Nadia* implies a shift away from Nature with a capital N toward nature, or rather, toward a series of natures. Moreover, since these natures are not separable from cultures or technologies, we might well use Bruno Latour's turn of phrase, and speak of natures/cultures.[1] Or we can think of them as techno-natures.

Nadia begins with a familiar narrative trajectory, by which the boy or young man leaves the safety of home to seek adventure in the outside world. Yet the trajectory of movement into the world gradually resolves into a pattern in which exposure to the natural world serves to enclose it on vaster scales. Jean and Nadia (and the lion cub King) flee Paris with Grandis and company close behind them (episode 1), and when these bumbling villains discover them at Jean's house, the children escape by flying out to sea in one of Jean's flying machines. Their plane, however, crashes at sea. Fortunately, an American warship (hunting the sea monster that allegedly killed Jean's father) rescues them (episode 2). When the "sea monster," which proves to be the *Nautilus*, destroys the warship, the children are once again lost at sea (episode 3). This time the *Nautilus* comes to their rescue (episode 4). Aboard the *Nautilus* they meet Captain Nemo, his first officer Electra, and the rest of crew. Despite Jean's plea to become a member of the *Nautilus*, Nemo sends them away in the repaired airplane. Unfortunately the children again crash, this time on an island where they adopt a little girl, Marie, whose parents have been killed by the Neo-Atlanteans (episode 5). The sinister Gargoyle, leader of cultish Neo-Atlanteans who sport long robes and shroud their heads in hoods with ghastly painted faces, is bent on suppressing the local human population as he commandeers island resources to construct a weapon of mass destruction, the Tower of Babel.

Because the Blue Water is the key to reactivating Atlantean technologies, Gargoyle seizes Nadia and holds her within a vast complex. Aptly, his seemingly vast garden turns out to be an enclosed park, and Gargoyle intimates that the stunning flowers are artificially produced and thus superior to the "real" flowers of Earth. While such a statement implies an ability to distinguish between the natural and the artificial, it is precisely such a distinction that the series as a whole gradually undermines. Eventually, entire islands prove to be spaceships, and nothing in the natural world can be definitively isolated from culture, artifice, or technology.

The children manage to undermine Gargoyle's plan. After an initial display of the power of his Tower of Babel (which directs a laser beam via orbital satellites to fire on the target), Gargoyle aims to blast the *Nautilus* with it. The children foil his plan, however. Jean teams up with Grandis, Hanson, and Sanson to rescue Nadia from Gargoyle, and they manage to interfere with the functioning of the Tower. This story arc (episodes 4–8) ends with the Tower self-destructing, and Nemo takes the children and Grandis and company aboard the *Nautilus*. These first eight episodes correspond fairly well in terms of their overall arc with the action of *Castle in the Sky*.

Early in the series then, the children confront a technological power that encloses the earth (circling it with satellites). Technological power has the ability to construct nature within this vast enclosure called Earth and the capacity to destroy all life within it as well. In other words, despite the children's exposure to the natural world and its harshness (rough seas and sea monsters), and despite the narrative trajectory of leaving home and meeting with an epic adventure, the natural world "out there" is time and again enframed technologically.

(I should note that the awkward word *enframe* stands in contrast to *frame*: to enframe is in the Heideggerian sense of transforming something into an image or a reserve, optimizing it for the sake of optimization, while to frame is, in the usual sense, to put a frame around something. Clearly, there is potential overlap or complicity between the two, depending on how one thinks about the technologies or techniques related to framing. Yet it is also possible to imagine a field at once "unframed" and "enframed." Bringing the multiple planes of the image to the surface (superplanarity), for instance, tends to break the frame of the image. Nonetheless, the resultant distributive field can entail a technological enframing. As we will see, in animation, especially in limited animation, the play between unframing and enframing becomes embodied in character design.)

In *Nadia*, the scale of enclosure or enframement expands throughout the series, until, in one of the final episodes, the newly rebuilt *Nautilus* flies into space, and Jean sees Earth from orbit. Marveling over its beauty, Jean wonders how humans can fight over something so marvelous. Yet the condition for this aesthetic reappraisal of Earth is technological distance and detachment, which serve to isolate and enframe the Blue Planet within space. In effect, the Earth appears like the Blue Water, a powerful gem reducible to whatever use we can make of it. This image of Earth from orbit builds on the sense of the natural world turning into a vast enclosure, into a giant park or reserve.

Such an image of Earth and the natural world recalls Heidegger's ideas about the technological condition in which techno-scientific instrumentality transforms the natural world into a standing reserve, and making the world into an image to be grasped and manipulated. Modernity for Heidegger is the "age of the world picture," or as Rey Chow glosses it, the "age of the world target."[2] The view of Earth from space makes of it an image and by extension a target, something that can be grabbed all at once, taken in a single look, blown to bits with a single shot.

Nadia, however, is post-Heideiggerian—not in the sense of coming after, breaking with, or overcoming the Heideggerian vision of modernity, but in the sense that Heideggerian modernity has become undeniable and irrevocable and thus indefensible, irredeemable. The irrevocable and irredeemable nature of the modern technological condition is reinforced by the transformation of humans into a standing reserve, and of humanity into a human picture: the whole of humanity, the human body and soul, is already subject to and available for instrumental manipulation, in the form of genetic engineering and brainwashing.

After all, an alien species has produced the human species, and has manipulated its beliefs and histories. Once the human species can be thus isolated and manipulated, the threat of its annihilation looms large. Peter Sloterdjik's rubric, the "human park," rings true here.[3]

In *Nadia*, the techno-scientific transformation of the world and humans into a standing reserve is already irrevocable, even though it is entirely indefensible. There is no way to make it go away or to redeem it. In fact, it is so much a condition of our world that we can no longer locate it exclusively in modern times. It is the stuff of myth, and operative at the origin of the species. Yet even mythologizing cannot redeem the "enframing" of the human. Significantly, it is the bad guys, the sinister secret society of Neo-Atlanteans, who cannot gain a free relation to technology. They wish to be gods. The Atlanteans may appear almost divine in their control over technologies, but the Neo-Atlanteans are not the new gods of whom Heidegger speaks. As in Miyazaki's worlds, in the world of *Nadia*, only children can save us now—children who rally around a girl, Nadia. Nadia is the new girl-god.

Unlike the idealized Sheeta in *Castle in the Sky*, however, Nadia becomes ever more petty and contrary in the course of the series. And her relation to technology is idiosyncratic to the point of contradiction. On the one hand, she poses as a nature girl: she loves animals, refuses to eat meat, disapproves of mechanical inventions, denounces ballistic technologies, and speaks against any form of violence. On the other hand, it turns out that she cannot live in nature, as a nature girl. She simply wants technology to give her what she demands, but without any negative impact on the natural world. This seems very far from Heidegger's ideas about gaining a free relation to technology. Indeed, because her love of nature entails a whimsical and inconsistent refusal of technologies, it looks like a variation on techno-scientific behavior. Recall that Heidegger and Miyazaki think of such behavior—both the acceptance and rejection of techno-scientific modernity—as self-defeating High Humanism, in which everything becomes measured and valued in terms of its impact on humans. Such a stance repeats and reinforces the logic of the standing reserve.

Still, even though Nadia's inconsistent behavior vis-à-vis technology is not exactly a free relation, it is not, for all that, merely technological behavior. Rather, in its maniacal, obsessive, and egotistic manner, it occupies a site where techno-scientific behavior betrays an excess that promises to tip it into a free or freer relation to technology—or vice versa. In effect, petty focal concerns, that is, self-stylizations that are personal to the point of obsession, make for a site where techno-scientific behavior coexists with a gathering and focusing of attention on technology to gain a free relation to modernity. This is not an illusion of free relation, any more than it is an illusion of techno-scientific behavior. The technological condition and salvation from it are paired face to face in a state of perpetual oscillation. It is in this respect that the world of *Nadia* is post-Heideggerian and post-Miyazakian. It might be dubbed a postmodern techno-logical condition, provided two things are kept in mind.

First, this postmodern condition does simply come after, break with, or overcome the modern. On the contrary, it is only as the modern technologi-cal condition, with its world picture and standing reserve, becomes ineluctable and irrevocable that such postmodern orientations emerge. Second, as a conse-quence of the enclosure of the modern condition, the postmodern condition is not a condition from which one can imagine salvation, even though, in Anno's animations, signs of spiritual and religious salvation become prevalent. Unlike the worlds of Heidegger or Miyazaki, such postmodern worlds do not imag-ine a macrostructural or macrohistorical outside or alternative (such as Nature, History, or myth). Simply put, you cannot be saved from the postmodern condi-tion, you can only diagnose it, and the diagnosis promises a temporary tipping of techno-scientific behavior into a localized free relation that may afford a micro-politics. As such, for all its large-scale modern gestures toward saving the world, *Nadia* offers not an alternative to the modern technological condition but a diag-nostics of the postmodern technological condition. It does not offer salvation but new ways of living. Subsequently I will discuss how the male otaku emerges as the tainted promise of a new lifestyle.

In light of its post-Heideggerian, post-Miyazakian, and generally postmodern trajectory, it is not surprising that *Nadia* continually folds the grand narrative back on itself, isolating its characters and dwelling on their petty focal concerns. A series of commentators on Japanese animation have noted a general move-ment away from grand narrative in anime, and in a manner reminiscent of Jean-François Lyotard's diagnosis of the postmodern in terms of the collapse of grand narratives, take anime as exemplifying postmodernity.[4] Ōtsuka Eiji, for instance, has called attention to the preference of anime consumers for organizing and consuming small narratives around an anime-related or manga-related commod-ity.[5] Azuma Hiroki builds on Ōtsuka's account, but instead of a shift from grand narrative to small narrative worlds, sees an initial transformation of grand narra-tives into grand fictions, followed by a complete break with narrative in organiz-ing consumption and communication around characters.[6] While I largely agree with these critics' sense of a movement away from grand narrative in anime, I do not see this shift in terms of generational breaks in patterns of consumption immediately registered in narrative structures. Nor do I see the relation between modern and postmodern in terms of a total rupture. Rather, in keeping with my emphasis on anime thinking technology, I tend to read such transformations in terms of technologies of the moving image and divergent series. As I will discuss in the Conclusion, these divergent series are precisely where economic concerns are brought to bear, precisely because there is a force to animation that invites disciplinization, or control, or both. This becomes evident if we pay attention to the mutation of grand narrative in light of the emergence of focal concerns, in the form of enclosed and enframed panoramas.

It is especially in the underwater sequences, where inside and outside become almost indiscernible because the ocean is an outside that encloses horizons, that the outward movement of epic adventure turns inward. Once the children and the Grandis Gang board the *Nautilus*, they are confined to fairly claustrophobic spaces, and the domestic squabbles and fantasies take precedence over the larger conflict "out there." Romantic concerns in particular come to the fore. Nemo separates Jean and Nadia, provoking awareness in them that they are of a certain age (episode 10). Grandis falls in love with Captain Nemo (from episode 9). New mysteries emerge, which promise to explain the larger action. After catching sight of Nadia's Blue Water, Nemo returns to his cabin without a word and opens a box to reveal his Blue Water, which is much larger, with a diamond-shaped indentation about the size of Nadia's jewel. Yet the action does not then open outward. Rather Gargoyle attacks again, and the feeling of entrapment inside the submarine increases. When Gargoyle drives the *Nautilus* into an undersea passage and blocks their exit with mines, Hanson and Sanson use the *Gratan* to clear the path (episode 10). Their demonstration of courage and loyalty results in the children and the Grandis Gang officially becoming new recruits on the *Nautilus* (episode 11). At the same time, the children struggle to understand the hard decisions and profound losses that are also part of this world of technological wonder. The children now truly inhabit this technological condition, whether they can accept it or not, and now it is the vehemence and inconsistency of their affective responses that promise fleeting depths of relation, personal fields of freer relation to the technological condition. This happens because there is not an "out there" into which they might escape, because the series relentlessly transforms the "out there" into an enclosure.

In the sequence in which the crew put ashore on an island to repair the *Nautilus* (where, to Nadia's distress, they kill animals for food), the island proves not only to be ringed by ocean but also by Gargoyle, the nemesis who personifies the technological condition. Moreover, the adventure ends with Nemo shooting point blank at a Neo-Atlantean about to fire on Nadia (episodes 12–13), which brings Nadia into an untenable relation to ballistic technologies, for she would have to prefer her own death to that of the enemy.

Underwater sequences further the sense of no outside: even when characters leave the submarine on various adventures, they are in the water, and this enhances the sense of being inside, if only inside the oceans. Many of the underwater adventures take place in tunnels, passages, or ocean trenches (in episode 14 in which Nemo and the boys seek medicine to cure Marie and Nadia), which reinforces the ocean as an enclosure. Of course, the overall trend of these submarine adventures is toward the discovery of marvelous underwater enclosures, the most notable being the ruins of the underwater city of Atlantis (episode 16). The sweeping views of the ancient metropolis—evidently destroyed in an event like nuclear holocaust—are astonishing not only for their scope and detail (and flat compositing of depth) but also for the fact that they are, for all their expansiveness, actually reached from the ocean, at the end of a long passage, hidden and removed from the world. In sum, even in the open air with vistas before us, we are still somehow inside. The panoramic experience happens within enclosures.

This combination of panorama and enclosure recalls Stephan Oettermann's study of the panorama in which he notes how the panorama, with its discovery of the actual horizon in the landscape, resulted in "a simultaneous liberation and new limitation of human vision."[7] Oetterman finds that the panoramic liberation of the eye "is also a complete prison for the eye," and the horizon comes to enclose the viewer. Put another way, he is attentive to how the apparently transcendent viewing position attributed to the Cartesian subject of geometric perspective transforms into an experience of imprisonment and enclosure, with a sense of the limited and fallible nature of the human body. Oetterman sees a sort of inversion of the panorama into the prison or panopticon.[8] This is akin to what Foucault sees as a historical shift from the classical transcendent subject and universal knowledge to the modern subject that is at once subjugated and subjectified through disciplinization—from panoramic liberation of the mind's eyes to panoptical imprisonment of the fallible body. It is interesting then that the operative perceptual logic of Nadia is that of enclosing of the panorama. Enclosure becomes the condition of possibility for access to panoramic knowledge. But this panoramic view is not truly universal knowledge. It is knowledge with a technological horizon, within a quasi-disciplinary regime.

It is entirely fitting then that the next episode (17) concerns otaku behavior and knowledge. The episode follows male crewmembers who organize a club devoted to an attractive young nurse on the Nautilus. This is a playful spoof of those men, young and not so young, who are reputedly too shy and unprepossessing to leave home and go "out there" into the world and date actual woman, who consequently remain fixated on a cute girl whom they idolize, producing images of her and knowledge about her. The result is an organization of knowledge production around the new god, a beautiful girl. This otaku episode is a beautifully apt follow-up to the enclosed panorama of Atlantis. Here, too, instead of a panoramic vantage and universal knowledge of the world guaranteed by God, there is an enclosed vantage and a knowledge whose horizon is delimited and guaranteed by a new little god, the idol. Despite the limitation of the horizon, however, the pursuit of truth within the otaku enclosure is as infinite and ambitious, as panoramic and encyclopedic as classical or Enlightenment knowledge.

In the otaku episode, in a lighthearted way, *Nadia* anticipates Okada Toshio's *Otaku no video*, with its darkly comic portraits of socially and legally marginal pursuits on the part of male otaku. But Anno's *Nadia* affords a very different angle on otaku. *Nadia* is, in effect, intent on "otakunizing" a classic tale of modernity, that is, otakunizing Miyazaki. As such, it enables us to perceive the connections between very modern structures of perception (panorama and panopticon) and allegedly postmodern otaku forms of knowledge and image production. In this respect, *Nadia* is unlike Okada (and subsequent otaku commentators like Murakami Takashi) who directly links postmodern otaku imaging with premodern or Edo practices, thus bypassing modernity and positing Japan outside and beyond it. In contrast, *Nadia* predicates the loss of an "out there" on the technological enclosure of the Cartesian subject. In a sense *Nadia* is a rewrite of the classic tale of the fall of God and the emergence of Man, in which God turns out to be space aliens, and Man turns into otaku guys. And the double bind of humanism, by which humans are at once the subject and object of knowledge and history, becomes the double bind of the otaku man, who is at once engineered and engineering.[9]

Jean eventually leaves the ship's fan club because he knows Nadia is his one and only. Nonetheless, the otaku episode casts its post-Enlightenment otaku light on Jean's pursuit of science and invention. Jean's immersion in science and technology is supposed to afford an absolute vantage on the world and a universal knowledge that will resolve all problems scientifically, but this is a post-Heideggerian world in which immersion in gadgets is already a basic technological condition—or enclosure, as it were. Jean's inventions tend to fail, but more significantly, his immersion in gadgets is merely another limited horizon, as if each invention was yet another in an endless series of technology-contingent, localized knowledge formations. It does not offer a more rational view or otherwise better vantage on world. It is one of many frames of reference. But now we see that different frames of reference, although relativized, are nonetheless productive of knowledge. In this respect, they are truly *fields*, whose potential depth and breadth comes in pursuit of the god, idol, icon, or the bullet, mecha, starship, or other invention, along a specific line of sight. Jean's inventions are all designed to please the new god, the girl Nadia. If universal knowledge is not possible, it is because the world is not out there; it is always in here, because it has been technologically pictured, enframed.

The episodes of the voyage to the South Pole in *Nadia* reinforce this feeling that the world has already been thoroughly pictured and enclosed. When the *Nautilus* arrives at the South Pole base, the new recruits naïvely dress to go out on the ice. It so happens, however, that the fantastical base sits beneath Antarctica (episode 18), and the team does not step out into the Antarctic cold but into another interior. There is an elevator leading to the surface, opening right onto the Pole. The elevator passes through translucent layers of ice in which are frozen on permanent display the bodies of extinct creatures, as in a museum of natural history. The layout of frozen creatures approximates an evolutionary history. This is an exploded view of the natural history of Earth. What might initially seem to be a linear and teleological progression of life forms proves to be a twisted record of fantastical deformations of terrestrial life. Life forms are arrayed in ice layers as if in an assembly diagram, as if to show how to put together natural history—and take it apart. In fact the exploded view of creatures remains as a record of how the Atlanteans have already disassembled and reassembled terrestrial existence. Life itself is a standing reserve of life elements to be unraveled and recombined like strands of DNA.

Such scenes encourage us to think of exploded projection as a structure that accommodates both (a) the soaring and liberating vantage of panoramic vision and (b) the imprisoning inversion of the panorama into the enclosure, park, or reserve. Where the material limit of the panorama is the horizon, the material limit of the enclosure is the human body. Exploded projection is a structure stretching between the "in here" of the body as horizon and the "out there" of the world as horizon. As such, it does not fix or stabilize the viewing position in the manner of the Cartesian subject. But it does not merely dispense with subjectivity either. I spoke previously of a subjectile—a projection along a line of sight that is neither fully subject nor entirely object. It is the structure of exploded projection that stabilizes the relation between panorama and enclosure, and the subjectile verges on a form of subjectivization that promises to be adequate to the exploded view. This is also how the backstory of Atlantean engineering of humans serves to fold the grand narrative of world salvation back on itself into petty focal concerns that take the form of lifestyles or personalized ways of living. In effect, everyone goes otaku.

As we have seen, personal concerns and domestic issues come to the fore from episode 9 when the children and the Grandis Gang board the *Nautilus*, pushing aside adventure narrative and large-scale conflicts. The little stories of characters frequently entail a radical inversion of expectations, which serves to diminish the scale of engagement, folding it into more egotistical concerns. Nadia, for instance, expresses her hatred of what she thinks Captain Nemo stands for: death over life, military duty over love, authority over cooperation, reason over feeling, and science over nature. Nemo turns out to be her father, however. He sacrifices his opportunity to destroy Gargoyle and save the world, in order to save the lives of Marie and Nadia. Nadia is thus left with a less grand set of ideas vis-à-vis Nemo. Romantic attachments also fold back on themselves. When Nadia explores her love for Jean, she finds him indifferent, and grows jealous of his attention to Electra. Grandis falls in love with Nemo, but Sanson loves Grandis. Hanson pines for Electra, while Electra loves Nemo. But it is especially after the spectacular confrontation in episodes 21 and 22 that *Nadia* fractures into even smaller stories.

The battle between the *Nautilus* and Gargoyle's Neo-Atlantean spaceship merits attention because the confrontation is a spectacular instance of the flattened ballistics discussed in chapter 11. Gargoyle tries to seize Nadia and crush the *Nautilus*. As magnetic fields strew debris, laser blasts energize surfaces, producing layers of military engagement in exploded views (Figure 30). The result is a distributive field in which multiple planes of ballistic movement are flattened into information fields. In narrative terms, too, there is exploded projection insofar as the confrontation brings all the characters together again, only to disperse them into smaller groups again: the children in one direction, the Grandis Gang in another, and the *Nautilis* in yet another, while the foiled Neo-Atlanteans go their way. In conjunction with these instances of exploded projection, it becomes more obvious that the behavior of characters follows suit. As the battle comes to a close, for instance, the first officer Electra turns on Nemo.

By this point in the series, we have learned that Nemo is responsible for mass murder: in the past, to stop a faction bent on total domination of Earth, he removed his Blue Water from their Tower of Babel just as his people prepared to launch a strike on the humans, and as a result, the Tower destroyed the city of Atlantis instead. He continues to track down this faction, the Neo-Atlanteans. Electra, whose family was wiped out in the explosion, blames the Neo-Atlanteans and follows Nemo to exact her revenge on them. In the course of the battle in episodes 21 and 22, she is outraged that Nemo chooses to save Nadia rather than destroy the Neo-Atlanteans; he is no longer the man intent on vengeance whom she loved, and to whom she has committed her life. Feeling doubly betrayed by Nemo, who cares more for Nadia than for Electra's vengence, Electra shoots Nemo.

As such rapid twists from large-scale military engagement to personal history demonstrate, the quasi-triumphant adventure story, in which the children

Figure 30. *Held in a magnetic field while under attack, the debris from the disintegrating* Nautilus *is arrayed in fields around the ship in this battle sequence from* Nadia. *This sense of an exploded projection of the ship is echoed in an exploded projection of the central characters, as they are scattered and gathered together again.*

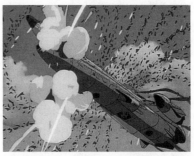

work with Nemo to save the world from Gargoyle and to free humanity, seems to promise but does not sustain a panoramic view in which we follow the adventure across obstacles to its successful conclusion. The series retains something of the teleological epic pattern but in the form of an exploded projection in which the grand narrative disperses into little stories whose character lines traverse the story world to form personalized fields. These character lines are not, however, different subjective points of view on the basic action. Nor do character lines function as side stories, minor inflections of the major theme. The characters' agonized choices, personal anxieties, questions, regrets, and impasses constitute affective or emotive fields whose movement produces potential depth. As we will see in the next chapter, this is where techniques of limited animation come into play, generating character types perfectly suited to this animated world built on superplanar relativity.

The flattened ballistics of the battles in episodes 21 and 22 is mirrored by an explosion of the whole narrative picture into a series of little events and focal concerns whose psychological depths do not produce subjective positions but affective loops and nodes. This tendency becomes pronounced in the island episodes (23–31) and Africa episodes (32–33).

Jean and Nadia wash ashore on a desert island with Marie and King. Jean sets to work building shelter and acquiring food, and more generally, singing the virtues of science, while Nadia proposes a return to nature. She refuses to eat any meat (even fish) and stalks off into the jungle. The life of nature, however, proves completely untenable, and in these episodes, Nadia appears at her most petulant and mercurial. Once she returns to Jean's camp, her moods continue to swing, but now from her reluctance to avow her feelings for Jean. At one point, even King is drawn into the affective loop: previously on the *Nautilus* Nadia grew jealous of King's preference for Marie, but on the island when Nadia kisses Jean, King is so heartbroken and angry that he runs away.

Subsequently, a "floating island" appears ashore, and the children find themselves reunited with the Grandis Gang and a character met aboard the American warship, Ayerton. What follows is a series of rivalries, romantic overtures, and misunderstandings: Hanson and Sanson bicker and fight like children, Ayerton woos Grandis, Nadia tries to win Jean's approval while Jean tries to win hers, but somehow everything misfires. In sum, these episodes deliberately do not depict humans struggling for survival. In fact, because they are on a floating island (which proves to be a camouflaged spaceship), they are not actually in the wild, in "Nature." And, despite their isolation and their complaints about privation, the characters do not experience any privation. On the contrary, this is a world of relative plenitude in which each character tries to construct her or his lifestyle, a sort of personalized nature-culture. To some extent, these self-stylizations echo the multiple frames of reference of the story and art design. And like those multiple frames of reference, these personalized modes do not congeal into viewing positions per se. Characters do not truly become subjects in the sense of a stabilized position whose depths derive from reflexive internalization of contradictions in their actions in the world. These characters bounce from symptom to symptom, complex to complex, their inconsistencies stretched so taut as to snap, as if only a little more pressure would push their maniacal behavior fully into madness. This is an exploded view of the rational bifurcating into the irrational, of reason unraveling into unreason. But the characters are never fully on the side of reason or of unreason. The trajectories of their actions and emotions constitute potential depths and affective fields. Each character thus verges on becoming an assembly diagram for a relative world.

Likewise, when the group leaves the floating island for Africa, a series of comic and trivial adventures occur. Nadia falls in love (while Jean frets), only to learn that her beloved is already promised in marriage. The scoundrel who married Grandis for her fortune makes an appearance, and the group must rescue King from him. Episode 34 resembles a collage of music videos: different characters sing songs accompanied by images drawn from the series thus far, in a sentimental look back over the emotional twists and turns of their adventures.

Across these episodes, one major plot twist occurs: the floating island turns out to be an Atlantean spaceship called Red Noah. Red Noah pulls Nadia into the control chamber and directs her to take command. But Nadia will not forsake her friends, and Red Noah lets her go. Gargoyle arrives at Red Noah just as Nadia and her friends depart in the *Gratan*, now a hot-air balloon, for Africa. The series concludes in episodes 35 through 39 with a final confrontation pitting Gargoyle and the Neo-Atlanteans against the children, the Grandis Gang, and the new *N-Nautilus* (now submarine and starship). Gargoyle captures Nadia and uses her Blue Water to reactivate Red Noah. The Grandis Gang manages to destroy the weapon that Red Noah is about to fire on the *N-Nautilus*, but Gargoyle captures Nemo, Electra, and Jean as they attempt to rescue Nadia. In the final sequences, Nadia sits on a throne alongside that of her brother, the Emperor Neo, both in a trance under the control of Gargoyle. Gargoyle commands Nadia and Neo to shoot Nemo, and as Nemo's blood flows, he asks Jean to shoot Neo and Nadia. Jean cannot bring himself to do it. Fortunately, however, the *N-Nautilus* manages to ram and destroy the control panel, releasing Neo and Nadia from their mind-control trance. Gargoyle, however, finds an opportunity to kill Jean.

In the concluding sequences, at the request of her father and with the encouragement of the women, Nadia uses the Blue Water to bring Jean back to life. She does this with the knowledge that the Blue Water will then lose all its power, and she thus cannot also save her father. The conclusion has all the elements of a clean resolution to family psychodrama. The daughter shifts her attention from the father to the future husband, literally giving up her jewel for the groom. The father steps aside for the husband. At the same time, Jean, who has lost his father, has gained an ideal spiritual father in Nemo. In sum, we have classic elements of the Oepidal complex in which the son must symbolically kill the father to become a man. *Nadia* also overtly evokes the Electra complex in which the daughter becomes libidinally attached to the father and imagines herself pregnant by him. In the end, the character Electra is actually pregnant with Nemo's child. In addition, Nemo's daughter figures—Nadia and Electra—both try to kill him in the course of the series. (It is Nadia and her brother who actually kill Nemo, albeit while in a trance.)

In sum, *Nadia* deliberately works into its character arcs a number of variations on classic psychological complexes, sometimes even referring to them by name. This gesture entails, once again, a multiplication of frames of reference. We have both the Oedipus complex and the Electra complex, and probably any number of other "normal" complexes that are alleged to underlie processes of sexual maturation. These different psychological trajectories are not integrated in a single complex or a unitary point of view. They are all relative movements of the soul or psyche, arrayed in such way that they can be taken apart, pieced together, recombined. This allows for an incessant twisting and perverting of small linear narratives (maturation scenarios). It is at once fitting and disturbing, then, that the series ends with little Marie, now grown, married to Sanson and pregnant with his child. The Victorian tone—the happy ending is a girl married to and pregnant by a mature man—rings flat in its pat and childish enthusiasm. The end also reaffirms the folding back of the grand narrative onto itself: world salvation culminates in a banal and slightly perverse relationship with echoes of the Electra and Lolita complexes, that of the little girl happily pregnant by a man old enough to be her father. Such gestures suggest a complete "otakunization" of the grand narrative of salvation from the modern technological condition.

In light of this otakunization, the island episodes are more important than they may initially appear. *Nadia* proved so popular with viewers that Gainax was instructed to produce additional episodes to stretch the series out, and the studio added the prolonged island episodes. For these episodes, the Gainax team wrote the basic story and farmed out the animation to other studios in Japan and Korea, which is still fairly common practice in animation production. Some fans complained (and still complain) that there is a drop in the quality of the animation in the island episodes, and the larger story almost disappears. What is more, Anno apparently became more and more distressed with his work on *Nadia* as the series progressed, especially because of the fan obsession with the girl heroine Nadia. It was also around this time that Miyazaki Tsutomu was arrested, and the media began to equate anime like *Nadia* with sexual pathologies and sociopathic behavior.

It is clear that *Nadia* marked a turning point for Anno in this respect, much as *Castle in the Sky* marked a turning point for Miyazaki. Interesting enough, the turning point for both directors occurred in the process of animating a certain kind of story about technology, in which weapons of mass destruction and global annihilation appear as the logical outcome of techno-scientific progress. What is more, both directors would come to see a boyish fascination with technology as a major part of the problem, and would associate this fascination with something like otaku activities. For Anno, the popularity of *Nadia*, its fans' intense erotic attachment to the character of Nadia, and the demand to stretch out the series were all surely crucial in his shift in attitude.

After *Nadia*, Anno fell into deep depression, refused to work for four years. He returned to animation with *Evangelion*, gradually fashioning that series into a critique of anime otaku. While a full account of *Evangelion* is not required here, it is important to note that *Evangelion* repeats and reworks most of the structures and questions that arise in *Nadia*. Particularly important is the involution of the grand narrative of world salvation into smaller focal concerns, again with human engineering as the mediator. *Evangelion* also shows a tendency to enclose panoramic views as part of the transformation of the viewing position into a subjectile line of perception. But clearly the construction of otaku worlds had begun to trouble Anno in the context of *Nadia*, and when *Evangelion* proved even more successful than *Nadia*, Anno had his opportunity. This time, instead of succumbing to the pressure to feed otaku fans what they wanted, he turned the series into an attack on them. As the series neared its conclusion, rather than offer a resolution to the battle to save the world from the unexplained invasion of Angels apparently bent on destroying humanity, Anno ended the series inside the head of its reluctant nonhero, Ikari Shinji, highlighting his insecurities and childish vacillation. Basically, instead of a conclusion, Anno offered his portrait of an otaku, confirming in interviews his dislike for the childishness of otaku behavior.

In fact, a recent interview suggests that Anno is now taking a tack reminiscent of Murakami Takashi, blaming the woes of Japan on its constitutive lack of adulthood.

> Japan lost the war to the Americans. Since that time, the education we received is not one that creates adults. Even for us, people in their 40s, and for the generation older than me, in their 50s and 60s, there's no reasonable model of what an adult should look like. . . . I don't see any adults here in Japan. The fact that you salarymen reading manga and pornography on the trains and being unafraid, unashamed, or anything, is something you wouldn't have seen 30 years ago, with people who grew up under a different system of government. They would have been far too embarrassed to open a book of cartoons or dirty pictures on a train. But that's what we have now in Japan. We are a country of children.[10]

Even though I feel it important to cite such statements, I also find them misleading, for they tend to shift attention away from many of the important questions about technology that are central to the animations associated with Anno. Attention falls instead on a moral and existential crisis in contemporary Japan, as if Anno's goal were to castigate people (or the current government) for its lack of discipline and responsibility.

Hints of such a moralizing stance crop up in both *Nadia* and *Evangelion*. The last episode of *Evangelion* in particular lingers on the existential crisis of its hero Ikari Shinji, as if to duck out of the questions about technology that the series effectively posed, and as if to make of Shinji's vacillation a moral failure. *Nadia* and *Evangelion* are not so different in this respect. Many commentators have noted the overlap between the two series, calling attention to the resemblance between Nadia and Ikari Shinji. If *Nadia* had ended at the moment where Nadia becomes paralyzed with insecurity and doubt, seeing herself as a nasty and petty person, unable to love or show her feelings, hardly qualified to save the world, then *Nadia* might well have been *Evangelion*.

Although it is possible to read these animations in terms of existential crisis or moral outrage, they are not particularly challenging in such terms. The interest of them lies in their articulation of such questions animetically, which inevitably

Figure 31. *Within the "frame" of Ikari Shinji's face in the last episode of* Evangelion, *the faces of other characters appear.*

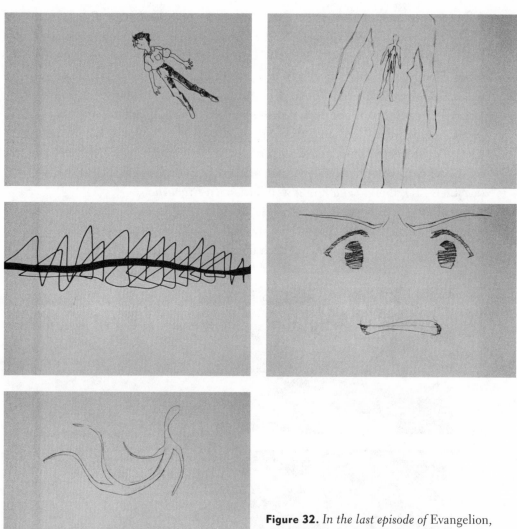

Figure 32. *In the last episode of* Evangelion, *Shinji's form gradually disperses into a variety of stances and then into modulating lines and shapes.*

brings questions about the modern technological condition into play. Simply put, because this is animation, even moral failure must be articulated animetically, which makes of it a question of technology. The last episode of *Evangelion*, for instance, in order to put us inside Ikari Shinji's thoughts and feelings, puts us inside animation. Existential crisis is technical crisis, and vice versa. The animation reminds us that this crisis is not just about a subjective point of view. Rather the animation gives us an exploded view of the psyche. Two procedures are especially important. First, for instance, a series of faces appear through the outline of Shinji's face, sometimes scarcely recognizable (Figure 31).

This makes Shinji's face by default the frame of reference, but it is a thoroughly relative frame of reference, serving largely to affirm how the flitting and sliding of flattened planes induces a sense of psychic movement. In conjunction with this flattened and dehierarchized image of the personalities inhabiting Shinji's soul, Anno uses either very rapid or very slow cuts from image to image, to the point that some viewers might think their television broken. Second, the Shinji frame of reference dissolves into long sequences of lines that unravel and recombine, as if the modulation of the outline of the character could no longer sustain his body, transforming into geometric shapes, contingent forms, and modulating lines (Figure 32).

If it is difficult to determine what such animation is telling us about the technological condition, about the enclosure of the world, the extinction of Nature, and the transformation of humans into a standing reserve, it is because Anno *optimizes* the very technicity in question, optimizing procedures of flat compositing, techniques of planar composition, and structures of exploded projection, as if seeking the material limit of the modern technological condition in the material limits of the distributive field. In the same way, he seems intent on unraveling otaku by pushing "otakunization" to the limit. This is also where techniques of limited animation, so important in Anno's works, function as something other than cheap or hasty approximations of full animation. Limited animation speaks to contemporary questions of technologies in ways unimaginable in full animation. As *Nadia* demonstrates with its relentless enclosure of the world, designed to produce inner natures that have no outside, limited animation becomes crucial in imagining how it is possible to live in a world in which the modern technological condition is both irrevocable and indefensible.

CHAPTER 15

FULL LIMITED ANIMATION

THE DISTINCTION between full animation and limited animation is central in the study of animation, and accounts of Japanese animation frequently characterize *anime* as a distinctive form of limited animation that began in earnest with the production of animated television series in the early 1960s.[1] The full/limited distinction is useful, yet certain problems arise. First, historically, there has been a tendency to think of full animation as *the* art of animation, and to depict limited animation as an *artistically* limited and even failed version of full animation. On the scene of Japanese animation today, Studio Ghibli in particular pushes such connotations, insisting that the works of its directors, such as Takahata Isao and Miyazaki Hayao, are not anime but *manga eiga* or manga films. The result is an entrenched *opposition* between feature-length full animation films (manga film) and animated television series (anime). Establishing an opposition between full and limited animation often has the unfortunate effect of eliminating the history of dialogue and exchange between different ways of making animation, in favor of a simple valorization of full animation.[2]

Second, at a more fundamental level, there is a tendency to think the distinction between full and limited animation in terms of *movement* versus *stasis*. Limited animation is not seen as a different way of animating, of generating movement, but as an absence of movement, a lack of animation, as a series of static images. Legendary animator Ōtsuka Yasuo captures this bias succinctly when he characterizes full animation in terms of *ugoki-e*—"dynamic image," "moving drawing," or "movement-image." In contrast, he suggests, limited animation entails *tome-e*—"static image," "stopped drawing," or "still-image."[3] This way of parsing animation carries the implication that, because limited animation does not strive to produce movement in the manner of full animation, it may not be animation at all. Limited animation might be closer to graphic design or manga than to animation (defined as full animation).

In some respects, it is true that the trajectory of limited animation has been to favor graphic design and character design over character animation.[4] Nonetheless, if we simply think of this tendency in terms of stasis versus movement, two problems arise. First, the distinction between movement-image and still-image tends toward a simplistic opposition and forecloses dialogue or interaction. Second, when limited animation is construed in terms of an absence of movement, a lack of animation, it becomes impossible to discuss the very evident dynamism of anime, not only the force of the moving image but also that which develops between "viewers" and so-called limited animations. There is surely a reason that the productive and generative activities of otaku are associated with limited animation.

If I put the term "viewers" in quotes here, it is because we have already seen, first in the discussion of Okada Toshio's otakuology and then in the context of Anno Hideaki's exploded view, anime often involves the construction of multiple lines of sight or perceptual trajectories. These do not entail a defined viewing position or a fixed subject who transcendently consumes anime objects or patronizes the anime world. Instead, we saw how anime techniques and structures imply an interactor whose pursuit of the potential depths that traverse the anime/manga/game world make of her or him a cooperator in the production and promotion of the expanded anime world. The pivotal role of the garage kit in Okada's apologia for otaku reinforces this sense of the fan as a producer, assembler, or fabricator, who engineers and navigates his or her path within the manga/anime/game world. Viewing anime frequently builds on or extends into fanzines, amateur production (dōjinshi), cosplay (costume play), conventions, fansubbing, toys, garage kits, and music venues. Anime thus becomes a nodal point in a culture industry that generates crossover, spin-off, or tie-in productions in the form of manga, light novels, character franchises, toys, music, video games, and other merchandise.

It is impossible to understand the dynamism of these anime networks if we continue to think of limited animation on the model of stasis or stillness. Thus, in this chapter, to counter the equation of limited animation with stasis, I will draw on Mori Takuya's 1966 discussion of full animation as "classic" in contrast to limited animation as "modern,"[5] in conjunction with Gilles Deleuze's distinction between "movement-image" and "time-image." I will propose that we understand limited animations (and thus varieties of anime) as modern, and in terms of the time-image. Full animation, in contrast, can be understood as classic, and in terms of the movement-image. Looking at anime from the angle of the time-image will allow us to see how the tendency toward producing "inner natures" characteristic of Anno's animations goes hand and hand with the tendency of character designs to move across media platforms. Here I wish to stress how the dynamism of anime interactions and anime-related networks is a matter of harnessing a specific potential of the moving image. Implicit in my approach is a challenge to the tendency to explain interactivity entirely by reference to media platforms or technologies that appear to be external to the moving image. Interactivity and the so-called "media mix" begin as a trajectory of the animated moving image.

Let me begin with Studio Ghibli's distinction between manga film and anime, which I will then pursue into the hyperlimited animation associated with director Anno Hideaki's work at Gainax Studios.

In 2004, in conjunction with an exhibition entitled *Nihon manga eiga no zenbō* (A complete view of Japanese manga films),[6] Studio Ghibli produced a documentary film on the work of Ōtsuka Yasuo called *Ōtsuka Yasuo no ugokasu yorokobi* (Ōtsuka Yasuo and the joy of making movement).[7] I have already discussed how Ghibli animation directors Takahata Isao and Miyazaki Hayao highlight the impact of Ōtsuka Yasuo on Japanese animation. Takahata and Miyazaki are adamant about situating their animated films in the lineage of *manga eiga* or manga film. For them, as both the exhibition and the documentary attest, Ōtsuka Yasuo is the pivotal figure.[8] Surprisingly enough, Studio Ghibli's "complete view of Japanese manga films" almost completely excludes those forms of Japanese animation that commonly fall under the rubric *anime*. Clearly, the goal of the exhibition and documentary is to shore up a lineage of Japanese animation (called manga film) that stands in contrast to anime.

Recall that, whereas histories of anime frequently begin with the emergence of animated television series in the early 1960s, taking as their point of departure Tezuka Osamu's adaptation of his manga *Tetsuwan Atomu* (*Mighty Atom* or *Astro Boy*) to the small screen, Studio Ghibli begins with the work of animators in the 1910s and 1920s in Japan and tracks the emergence of feature-length animated films for theatrical release. Central to this lineage is Tōei Dōga, an animation studio established at Tōei Studios in 1956 by its first president Ōgawa Hiroshi, who envisioned making animated films to rival those of Disney, with an eye to exporting Japanese culture to the world. Ōtsuka Yasuo emerged as one of the most important animators at Tōei Dōga, and both Takahata and Miyazaki worked with him there. The linchpin in this history of Japanese animation is a Tōei animated film called *Taiyō no ōji Horusu no daibōken* (Prince of the sun:

Hols's great adventure, 1968; released in English as *Little Norse Prince*), which combined the talents of Takahata as director, Miyazaki as key animator and scene designer, and Ōtsuka Yasuo as animation director.

This distinction between manga film and anime, with its tendency to elevate big screen animation over little screen, is built on a distinction between full animation and limited animation. Ōtsuka Yasuo sees Studio Ghibli as the only heritor of full animation in Japan today.[9] Even though Miyazaki, Takahata, and Ōtsuka collaborated on a number of television series (most famously *Lupin III*), the exhibition does not link such series to broader currents in Japanese animation (and thus to limited animation and anime). It situates them within the lineage of manga film and thus full animation. There is an overall tendency for television anime either to drop out of Ghibli's story of manga film or to reinforce a commitment to full animation under difficult circumstances.[10]

Full animation, as discussed in chapter 6, refers primarily to the number of drawings used to animate movement. The projection rate for film is 24 frames per second, but you can produce cinematically full animation with 12 drawings per second. This is called "on twos" because you use a drawing for two frames. Faster movements may require "on ones," or a drawing for each of the 24 frames per second. The Disney average was 18 drawings per second. The full animations of Tōei are generally described as "on twos."[11]

The story of limited animation in Japan usually begins with the formation of Mushi Pro by Tezuka Osamu in June 1961, to make animated series for television. As the story goes, Tezuka had long wanted to make animated films (and he also worked on a couple of Tōei Dōga productions), and the popularity of his manga gave him enough visibility and credibility to propose an animated adaptation of his popular manga *Tetsuwan Atomu*. To sell the project to Fuji Television, he presented such a low budget that no one really thought he could pull it off. He proposed to make thirty-minute programs at roughly one third the expected budget (at approximately ¥500,000 each).[12] The solution of his team was, simply put, to animate "on threes," to work with approximately eight drawings per second.

Full animation is frequently treated as *the* art of animation, while limited animation is seen as cheap and slapdash. Today we are accustomed to thinking of limited animation in terms of the production of the low-budget television animation that were popular in the 1960s—Hanna-Barbera series such as *Top Cat*, *Yogi Bear*, *The Flintstones*, and so on, as well as a number of Japanese animated series that made their way into syndication in North America and Europe, such as *Astro Boy*, *Tobor the Eighth Man*, *Kimba the White Lion*, *Speed Racer*. In an introduction to animation written in 1966, however, Mori Takuya reminds us that it was the former Disney animators who founded UPA (United Productions of America) who initially experimented with limited animation techniques.[13] They saw it as an art movement in animation that employed a simplified graphic mode of expression in contrast to the simulated naturalistic worlds of Disney Studios. Stylistically, the idea was to move away from elaborate detail in drawing, reducing images to graphic designs and iconic figures, while limiting the number of drawings per second. Because such techniques proved useful in cutting costs in production, major Hollywood cartoon studios gradually turned to limited animation in some guise or another. Animation, especially television animation, gradually abandoned its emphasis on painterly worlds and cinematically inspired movement.

The interest of Mori Takuya's account is that it tries to some extent to invert the valorization of full animation over limited animation: limited animation, not full animation, is the future of animation for him. He sees limited animation not merely as a cost-cutting measure (although he is aware of this potential) but as a modern art of animation in contrast to the classicism of full animation. In fact, Mori Takuya goes so far as to suggest that live action has become boring, and to speak of the fascination of line tests.[14] His account thus reminds us that limited animation is as artful and experimental as full animation, and, even more importantly, with limited animation, it is impossible to establish a divide between commercial and experimental fare. Formal distinctions between mass culture and avant-garde art have no purchase here. In fact, at the first screening held at Mushi Pro in 1962, Tezuka presented one of his new experimental animations *Aru machikado no monogatari* (Tale of a certain street corner, 1962) and an animated short *Osu* (Male, 1962) alongside the first episode of the *Astro Boy* television series.[15]

In sum, the distinction between full animation and limited animation is not explicable in terms of clear-cut formal distinctions between experimental art (avant garde) and studio production (mass culture). Nonetheless, it is precisely this kind of distinction that Studio Ghibli wishes to mobilize in its bid to separate its manga films from anime. Ghibli has been very successful promoting its animation as art animation and as national cinema, consistently striving to distinguish its works from the mass culture industry and transnational subcultures. Needless to say, this gesture dovetails nicely with Miyazaki's take on the modern technological condition: his effort to think a free relation to technology animetically tends to posit Nature as a universal frame of reference for a postapocalyptic return to a slower human-scaled world, which demands constant vigilance, protection, and conservation. He thus risks repeating the very enframing that he posits as the condition demanding salvation.

When one looks at the actual films in Ghibli's manga-film lineage, however, limited animation techniques are abundant. The jewel in the manga-film crown, *Prince of the Sun*, has extended sequences deploying techniques of limited animation. For instance, the first two attacks on the village are rendered with a montage of still images; in the midst of more fluidly animated sequences, rapid cuts from still to still showing violence enhances the sense of shock and violence. What is more, in a scene of Hilda in reverie, the camera pans slowly from the reflection of the landscape in a lake, up the image to show Hilda in the landscape, and then the camera moves on to show the landscape that was reflected in the lake at the start of the sequence. This is a beautiful, concise, and low-cost way of rendering a scene of reverie, by moving the viewing position rather than drawing the movement.

What is more, Takahata, Miyazaki, and Ōtsuka spent a significant number of years producing television animation, which obliged them to work closely with limited animation techniques. In fact, one of Mori Takuya's prime examples of limited animation is a 1963 television series, *Ookami shōnen Ken* (Ken the wolf boy), on which Miyazaki worked as an in-between animator and Takahata as a director. Interestingly enough, *Ookami shōnen Ken*, loosely based on Kipling's *The Jungle Book*, came as a response to the success of Mushi Pro's *Mighty Atom*.[16] In effect, Tōei's full animation was not leading but following, and as it entered into television animation, its full animation "on twos" (12 sheets per second) gave way to "on threes" (8 sheets per second).[17] It is, of course, possible to insist that, behind the scenes, Tōei animators and the future Ghibli team remained committed to full animation. Ghibli researcher Kanō Seiji, for instance, points to the steady increase in the number of sheets used in Miyazaki's television animations, and to an emphasis on full animation techniques.[18] But such a history forecloses dialogue and interaction, reducing them to a simple story about Miyazaki-Ghibli's resistance to an economic degradation of the true art of animation.

Miyazaki's animations have always been in dialogue with limited animation and cannot actually reject or overcome it. We have seen that two techniques are crucial to a sense of his animations as full rather than limited: the use of painterly backgrounds, which are in Miyazaki's films ever more painterly in recent years, and an emphasis on the dynamism of character movement. Interesting enough, because the defense of full animation depends so much on full animation of characters, those commentators who wish to praise the fullness of Miyazaki's animations tend to stress the movement of characters rather than the painterly backdrops. Ironically, however, Miyazaki's characters do not move all that much; their motion is rarely that of classic full animation. His character animation shows the impact of limited animation. This is where Ōtsuka Yasuo's techniques for producing a limited version of the dynamism of full animation come into play. We have seen in chapter 6 how Ōtsuka introduces a slight tilt into each successive image of the character to impart a sense of roughness and energy into animation. Thus, despite the limitations in drawings per frame, techniques of angling the image allows for a sense of fully animated dynamic characters. We might think of such techniques as *limited full animation*. Or, given the brand emphasis of Ghibli, we might think of this as "full animation, ltd."

A contradiction emerges with the full animation of characters, however. In effect, full animation of characters works to mask the animetic interval that becomes palpable with the multiplanar image. As such, it lessens a sensation of the world in motion, of a dynamic natural world, displacing that energy onto characters. Nature thus risks appearing as a lush backdrop for action, as a standing reserve, at the very moment when its dynamism is supposed to provide the universal frame of reference to ground our movement beyond the modern technological condition. Angling characters helps to impart a sense of characters dynamically orientated earthward, and yet the reliance on painterly backgrounds tends to reify Nature rather than continue the experiment with dynamism, with the force of the moving image. As such, painterly landscapes run the risk of becoming the ultimate *tome-e* or stills. I tend to think that this is why the Ghibli team is adamant about rejecting limited animation, about presenting it as stasis: such a gesture allows them to disavow their own moments of reification. But are they not selling a relation to Nature in precisely the way that limited animation, with its emphasis on character design, sells a relation to character?

The Ghibli bias against limited animation takes an unusual turn in one of the final sequences of the Ōtsuka Yasuo documentary in which character designer and manga artist Sadamoto Yoshiyuki makes an appearance. One of the original team who founded Gainax Studios, Sadamoto Yoshiyuki lent his talents to major Gainax productions from *Wings of Honneamise*, through *Gunbuster* and *Nadia*, to *Evangelion* and *FLCL*, and his collaborations with director Anno Hideaki on such television series as *Nadia* and *Evangelion* have especially contributed to his fame. Needless to say, Gainax Studios and Anno's animated series, famous for taking limited animation to an extreme, might be considered the antithesis of the Ghibli manga film. In the Ghibli documentary, with a tone of surprise and concern, Ōtsuka asks Sadamoto about his shift from animation to character design. Sadamoto diplomatically replies that such is the work that has come his way. Brief as it is, this exchange evokes an important tension. For Ōtsuka, character design is not animation; *the* art of animation is the *ugoki-e* or movement-image.

Yet, if we approach this tension between the movement-image (full animation or manga film) and the still-image (limited animation or anime) without the assumption that limited animation is an absence of movement and thus a lack of animation, we can understand anime as generating movement in a very different way, one whose dynamism opens the image in very different directions.

In limited animation, for instance, there is a tendency for the viewing position of the "camera" to slide over the image (even if this is produced by sliding the image instead of moving the camera), and its speed and direction impart a sense of movement. This is different from the sense of a viewing position imparted through Cartesian perspectivalism. It is closer to an art of describing, unfolding, or scanning the world.[19] In addition, in limited animation, cutting from image to image increases in importance, as do the rhythm and speed of cuts. Cutting between static drawings tends to work well with scenes of characters talking (a variation on shot with reverse shot), and voice-overs (exchanges of dialogue and monologues) become more important in introducing a sense of continuity across cuts. There are also the sliding planes of the image: Tsugata Nobuyuki calls this technique *hiki seru* or "pulling cels."[20]

Yet, in contrast to accounts of animation that provide lists of formal features associated with full animation or limited animation, I have adopted something of the stance of experimental science and technology studies, giving priority to the force of the moving image in understanding animation. This has led me to stress the importance of multiplanar animetic machine, and of the animetic interval. Giving ontological priority to movement has led to an emphasis on compositing or "editing within the image" over character action. In effect, compositing is analogous to camera mobility in cinema, and character action is analogous to montage. This is not to say that camera movement and montage in animation have no importance. Rather, with reference to the force of the moving image, I see a priority of (a) compositing over character animation, and of (b) compositing and character animation over camera movement and montage. It is in compositing first and foremost that the force of the moving image (animetic interval) is harnessed and directed within animation, and character animation is always done with a sense of the multiplanarity of the animated moving image.

This is why I began my account of limited animation with an emphasis on flat compositing rather than limited character movement. Such an approach has the advantage of not positing a divide between full animation and limited animation on the basis of movement versus stasis. From the angle of compositing, we see that limited animation tends toward iconic or schematic expression across the planes of the image, which leads to a flattening of multiplanar depth, bringing the animetic interval to the surface of the image. Even when there are gestures toward depth such as darkening the background layers or sketching perspective lines (gestures common in limited animation), these remain schematic or iconic depths, close to the surface. In sum, in limited animation, movement does not merely stop or disappear. Instead, it comes to the surface of the image, as potentiality. And so, rather than insist that the characters of limited animation do not move, we need to look at how they harness and direct the force of the moving image that compositing has transformed into potentiality on the surface of the image, in a distributive field.

When it comes to animating characters, it is true that limited animation tends to move as little of the figure as possible and to reuse as much of the figure as possible. With faces, for instance, the eyebrows, eyes, or the mouth may move but nothing else; and drawings of the face seen from a couple different angles are used again and again. Likewise with the animation of bodies, the legs and arms may move, but nothing else. Limited animation tends toward the production a series of cel copies of the same body or face, and minor additions are made to them as you use them. The best way to assure maximum reuse of figures and bits of figures is to develop a cel bank, so you can piece together different scenes and different movements by assembling elements already drawn.[21] The cel bank prepares the way for a relation to characters based on assembly—it forms the basis for the overlap between animation and garage kits and models (self-assembled characters) as well as an overlap between cel animation and the customizable characters of many videos games. It goes hand in hand with the sense of a transformation of humans and other life forms into a standing reserve or human park, as in exemplified in *Nadia* and *Evangelion*. The cel bank provides the assembly diagrams for taking apart and piecing together animated life forms. The character form becomes, in effect, a site and mode of technological enframing.

A commonly cited precedent or source for limited animation is *kamishibai* or "paper theater," which consists of drawings on paper board that are loaded into a wooden frame, often conveniently mounted on bicycles to allow the narrator to take his story on the road.[22] Using these images, the narrator would recount a story or joke, sliding the upper image out of the frame at various speeds to reveal the image below, building from image to image toward the denouement or punch line. Tezuka's *Atom* was commonly referred to as "electric kamishibai."[23] Frequently, the idea of kamishibai sources also encourages commentators to ignore the force of the moving image in limited animation, resulting in an emphasis on stasis and apparently native traditions of storytelling. Kamishibai, however, also has a profound relation to technologies of the moving image. Not only did paper theater serialize stories that sometimes reprised or evoked film scenarios and later television stories, but also the narrators were frequently silent film narrators (benshi or katsuben) who had lost work with the advent of talkies, and not surprisingly their image sequences recall those of silent films.[24] Clearly, this cardboard theater, with its sliding drawings and live narration, had a profound impact on limited animation, leading to an emphasis on moving the drawings and on supplying voice-over narration or explanations. Nonetheless, even if we locate the sources of sliding planes and moving the drawings in the sliding paperboard panels of kamishibai, those kamishibai techniques, already profoundly related to technologies of the moving image, occur under conditions of movement in limited animation, wherein the flattened compositing of celluloid layers pushes depth and movement to the surface of the image in specific ways. Thus when Anno Hideki's hyperlimited animation is characterized as hyper-kamishibai, this should not be an invitation to avoid questions about the moving image, but to consider how the force of the moving image is specifically channeled and orientated in Anno's animations.[25]

In conjunction with very limited character movement, Anno Hideaki's animation is famous (or notorious) for taking limited animation to an extreme. His animations frequently use techniques of "pulling cels" or "sliding planes," thus producing a sense of movement by sliding the layers of the image, as in the example from the first episode of *Nadia* presented in chapter 13. Let me look at some other examples, these from Episode 13 of *Nadia*, which verge on hyperlimited animation. The little girl Marie and a pet lion cub King, wandering into the interior of the desert island on which the *Nautilus* has put ashore for repairs and food, discover a network of railroad tracks. As they walk happily down the tracks, we see their movement laterally (Figure 33). Pulling the foreground layer of grass backward creates the sense that the characters are moving forward. The background layer of clouds moves backward too, but only slightly. Yet the little girl's layer does not move, and for the most part, her body does not move. Every couple of frames, however, her arms and legs are put in different positions, and the result is a sense of her walking. Such character animation is exceedingly limited or hyperlimited not only because it uses so few drawings per frame but also because it slides the layers of the image to move the character.

The result is a perfectly serviceable rendition of walking, which is fundamentally different from Ōtsuka's limited full animation in terms of its sense of dynamism. Some of the sequences of walking feel too long, and we become keenly aware of repetition. The sense of repetition suits the sequence in question: the girl and cub walk on and on, eventually losing all sense of direction. The episode as a whole is a brilliant illustration of action based on limited animation: the characters repeat their steps, going in circles. When their enemies'

Figure 33. *In this sequence from* Nadia *of the girl Marie and the lion cub King walking along railroad tracks, we see how hyperlimited character animation places renewed emphasis on the sliding of layers to produce a sense of movement.*

robot discovers them and chases them, their leaps and bounds repeat again and again. Hyperlimited animation results in rhythms that are as exhilarating and hilarious as anything in full animation, precisely because we become aware of skips and jumps internal to character movement. These become a source of surprise. In conjunction with the expectations that come with literal repetition, the inherent yet almost subliminal jerkiness of character movement makes for a world of action in which you cannot be sure what will happen next, or where it will come from.

I previously mentioned a sort of anime rhetoric, certainly familiar to those who have seen some of the mecha or space opera series that were a source of inspiration for Daicon and Gainax animations (*Galaxy Express 999, Yamato, Macross*), or even to those who know *Pokémon*: figures pop abruptly on and off the screen, or heads poke into a scene, or screens suddenly split into two, three, four, or more planes. Usually the planes are articulated diagonally to emphasize a field of multiple actions, and there occurs angular slipping of planes of actions with sudden and sometimes incongruous apparitions—as when the giant robot chases Marie, King, and Sanson (Figure 34).

Here the animetic interval implicit in the sliding planes is embodied in the character. But the invisible interval between planes (the force of the moving image) is not channeled into dynamic character movement as in classic full

Figure 34. *In these two sequences from episode 13 of* Nadia *in which a giant robot with red pincers chases Marie, King, and Sanson, we see how the repetition of character movements implicit in the cel bank, in combination with the repetition of backgrounds, allows characters and other entities to jump from field to field, giving precedence to rhythms of appearance and disappearance over continuity in movement.*

animation. Instead, the gap between planes comes to the surface of the image, which makes for the image composed of multiple fields. Now characters do not simply move gracefully across the image; they can literally jump into and out of the image along angular trajectories that follow one or more of multiple fields of action crisscrossing the image. The animetic interval directs the force of the moving image in a manner that allows for leaps from field to field. At the same time, the character is at once unframed (the flattening of the relation between foreground and background makes the figure take priority over background) and enframed (a cel bank–like assembly of passions and actions available for technical manipulation). This makes for a character whose integrity does not depend on the unity of space of an image, which makes it available for disassembly and reassembly across images.

Another striking feature of Anno Hideaki's hyperlimited animations is the rhythm of cuts. Anno often tends to cut from simplified image to simplified image—from a static face, for instance, to a printed word; or, as happens in *Nadia*, as a character speaks of something, an image of it flashes on the screen. Anno plays with the relation between images by making the cuts feel too slow or too fast.[26] This procedure reaches dizzying proportions in the last episode of the *Neon Genesis Evangelion* television series. At times you suspect that either your TV or your disk is not working properly, that something is catching or skipping. Images remain still far too long, and sometimes the cuts are far too rapid. Obviously, however, such stillness and the effect of surprise that it produces happen within a field of movement. Animation has not broken with the moving image. Rather such rhythms of editing come from an explosion of the animetic interval across images, analogous to the jerky looping movements of limited animation characters. It is as if the stacked cels, the multiple planes that compose the anime image had been spread flat across the sequence of images. One might think of this sort of editing as "superplanar editing," for it follows directly from the flattening of planes that forces movement to the image surface.

In sum, Anno Hideaki's animations place dramatic limits on character action and continuity editing, yet these limitations imply a confrontation with the moving image. It is not a matter of stasis in opposition to movement. Hyperlimited animation entails a very different way of dealing with the animetic interval, a distinctive relation to the multiplanar machine. Needless to say, because it has its specific way of channeling the force of the moving image, hyperlimited animation also implies a specific manner of thinking the question of technological condition. This is where the distinction between movement-image and time-image proposed by Gilles Deleuze in his two-volume *Cinema* proves useful, for it does not arrest thinking at the level of stasis versus movement but forces an encounter with the material essence of the moving image as harnessed and orientated in cinema.

Across two volumes, Deleuze presents what initially appears to be a historical divide between the movement-image and time-image. His discussion of the movement-image largely deals with films and directors before World War II, and the time-image emerges in postwar Italian neorealism and French new wave cinema. He associates the movement-image with classic cinema, and the time-image with modern cinema. In his analysis of cinema, Deleuze thinks in terms of orientations (prehensions of time and space) that are prior to narrative. He sees in classic cinema the emergence of a "sensorimotor schema" that coordinates our sensory and motor faculties, laying down patterns of interconnection between our senses and movements, and shaping a commonsense world.[27]

What Deleuze calls classic cinema is not unlike what other film scholars call the classical style—which entails an emphasis on cause-and-effect, goal-orientated movement through a subordination of time to space.[28] Simply put, cinema develops a set of conventions to impart a sense that movements clearly begin and end somewhere, and we can trace their course coherently. This often translates into narratives in which protagonists pursue and attain a goal. Unlike commentators who associate such conventions almost entirely with Hollywood and speak of a classical Hollywood style that becomes the international standard, Deleuze offers a variety of movement-images (and non-Hollywood cinemas). *The* movement-image (classic cinema) actually comprises different ways of coordinating a variety of movement-images (perception-image, affection-image, action-image, impulse-image, and others).[29] Likewise, within classic cinema are different national cinemas (and within these, different directors and schools). Nonetheless, among varieties of movement-image coordinated within classic cinema, the action-image is the one that tended to shape the conventions for cause-and-effect, goal-oriented action that came to dominate classic cinema. It is a crisis in this specific kind of movement-image (the action-image), within the overall coordination of cinema called classic cinema, which spurs the emergence of the time-image.

Because Deleuze sees this crisis most clearly in Italian neorealism and French new wave cinema, many commentators read this cinematic transformation in terms of a historical rupture. In my opinion, the interest of Deleuze's study lies in its emphasis on the ontological force of the moving image rather than its film history. Thus I read Deleuze from the angle of Gilbert Simondon's philosophy of technology (with its emphasis on the force entailed in the "individuation" of technical objects), which is the source of my general emphasis on the force implicit in technologies of the moving image. For Deleuze, it is the emergence of the time-image that shows the force of the moving image pushing beyond its initial schematization in classical cinemas. The time-image, then, does not break with the movement-image, because the time-image is incipient in the movement-image. The time-image is inherent to cinema, to the moving image. Thus Deleuze asks, "can the crisis of the action-image be presented as something new? Was this not the constant state of cinema?"[30] The time-image is a transformation or mutation in the movement-image that brings forth a force inherent to or incipient in the moving image.

Deleuze's way of linking the *classic* movement-image and the *modern* time-image recalls some distinctions that have thus far been central in this study of animation. First I challenged the idea that the Cartesian subject associated with geometric perspective, panoramic vision, rationalism and universalism is *the* modern subject. Instead, following Foucault, Crary, and Kittler, I presented the Cartesian as a classic subject or the classical modern subject. Second I stressed Miyazaki's work on animated adaptations of classic children's literature, which is part of a general tendency to ground a critique of the modern technological condition in a classical or premodern worldview. Of course Miyazaki does not embrace classicism or Cartesianism, or propose a return to the early modern or to rationalism. Rather he wishes to sustain, however tentatively, some stable frame of reference to impart a sense that something new can coalesce beyond the modern technological condition—minimized Cartesianism or hypo-Cartesiansism, as it were. Finally, in the discussion of superflat theory in particular, I suggested that the superflat distinction between modern and postmodern frequently repeats the Foucauldian distinction between the classical (Cartesianism and Enlightenment thought) and the modern (disciplinary compensation for the breakdown of universal knowledge). My aim is not to reify these classic/modern distinctions. On the contrary, my aim is to avoid positing a divide or rupture between different formations of modernity.[31] Thus, while I think it justified to think of superflat or otaku or hyperlimited animation as postmodern, it is on the condition that we think of the postmodern not as something after or beyond the modern but as a moment when formations of modernity appear at once intractable and irredeemable as well as a site where forces incipient in the modern emerge again.

Deleuze makes an analogous gesture in his thinking of the relation between the classic movement-image and the modern time-image. His use of taxonomy and natural history invites us to read this transformation in terms of (creative) evolution, or more precisely, individuation. In effect, the movement-image is the body of cinema, and the time-image is the soul and brain of cinema. With the emergence of the time-image, cinema is learning to think. Or more precisely, just as we see in the record of evolution a trend toward encephalization (the development of centralized nervous systems and the brain), so the creative evolution of cinema is toward increased encephalization. Deleuze reinforces the point, writing that the brain is a screen.[32]

With the crisis in the action-image and the emergence of a modern cinema that coordinates various kinds of time-image, Deleuze sees a tendency toward protagonists who are confused about which way to go or unable to act effectively, and toward stories in which orientation gives way to disorientation, and action gives way to reflection, recollection, memory, and other emotional and affective tendencies. The break between modern cinema and classic cinema, then, is not a total rupture. The (cinema) brain cannot go on without the (cinema) body, so to speak. Yet the emergence of so much feeling and thinking make for a different relation to the body, to action. Put another way, the time-image is the nonrelation at the heart of all cinematic relations and relationality, which opens them to thought.

When Mori Takuya presents full animation as classic and limited animation as modern, he invites us to think in similar terms. In his account, limited animation is not only the product of a historical and economic crisis. Limited animation was, in fact, an art movement first and a response to economic concerns second. It was a creative transformation. At the heart of animation's creative and economic crisis was a breakdown in both the desire and the money to produce fully animated character movement. But, as with Deleuze's account of the crisis in cinema, this crisis in animation is not a total rupture with animation. Limited animation entails an individuation of the force of the moving image as embodied in classic full animation, which individuation opens the potential of the animated image into new possibilities. It is an individuation in which the animetic interval, which is but a by-product, artifact, or accident in one formation, becomes operative in transformation.[33]

We have seen how human evolution and "Nature" are subject to engineering in Nadia, making of the human a standing reserve or human park. We have seen how the panoramic viewing position of the Cartesian subject is relentlessly enclosed, and how the grand narrative of world salvation folded over on itself, to be refolded into minor focal concerns. This is also where the action-image enters into crisis; heroes or protagonists emerge who are less and less sure about their goals. Inaction and disorientation undermine goal-oriented action, to the point that we are not sure where this is going and what a good resolution would be. This is precisely where the famous (or infamous) episode 26 of Evangelion takes limited animation: the action-image opens up from within, exploding into anxiety, uncertainty, disorientation, and also reverie, recollection, love, and confidence.

But for this to happen you must first lose all sense of where this character is going, and even of where this series is going. The action-image is not only stretched out; it becomes populated with affective responses, mood swings, and emotional values. We are then shocked into thought and remembrance.[34]

In Anno's animations, the emergence of the time-image is thus associated with the optimization of the modern technological condition. It appears at the moment when Nature is thoroughly enclosed, the lifeworld is enframed, life-forms are engineered, and humanity becomes a human park, a standing reserve of genetic elements (which echoes the cel bank of limited animation). In Anno, limited animation allows for an optimization of the animetic machine, which provides the impetus for thinking the optimization of the modern technological condition. Simply put, hyperlimited animation implies technical optimization. Flattening and dehierarchizing the planes of the image brings the animetic interval to the surface, where it is optimized in the limited animation of characters, which makes for characters whose inaction is not merely stasis. Their operative and optimized inaction affords a time-image.

It would be impossible, of course, to produce a pure time-image. It would be like trying to produce a brain or soul without a body. The production of an autonomous time-image nonetheless remains one of the dreams of animation—a brain or soul or consciousness that is somehow free of the body or flesh, and there is a long line of efforts to think in animation the disembodied mind—a ghost that can move from shell to shell; or a robot or computer that develops a heart, mind, or soul; or a mecha or giant robot that somehow communicates with its pilot via empathy, via psionic connection or some other kind of quasi-spiritual bond. If animation frets a great deal about the connection between the body and the soul, it is because the centrality of compositing—and this is where cel animation and digital animation continue to overlap and intersect—forces a confrontation with the animetic interval in the bodies of characters.[35] Full or classic animation tends to manage the animetic interval through "closed" compositing and through the production of action-images that serve to mask the gap that cannot be entirely closed. In response to intimations of a crisis of the action-image or hints of character breakdown, the tendency of classic full animation is to step on the gas, or to pour on the sentiment. In other words, the tendency is toward a cinematism that feels okay in the end, even if it entails a disturbing hypercinematic instrumentalization of the lifeworld. Hyper–full animation will push toward total war that ultimately works out, for sentimental reasons as much as for justice.

If limited animation feels the crisis in the action-image and takes it more seriously than does full animation, it is partly because techniques of flattening and of schematization are less willing and able to mask the appearance of the animetic interval. The crisis of the action-image is a spreading of the animetic interval across the surface of the image, where it transforms the dynamics of character animation, making for inaction or inoperative action, or a crisis of body and soul, or both. This crisis in action does not simply result in inertia or stasis, however. Instead of fluidly cinematic movement across the screen or within a world, limited animation allows bodies to leap from field to field, from image to image, and even from medium to medium. In this respect, the time-image also entails some manner of capture of the animetic interval or force of the moving image. It has its instrumentality. Yet this tendency in animation toward the time-image is less prone to disavow the force of technologies. It is prone to a prophetic annunciation and revelation of the material limits inherent in the animated moving image. In sum, in limited animation, the crisis of the action-image does not necessarily result in the emergence of a pure time-image, that is, pure mind or pure soul. Yet it may tend to linger obsessively on questions about disembodiment and spiritual immortality, gravitating toward them but in the form of an ideal that has become a technical problem.

Limited animation tends toward the production of "soulful bodies," that is, bodies where spiritual, emotional, or psychological qualities appear inscribed on the surface. Limited animation encourages the leaping of bodies into and out of images, but only certain kinds of bodies are effective leapers. This is where character design becomes all important, taking precedence over character animation, which returns us to the difference between Ōtsuka Yasuo and Sadamoto Yoshiyuki, and to the contrast between Ghilbi's commitment to full character animation (however limited) and Gainax's emphasis on character design and otaku-related character products. This is also where the emergence of the time-image in limited animation differs from the conditions that Deleuze sees in cinema.

For Deleuze, writing on cinema in the early 1980s before the widespread use of VCRs and large-scale distribution of films on video, it was easier to sustain a distinction, however tentative, between the time-image and the cliché. It was easier to imagine the "beyond movement" of the time-image in terms of a movement beyond clichés. He closes the first volume of *Cinema* with these remarks about the conditions for the postwar mutation of cinema:

> On the one hand, it would require and presuppose a putting into crisis of the action-image, the perception-image, and the affection-image, even if this entailed the discovery of "clichés" everywhere. But, on the other hand, this crisis would be worthless by itself, it would only be the negative condition of the upsurge of the new thinking image, even if it was necessary to look for it beyond movement.[36]

Similarly, when limited animation put full classic animation into crisis, it discovered clichés everywhere—stock situations, generic locations, dependable gags, iconic characters. This is a kind of negative condition for the appearance of a new thinking image, manifested in characters whose heroics are empty, whose feelings undermine the resoluteness of their actions, and whose loves and wars gradually intertwine into rivalries that are at once cosmological in scale and petty in tenor, precisely the sort of action that *Evangelion* takes to the limit in optimizing limited animation into hyperlimited animation. Yet, as the emphasis on the VCR in discussions of otaku attests, this "beyond movement" of the animated time-image, this emergence of a new thinking image, is also linked to the upsurge of a new business model, a new corporate entity, a condition that is better captured in Deleuze's later remarks (in 1990) about the soul of corporations: "We're told that businesses have souls, which is surely the most terrifying news in the world."[37]

The male otaku lineage of anime similarly reminds us that clichés, too, may today have souls. As limited animation produces the crisis of the coordinating action-image of classic animation, the resulting emphasis on character design generates soulful bodies, bodies designed to embody the potentiality of the moving image and thus to make the leap from field to field. These are time-images that stick very close to the negative conditions for their production. Thus they show an affinity for the new soulful corporation (such as Gainax) that incorporates the hearts and souls of fans into its productions.

A number of factors affected the use of character design within limited animation in Japan. For instance, Tezuka's adaptation of his manga set a precedent not only at the level of studio structure and technical skills but also in terms of an emphasis on producing anime based on manga.[38] Even subsequently when studios had larger budgets, animation teams tended to adhere to the precedents for limited animation set up in the 1960s, which had begun with *Astro Boy*, continued into *Eight Man*, *Gigantor*, and into additional series based on Tezuka's manga, and finally resulted in *Mazinger* Z. Although anime based on toys or designed to promote toys and other anime-related commodities became more prominent in the early 1980s (*Macross* is frequently cited as the turning point), *Astro Boy* already succeeded in stretching its loveable little robot character across a variety of commodities, spawning toys and populating ads.[39]

Limited animation lends itself to this movement of the character from manga to television screen to toy store (and subsequently limited animation would become as central as manga to multimedia production), precisely because the crisis of the action-image tends to produce a character detachable from one field of actions, which can be inserted into other fields. We have already seen how, in the Daicon animations and in Anno's Gainax animations, the flattening of the multiplanar image produces an image traversed with planar energies, generating multiple fields of action with characters popping on and off the screen, which exploded projection managed tentatively to capture in a structure that dispersed viewing positions while integrating them into lines of sight. In *Nadia* and in *Evangelion*, the dispersion of viewing position was accompanied by its technological enclosure, which tended to integrate the lines of sight across the anime world into otaku-like affective fields associated with characters. In effect, Anno's hyperlimited animation responds to the crisis in "full" sensorimotor integration (the action-image) by optimizing the crisis. The result is an exploded projection of the character, and the character appears as a do-it-yourself kit, as an assembly diagram for taking bodies and souls apart and piecing them together again. As such, the character is free not only to leap in and out of the animated field of action. It is also free to leap across media fields. It can disassemble and reassemble from one media platform to another.

By optimizing the crisis of the action-image (already inherent in its Miyazaki sources), *Nadia* shows us how flat compositing can generate "inactive" characters, at once unframed and enframed, which are then available for reassembly and reanimation across multiple media. Operating on characters across media becomes not only possible but also desirable, especially from the vantage of the corporate soul. It is as if all the depth brought to the surface became condensed into one soulful figure, allowing it to flash from media to media, convulsively. Optimizing limited character animation heightens this potential, not only spurring official products or authorized spin-offs and tie-ins, but also inciting fans to rework the stories and characters, to adopt their dress and manner, and to work with garage kits. There is even a new relation to voice acting, in which vocal qualities and verbal explanations stand in for action, and voice actresses in particular become stars in their own right in the anime world. Above all, however, it is character design that plays a pivotal role, for there must be a diagram for the character that is expressive of both its potential as an action-image and as a time-image.

In keeping with the crisis in the action-image, it is the time-image—that is, a coordination of time-images—that must appear on the surface in character design. The movement of the soul or brain or psyche—feeling, thinking, discerning—is written on the surface of the character. This is how character design in limited animation captures and directs the force of the moving image surfacing as potentiality. You then see in the character not only a potential movement of the limbs but also a potential movement of the heart and mind. Character design thus begins to stress affective expression or emotion in a state of physical inaction. Character design becomes a coordination of varieties of time-image, and its rhythms are at once erratic and predictable; it pops up everywhere on almost anything, which is pretty much what you expect it to do. But then, if the character works well, it does not always pop up how or when you expect it.

With his post-Disney-esque obsession with cuteness, Tezuka seemed to anticipate this tendency with Astro Boy, with his expansive eyes, his hair coiffed like horns or bunny ears, and his frail yet mighty limbs. Subsequently, in such series as *Galaxy Express 999*, *Yamato*, and *Sailor Moon*, characters began to take on new density, with quasi-modeling effects in etching that imparted a sense of autonomy and agency, even though the characters moved very little. This made the character appear to operate on a plane independent of the background world at the same time that the inaction of the character, in conjunction with the echoes of its lines in schematized backgrounds and its positioning to emphasize negative space, thoroughly flattened and dehierarchized the multiplanar image. As Okada Toshio stresses with his examples from *Getter Robot*, this is also when anime viewers began to detect how different animators rendered the character differently. This is how the anime character begins to operate in different avatars and renditions, preparing for its leap across media.

Needless to say, the history of limited animation in Japan presents such a rich array of character designs that I can only scratch the surface here. Suffice it to say, as limited animation deemphasized full animation of characters, it increasingly stressed character design, and the degree of detail and the density of information became as important as line, implied depth, and implied mass. Character design became so crucial to this kind of animation that even today fanzines typically include character designs in their synopses, discussions, or reviews of a series; and reviews usually give as much weight to character design as to story or other aspects. In this context, Sadamoto Yoshiyuki's comments on his character designs are very telling.

Sadamoto's is a recognizable style, partly because his characters tend to be spindly and peaked rather than roundly cute, and partly because he is renowned for his personalization of characters. He comments, "An easily recognizable silhouette is also important, but I designed the characters (for *Evangelion*) so that their personalities could be more or less understood at a glance. For example, even the color and length of hair expresses personality."[40] As his remarks suggest, Sadamoto is famous for his ability to inscribe the personality of the character—even its flaws and conflicts—on the character surface and across the entire figure. It is not only the face that expresses withdrawal, for instance, but also the entire posture and stylization of the figure. There is a combination of potential action-image and potential time-image. What is more, Sadamoto implies points of resistance to withdrawal within the withdrawn characters, points of insecurity in the confident characters, and so forth. His design for the character of Ayanami Rei, who first appears in *Evangelion* wrapped in bandages, became *the* sensation of the series, selling an unprecedented number of figurines and spurring extensive speculation about her character in the press and the world of anime criticism.[41] Ayanami Rei may be the ultimate instance of the inactive character as time-image, the quintessentially soulful body (Figure 35). Like so many of Sadamoto's characters, she tends to be all soul to the point of losing the

Figure 35. *The first panel shows Ayanami Rei as she appears in the first episode of the* Evangelion *series, and the second panel shows Rei in* Evangelion: 1.01 You Are (Not) Alone (2008). *The third panel presents sketches for three of Sadamoto Yoshiyuki's* Evangelion *characters from the title sequence of the animated series. Sadamoto was also illustrator for the subsequent manga edition of* Evangelion, *and his cover work for volume 9 of the manga displays his characteristic style of soulful bodies.*

body and dropping out of action altogether, but only to turn up everywhere, her soul stretched across innumerable platforms and fields.

As such, Sadamoto's character design is not typology (normalization or disciplinization of types) or psychology (exploration of the unconscious depths of the psyche). By taking the modern "inaction" of character inherent in limited animation to a certain limit, he conjures from within it a portable animus, an image of the soul that can attach itself to anybody or anything. You don't have to believe in the character or even like it to feel its powers of attraction, to know it may stick with you a long time. Such is full limited animation.

PART III. GIRL COMPUTERIZED

CHAPTER 16

A FACE ON THE TRAIN

RECEIVED WISDOM HAS IT that little boys gravitate toward playing with cars, planes, trains, and other vehicles, while little girls show a preference for dolls and other cute little humanoid figures. Boys are supposedly interested in building and dismantling, tinkering with and destroying their toys, while girls are allegedly focused on clothing, feeding, and otherwise nurturing their toys. Thus boys are enjoined to become mechanically minded adults, as engineers, architects, or scientists, and girls to become nurture-orientated adults, as mothers, nurses, or some other types of service provider whose work entails affective response. In other words, such wisdom is not merely an observation of gender preferences. It functions as an injunction: boys will play with vehicles, and girls will play with dolls! It is an injunction calculated to direct libidinal energies.

When posing questions about gender in the context of anime, commentators inevitably raise questions about shojo, and frequently the emphasis falls on a gap between actual girls and the shojo image. Yokokawa Sumiko, for instance, stresses the literary quality of the term *shōjo* in Japanese, which implies a gap between shojo and girls *(onna no ko)*.[1] In other words, the question of shojo tends to be posed first and foremost in terms of a gap between girl and image, which can be read in terms of representation or misrepresentation, normative regulation (social codes and norms), or a filling-in and transforming of the image by girls (performance). In sum, questions about gender tend to work in the gap between world and image.

Without denying the importance and explanatory power of such approaches, and without trying to dispense with the sense of a gap between real girls and images of girls, I will in the following chapters focus attention primarily on what happens within the moving image (rather than what happens between girls and images). I will look at the impact of the animetic interval on questions of gender and sexuality. Looking at gender from this angle tends to rely less on questions about representation and misrepresentation and more on questions about how imaging can affect the patrolling of boundaries, the theater of operations, in which the perimeters and parameters of gender are deterritorialized and reterritorialized.

From such an angle, it seems that, even though both *Castle in the Sky* and *Nadia* appear to offer new types of shojo, they remain intent on exploring the implications of shojo for the mechanically minded boy. Indeed, although they sometimes trouble clear-cut gender dichotomies in adult bodies (notably the warrior woman), Miyazaki's films are fairly consistent in associating boys with mechanical devices, and girls with communicative devices.[2] Boys are largely engineers, and girls primarily communicators. Boys tend toward the mechanical and the active, and girls the biological and the receptive. This is even true of Nausicaä, whose courage and skill with both glider and sword make for a girl unlike any other: the burden of communication, biology, and even Nature falls on her. As Murase Hiromi notes, she reigns almost as a "god," insofar as her existence goes beyond sexuality.[3] As we have seen, establishing the shojo as god, as a being beyond girl and sexuality, constitutes an attempt on the part of Miyazaki to stabilize, or to find a cultural paradigm for stabilizing, a freer relation to technology. He associates this freer relation to technology with a moment that is "earlier" in terms of development or maturation. He dwells on relations between boys and girls, avoiding those between men and women. With respect to masculinity, he favors boyish high spirits and undercuts the gender authority of men in their prime.

Recall that Miyazaki and Ōtsuka Yasuo show a passion for designing aircraft, tanks, cars, and other vehicles. In fact, the documentary devoted to Ōtsuka's work as an animator stresses his boyhood passion for trains. Apparently, Ōtsuka so loved trains that when he finally had an opportunity to leave his small town and visit a larger town, he lingered for hours around the train yard, questioning the engineers and producing very detailed sketches of the various kinds of engines. Ōtsuka not only learned how steam engines function but conveyed it in his sketches, and the Ghibli documentary lavishes attention on the accuracy of Ōtsuka's sketches and on his enthusiasm for military vehicles. We even see him happily driving his army jeep! Given that the trains that Ōtsuka so meticulously sketched were also those sending young men off to war, it would seem difficult to avoid questions about the overlap between wartime mobilization and Ōtsuka Yasuo's boyish passion for the mechanical. Yet, in keeping with Miyazaki's efforts to separate the boyish enthusiasm for vehicles from masculine authority and military might, the documentary enjoins us to avoid such questions.

Ōtsuka Yasuo's mechanically detailed drawings of trains and military vehicles fit neatly in the lineage of what manga writer, critic, and editor Ōtsuka Eiji (not to be confused with Ōtsuka Yasuo) calls "weaponry realism." Ōtsuka Eiji tracks the impulse to produce realistic depictions of weapons from the late nineteenth century, into manga and anime produced during World War II, and into the mecha in post-war anime and manga.[4] Weaponry realism, in Ōtsuka Eiji's genealogy, grew out of military nationalistic ideologies that called for scientific accuracy in diagrams and designs of weaponry, which were deemed necessary to assure Japan's technological supremacy. Ōtsuka stresses the importance of geometric perspective in weaponry realism, to which I would add techniques of exploded projection. In other words, for Ōtsuka, these Japanese calls for techno-scientific accuracy in mechanical drawing agree with the modernization theory implicit in Samuel Edgerton's account of geometric perspective presented in chapter 10: techno-scientific modernization is built on such drawing techniques. Ōtsuka points out that, with the steady militarization of everyday life in prewar Japan, the calls for weaponry realism gradually became injunctions, codified into education guidelines established by the national censorship board for the benefit of editors and others responsible for publishing manga and animation. He writes:

> When "true sketching" (shinsha) or "realism" based on perspective was initially used in modern Japan, it was at the demand of the Army and Navy as a drafting technique. Immediately after the Meiji Restoration (1868), art schools were under the jurisdiction of the Ministry of Industry (Kōbushō). Artists who accompanied the military during the Sino-Japanese War (1904–5) further developed realistic drawing techniques. Realistic representation and perspectival techniques became the preferred ideology for drawing and painting in times of war and, in the course of the Fifteen-Year Asia-Pacific War, came to be sought after in manga too.[5]

For Ōtsuka, such is the genealogy of mecha. Typically, we think of mecha as bipedal vehicles, usually piloted—running the gamut from giant robots to tactical armors—and usually associated with grand fictions of world destruction and human salvation, which are also associated with the otaku lineage of television. The mecha is commonly said to begin with the remote-controlled robot popularized in *Gigantor*, which subsequently morphed into the bipedal piloted vehicles that came to constitute a distinct genre by the 1970s. While such 1970s and 1980s series as *Mazinger*, *Getter Robo*, *Gundam*, and *Macross* are often evoked as characteristic mecha series, there is such a proliferation of mecha anime that it defies tabulation, especially from the 1990s. What is more, as Ōtsuka Eiji notes, mecha comprises a broader range of vehicles. For him what is important is that the fighter planes and military vehicles of wartime animation set the style and tone for postwar mecha.

Ōtsuka Eiji also detects a tension and potentially a contradiction between ways of rendering mecha (scientific realism) and ways of drawing characters. He stresses the profound impact of Disney's animations on characters in Japanese manga and animation, noting an antirealism or nonrealism in the fluid lines and shape-shifting characters, which also makes for a deathless body that survives the most cruel and unusual deformations. In effect, Ōtsuka's essay locates a tension between the mechanical and the biological, or between mecha and human, in the register of drawing. It appears as a tension between deadly weaponry and deathless human bodies. All in all, what Ōtsuka calls weaponry realism is a form of Cartesianism (geometric perspective and techno-scientific rationalism) that stands in contrast to the non-Cartesian "squash-and-stretch" techniques associated with Disney animation.[6] At stake in Ōtsuka's essay is what one might call male "mechaphilia," a variety of technophilia directed toward the mechanical. Ōtsuka implies that, underlying the tension between scientifically rendered deadly mecha and fluidly drawn immortal humans (well, men) is a fascination with techno-scientific modernity that literally draws boys into militarism, spurring totalitarian forms of identification with the nation-state.

The association of boys with mecha and the mechanical, and particularly the "wisdom" that boys will direct their energies into the mechanical, adds another twist to the question of technology. Because mechaphilia is still largely associated with boys, questions about gender, sexuality, and the organization of libidinal energies become inseparable from questions about technology and technological condition. If we read Ōtsuka's account of weaponry realism and squash-and-stretch animation from the angle of gender, it appears that masculine militarism is a sort of Cartesianism or hyper-Cartesianism (consonant with Virilio). Once again, we confront the questions about the status of non-Cartesian structures or modes of perceptual organization in manga and animation. Should we associate the non-Cartesian with feminine modes of being in contrast to masculine instrumentalization? This is, in effect, what Miyazaki's animations tend to do, imparting nonexertive, quasi-magical energies to shojo bodies, as if shojo were *the* point of crisis in the action-image. This is also where psychology and psychoanalytic theory enter the mix, especially in their feminist inflections, adding a new set of questions about technology that may not always sit comfortably with the phenomenological or postphenomenological lineage of thinking technology evoked thus far.

To situate what will follow in relation to prior discussion, even at the risk of constructing an overly reductive theoretical schematization, let me provide a brief summation. In the first section I stressed the resonance between Miyazaki and Heidegger in thinking technology. While I did not explicitly take on the Heideggerian legacy in Japanese philosophy, which is especially pronounced in Kyoto School Philosophy, I implicitly situated Miyazaki on a Japanese Heideggerian trajectory in the critique of modernity and modernization theory (especially that of Watsuji Tetsurō). In the second section, it is not a coincidence that I evoked post-Heideggerian theorists such as Foucault, Deleuze, Derrida, and others who have drawn on their work (Crary, Kittler, Chow, Azuma). Needless to say, Foucault, Deleuze, and Derrida have very different ways of thinking technology and of taking on the Heideggerian legacy. In the context of Anno Hideaki and Gainax, I leaned toward Foucault (or a combination of Foucault and Deleuze), because this allowed me to deal with the connections between knowledge production and perceptual evolution that appear in *Nadia* and *Evangelion*, and in otaku discourses.

In this section, I turn toward psychoanalytic theory, especially that of Jacques Lacan and its aftermath in feminist criticism and film theory as well as in Japanese psychoanalyst Saitō Tamaki's discussions of otaku. Although I will continually highlight the impasses of psychoanalytic theory in theorizing technology, I also find that postphenomenological theory frequently comes to an impasse when dealing with gender and sexuality. Consequently, in this section, to address the complexity that appears when gender and technology come face to face, I develop a dialogue between psychoanalytic theory and its deconstruction, which works at one level through a contrast between the Lacan-inspired Saitō and the Derrida-inspired Azuma. At another level, I take up a range of feminist considerations of Lacan (Laura Mulvey, Joan Copjec, Anne McClintock, Judith Butler) that have had a profound impact on film theory, while evoking postfeminist approaches that resonate with the deconstruction of psychoanalysis and open different relations to technology (Donna Haraway and Kotani Mari). In case there are readers who wish to posit Western theory as somehow alien to Japanese ways of thought, I should add that an exceedingly broad range of Western philosophical formations have been seriously debated in Japan for well over one hundred years. Nevertheless, my aim is not to introduce or reconstruct theoretical debates in Japan (which easily degenerates into a catalog of different positions) but to explore how anime thinks technology, animetically. And so let me return to a less theoretically program-matic tack.

Significantly, Heidegger's theory of gaining a free relation to technology does not broach questions about gender, but Miyazaki's Heideggerian take on the modern technological condition definitely does. Miyazaki's animations con-sistently differentiate boy and girl energies, which is partly due to the legacy of

Ōtsuka Yasuo and Tōei *dōga*. But, even if the Ghibli documentary overlooks the connections between war and Ōtsuka Yasuo's boyhood mechaphilia, the remnants of hyper-Cartesianism within boyish mechaphilia trouble Miyazaki, precisely due to the connections he imagines between mechaphilia and global annihilation. His animations strive to redirect boyish energies and to prevent the development of boyish mechaphilia into masculine militarism. Because Miyazaki either does not want to surrender boyish mechaphilia or because he considers it an irrevocable fact of nature, he strives for a free relation to technology that will minimize technologies, thus directing mechaphilia into human-scaled, environmentally friendly technologies. Techniques of the multiplanar image, of sliding planes over depth, allow Miyazaki to think this salvation from the technological condition animetically. Yet we are left with the suspicion that, even though only a girl can save us, it is primarily boys who need, even demand, salvation at the hands of shojo.

In *Nadia*, building on a scenario reminiscent of Miyazaki's *Castle in the Sky*, Anno nonetheless thinks the technological condition differently from Miyazaki, striving for an animetic optimization of the multiplanar machine that brings with it precisely what Miyazaki and Ghibli reject: anime otaku technophilia. Anno remains ambivalent, however, sometimes attacking and rejecting exactly what his animations optimize. To counter his ambivalence (equally prevalent in Murakami's superflat), I suggested that the critical potential of Anno's animations lies in their thinking the "postmodern" irrevocability of the modern technological condition, which stands in contrast to Miyazaki's striving for an animetic experience of minimizing modernity.

Significantly, both Miyazaki and Anno bring gender and sexual development into the mix. Miyazaki prefers to keep his children presexual yet protosexual, on the edge of maturity, with beautifully innocent yet intimate relations between boys and girls, as exemplified in *Castle in the Sky* or *Kiki's Delivery Service*. But this strategy lends itself to otaku appropriation, so to speak. Ōtsuka Eiji reminds us that, for all of Miyazaki's desire to differentiate his work from the world of anime, otaku, and subculture, prior to the mid-1980s, anime fans saw Miyazaki Hayao's work in this lineage.[7] The 1979 film *Rupan sansei: Kariosutoro no shiro (Lupin III: Castle of Cagliostro)* is a prime example. Not only did animator Ōtsuka Yasuo and Miyazaki Hayao lavish attention on vehicle thrills, but also the shojo character Clarisse proved a favorite with otaku. But is otaku appropriation truly a misunderstanding of Miyazaki?

Anno's animations help to clarify the problem. In contrast to *Castle in the Sky*, Anno's *Nadia* tends toward "angry love" in which the kids bicker and fight as they gradually bond, and it is likewise with *Evangelion* and *His and Her*

Circumstances (*Kareshi kanojo no jijô*, 1998–99).[8] Aptly, *Nadia* culminates in a perverse combination in which Victorian ideals of marriage and Electra-Lolita complexes are dutifully paired.[9] Yet, as in *Castle in the Sky*, such perversity derives from a displacement of the question of the modern technological condition onto the girl, such that her communicative power and biological heritage (embodied in the jewel as techno-nature) operates as both problem and solution, or rather, condition and salvation. Miyazaki and Anno negotiate the place of gender in different ways, which Ōtsuka Eiji's notion of a tension between Cartesian weaponry realism and non-Cartesian character animation can help us to parse. Miyazaki, via Ōtsuka Yasuo's approach to character animation, will make the non-Cartesian moment depend on shojo energies in character animation (rather than squash-and-stretch, a natural buoyancy), which responds to the sliding planes of the animetic world. Anno Hideaki, via Sadamoto Yoshiyuki's soulful bodies, will rely on shojo energies inscribed in petulant contrariness, as potentiality on the surface of design, which optimizes the crisis of the action-image, in response to the enclosure of the lifeworld. Nonetheless, when seen from the angle of gender dynamics, the difference between minimizing and optimizing the technological condition crystallized in the "jewel" seems to amount to the same thing. Shojo appears to enable a *displacement* of technological boundaries, allowing for an exploration of the perimeters of boyish mechaphilia, whether that manner of displacement is quasi-redemptive (Miyazaki) or quasi-deconstructive (Anno). What's not for a male otaku to like in either situation?

There is yet another situation in which technology and gender become inextricably meshed—that of the female cyborg, woman robot, or "gynoid."[10] *Castle in the Sky* and *Nadia* already hint at this situation in their presentation of the girl–jewel interface, in conjunction with the alien origins of the girl: their shojo is almost like a robot in that she is subject to remote control, and she is like a communicative technology in that her jewel is the telecommand for the activation of weapons of mass destruction. By collapsing the gap between jewel and girl, the gynoid poses a new question: What happens when the girl actually is the technology, not merely the pivotal subject of and for it? How does the force of the moving image then affect questions of gender and sexuality? What happens when you can't separate the force of destruction (jewel) from the girl-savior?

There are many variations on the scenario in which girl and technology are fused, so that I will give only a handful of examples of the fusion of mecha-destruction and shojo-savior, which are relevant to later discussion.

On the one hand, in the mecha genre itself, which is usually said to begin with stories of remote-control robots à la *Gigantor* only to transform rapidly into stories about giant bipedal robots piloted by boys or young men,[11] there is a gradual "shojo-ification" of the boy–mecha interface. Gradually, with the emergence of psionic interfaces, control of the giant robot becomes less a matter of masculine will and physical abilities and more a question of an empathic connection, of feelings and emotions. Boy pilots become gradually feminized in the sense that operating mecha demand that they be in touch with their feelings and prone to affective communication in a manner previously coded as feminine. The crisis in the movement-image (in the overall coordinating action-image) implies a crisis in masculinity. Girl pilots become more common—and sexy (as in *Bubble Gum Crisis* OAV, 1987–91). *Evangelion* takes this scenario to its logical extreme: most of the ace mecha pilots are girls, and the one boy pilot, Ikari Shinji, is the antithesis of masculine virtues. What is more, the boy–mecha interface begins to imply a maternal bond, not to mention a biological predisposition in the interfaces based on genetic compatibilities. As the boy pilot becomes shojo-ified, the giant robot becomes a quasi-maternal biological matrix.

On the other hand, there are gynoid entities, that is, nonbiological mechanical entities that appear in the form of girls or women. Typically, the gynoid looks and acts like a woman but is not truly a woman. Gynoid scenarios run the range from cosmologically derived women (goddesses) to full metal women (female robots and cyborgs). Between the goddess and the gynoid robot is the mechanically produced girl image. For instance, in *Video Girl Ai*, a videocassette spawns a "video girl," a girl image that leaps from the screen into real life; although she looks utterly real, she remains "alive" only as long as the tape plays in the VCR. When it comes to full metal women, stories tend to oscillate between law enforcers (policewomen, female combat soldiers, special operations gynoids) and service workers (robot sex slaves or sexroids, idol songstresses, newswomen). Often the gynoids oscillate between law enforcement and "service" (affective and communicative labor). *Armitage III* OAV (1995), for instance, tells of a planet without women (Mars) where men find solace in gynoid companion robots. A male detective from Earth teams up with a girl cop with a bad attitude to investigate a murder. As they solve the case and fall in love, the secret of the murders hinges on the production of gynoid robots that are capable of giving birth.

As such examples imply, the gynoid scenario frequently addresses male viewers directly, either boys (shonen), or young men (seinen), or both. Thus the gynoid is often associated with what might be called a male-directed mode of address, in which the primary concern is to present women to men, and to figure out what women are or can be for men. In this respect, my passing use above of the word "service" to characterize the gynoid scenario was not coincidental. The term *service (saabisu)*, often rendered as "fan service" in English, refers to images of girls or women, usually sexually provocative or explicit, which are dropped into anime almost arbitrarily, simply as eye candy for boys and men. In other words, service implies a male-directed mode of address. Such an address is echoed in the doubling of gynoid cop and sexroid. While the oscillation of a gynoid's function between police work and "service" may initially seem to present a contradiction, it is also possible to see in this oscillation a variation on the long-standing prejudices about women's work and the female condition: after all, the gynoid is protecting and nurturing humans.

Nonetheless, the gynoid scenario does not merely reproduce received wisdom about boys and girls, men and women. It entails a displacement of traditional roles, often a violent one, which in turn implies a new exploration of perimeters, in which gender becomes central to the theater of operations. Much of the violence stems from the difficulties that arise when the female form is imposed on, or taken up by, mecha. Again, Ōtsuka Eiji alludes to this problem when he calls attention to a tension between hyper-Cartesianism and non-Cartesianism running through anime and manga. The displacement of male mechaphilia, implicit in the girl–jewel interface, takes the form of a quasi-redemptive minimalization of anime technology in Miyazaki, and the form of quasi-deconstructive optimization of anime technology in Anno. In both instances, it is the relation of character animation to compositing that stabilizes the technology–sexuality interface. The process of harnessing and orientating the force of the moving image is stabilized through recourse to shojo. In this sense, the crisis of the action-image may find its material limit (and a comfortable perimeter) through recourse to gender metaphysics.

The challenge of gynoid scenario, then, lies in how it inhabits the crisis of the action-image, how it plays the asymmetry between the shojo and the mecha.

Because mecha commonly implies weapons of mass destruction (just as the jewel does in *Nadia* and *Castle in the Sky*), it is as if the girl had become a weapon of mass destruction, or the weapon of mass destruction a girl, with no hope of the global resolution or world salvation that are offered in *Nadia* and *Castle in the Sky*. A fairly recent manga and anime series, *She, the Ultimate Weapon* (*Saishū heiki kanojo*, 2002), explores precisely such a scenario: the boy falls in love with a girl who each night transforms into a weapon of mass destruction. Things don't exactly turn out for the best: the world is destroyed, and while the girl WMD apparently manages to save the boyfriend, he survives utterly alone in a devastated world.

While it is possible to read such a scenario entirely in terms of a male-directed mode of address (asking what women can be for men), an address to girls and women can also be read in the gynoid displacement of male mechaphilia. This is what Donna Haraway strives for in her "Cyborg Manifesto," in which she boldly draws out connections between information society, the postmodern condition, and the global feminization of labor. She takes the figure of the cyborg to another direction, concluding, "I would rather be a cyborg than a goddess."[12] In other words, Haraway finds something empowering or enabling in the female cyborg. She does so by stressing what might be dubbed the "mecha-ification" of the woman rather than the "gynefication" or shojo-fication of mecha. In the combination of woman and machine, she finds a site where the distinction between woman and machine is blurred, which implies for her a moment of potential inversion and deconstruction of received hierarchies pertaining to women.[13]

But is it so easy to invert and deconstruct the male-directed modes of address associated with the gynoid scenario in manga and anime? In other words, as is implied in the very idea of a mode of address, is there a material limit to the gender deconstruction implicit in the gynoid scenario, and how does the force of the moving image affect it?

This question comes to the fore brilliantly in *Chobits*, a manga series produced in 2001 by CLAMP. Initially a team of eleven art students who worked together on dōjinshi, CLAMP transformed into a four-woman studio comprising Igarashi Satsuki, Ohkawa Ageha (formerly Ohkawa Nanase), Nekoi Tsubaki (sometimes Nekoi Mick), and Mokona (sometimes Mokona Apapa) who over the past twenty-odd years have produced over twenty-two popular manga series, among them *X, Angelic Layer, Tokyo Babylon, Magic Night Rayearth, Cardcaptor Sakura, xxxHOLIC, Reservoir Chronicle*, and *Tsubasa Reservoir Chronicle*. Like many other CLAMP manga, *Chobits* quickly spawned a television anime series (dir. Asaka Morio, 2002). CLAMP describes *Chobits* as a variation on the genre of "boy living with mysterious girl";[14] in this instance, the mysterious girl is a personal computer with the form of a sixteen-year-old woman, and the tale is that of a boy who lives with, and gradually falls in love with, "her." Serialized in Kōdansha's *Young Magazine* between February 2001 and November 2002, the *Chobits* manga received attention as CLAMP's first foray into *seinen* or "young adult" genres, typically geared to young men between the ages of eighteen and thirty, with an *ecchi* or sexually risqué edge. The CLAMP team had already garnered a reputation for its shojo fare and for comics that cross gender and genre lines of shojo manga and *shōnen manga* or "boys comics." Yet *Chobits*, like other CLAMP titles, mixes genre conventions, and it proved equally successful with girls and boys. As I will discuss in greater detail in subsequent chapters, part of its appeal for both boys and girls lies in its dexterity in propping up and humorously deflating male otaku-like fantasies about the gynoid personal computer, fantasies about what sexy mechanical girls can do for men.

Chobits thus introduces another way of thinking technology. It focuses on how we look at and interact with the surfaces of technology, rather than dwelling on how mecha are put together (the exploded view). We never really see the underlying mechanisms, only the adorable shojo surfaces. In other words, fantasies and structures of desire become the key to thinking the technological condition, and in this respect (and a number of others), *Chobits* poses questions more in the register of psychology and psychoanalysis than Heideggerian postphenomenology or post-Heideggerian theory. Nonetheless, I will keep open both lines of inquiry, both the post-Heideggerian question of *how technologies of perception structure our fields of knowledge* and the Lacanian question of *how the ontological lack constitutive of the human structures the visual field.*

To put it another way and to anticipate later discussion, *Chobits* is exceedingly attentive to, and canny about, the mechanisms of male fantasies vis-à-vis the gynoid. It tries to turn the male-oriented mode of address back on itself, not merely to expose the fantasy but to open a site where female fantasies of mechanical perfection and autonomy might also be addressed. This is where shojo-oriented modes of address tentatively emerge. *Chobits* does indeed strive to invert and deconstruct the male-directed mode of address. Yet that deconstruction is not so complete or radical as that imagined by Haraway. Rather *Chobits* tends toward a relentless displacement of male desire, which aims to twist and deform male perversion into a truly female perversion.

In sum, the gynoid scenario, in which shojo and mecha are somehow indistinguishable, raises a very basic question, one that returns us to the start of this chapter: what happens when you put a face on the toy train?

Take the example of *Thomas the Tank Engine*, in which each little train has a face and a personality. Is the train now a doll? Should the child play with it as a train or as a doll, or both? Is the boy less likely to smash it to bits because it has a human face, and more likely to cradle it and talk to it? Would the girl start to think of her dolls as technological devices to take apart and put together?

The first scenario plays out in the images by manga artist Takekuma Kentarō in which he puts Thomas the Tank Engine on the tracks in the Tokyo commuter network, to discourage people from committing suicide by throwing themselves in front of the train, as in his "A Dream-like Plan for the Thomas-ification of the JR-Chūō Line."[15] In effect, because it is largely middle-aged businessmen throwing themselves in front of trains on the JR Chūō Line, Takekuma's scenario addresses the very male mechaphilia in which Ōtsuka Eiji, Miyazaki Hayao, and Paul Virilio detect an accelerated instrumentalization or hyper-Cartesianism, a deadly fascination with ballistic technologies, in which self-annihilation on the rails of the train speeding like a bullet is part of a fleeting bid for immortality in which the shredded body seeks eternal life in the temporary but widespread suspension of the techno-scientifically ordered and measured urban network.[16] In putting a face on the train, Takekuma strives literally to put a human face, a happy face, on the technologically ordered world, apparently to deflect the violence of male technophilia. Yet, if scenarios like that of *She, the Ultimate Weapon* are any indication, the human face on the deadly mecha may equally spur fantasies of personal salvation amid world annihilation.

Chobits plays with the second scenario: once the face on the mecha is a girl's, once mecha becomes indiscernible from the feminine body, is there any reason to suppose that dressing up or playing with dolls is any less technological behavior than engineering the train? We are compelled to ask whether fashion or cosplay is any less part of the modern technological condition than building a train, and whether playing with dolls in the information age is not thoroughly compatible with technological optimization. These are, needless to say, decidedly perverse takes on the modern technological condition, but that is precisely where the computerized girl leads.

CHAPTER 17

THE ABSENCE OF SEX

THE CRUCIAL SCENE OF *CHOBITS* occurs right at the outset, in the first chapter of the manga and in the first episode of the animated series. It occurs just after the male protagonist, Motosuwa Hideki, finds a gynoid "persocom" (a personal computer in female form) abandoned in a pile of garbage, its sexy young body alluringly wrapped in tape. It is as if his wish had been granted, and overjoyed at his find, Motosuwa lugs "her" home. Alone in his room in a boarding house, he looks for the switch to turn her on. Four hours later, after exploring every square centimeter of her, he still cannot find the switch. There is only one place he hasn't checked. And as he slides his fingers between her legs, he tries to reassure himself that there are no sexual motives behind his action.[1]

Apparently, there is a switch (or something) between her legs, because the persocom instantly comes alive, and the wrappings fly from her body, leaving her exquisitely exposed. Yet the reader-viewer never sees or knows exactly what Motosuwa finds between her legs. Motosuwa himself does not *see*. His eyes are tightly shut as he turns on his newly discovered persocom. It may look to us as if he inserts a finger into "her" genitals, but there is no image of female genitalia or of the switch. The anime version even includes a shot of his hand seen from between the persocom's legs, but we do not know what is looking at his hand while he closes his eyes. The operative image is that of his hand between her legs, fingers crooked (Figure 36).

This is the critical scene and the crucial image for the entire series. It establishes the question that activates the series: is this a sexual relation? It definitely looks like sex. The reader or viewer has constant reminders, however, that it only

Figure 36. *After searching everywhere for the gynoid persocom's "on" button in the animated version of* Chobits, *Motosuwa Hideki resolves to check the last possible place, and, turning his head and shutting his eyes, he puts his hand between "her" legs.*

looks like sex. In fact, Motosuwa is just turning on a computer—nothing sexual about that switch between her legs, just a button to turn her on. There's nothing dirty about it at all. Yet the scene is at once comedic and *ecchi*, funny and risqué: it looks like a sexually intimate moment, and the conceit of Motosuwa "turning on" his very personal computer reinforces our sense that something sexual is happening.

The way *Chobits* sets up our view of the boy turning on his gynoid PC recalls Lacan's quixotic formula about sexuality: despite all appearances, there is no sexual relationship.[2] For Lacan, as Slavoj Žižek points out, existence is synonymous with symbolization, and the absence or nonexistence of the sexual relationship means that it resists symbolization.[3] For CLAMP, the so-called "absence of the sexual relation" has a pragmatic valence. When asked about the anime adaptation of the manga, Ohkawa Nanase says that the idea was to make an anime that wouldn't embarrass girls.[4] In other words, although the manga is clearly addressed to young men at one level, CLAMP addresses girls at another level, whence the relative modesty in portraying bodies and genitals—no money shots, as it were. The combination of a *seinen* mode of address with shojo sensibility results in sexual situations without actual sexual relations—sex without sex. In sum, it is partly due to CLAMP's resistance to depictions of sex that *Chobits* proves uncannily in sync with Lacan's ideas about the nonexistence of the sexual relationship. But the absence of sex also becomes a way of thinking about sexuality, and especially about gender and technology, as we will see.

In fact, due to the location of her switch, Motosuwa can never have sex with his gynoid PC. Sex would push her reset button and wipe her memories and identity. The original manga makes this problem explicit. The anime adaptation never states the problem explicitly, even though it presumes such a situation. The anime may show greater modesty and propriety because the television anime are thought to address a more general public than manga. In any event, in both manga and anime, the sexual relation is predicated on a literal absence of sexual relationship.

Moreover, strictly speaking, there is no woman in this relationship. The girl persocom is not human, and thus not a woman. This is why Motosuwa can insert a finger between the computer's legs and turn it on, while claiming that there is no actual sexual interaction with the "girl." Nonetheless, the situation remains perverse, because (as the manga tells us) the computer has the physique of a fifteen- or sixteen-year-old girl or young woman. This is why Motosuwa cannot immediately bring himself to feel between "her" legs. Likewise readers-viewers cannot quite believe that these images of a nineteen-year-old youth[5] with a sixteen-year-old girl in his arms, with his hands exploring what appear to be the most private parts of her body, are not images of a sexual relationship. In an almost classic psychoanalytic fashion, *Chobits* sets up the truth as unbelievable. There is no way to believe that this is not sex! The situation produces a desire to see the truth from a believable angle, to set it straight or get it right. This is what sets the story in motion. Is this a computer or a girl? Is this sex or not?

This brilliant set-up allows CLAMP to pose the question of what a woman is. While it may seem that the answer lies between the legs of the gynoid persocom (that is, the truth lies in female anatomy), *Chobits* does not allow for such a simple answer. Instead, it shows "woman" as an effect of socially structured relations. Which to say, the persocom is a woman insofar as Hideki treats her as one. The question "computer or woman?" turns into a question about the construction of "woman." Will Motosuwa treat it/her as a computer or as woman?

Here *Chobits* also presents us with a parable that opposes love to instrumental use. It would seem that love for the gynoid as girl can triumph over instrumental use of the gynoid as computer—simply put, love over sex. Yet the series never clarifies the relation between love (as noninstrumental) and sex (posited here as instrumental). On the one hand, the series tells us, humans may use computers as instruments, but men should not use women that way.

Consequently, even though Motosuwa Hideki dreams of using his female computer as an instrument to access e-mail, surf the 'net, and most importantly, to download porn, nevertheless he cannot simply "use" her because he sees her/it as a woman. On the other hand, real women unnerve Motosuwa, and it is only because his computer is not a woman but an instrument that he can treat her/it as he should treat a woman, with love, respect, and affection. He can't treat a woman like a woman but he can treat a computer like one. If *Chobits* consistently wheels around this paradox, it is in order to pose and pose again the crucial question: what is a woman?

This is why the crucial scene for the series is the one in which Motosuwa turns her/it on. *Chobits* toys with our inability to see what lies between the persocom's legs. What do persocoms have down there? Is the female persocom really (that is, anatomically) like a woman? We cannot see what the persocom "really" is. Is "she" a computer or a woman? Apparently Hideki knows, but even if he told us what he found there, we could not believe him, for the story insists on his complete lack of experience with women. *Chobits* presents him as an anomaly: a nineteen-year old virgin who is continually embarrassed by his lack of experience. What's more, he closes his eyes as he reaches for her switch. Would he really know the difference between an on switch and, say, a woman's genitals? Does he know what a woman is? What is more, we subsequently learn that he knows nothing about computers. *Chobits* deftly mobilizes Hideki's lack of experience with women and with computers to pose very basic questions. How does anyone know what a woman is? Who can say for sure? Is it just a way of looking at things? From what angle can you determine what a woman is?

By not allowing the reader-viewer to see or know, *Chobits* implies that there is a deeper structure, a secret to be revealed. The first sequences of *Chobits* thus expand the aura of mystery around the female persocom. At the end of the second episode Hideki names her Chii, for "chii" is the only sound she can initially utter. In the second episode, a fellow tenant, Shinbo Hiromu, assists Hideki, showing him how to connect her/it to the television set in order to see what operating system or OS she runs. But they are left with a puzzle, for the television indicates no data, and it seems impossible for a persocom to walk and talk without an OS. Connecting Chii to Shinbo's tiny gynoid persocom, a perky little machine called Sumomo, crashes Sumomo. The distressed Shinbo then sends Hideki to ask the advice of Kokubunji Minoru, who is something of a computer wiz. The twelve-year-old Kokubunji lives in a mansion with an entourage of lovely female persocoms in maid uniforms, each of whom crashes when connected to Chii. Finally, Kokubunji's very special custom persocom, Yuzuki, learns something (although she/it too crashes): Chii's data are heavily protected. Kokubunji speculates that Chii may be one of the legendary *chobits* series rumored to possess true intelligence (beyond what is programmed into them) as well as an ability to feel emotion and evolve. In sum, the "mystery" between Chii's legs, that thing we cannot see or know, is gradually displaced onto other aspects of Chii—her OS, her software, her data protections, her mysterious origins. A circle of mystery expands around her.

Even though in the end *Chobits* (especially the manga) offers very concrete answers to these questions about Chii, the solution is as bizarre as the problem: sexuality without sex. If we think of the technological problem posed by Chii in particular or by persocoms in general (how to live with advanced communications technologies such as computers), it is clear that the structure of this manga/anime is not that of a problem with a solution. Again, as in Heidegger, as in Miyazaki and Anno, there is a technological condition. Technology is not about finding the solution to a problem. It is about a condition from which one seeks salvation or redemption. What distinguishes CLAMP's approach from Miyazaki's quasi-redemptive minimization of technology, and from Anno's quasi-deconstructive optimization of technology, however, is their greater emphasis on family drama-trauma, sexuality, and psychological projection. What gathers and focuses attention on technology—what promises to transform our relation to technology—is sexuality, the question of our erotic attachment to technological devices. Ultimately, however, the sexual relationship is not the path to "salvation" from the modern or postmodern technological condition. If there is redemption, it lies in the weird absence of the sexual relationship: it is only because Hideki agrees never to have sex with Chii that the man–machine interface becomes fully operative and personally satisfying. In other words, instead of salvation or redemption per se, *Chobits* provides a process of psychological maturation, yet maturation here implies a normalization of perversity, an acceptance of perversion as a normal state of affairs. *Nadia*, of course, had its share of perversion, in the "angry love" between Jean and Nadia, and in the coupling of Electra and Lolita complexes. *Chobits*, however, consistently situates or triangulates the strange twists of romance in relation to gynoid love. In other words, techno-erotic formations of male mechaphilia are always under scrutiny in *Chobits*.

As the series progresses, a number of characters appear who have also experienced some sort of emotional turmoil and romantic loss vis-à-vis persocoms. In episode 3, in which Hideki begins attending a cram school (*yobikō*) to prepare him for college entrance exams (which he previously failed, whence his status as an unaffiliated "rōnin" in Tokyo), we meet Shimizu Takako, a young woman teacher, whose kindness and attractiveness throw Hideki into a state of reverie. In later episodes, it turns out that Hideki's friend Shinbo and Ms. Shimizu have fallen in love (episode 15), but they hide their relationship because she is, after all, his teacher. What is more, she has already been married. But her husband became so obsessed with his female persocom that he simply ignored her!

Also in episode 3 we meet Yumi, the daughter of the owner of an *izakaya* or "pub" where Hideki fortuitously finds part-time work, which he desperately needs to support him and Chii. In his characteristic fashion of voicing aloud his thoughts, which never fails to embarrass him, Hideki cries out, at the top of his lungs, his appreciation for Yumi's large breasts. The series presents such asocial outbursts as part of a disarming naïveté and youthful enthusiasm. In particular, Hideaki is an asocial mess with women and even with gynoids: he instantly begins to fantasize about them and usually gives voice to some part of his fantasy, which means that he is always caught out. He is constantly exposing his fantasies and humiliating himself. This naïveté endears him to women and other characters, yet it also seems to prevent him from pursuing any romantic relationship seriously. He does go on a date with Yumi, for instance, but ultimately, because he and Chii are clearly meant for one another, things don't work out for Hideki and Yumi.

In any event, Yumi's situation is also triangulated with male mechaphilia or gynoid love. She suffers from a sense of inferiority vis-à-vis female persocoms. She does not believe that any man could prefer a woman to a persocom; gynoid computers are too perfect. When romance promises to bloom between her and Ueda Hiroyasu, the owner of the bakery where Chii eventually finds employment (episode 8), Yumi is unable to respond appropriately because she knows that Ueda once loved and married a female persocom (episode 22). There is a third plot that also circles around the problem of loving the gynoid computer. Kokubunji Minoru, who lost his beloved sister at an early age and has built the custom persocom Yuzuki in her image as a replacement, must work through his bias against the persocom as an inferior substitute for his sister. He eventually learns to love the persocom on its own terms, for what it is rather than as a failed imitation.

In sum, in all these romance stories, although love for the gynoid initially appears as an obstacle, it does not ultimately prove insurmountable. Kokubunji learns to love his gynoid, Shinbo and Ms. Shimizu overcome the difficulties of her husband's love of his gynoid, and Yumi and Ueda work past her worries about his prior marriage to a gynoid. The rather pat moral is that love is love, and it matters little whether it is love of a human or of a humanoid. What is strange, however, is how these very sentimental gestures—love will find a way, love is wonderful enough—serve to normalize male mechaphilia in the form of erotic attachment to the gynoid. Thus the smaller romance stories serve to support the major arc of the "boy lives with gynoid" love story.

Because the romantic side stories hinge on some kind of traumatic loss (death of a sister, death of a persocom wife, loss of a husband to a persocom), we are encouraged to ask what Hideki's problem is. Is there some kind of underlying trauma implicit in his anxiety about living with Chii, which he expresses by constantly disavowing his deepening affection for her and his erotic interest in her?

Everything hinges on the mystery between Chii's legs. This set-up, in which no one can see or touch her button, is eerily reminiscent of Freud's discussion of the traumatic structure of fetishism. Freud argues that the sight of the woman's genitals proves disturbing for men, because the sight is suggestive of castration. The fetishist disavows the female genitals by focusing his attention on other parts of the woman's body—feet, hair, breasts, neck, or any other part of the body, or clothing, something that can be compulsively idealized in its beauty and attractiveness in order to counter the traumatic experience of the perceived "ugliness" of the woman's genitals.[6] In effect, the fetishist cannot accept the bare facts of sexuality and strives to cover this naked or exposed truth with excessive adornment of the woman's body, or obsessive attention to certain parts of the woman's body, or both. Sexuality becomes organized around an idealized or fetishized part of the body, to the point where interest in the fetish replaces genital sexuality altogether.

Hideki is an avid reader of pornography. He only knows the idealized images of women found there. From the outset he frets about covering Chii's body, and especially worries about underwear, that is, about hiding her crotch. No sooner does Hideki's beautiful landlady, Ms. Hibiya, give him clothes for Chii than he thinks of underwear. At the end of episode 2, for instance, Chii leaps onto Hideki in a hug, knocking him to the floor with her on top of him. In this sexually explicit position, the first thing Hideki thinks (and yells out) is that Chii needs underwear: anything to cover the mystery between her legs. Of course, we are supposed to think that Hideki is being courteous and modest, unwilling to take advantage of Chii. In the same episode, when Shinbo brusquely searches Chii's breasts for a brand name and then opens her legs to find the model number, Hideki leaps on Shinbo to stop him. Shinbo wonders how Hideki will manage to use a persocom if he is such a prude.

A great deal of attention falls on how to dress Chii, how to assure her modesty. In the first scenes, her body is perfectly wrapped. When the wrappings fall away, her excessively idealized hair enters into the act. Subsequently, whenever she loses her clothes, her long flowing locks swirl around her body, beautifully clothing her. Yet it is her crotch above all that worries Motosuwa. Indeed an entire episode (episode 4) deals with Hideki's embarrassment about buying women's panties. Because he cannot build up the nerve to enter the lingerie store and request panties, he decides to send Chii, first showing her what she needs (what he wants for her) in skin magazines. After Chii fails, Hideki musters the courage to buy panties, only to go into wild antics about being taken for a pervert *(hentai)*.

Subsequently, throughout the series Hideki delights in seeing Chii in a variety of garbs, some evocative of fetish wear (such as her French maid attire for the bakery). The manga and anime linger over Chii posing in different costumes. It often seems that the point of various episodes is primarily to explore different garb for Chii, to develop little stories that revolve around seeing Chii sweetly posed in new attire. This is where character design takes on great importance.

Ohkawa Ageha, who functions as the producer/director of the CLAMP artists, takes on the task of establishing a visual style for a manga series.[7] She also chooses which artist will be responsible for which character. Due to their flexibility as artists and the different placement of individual skills on different manga, CLAMP manga present a broad range of graphic styles and an equally broad range of genres. There is nonetheless a CLAMP feel that is consistent across different genres and graphic styles, which stems from the delicacy and clarity of their line work, with an emphasis on curvilinear flow that serves to tie the image together even as it enables a proliferation of graphically distinct zones within the image. These tendencies frequently come together in flowing tresses and billowing frocks that characterize many of their popular girl characters. Chii is a prime example with her slight, slender, largely undefined body, which functions primarily as a rack upon which to drape clothes. But these are no ordinary clothes. Her clothes, like her hair, appear as if full of wind and air, as if breezes naturally arose around her body, as if her body emanated invisible yet powerful currents that sent ripples coursing through her ethereal dresses and locks, generating a voluminous and shifting force field around her. Hers is an expansive and powerful delicacy, that of a fine line that can bend all space to its undulating contours.

This is a variation on the "soulful bodies" discussed in chapter 15, bodies on which supposedly inner states, spiritual, emotional, or psychological tensions and conflicts are directly described, appearing on the surface in character design, implying potential movement of the body and of the soul. Chii's design does not imply great potential for physical movement. In the fuller color illustrations for the manga and other covers (CD and DVD), Chii usually appears lounging or reclining, or curled up like a cat (an impression reinforced in her cat-ear-like portals), looking pensive, vaguely attentive yet distant, not drowsy or sleepy, with her soul somehow veiled in her eyes (Figure 37). In conjunction with her delicately layered volumes of clothes and hair, these features make for a

Figure 37. *The covers for the first two volumes of the* Chobits *manga demonstrate CLAMP's sense of design for Chii. Shown here are the Kodansha bilingual editions, which reprise the original covers.*

girl designed to float or hover. Indeed, in the anime, Abe Hisashi's character design nicely reprises CLAMP's, but in terms of character animation, the result is a highly limited Chii who walks stiffly and pointedly, but usually with garments drooping, trailing, or swirling.

We might conclude that, because CLAMP delights in girls who change clothes a lot (as in their *Card Captor Sakura*), costume design is taking over character design. In fact, character design, especially when it comes to soulful bodies, always implies an intimate relation to clothes and accessories. Think of Ayanami Rei and her bandages. But if we contrast Chii with Ayanami Rei or Nadia, we detect a crucial difference. The suits worn by these Sadamoto Yoshiyuki characters serve to enhance the sense of an underlying physical contour, as if they were a second skin, which may be construed as revealing or concealing the girl's body, depending on how you look at it. It is a matter of eyes sliding over surfaces. In contrast, with Chii, there is little sense of an underlying morphology or contour. Rather, her body is a rack. What is more, her lacy fluttering dresses echo the billowing tresses, as if a second hair. Yet, for all its delicate lines, hair is structurally closer to "skeleton" *(hone)* than "flesh" *(niku)*.

As the Japanese glosses indicated, I use these terms *skeleton* and *flesh* in their calligraphic sense. I do not mean simply to imply that Sadamoto's Nadia and Ayanami Rei are fleshly, while Chii is boney, in a physiological way. After all, these girls are all woefully thin. Rather it is a matter of very different abstract tendencies related to techniques of the line. Ayanami Rei's lines draw the eyes in and across the surface, implying a sort of reticence and even withdrawal that is belied by force of massed shadings and exuberant contour, whence the sense of youthful energies in anxious withdrawal that might find their outlet in resentful and angry outburst. This is an exploded view of the soul and body laid out in "fleshy" lines. Chii's lines encourage the eyes to sweep outward and downward, implying an ethereal lightness to Chii, as if she might float away. At the same time, the sweep of the lines also imparts a sense of unveiling something, maybe her body. The curvature implies the construction of a haven, as if one might dwell peacefully within those lines, and yet, as soon as the eyes try to inhabit the space within the curvilinear flow, they are instantly swept out again. Also, because movement is concentrated in draping, blooming, lacy, frilly lines, the impression is that the soul itself is the source of the currents that unfurl in hair and dresses. Yet the design gives us only the traces of the soul's flight, rendering it in very fine but exceedingly structured lines. This is "boney" or "skeletal" insofar as the lines, despite the emotion implied in their fluidity, remain impassive and structural. In sum, in Ayanami Rei and Chii, we have two different varieties of soulful body, and in both instances, the soul, that is, movements of feeling and thinking, is inscribed on the surface, explicating itself in advance of any narrative explication.

The basic question of *Chobits* is whether young men see those lines differently from girls or young women. There is something odd about *Chobits* in this respect, because the design for Chii, which the CLAMP team posits as the inspiration for Motosuwa's manic and anxious fetishization, is not so unlike the design used for girls in their shojo manga addressed to girls. Consequently, male fetishism feels compromised in advance, somehow forced to inhabit ways of looking that are not entirely in male control. In other words, the seinen mode of address may not be entirely incompatible with a shojo mode of address. But can the seinen mode of address be subordinated to the shojo mode, or at least somehow mitigated by it? Or how do these coexist? These questions emerge even at the level of CLAMP's design for Chii.

At the level of story, however, there is no doubt that in *Chobits* the CLAMP team initially focuses the reader's attention on how Motosuwa responds to Chii.

Gradually, we begin to sense that Hideki is not merely modest and courteous. If Hideki gravitates toward a "girl" with whom he can never have sex, it is because he truly cannot deal with women at the level of the "truth" of sexuality and sexual difference; he is the ultimate fetishist, entirely successful in his desire to linger over the trappings of femininity without ever confronting the woman's genitals. With its array of Chii poses and costumes, with its story of the boy who chooses to live with his girl computer, *Chobits* is not merely repeating the mechanisms of fetishism but exposing them, making them too obvious to ignore. In fact, it is as if CLAMP were here intent on locating the secret of the appeal of their shojo manga for men, and finding, in the design for Chii, the fault lines that run between girls' fashion obsessions and male fetishism (drawing the eyes into the body only to sweep them out again, by enhancing the flow of adornment in a play of veils).

The circles of mystery that expand around Chii at the level of narrative are analogous to the billowing hair and sweeping dresses. This is a highly structured delicateness and thoroughly obdurate courtliness. For instance, in episode 5, as Hideki studies for a practice exam, he realizes that he has not brought his English–Japanese dictionary to Tokyo with him. He and Chii go to a bookstore where she discovers an illustrated children's book, *Dare mo inai machi* (literally, "a town where there is no one," but figuratively, "a town with no one for me"). Even though it means that he cannot buy the dictionary that he needs for his studies, Hideki buys the children's book as a present for Chii. As the series progresses, we learn that Chii is drawn to the books because they are written expressly for Chii, and each installment tells Chii (and us) a bit more about her origins and destiny, but in cryptic form.

This illustrated book and subsequent installments teach Chii that she must find the one who will love her for herself, who will be her one and only. Even though we suspect that Hideaki will be her one and only, subsequent episodes raise questions about what will happen if Chii does find her love. There are, for instance, two mysterious security persocoms, Dima and Zita, who track Chii. They hint that if something goes wrong, if Chii finds her love, the result could be catastrophic, apocalyptic. In other words, as in *Nadia* and *Castle in the Sky*, the girl is associated with a power of great magnitude with potentially world-destructive capacities. The girl, in all her innocence, is the site for activation of a mystery that can lead to world salvation or annihilation. *Chobits*, however, has a very different take on girl's relation to the modern technological condition.

The illustrated books awaken something within Chii. As she reads the first book, she enters into trance-like state, and her body begins to float and radiate light. Recall how Sheeta's jewel in *Castle in the Sky* glowed and protected her, slowing her fall and allowing her to float. Recall how Nadia's Blue Water in *Nadia* emitted flashes of light to warn her of danger. The jewels of both girls were at once blessing and curse, a biologically inherited ability to control a power of great magnitude, which the girls must ultimately relinquish to save the world. Both girls were, in effect, mecha-shojo, but in the end, they give up their mecha-jewel powers to save humanity—or rather, to save *mankind*. The final scene of *Nadia* underscores the relation between "giving up the jewel" and the female condition: her father and the other adults around her encourage her to give up the jewel to save Jean, although it will also mean the death of her father; even the women tell her that this is what women do. In other words, the daughter lets go of her attachment to the father and "gives up the jewel" to the future husband, the boy who has helped her to protect her jewel until now. So mankind is saved.

Chobits makes explicit the techno-erotic connotations inherent in *Nadia* and *Castle in the Sky* by placing the mysterious jewel of world destruction between Chii's legs. In *Chobits*, too, the boy must help the girl protect her jewel, to make sure that the men in pursuit cannot get their hands on it. In episode 7, Chii seeks work in order to help support her life with Motosuwa. A pornographer who stages peepshows persuades her to work for him. He sits Chii in a room full of peepholes for live viewers, and instructs her to undress and play to the audience. He also films the performance for online, real-time transmission. When he instructs Chii to put her fingers between her legs, a voice sounds in Chii's head, warning her not to do so. At this moment, her black-clad "double"—the image of a young woman whom we will later learn is her sister Freya—appears to explain that only her true love may touch her there. Meantime, disappointed that Chii will not do as he asks, the scurrilous pornographer comes to her side and slips a hand between her legs to show her how to masturbate for the audience. Suddenly, Chi begins to glow and float, and lapsing into a dreamlike state, she skips and flies over the rooftops, alighting here and there in the city, all the while emitting a weird radiance. As she lingers in her amnesiac state, all the other persocoms in the city go dead. In other words, her jewel, like Sheeta's and Nadia's, comes with apocalyptic powers. But *Chobits* makes the metaphor of the jewel exceedingly concrete: what lies between her legs is a sex/reset button that threatens the very technological fabric of urban existence.

Because in Chii the line between shojo and mecha has collapsed, the girl cannot remove the jewel pendant. Nor can she destroy it in order to break her link to the mecha world. Rather the girl herself takes on the characteristics of weapons of mass destruction. In this respect, the Chii of *Chobits* who flits over the city like an angel of protection/destruction bears comparison to the girl in *She, the Ultimate Weapon*, who actually turns out to be a WMD. Chii also recalls the "battle angels" (*kidō tenshi*) of CLAMP's manga *Enjerikku reiyaa* or *Angelic Layer*, which are custom-designed dolls deployed in a game wherein they battle upon fields called layers. *Chobits*, in fact, is set in the same world as *Angelic Layer*. There are many other examples of fictions that conflate the destructive power of WMDs with the protective, affective, and communicative functions associated with women, generating a range of gynoid figures who are at once angels of destruction and goddesses of protection and mercy. What demands special attention in the context of *Chobits* are the echoes of family drama and sexual trauma that surround Chii as "daughter" in search of a home.

Like *Nadia*, *Chobits* ends with the passage of the daughter from father to husband under the tutelage of a mother figure. The landlady Ms. Hibiya turns out to be Chii's "mother," and it was her husband who made two chobits as children for his wife and him, naming them Freya and Elda (Chii). Unfortunately, Freya fell in love with her father creator and chose to die rather than live with the heartache of this impossible love. Apparently, after Freya's death, the "father" endowed Chii with special abilities, apparently placing the reset or on/off switch between her legs to assure that she would only thrive in a relationship of love free from demands for sex. After the death of the father, the mother could not bring herself to destroy Chii, and so she reset her and abandoned her. All the while, however, she continued to watch over her, guiding her with illustrated books reminding her of her destiny.[8] In sum, this is an almost classic story of filiations, in which the boy "wins" the girl from the father with the mother's assistance. Significantly, however, there is no "giving up the jewel" to the husband.

Fetishism in *Chobits*—wrapping and rewrapping the girl's body in layers of hair, clothing, conspiracy; drawing in and deflecting the eyes—also evokes grand masculinity (father creator) and grand fictions of world salvation and destruction (apocalypse), only to turn them into ornate veils that promise finally to part and reveal the girl's truth, but never do. The entire world comes to revolve around Chii's mysterious hidden "nothing," shielding and covering her, amplifying her with voluminous folds of soulful existence. Clearly, there are intimations of feminine power here, and Chii is a source of awe and wonder. Nonetheless, this set-up also raises the possibility that Chii is nothing but a symptom of the man, of male desire. To take on the challenge of this variation on the mecha-shojo, we need to consider how Chii potentially operates as a symptom of Hideki.

CHAPTER 18

PLATONIC SEX

N THE GYNOID SCENARIO, the combination of mecha and woman implies a double or two-fold relation for men. Men address themselves at once to the technological and to the feminine. There are a variety of scenarios, as we have seen. While mecha or giant robots stories do not present a gynoid scenario per se, there is in such genres a gradual feminization, biologization, and informatization of the pilot–mecha interface. In a very general way, such transformations in the mecha genre speak to larger socioeconomic transformations, from industrial modes of production to information modes of production. Significantly, as the relation between man and machine becomes "informationalized," there is also a tendency to biologize and feminize it, as if the woman's body (often the maternal body) were being dispersed or spectralized, as if new material conditions or new materiality could only be imagined in terms of a new matrix, that is, a new *mater*-mother-matter spread across the social. A fascination with the mothering machine, with the mecha that can give birth to humans, comes to the fore. Apparently, as information technologies begin to inhabit and transform human interaction with industrial machinery, there is a shift away from imagining machines that are under male physical and intellectual control, whose flaws or malfunctions can be resolved by a combination of male heroism and engineering. The interface becomes decidedly "softer," in the sense that the technological device makes emotional demands, and the man is asked to negotiate with the mecha not through brute strength or mental control but through feelings, physical tendencies, or corporeal inclinations.

In the actual gynoid or full mecha woman scenario, in which the mecha takes on feminine form, the conceit is usually that of man addressing a mecha that is *almost* indistinguishable from a real woman—even when the mecha is entirely indistinguishable from a real woman, there is always the moment of confrontation with mecha truth. Here, too, in conjunction with the informationalization of machines, there is a gradual tendency toward a less obviously instrumental relation to technology, and toward mecha women who make greater emotional demands on the man. The straightforward fantasy of a completely instrumental control over women—the sex machine or sexroid—becomes fraught, and the question of how men treat women becomes entwined with the question of how humans interact with machines, to the point that it is difficult to say whether sexual relations are becoming thoroughly instrumentalized (in the information mode) or whether human–machine relations are becoming completely eroticized.

In one important variation on the gynoid scenario, the central question is whether a man can live with a woman who is not really a woman. Sometimes it boils down to a choice between a real woman and a mecha woman, as in *Saber Marionnette J*, in which the central dilemma is whether the man will rest content with the familiar and seemingly authentic mecha copy of woman or to make the effort to bring back the original biological woman. In other instances, for a man to live with a mecha-woman demands a significant retooling or upgrading of the gynoid. This is the case in *Armitage III*, in which the gynoid proves as functional as a human woman, that is, capable of giving birth. Nonetheless, the central question is "can a man live content with a mecha woman?" Put another way, can a man live with a woman who is not a woman? This is precisely the question that *Chobits* pushes to the fore with its story of a young man living with a gynoid computer. Its challenge lies in its treatment of the man–gynoid romance as a general problem of male sexuality rather than a problem specific to the man–machine interface or information technologies. In *Chobits* it is a girl mecha that exposes the mechanisms of male sexuality, offering a concrete instance of Lacan's proposition, *il n'y a pas La femme*, that is, "woman does not exist" or "there is no such thing as The woman."[1]

Chobits provides ample reminders that Chii is a computer not a real woman. For instance, the series shows how, for many humans, persocoms do not demand the same courtesies as humans. Hideki's friend Shinbo does not hesitate to examine Chii's breasts or to look between her legs, because she is a PC not a woman. Hideki stops him from going between her legs, because, for Hideki, the form truly matters. Confronted with the form of a young woman, Hideki feels compelled to sustain the form of male–female interaction. This is also why Hideki cannot face the reset button: he refuses to break with his ideal of feminine form. At the same time, Hideki is free to project his idealized vision of woman onto

Chii, to shape and develop her. Chii's learning software is intact, and so *Chobits* is also a Pygmalion story, of the *My Fair Lady* variety in which the man has the opportunity to shape the perfect woman through patient instruction. Not only does Hideki teach Chii to speak, but also from the outset Chii mimics Hideki's every gesture and emotional expression, smiling, raising a ruckus, rolling around on the floor in a tizzy, and so forth, whenever he does. If Chii proves ideal for Hideki, is it not because he shapes her in his image of the ideal woman? Chii also learns a great deal from Hideki's porn collection, and he refers to them to show her what underwear to buy.

Chii is almost a tabula rasa on which Hideki writes and projects ideal feminine attributes. Of course, because she is already shaped like a girl, she is not entirely a blank slate. There is already femininity or girlness there. And, insofar as her "father" initially constructed her as the perfect daughter, the femininity of Chii appears as an effect or symptom of men. This is what Lacan means by the proposition "Woman does not exist." As Lacanian critic Slavoj Žižek puts it, "she is nothing but the symptom of man, her power of fascination masks the void of her nonexistence."[2] Hideki's treatment of Chii often recalls that of a pet owner with a pet (he pats her on the head in approval) or a father with a child (his paternal concern) rather than a man with a personal computer or a boy with a girlfriend. When Chii takes on a part-time job and offers him the money, Hideki magnanimously and paternalistically explains to her that this is her money. The overall tone of Hideki's education of Chii is that the ideal woman is at once pet, child, partner, and feminine in appearance. In other words, the gynoid has no essence, no essential identity, other than that ascribed to her by men. Some feminists see this condition as the fundamental truth of women. Luce Irigaray, for instance, writes of woman as the "sex that is not one."[3]

Such insights about "Woman" as a male construct, as a symptom of male desire, can be taken in a number of directions, and there are intense debates about how to follow through with them. It is, however, characteristic of psychoanalysis to treat male desire as the unity underlying the construction of sexual relations. As we will see, psychoanalysis sees Man, like Woman, as a construct, but Woman appears as symptom of male desire as the man strives for ontological consistency. Simply put, psychoanalysis insists on a fundamental asymmetry within sexual desire, which tends to position Woman and Man very differently, which difference persists even across historical and cultural formations.[4] As such, the question of Woman is an ontological question more than a sociohistorical question. Žižek, who derives a great deal from Lacan, puts it this way: "*man himself exists only through woman qua his symptom*: all his ontological consistency hangs on, is suspended from his symptom, is 'externalized' in his symptom."[5]

If I linger on psychoanalysis in the context of *Chobits*, it is not because I wholeheartedly endorse the psychoanalytic interpretation of sexual desire.[6] On the contrary, I find that psychoanalytic theory is rather limited in its thinking about technology in general and about the moving image specifically. What is more, in its emphasis on the ontology of the human, psychoanalytic theory tends to ignore the social institutions that invest men with power in the first place, and thus as feminist scholars have noted, the theoretical centrality of male desire also becomes a problem, because it may unwittingly work to reify and reinforce precisely the male centrality it aims to challenge. Anne McClintock summarizes the problem succinctly, "Lacanian psychoanalysis therefore cannot challenge the subordination of women precisely because it constantly reproduces women as inherently and invariably subordinate, destined to reside permanently under the false rule of the pretender phallus."[7] Nonetheless, I think it important to begin with psychoanalytic theory in the context of *Chobits* for a number of reasons.

Because it adopts and troubles the seinen mode of address, the stance of *Chobits* is eerily consonant with psychoanalytic theory in its exposure of shojo as a symptom of man. This is often the case with the gynoid scenario. Now, I have not thus far differentiated the terms *woman, girl,* and *shojo*. There are of course commonsense distinctions in age between woman and girl, and the shojo is supposed to present a moment of passage from girl to woman. Yet what gives shojo its power in manga, anime, and games stems from the presentation of the shojo as neither girl nor woman, while maybe both at once. In other words, the world of manga and anime encourage us to see shojo in something other than simplistic social terms, as something other than a social category that refers to females of a certain age.[8] Manga and anime thus encourage us to see shojo as a *metaphysical* construct with cosmological implications, precisely because she/it is a woman that is not one. As *Chobits* works through the seinen mode of address, it exposes how the woman that is not one may function as a symptom of male desire. Yet, to anticipate later discussion, *Chobits* also tries to construct shojo ontology, by which shojo would operate independently of male desire, which promises other configurations of sexuality and gender.

Recall that Hideki fails his college entrance exams and leaves his hometown in rural Hokkaido for Tokyo, to attend a cram school to prepare him to take the exams again. He is "rōnin," that is, a student without an official affiliation. Naïve and ill equipped for city life, Hideki yearns for a life and an identity that for him is symbolized by owning a gynoid persocom and/or having a girlfriend. He has no ontological consistency. The anime version comically evokes Hideki's lack of ontological consistency by having him first appear as a voice-over for a cow. It is through Chii (as persocom and then girlfriend) that Hideki takes on ontological consistency; through Chii, he learns and becomes who he is.[9]

Everything depends on Chii, or to evoke Žižek's deliberately provocative phrasing, everything *hangs* on Chii, or everything depends from her. As symptom, Chii places a constant demand on Hideki. At school he worries about her when he should focus on his lessons. He frets about spending so much time at the izakaya where he works part-time. He incessantly voices aloud his concerns about her, and he rushes home to check on her. When Yumi invites him for a home-cooked meal, for instance, he must dash out to rescue Chii from the pornographer. He fears that Chii will disappear, and in fact near the end of the series, Chii is kidnapped. Everything conspires to force Hideki to admit that he cannot live without Chii. His existence, his ontological consistency, depends on her.

In Lacanian theory, woman, however, does not truly exist, which is say, her consistency is as a symptom of man. Her apparent ontological consistency is thus prone to dissolve. For Žižek, the film form that best expresses the nonexistence of woman is film noir. He writes, "The destiny of the femme fatale in film noir, her final hysterical breakdown, exemplifies perfectly the Lacanian proposition that Woman does not exist: she is nothing but the symptom of man, her powerful fascination masks the void of her nonexistence, so that when she is finally rejected, her whole ontological consistency is dissolved."[10] Žižek refers to the tendency in film noir for the hardboiled guy to reject the woman whom he finds so seductive in her overt challenge and appeal to men. In Žižek's opinion, the film noir woman's response to sexual rejection, which typically occurs in conjunction with her becoming entrapped in her own plot, entails hysterical breakdown in the sense of an emotional excess, panic, and utter disorientation.

Chii might be considered something of a femme fatale in that, even as her cuteness proves thoroughly seductive to Hideki, she must withhold her body. Ultimately, however, despite some of the echoes of film noir in *Chobits* (seductive woman of mysterious origins, with hints of conspiracy), Chii doesn't fit the femme fatale or film noir mode. Even though she is a symptom of Hideki, and even though Hideki evidently takes on ontological consistency through his symptom, Chii does not suffer a hysterical breakdown. There are moments in the series at which she thinks that, despite her attachment to him, Hideki may not turn out to be the one for her, and threats of a catastrophic breakdown loom on the horizon. Yet, somehow, oddly enough, Chii appears to be as happy with her symptomatic consistency as Hideki is. Both enjoy his symptom, so to speak.

This mutual happiness does not arise merely because *Chobits* is, after all, a romantic comedy laced with risqué moments, which implies a happy ending in contrast to the darker world of crime and seduction in film noir. In many ways,

Chobits is far stranger and darker than noir. *Chobits* is exceedingly perverse, so perverse that the anime persistently glosses over what the manga makes explicit: here is a young couple whose love life hangs on not having sex. Were Hideki to touch her between the legs, he would reset her, and she would lose all memory and identity, and cease to be the Chii that he loves. Aptly, at the end of the series, Motosuwa has again failed his entrance exams and will remain safely in limbo, a student without official status, blissfully content with his "sexless" sex life with Chii.

This resolution makes concrete the original conceit of the series: there is no sexual relation here, and woman does not exist. At the same time, unlike Lacan for whom the absence of the sexual relation and the nonexistence of woman are ontologically true of sexual relations in general, *Chobits* presents Chii's relation to Hideki as something special, as a potentially truer, superior form of love. Chii needs someone who will love her for herself not for her body, and this need is apparently built into her hardware (due to the switch placement), programmed into her memory by her father. Since she has lost her memories, however, she needs the coaching of her mother's illustrated books to awaken her. In episode 10, as Chii reads the second installment, *Atashi dake no hito* (A person only for me), her memories resurface, taking the form of a dialogue with her "double" Freya (whom we do not yet know as Freya but only as a mysterious darkly Gothic version of Chii). Again, the gist of her parents' coaching is to assure that Chii will be loved for herself not her body. It is as if she could only come to know herself and develop a sense of identity in the absence of physical love. Naturally, because the context is one in which Chii is thing to be owned, the idea is to assure that Chii is not to be "used" sexually.

At this level, *Chobits* recalls the romantic conceit popularly referred to as Platonic love, that is, nonsexual love between heterosexual friends, implying a deep and intimate friendship. The popular understanding of Platonic love is not consonant with Plato's theory of love: Plato's theory of love does not entirely reject sex and depends on love between men.[11] Nonetheless, the popular understanding of Platonic love is important in the context of *Chobits*, insofar as it presents the ideal of loving someone for their character rather than their physical charm. Hideki must prove that he loves Chii for herself not her body, and Chii cannot retain her identity unless she is loved "platonically." Hideki and Chii must achieve a higher union—higher in the sense of transcending bodily impulses and interactions. In this respect, *Chobits* recalls the tradition of respect for the woman, and ideas of love for her spirit, which coalesced in ideals of courtly love in medieval Europe and became central to Romantic and Victorian conceptions of love. Such ideals take a number of twists and turns in Japanese literature from the Meiji era onward, with a range of debates on Love *(ren'ai)* versus bodily allure and affective response, described with diverse terms with varied connotations *(koi, iki, shikijo,* to name a few).[12]

In any event, just as Plato's theory of love is more complicated than passionate yet nonsexual friendship between man and woman, so the effort to transform male–female relations in *Chobits* is more complicated than a simple endorsement of love without sex. *Chobits* is overtly *ecchi*—that is, risqué, naughty, or dirty— and pornography plays a major role. There are, on the one hand, all the *okazu* or porn magazines lying around Hideki's room. Aptly, even though the term *okazu* itself euphemistically suggests that these mags are "side dishes," there is actually no "main dish" in Hideki's life. Living with him, Chii quickly becomes familiar with his porn collection. In episode 10, in which Chii goes shopping to spend the wages newly earned at her bakery job, not only does she buy Hideki a porn magazine as a present but she also rifles expertly through the rack of magazines, ruling out all those he already possesses. Also, Hideki uses examples from his skin books when he needs to explain certain matters to Chii. Chii is so familiar with these images that when Hideki explains the bathhouse to her in episode 9, she points to an image of women posing nude at a hot springs. Pornography for men and the male-directed mode of address is simple reality for Chii.

Everyone else seems to think that Hideki's stacks of *okazu* are normal, too. When other women catch sight of porn in his apartment, Hideki goes into paroxysms of embarrassment, yet the women treat pornography as perfectly normal for a young man. Presumably this acceptance of pornography implies an acceptance of masturbation, but the series is not that frank. Solitary sex is implied, not shown or discussed. But there are sly references to men having sex with persocoms. And you cannot help wonder whether persocom sex is like pornography. The female persocom may be nothing more than a male pornographic fantasy, raised to a new level of technological sophistication. In response to this pornographic condition, the goal of Chii and the triumph of Hideki lie in going beyond the use of gynoid persocoms as sex toys. Yet sexual stimulation is everywhere. Chii is a turn-on for Hideki; she even notes his erections. In one sequence (episode 9), when Chii leaps on him like a large dog greeting its master, she nudges his crotch with her knee, and Hideki goes into sexual rapture.

In fact, Hideki becomes aroused in proximity to anything that recalls his pornography. His coworker Yumi, his landlady Ms. Hibiya, his teacher Ms. Shimizu, and even Kokubunji's sexy persocom maids turn him on. It is part of the comedy that Hideki is easily aroused—and funnier still, he has no idea how to follow through. This situation is one that I think appropriate to call "Platonic sex." Sexual arousal is everywhere, happening all the time, but there are no sexual acts in the conventional sense of genital sex. Simply put, it is a world of pornography without sex—by implication, a world of male masturbatory pleasure, a world of sex without actual women.

The scandalous and shocking implications of *Chobits* come from its suggestion that pornography is not a side dish, *okazu*. It is the main dish and every dish. What is more, Platonic sex—sex with images of woman rather than with actual women—appears as a fitting conclusion to the Lacanian theory of sexuality. After all, the nonexistence of woman implies that, potentially, any substitution in the shape of woman might do. The path is clear for endless substitution, for perversion. As Linda Williams notes, "As even a cursory reading of Freud shows, sexuality is, by definition, perverse. The 'aims' and 'objects' of sexual desire are often obscure and inherently substitutive."[13] The implication of *Chobits* is that the nonexistence of woman is the oldest trick in the book, and perversion is the normal state of affairs.

Yet it is important to note that *Chobits* at once liberates and restrains perverse substitution. After all, it is images of women (or more precisely, girls) that substitute for actual women; there is a heterosexual pretext. And it is new technologies (humanoid personal computers) that set the scene for perverse substitution, which raises the question of whether technologies place material limits on sexuality. In sum, *Chobits* encourages us to see Hideki and Chii's relationship in two ways at once: (a) as a fundamental (ontological) condition pertaining to human heterosexuality; and (b) as a new technological condition linked to communications technologies that enhance possibilities for substitution. As a consequence, we must now explore the relation between perversion and technology, particularly if we are to consider what is in this situation for women, and address why *Chobits* toys with but does not end with the hysterical breakdown of Chii.

CHAPTER 19

PERVERSION

BECAUSE IT DEALS FIRST AND FOREMOST with what Žižek calls the "weird substance of enjoyment,"[1] psychoanalysis tends to look at technology from the angle of sexuality, and the emphasis is on the ontology of the human and human existence. Technology does not have ontological consistency for psychoanalysis. Confronted with new technologies or new material conditions, psychoanalysis stresses that we never have an immediate or nonmediated relation with them. Our relations to such technological devices as the personal computer or the cell phone are always already mediated, and psychoanalysis stresses the mediation of the unconscious, of those structures that shape us without our knowing it. Particularly important is enjoyment. If Žižek refers to enjoyment as a "weird substance," it is because we can never quite be sure what it is that we are enjoying (or why): something of our experience always remains obscure to us, remains unconscious. Yet enjoyment for him is a substance, which is to say, the mechanisms of desire are not merely airy fantasies, easily blown away.

In its approach to technologies, psychoanalysis thus avoids simplistic empiricism, positivism, rationalism, or mechanistic worldview: the effects of technology cannot be calculated or predicted on the basis of their mechanisms (or how they operate), because our experience of them is not fundamentally rational or measurable. This is not to say that our experience of technology is utterly irrational. The unconscious has its logic, but it is not that of reason (in the traditional Enlightenment sense).

When Žižek, for instance, considers the impact of the PC, he treats it largely in terms of fetishism.[2] *Chobits* also shows how the persocom may serve as fetish, and Hideki's fuss over dressing his female persocom is textbook fetishism: a delight in ornate trappings to shield himself from the naked truth. But to understand what it means to say that technological devices function as fetishes, I need to introduce, if only in a cursory fashion, Lacanian ideas about lack and desire. Such ideas have some currency in Japan, and one important theorist of otaku and anime, Saitō Tamaki, is explicitly Lacanian in his analysis. My cursory remarks on Lacan are also intended as an introduction to Saitō Tamaki, whose approach to anime otaku appears in the next chapter.

For Lacanian psychoanalysis, humans are constituted by lack; they are born too early and are unable to function in the world in a truly independent manner. In the course of their development, humans strive ceaselessly to stave off and deny lack. They produce and try to sustain an image of themselves as whole, powerful, and autonomous; the symbol of this wholeness and potency is the phallus, which is (as the dictionary definition of *phallus* implies) not the penis. Thus need turns into desire. The lack is no longer purely physical but largely psychological. A person will latch onto various little objects (referred to as *object petit a*) that promise to make him or her feel whole. These are often dubbed partial objects. Fetishism then is one way of latching onto a partial object or a set of partial objects in order to deny one's fundamental incompleteness in the world.

If fetishism is deemed to be somehow "abnormal," it is because partial objects are supposed to function in the context of sexual development as "transitional objects," as objects that ease the transition from an imaginary sense of wholeness and completion (that comes of being with the mother or some other caregiver) into the bigger world where one can only fit in by acknowledging and working through one's "castrated status," that is, one's incompleteness in relation to the social formation, a realm of law, language, and paternal authority, which for Lacan is symbolized by the Phallus. The basic scenario is written in highly gendered terms—in terms of the Oepidal movement of little boys from a cuddly infatuation with mothers into a world of law symbolized in the father's prohibition, his "no, the mother is not for you." Even though gendered terms such as *mother* and *Father* are, in theory, symbolic placeholders and open to any gender, it has proved very difficult in practice to get beyond them. The psychoanalytic scenario tends to presume the unity of male desire, which is why *Chobits* most resembles psychoanalysis when it centers attention on Hideki, shrouding Chii in mystery.

What also demands attention is how psychoanalysis situates technology, especially technological devices like the PC. In the psychoanalytic scenario, technological devices function as partial objects, to which the subject adheres in an attempt to avoid a confrontation with lack, and thus to avoid the realm of law, prohibition, and authority. The association of personal computers with the home and with personal communication, for instance, might be taken as a prime example of how technological devices reflect a desire to remain in the realm of cuddly domestic intimacy rather than go out into the world. This is true of Hideki: he is presented as a young man who is as yet unable to enter the bigger world. He has left his parents' home but remains immature in the sense that he still cannot address the task at hand: to study for and pass the entrance exams, and enter society. Chii remains at home, and when she takes on a part-time job, the arrangement is thoroughly domestic. In this sense, she/it is symbolic of Hideki's desire to stave off or deny his entry into "castration," that is, into the bigger world of law, authority, and prohibition.

Inevitably, social realities interrupt his fantasy, in the form of a need for money and a desire for a "normal" path of development (girlfriend and college), and as he overcomes these intrusions of the symbolic into his fantasy life, there occur stranger, more fantastical and violent disruptions. Chii is kidnapped, and there are signs of mysterious organizations conspiring all around him—signs that the social cannot be entirely denied. Ultimately, however, Hideki defeats these obstacles and opts to *remain in transition*. In sum, if we look at Hideki's attachment to Chii from the angle of the technological device as a partial object, the persocom or PC appears as a specific instance in which the partial object functions as a *transitional* object. But rather than allow a transition to the next phase, Hideki's transitional object assures a permanent state of transition. In effect, the fascination and obsession with the PC amounts to a desire to remain in transition, to construct a realm that is no longer that of the parental domestic scene but does not entail entry into the symbolic social realm either. This state of perpetual transition is precisely the realm of perversion.

In their introduction to a book on perversion, Molly Anne Rothenberg and Dennis Foster argue that perversion is about polymorphous pleasures (or avenues of cathexis) that come before the law, pleasures that are not yet organized or legalized, "the category of polymorphous perversion suggests that we are highly motivated to have varying forms of satisfaction and attachment to objects, including both human and non-human relations."[3] Polymorphous perversion implies a loosely organized, somewhat chaotic and inconsistent set of attachments. Hideki's responses to women, for instance, are consistent with polymorphous perversion in the sense that he finds satisfaction in anything with female attributes, running the gamut from human women (his coworker Yumi, his teacher Shimizu, his landlady Hibiya), through images of human women (porn magazines and films), to nonhuman women (Kokubunji's persocoms and Chii). In such perversion, there is not yet a "full substitution," that is, an object of desire around which to organize desire and impart ontological consistency in the form of a recognizable commitment.

Hideki's general excitability around women and images of women underscores that his is a not yet entirely localized interest in actual women, let alone a woman; Hideki projects Woman everywhere, and the implication is that almost anything womanish will do. Pornography is key here, because it straddles the realms of human and nonhuman. Above all it is the image that excites Hideki, or more precisely, as is implied in polymorphous perversion, there is a general delight in bodily movements, patterning of words, babbling, ogling, gobbling. In the episode in which Yumi invites him to dinner (7), for instance, Hideki goes into a rhapsody as he envisions himself in the position of having a cute girl cook for him. When she remarks that they are like young newlyweds, he replies that he always liked a certain television series about newlyweds, which, as it happens, is a porn series. She does not get the reference, and Hideki, suddenly aware of his inference, stammers and babbles. In brief, Hideki is in a zone of heightened affective response, in which he reacts intensely to the tiniest patterns or slightest insinuation of sexuality. The running joke of the series is that he invariably responds with erotic gusto only to fall into paroxysms of embarrassment.

There is a kind of image associated with Hideki's paroxysms and manic reactions. We see Hideki in bold outline striking an extravagant pose of heightened emotion—bold determination, abject embarrassment, rapture, fear, courage, to name a few. Behind him is an abstract optical pattern of motion, usually in white and a bright almost fluorescent color (electric blue, shocking pink, neon green, dayglow yellow), composed of vertical, diagonal, or zigzag stripes that run across the background, or radiating circles (Figure 38).

This is a kind of affect-image that evokes yet breaks with the action-image. Hideki is frozen in action, as if paralyzed by his affective response. This is an image of sheer patterning and behavioral response. Later I will consider how this kind of image presents a crisis not only of the action-image but also of the time-image. It also recalls the patterns of behavioral response that Azuma Hiroki associates with the "grand database." First, however, it is important to note that, for all the babble, ogle, and gobble associated with polymorphous perversion, perversion is characterized by an orientation toward the law.

Hideki is exceedingly scrupulous with Chii, not only taking care to dress her, protect her, and teach her, but also insisting that she keep the money she earns. A strong sense of propriety accompanies his *ecchi* behavior. Episode 4 in particular highlights his anxiety about being seen as a pervert *(hentai)*. Hideki wishes to buy panties for Chii but cannot enter the store; he stands in front of lingerie store, hearing the women whispering and muttering about him. Subsequently, when Chii fails to get panties, he finally musters the courage to march into the store and ask for panties, only to run home and bang his head on the

Figure 38. *A series of images of Hideki's manic responses drawn from the animated* Chobits, *in which he suddenly appears in emotive poses against a background of pulsing geometric patterns. In the last panel, Chii leaps onto him, and the embarrassed Hideki remembers nonetheless to pull her skirts down to cover her lack of panties.*

floor screaming abjectly that he is *hentai*, a pervert. While Hideki never fails to imagine the naughty possibilities of any situation with a woman, he never fails to behave properly. Vis-à-vis Chii, for instance, each time he feels forced into a situation wherein he must see or touch her naked body (as in the bathing episode [10] or in the seashore episode [13] in which he learns he must apply special lotion to Chii's body), Hideki ultimately defers to a woman to sort things out for him. In these instances, the landlady Hibiya comes to the rescue—*mater ex machina*. In other words, even when nothing prohibits him from doing whatever he wants to do with or to Chii, Hideki acts *as if* rules and prohibitions existed.

Psychoanalytic theory reads such "as if" behavior as a neurotic suppression of lawlessness, designed to avoid suspicion that law does not exist. Ultimately, however, there is no effective law or binding authority for perversion. Consequently, even if the pervert is caught in the act, being caught does not signal the effectiveness of the law but confirms its impotence. Hideki, for instance, finds himself repeatedly caught in embarrassing or compromising positions with Chii, but it is easy for him to say that things are not what they appear to be. The sensation of being caught does not end the fantasy but propels it forward. In a world in which there are no prohibitions against sexual relations with persocoms, Hideki perversely and neurotically posits them for himself, but the projected prohibitions do not curb his fantasy, they spur it.

Hideki also frets incessantly. He frets about being seen as a pervert, about being recognized as a virgin, about not having a girlfriend, and about not moving ahead with his studies. In episode 13, he receives a D on his practice exam and vows to study all summer, but soon he is at the beach with his friends; when he returns, he frets about studying, but the results are worse, an E. In his discussion of perversion, Bruce Fink sees the perverse sexuality as dominated by anxiety, because the pervert has undergone alienation but refuses separation.[4] Separation for Fink means symbolic separation from the mother, and the refusal of separation means that the pervert wishes to remain cuddly, content with masturbatory pleasures. At the same time, perversion entails a sense of alienation vis-à-vis cuddly masturbatory pleasures, as with Hideki's simultaneous delight in and humiliation over pornography. He will not give it up, yet it produces a sense of anxiety. This is why Fink speaks of a splitting of the ego in which contradictory ideas are maintained side by side. The ultimate expression of this splitting in *Chobits* is Hideki's stance toward Chii: she is a girl, she is not a girl; she is just a computer, she is not just a computer.

For Octave Mannoni, such a perverse maintenance of contradictory ideas often amounts to insisting that something untrue is in fact true in a different way. A simple example is a belief in Santa Claus. While adults know that there is no such being, they believe in it for someone else, accepting it as true in a different way, even presenting it to the enlightened child as true at some other level. Mannoni thus concludes that perversion is not so much about a belief in magic as about the magic of belief. He draws attention to how belief makes something out of nothing, and the refrain of perversion becomes "I know well, but all the same . . ."[5] So it is with Hideki in *Chobits*: he knows very well that Chii is not a girl and yet all the same he acts as if she is, and eventually he must believe she is a girl for someone else's sake, for Chii herself. Of course, the entire series conspires with Hideki, with its legends of chobits, that is, computers with the capacity to feel emotion and think for themselves. Gradually, even though everyone knows Chii is a computer not a girl, they gradually begin to accept that, in some other way, she is a girl. They know very well she is not a girl, but all the same . . .

The situation recalls that of *Video Girl Ai*, one important precedent for *Chobits*. The boy in that series knows very well that Ai, the girl who leaps out of the TV screen from a porn video, is not a real girl. He knows that Ai is programmed to aid him and then to vanish when the tape is through. Yet, as he treats her as a girl, he falls in love with Ai, and his love awakens hers. By the terms of the gods who send video girls to those young men who merit them, video girls are not designed or permitted to fall in love. Ai's love of the boy thus runs counter to the order of things, and gods set up obstacles to foil their love. In *Video Girl Ai* as in *Chobits*, the situation is perverse at a number of levels. In the absence of actual prohibitions, a neurotic anxiety about propriety sustains a relation to law, but only to carry out the fantasy. The male hero comes to enjoy the "fake girl" and the solitary eroticism associated with pornography more than the real girl. At the same time, the hero and other characters come to accept contradictory ideas: she is not a girl but all the same . . . But *Chobits* goes beyond *Video Girl Ai* in its commitment to perversion. In effect, *Chobits* takes the idea of otaku commitment to the anime shojo to a logical extreme.

In chapter 12, in the context of Okada Toshio's "otakuology," I discussed the social panic that arose in Japan vis-à-vis otaku with the arrest of the "otaku serial killer" Miyazaki Tsutomu in 1989. Otaku culture had already been around for some time. If we adopt the standard chronology for otaku, the first generation was born between 1955 and 1965, and the first wave of television anime otaku culture appeared in the 1970s. In wake of the Miyazaki Tsutomu incident, however, those who wished to defend or sustain otaku-type culture were forced to address the relation between the otaku images of girls and actual girls. Recall how Gainax's *Otaku no video* responded with portraits of otaku that played up the pathos of disconnection between otaku and the real world, stressing that male otaku tend to become caught up in pornography at the expense of developing relations with actual women. It appeared safer, and maybe truer to the situation, to present male otaku as losers who cannot or will not date real women, preferring or merely settling for idealized porn images, fantasy narratives, and masturbatory pleasures. Gainax set the precedent and the tone for a view of male otaku that highlighted the disjuncture between their connoisseurship of girl images and their relations with actual girls. Gainax thus assured viewers that the male otaku's delight in little girl images did not lead out into the real world, to crime or violence against girls. Male otaku appeared as the site of pathology, but of harmless, even pathetic pathology. Needless to say, such a view of the male otaku completely ignores the exploitation of women within the pornography industry, which came to the public eye about the same time as Okada's *Introduction to Otakuology* in a spectacular way with the publication of the book

AV *joyū* (Adult video actresses, 1996), in which women from porn industry spoke directly about its brutality.[6]

By the mid-1990s, however, as the commercial success of *Evangelion* made all too evident, otaku-related activities had to be recognized as an economic opportunity if nothing else. Interest in otaku was renewed, but with greater emphasis on otaku-type *consumption*. With the global boom in the popularity of Japanese animation, some commentators began to see in otaku-related production and consumption a different business model. Suddenly, otaku-related consumption promised to redeem or save postbubble Japan, whose glacial economy promised nothing but eternal zero growth. In an essay published in 2002 in *Foreign Policy*, Douglas McGray gave an aura of authority to the idea that Japan had developed a unique mode of cultural production and consumption, a globally viable "national cool."[7] Soon it was common to see articles with such proclamations as "Japan is transforming itself into Asia's cultural dynamo—and might just reinvent its economy in the process."[8] In the first decade of the new century, the Japanese government has begun to act on such ideas, developing public policy to promote manga, anime, and video games under the rubric of Japanese culture, and sponsoring conferences on the topic of the Japan's national cool as well as the contents industry. Thus the economic success of otaku-related production and consumption have become part of a neoliberal imaginary of Japanese economic recovery and ascendancy.

Nonetheless, precisely because otaku are not cool, at least not in any usual sense of the term, anxiety has persisted about the male otaku. The image of the male otaku needed a thorough makeover if it was to jive with the idea of Japan's national cool. How is it possible to redeem the social dropout who is fixated on the girls of manga, anime, and games? Is it possible to have him grow up, to move beyond those girl images? One solution to this perceived crisis in the sexual development of young men is to treat otaku fixations as transitional objects. The young man's obsession with porn is construed as an expression of a normal, healthy sexuality, and above all, heterosexuality. His is a sexuality stuck in transition, due to his shyness or awkwardness, and due as well to a lack of social rituals to assist him in his rites of passage. The hope is that, with a little help, the guy will find a girlfriend and leave his collection of little sexy girl things behind him. This is basically the stance of *Densha otoko* or *Train Man*, which, as I discussed in chapter 12, recently generated something of a multimedia craze in Japan, appearing as a book, a film, a television drama, and in multiple manga serializations.

Through a series of internet exchanges on 2channel (*ni-chaneru*), *Densha otoko* tells the story of a young male otaku who stands up to protect a young woman on the train when a bully harasses her. The otaku falls in love with her but has no idea how to go about courting her. So he writes into 2channel for advice, and a number of people begin to send messages, assisting him through every step of his courtship. Ultimately, with their aid, the male otaku casts off his geeky attire, moves past his obsession for anime girls, and wins the girl. *Densha otoko* can be seen as a kind of Cinderella story, with the guy in the Cinderella role and the Internet community playing the fairy godmothers who help him dress for the ball and move up in the world through courtship. The overwhelming popularity of this story is surely due in part to how it holds out a potential solution to social anxieties about the inability of young men to grow out of their fantasy worlds and pornography. *Densha otoko* offers the portrait of a socially redeemable otaku, one better suited to neoliberal ideas about gross national consumption and production.

At another level, however, because it is the Internet that mediates the male otaku's transition from anime girls to real girls in *Densha otoko*, we have to wonder about the male otaku's relation to these helpers, who are, after all, just images and signs of humans somewhere out there. If *Densha otoko* appears to solve the problem of boys' erotic attachment to images of girls (the virtual girl), it does so only by displacing the problem of attachment to images of magical girls onto images of magical community (the virtual community). *Densha otoko* thus invites two readings, almost diametrically opposed. On the one hand, it would seem that society, in the form of the public sphere, has intervened to reintegrate the little otaku world into the larger social community. On the other hand, because the status of the anonymous computer helpers remains in question, *Densha otoko* also implies a collapse of the public sphere into a network of personalized little worlds.

Chobits also plays the otaku scenario both ways, yet ultimately, through its emphasis on Hideki's perversion, *Chobits* pushes the second scenario to the fore. On the one hand, Hideki's interest in having a girlfriend and his reluctance to think of female persocoms as adequate substitutes for girls holds out hope for Hideki's "normal" development and social integration. On the other hand, the insistence on perversion in *Chobits* plays havoc with the logic of full, adequate, or normal substitution. It troubles the logic of organizing desire around an object that puts an end to unconstrained substitutability of polymorphous perversion in which almost any partial object will do. *Chobits* thus challenges viewers-readers in a way that *Densha otoko* does not: where the Train Man finds a full substitution in a real girl "Hermès" (whose nickname, derived from a classy product, nonetheless exposes the perversity underlying neoliberal operations of normalcy), Motosuwa Hideki finds Chii.

Chii is the substitution that promises to bring consistency to Hideki's babbling ogling chaos.[9] The series ends with the symbolic union of Hideki and Chii, sanctioned by parental authority. Yet this substitution remains genuinely perverse. Rather than an integration of the subject into the symbolic (law, authority, prohibition, the social), we have a subject (Hideki) who sustains a relation to the social only to tighten his grip on his fantasy. In the end, the public sphere exists only to abet perversion. But we have seen this all along: whenever Hideki wanders into crowds in large public areas, he sees myriad instances of men and women happily and intimately focused on their persocom, as if the world had already confirmed his fantasy. In contrast to *Densha otoko*, which holds out hope that anime girls will function as transitional objects on the male journey to find an actual girl surrounded with high-end products, *Chobits* populates the public sphere with gynoids, leaving Hideki and the reader-viewer in perpetual transition, in eternal perversion, in the realm of babble, doodle, and ogle.

Such a scenario depends on a specific kind of relation to technology. Hideki's perverse relation to the gynoid Chii makes both women and technologies appear as partial objects, as transitional objects that remain "stuck" in the register of the fetish, at once promising full "normal" substitution and deferring it endlessly. Because girl and computer are equally portrayed as fetishes for Motosuwa, it is difficult to gauge the impact of technologies, because the emphasis falls almost exclusively on the mechanisms of male perversion. It is difficult to say whether computerization has generated new forms of male perversion, or whether computerization has merely spurred and enabled received forms of male perversion. Simply put, the emphasis on sexuality in *Chobits* makes it difficult to focus directly on questions about the impact of technology, even though computer technologies are integral to the story. Similarly, the emphasis on successful romance and "full" substitution in *Densha otoko* at once highlights and obfuscates the role of computer technologies. Nonetheless, *Chobits* is more interesting and challenging than *Densha otoko* precisely because its emphasis on the perverse mechanisms of male desire in the context of the gynoid makes for a girl who is at once psychologically fetishized and technologically spectralized. It is this technological spectralization of the girl that now merits attention, alongside the mechanisms of perversion and fetishization.

CHAPTER 20

THE SPIRAL DANCE OF SYMPTOM AND SPECTER

SAITŌ TAMAKI'S ANALYSIS OF OTAKU draws inspiration from Lacanian psychoanalytic theory. He has written so many books that it would be impossible to address all of them here. His 1998 book *Shakai teki hikikomori: owaranai shishunki* (Social withdrawal: endless adolescence) introduced the concept of social withdrawal as an explanatory framework for otaku-related tendencies, popularizing the term *hikikomori*. His 2000 book *Sentō bishōjo no seishin bunseki* (A psychoanalysis of beautiful girl warriors) also had a profound impact on otaku debates, for in this book Saitō analyzes male otaku fantasies that are structured around *sentō bishōjo*, that is, the beautiful girl warriors, the "battling babes" or "fighting foxes" prevalent in anime and manga catering to boys and young men. Saitō styles these battling babes as "phallic girls."[1] This book deals exclusively with male otaku fantasies, but in subsequent works, especially in the essay "Otaku Sexuality" included in a collection of essays entitled *Hakase no kimyō na shishunki* (The doctor's strange adolescence, 2003), he takes on female otaku sexuality and takes into account some of Azuma Hiroki's ideas about database structure as well.[2]

In Lacanian fashion, Saitō begins with the asymmetry between male and female desire. The orientation of male desire differs fundamentally from female desire, and this structural difference is explained in terms of different relations to castration. In Lacanian fashion, he insists on the *ontological consistency of male desire* and the *symptomatic consistency of female desire*. He writes, "Woman can locate themselves only as beings lacking from the symbolic world, where women do not exist, and it is from this position of lack that women desire the phallus they do not have."[3] In other words, the woman as such does not exist except as a symptom of male desire, and women can locate their desire only in relation to the nonexistence of Woman. Saitō's account of male desire follows suit. The battling beauty is a variation on the nonexistent Woman. She is the "phallic girl" from whom everything hangs (to evoke Žižek's turn of phrase). Saitō describes the phallic girl as thoroughly hystericized. She is a bundle of male symptoms without ontological consistency. In sum, this is the familiar psychoanalytic scenario in which men strive for ontological consistency, while women are stuck with symptomatic consistency.

Of course, in psychoanalytic theory, this asymmetry is a result of structural positioning, not inherent essences. As such, the structure of male desire is as fragile and lacking as female desire. This is why Jacqueline Rose, for instance, underscores that Lacan's importance lies in his insight that the phallus is an "impostor."[4] Nevertheless, what bothers feminist critics of Lacanian psychoanalysis is the ontological priority of male desire over female desire in relation to lack. Even if the ontological consistency of the man is a ruse, and even if the phallus is a pretender or impostor, the consistency of women is always twice removed from the phallus; "she" is a symptom of ontological lack in men.

Saitō embraces this asymmetry of male desire and female desire, which is fundamental to psychoanalytic theory: "when a male desires a female, she is hystericized."[5] In his opinion, the warrior girl or battling babe presents many features that correspond to actual hysteria, but the difference is that the battling babe can enjoy battle without trauma, and in this respect, "she presents the mirror image of actual hysteria."[6] If she can also be styled as a phallic girl, it is because her symptomatic consistency (hysteria or its mirror image) works to impart ontological consistency to the male. For Saitō, what characterizes the male otaku is a keen awareness of the fictional status of the warrior beauty, and of the anime fantasy girl more generally. In effect, her hystericization is redeemed in his fictionalization—which affords him ontological consistency.

Now, as we have seen, the backstory for Chii is eerily reminiscent of Saitō-Lacanian ideas about female desire. As *Chobits* unfolds, we learn that the "father" initially created one chobits persocom, as a girl child for his barren wife (Hibiya). Later, noting an undercurrent of sadness in this gynoid child Freya, the parents produced another persocom girl, Elda. Already the girls appear in a field of substitution, in which the one might substitute for the other. Freya's sadness persisted, however, and eventually the wife realized that it was because Freya had taken the father as her one and only. Freya had fallen in love with her "father." Confronted with this impossible situation, rather than allow her memory to be erased, Freya chose not to exist. Grief stricken, the father fell ill and died, leaving the mother and Elda. Unable to bear the thought of terminating Elda, the mother reset and abandoned her, hoping for the best. Fortunately, it was Hideki who found Elda, naming her Chii. Also fortunately, Chii remembered just enough of her programming to find someone who would love only her. In this way, Chii succeeds in avoiding her sister's mistake by transferring her attachment from the father to another man, Hideki.

Initially then, the male and female scenarios in *Chobits* appear to some degree symmetrical. In the Oepidal scenario, when the father prohibits the son's erotic attachment to the mother, the boy seeks substitutes (looking for his own woman), gradually moving into the position of the father. In Chii's case, the mother prohibits the daughter's erotic attachment to the father, and the girl thus seeks a substitute (her own man), moving into the position of the mother. Again however, *Chobits* proves oddly consistent with Lacanian thinking, by positing a profound asymmetry between male and female desire, between Chii's desire and Hideki's desire.

Chii's symbolic mother, Ms. Hibiya, is on hand to offer her "daughter" instruction on how to move into the mother's position, teaching her how to cook for Hideki, for instance. The one man in *Chobits* who appears, rather fleetingly, as a symbolic father for Hideki is Yumi's father, his boss Mr. Omura. Omura offers him a DVD player and tips on buying porn videos, and when Hideki does not immediately buy porn videos, he lends him some of his favorites. In other words, male desire entails gaining the phallus, and consequently it does not put an end to desire for the mother, but disperses her attributes across a series of woman objects, with an emphasis on parts of the woman (partial objects), which here become fetishes. In contrast, female desire in *Chobits* does not operate through pornographic images of men. Chii configures her desire through Hideki's pornographic images of women, and through her mother's illustrated book about love. She locates herself in the position of that which is desired by Hideki. She locates herself as that which does not exist symbolically; she locates herself as Woman. That in the end Chii and Hideki cannot ever have sex seems to confirm the Lacanian view: it is precisely because of the asymmetry between male and female desire that there is no sexual relation between man and woman. Or, as Saitō puts it, "love is nothing more than an exchange of illusions."[7] Desire is a matter of positioning oneself in what feels like a stable relation, but the sense of stability derives from the relation to the phallus (castration) not directly to the sex partner. Castration appears to mediate everything.

In sum, *Chobits* seems to fit perfectly with the Saitō-Lacan scenario of the fundamental asymmetry of male/female desire by which men strive for ontological consistency and women for symptomatic consistency, but only when we stress specific frameworks within the series—such as the "master narrative of the western family romance" (to cite Anne McClintock) and the "modern heterosexual matrix" (to cite Judith Butler). McClintock argues that the logic of castration is operative only where specific institutions shore up and invest authority in the male. Behind the Oedipal romance of psychoanalytic theory, she sees institutions of family, specific to the modern West.[8] In contrast, Judith Butler calls attention to modern institutions that made heterosexuality not only normal but also compulsory.[9] It is precisely such institutions that the psychoanalytic theory frequently presumes.

What of technologies? It is clear that when we read *Chobits* psychoanalytically, or in terms of the institutions that invest authority in men (family, school, company) and make psychoanalytic paradigms operative, we get only half its picture. We might as easily say that, in *Chobits*, computer technologies mediate everything, and not castration or the institution of the family or the heterosexual matrix.

Interestingly enough, this is where Saitō Tamaki takes a strange turn. On the one hand, he insists that otaku activities are not pathological or abnormal but therapeutic and normal, that is, thoroughly heterosexual at heart. His reason for resisting the pathologization of otaku is, not surprisingly, Miyazaki Tsutomu. To avoid such pathologizing views of otaku, Saitō takes care to assure readers that women who enjoy stories of male homosexual love (*yaoi* or *bishōnen ai*) are not gay but heterosexual, that men who delight in "phallic girls" are not perverts, and that men and women who read and write fantasies entailing sex with children (*shōta*) are not pedophiles. He repeatedly assures us that otaku sexuality is not perversion (*tōsaku*).[10] On the contrary, he reassures us, these fans are all average heterosexual citizens. Saitō finds that the fantasy worlds of these otaku men and women are entirely separate from their everyday existence. Men and women who like manga and anime about same-sex love, or robot sex, or adult–child love, do not depart from "normal" sexuality in their daily lives.

This is also where Saitō's psychoanalytic approach begins to falter, leaning toward a simple defense of normalcy. Above all, Saitō wishes to highlight the creativity of otaku, but oddly enough, creativity is always in keeping with normal sexuality, which to him means heterosexuality. In Saitō's opinion, otaku sexuality differs from ordinary daily sexuality primarily in its self-conscious delight in fictionalization, in fictionalized contexts. He stresses that otaku are people who love fiction, who have an erotic attachment to texts and narratives, and hence to fictionalization and texts with multiple orientations, which increases the sense of fictionalization. He even refers to "drawn sexuality," which is his way of putting emphasis on how fans write and draw their amateur productions.[11] His account thus mobilizes a distinction between techniques (or low tech) and technology (or high tech), which is highly questionable in the context of otaku activities. But this dubious distinction suits his overall purpose, which is to posit otaku creativity as a form of resistance to what he calls, with a nod to Azuma's discussion of database structure, "data-ification."[12] In sum, he wishes to establish human creativity and fantasy as resistance to the leveling forces of information technology. Ultimately, what begins as a Lacanian theory of otaku desire ends as a quasi-Jungian apologia for the creative force of fantasy.

What is disturbing about Saitō's approach is that, in his eagerness to prove the normalcy of otaku sexual fantasies, he reinforces normative ideas about sexuality. As a corollary to his insistence on the normality or normalcy of otaku, Saitō Tamaki posits heterosexuality as a normative force. Even as he champions the ways in which the otaku creativity resists the leveling effects of data-ification by unfurling unlimited fantasies, he leads all those fantasies back to the maintenance of normal, that is, heterosexual lives. Ultimately, the heterosexual matrix regulates the allegedly unconstrained realm of fantasy, structuring its movements. Paradoxically then, in Saitō's account, otaku resistance (fantasy) sustains the status quo (heterosexual normativity). What is more, the initial positioning of woman as symptom, as Woman, assures that, underneath all the different fantasies, male desire maintains its ontological priority, as the ground for the heterosexual matrix.

Equally disturbing is Saitō's inability to deal with the materiality of technology. Frequently, psychoanalytic approaches will stress the symptomaticity of technologies, positioning such devices as computers or mobile phones as partial objects designed to stave off a confrontation with constitutive lack. Thus a computer, for instance, becomes a fetish. Saitō, however, does not even try to address questions of technology. Instead he champions seemingly nontechnological techniques (drawing and writing) and rejects data-ification and information technologies. This fits perfectly well with his agenda: basically he remains committed to the promotion of fantasy and fictionalization as a process that shores up "full" or "normal" substitution. To wit, let your fantasies run wild as long as they lead you back to bed with your socially legitimate partner. Apparently, for Saitō, data-ification threatens such normal substitution by allowing for a general regime of incessant substitution, due to its tendency toward fragmentation, multiplication, recombination, and exchangeability, in which anything and everything becomes a partial object, but no partial object has the power to stabilize or organize the subject.

What drops out of Saitō's account is precisely what Žižek introduces: value. Where Žižek explicitly evaluates regimes of substitution (usually favoring regimes that force an awareness of alienation under capitalism),[13] Saitō mobilizes substitution (fetishization or fictionalization) in the service of received sexual norms. As Anne McClintock reminds us, "Fetishes may not always be disruptive or transgressive and can be mobilized for a variety of political ends—some progressive, some subversive, some deeply reactionary."[14] In Saitō's case, although he follows Lacan in speaking of a constitutive lack that is constantly deferred, Saitō stresses how fictionalization allows subjects to cope creatively and successfully sustain normal relations in a data-ified world of intensified exchangeability. His is a profoundly conservative mobilization of otaku fictions as heterosexual therapy for the computer age.

We must then ask, how does *Chobits* mobilize the male fetishization of gynoid computers? Are its tactics of fictionalization, like Saitō's, designed as heterosexual therapy for those who feel anxious about the future of masculinity, femininity, and heterosexuality in an era in which digitalization promises endlessly perverse possibilities for substitution, in which men may find sexy girl images more companionable than actual women? After all, *Chobits* offers a nice heterosexual couple with substitutions that are in keeping with the institutions inherent in the modern family drama. This is where the questions about technology come to the fore again. Does *Chobits* entail a conservative domestication of information technologies, assuring us that new technologies will not change the fundamental heterosexual order of the world, by which men and women form households? Or does it invite us to assess the impact of "data-ification" or informatization on the formation of the households, on domesticity?

Here the double-edged household connotations of the word *otaku* come to fore. *Otaku* refers at once to a residence or household and to a solitary housebound individual. The male otaku is both a family of one, and one of a family.[15] This is why *Chobits* can play Hideki's situation two ways. Is Hideki an otaku happy to live alone with his computer? Or is he a man living with a woman? *Chobits* also encourages us to see information technologies as central to the production and maintenance of the otaku entity—that is, one of a household, and a household of one. A great deal depends on what the contours of the household are. Are they those of family or of something else?

This is where Azuma Hiroki's theory of the "grand database" proves of interest, partly because it deliberately runs counter to the psychoanalytic approach. Azuma initially worked on the philosophy of Jacques Derrida, and in his first book, *Sonzaiteki, yubinteki: Jacques Derrida ni tsuite* (Ontological, postal: On Jacques Derrida, 1998), he traces Derrida's usage of the logic of the postal in order to lay the grounds for a new theory of communication. Already in his second book, *Yubinteki fuantachi* (The Postally anxious, 1999), a collection of diverse essays and reflections, Azuma pushed his Derridean-inspired theory of communication further in the direction of an analysis of subculture, particularly in his discussion of *The End of Evangelion*. Yet it is in a collection of interviews and exchanges,

Fukashina mono no sekai (Overvisualized world, 2000) that Azuma came to the fore as one of the most important commentators on contemporary Japanese popular culture and subcultures, especially on anime and otaku.

Azuma's background in deconstruction initially made him an especially keen observer of the autodeconstructive tendencies of anime and otaku subculture. As his work progressed, however, he began to see such tendencies in terms of the emergence of a new structure of communication and control. It is in *Dōbutsuka suru posutomodan: otaku kara mita Nihon shakai* (literally "Animalizing postmodern: otaku and postmodern Japanese society," 2001; recently published in English as *Otaku: Japan's Database Animals*) that Azuma persuasively argues that otaku are not merely a site where one might deconstruct Japanese culture; rather otaku subculture presents the emergence of a new "database structure," which he links to a new mode of cultural reception dubbed "animalization."[16]

In an essay introducing the basic framework of thinking about animalization and otaku, which was written in the context of a debate among Japanese intellectuals about otaku, Azuma explicitly distinguishes his approach from psychoanalytic theory.[17] He prefaces his essay with some remarks about how his approach differs from that of Saitō Tamaki, pointing out that analysis centered on sexuality tends to posit the human subject as the beginning and end of analysis. In contrast, Azuma's discussion centers on consumer behaviors and media structures rather than on desire and symptoms. Countering Saitō's conservative resistance to (and disavowal of) computerization, Azuma makes information technologies central to the analysis of male otaku activities. His is a more detached, almost cognitive or behaviorist diagnosis of contemporary inflections of the postmodern condition. Let me briefly introduce his model of the two-tiered mode of consumption characteristic of the grand database.

On the one tier, he submits that consumers no longer look to anime or games for grand fictions or worlds. Instead, they have withdrawn into little narratives that are organized around "animalized" responses, that is, affective responses to characters. Azuma discusses how consumers today construct databases of their favorite character elements, disassembling and reassembling the characters in new and creative ways. The key term is *kyara-moe* or simply *moe* (pronounced *moé*). *Kyara-moe* refers to the *moe* elements of *kyara* or characters. *Moe*, which can be written either with the characters for "sprouting/budding" or "blazing/burning," refers broadly to the affective responses to elements that appear to sprout from manga, anime, or game characters, such as cat ears, colored hair, rabbit tails, eyeglasses, costumes or uniforms, and poses, gestures, or situations.[18] There is a broad range of discussions of *moe*, some speaking of sexual stimulation, others seeing in *moe* a passionate self-forgetting, and still others speaking of maternal nurture. In Azuma's account, *moe* recalls the logic of affect insofar as *moe* refers to perceptual elements that strike consumers, wowing them, completely capturing their attention.

Azuma sees in *moe* an automatic behavioral response that makes otaku prey to technologies of statistical control, which he likens to brainwashing and drugging. It is as if *moe* entailed a complete collapse of perceptual distance between user and computer, and as a consequence, the computer used the user rather than the reverse. Entering into a regime of pure mimicry, the user becomes subject to programming by the computer; the user's responses are, in effect, programmed. On this tier, Azuma sees otaku as simultaneously isolated by technology and exposed to it. Such an approach does not presume a subject. In fact, Azuma does away with the subject-object distinction. Nor are *moe* elements partial objects or fetishes in the usual psychoanalytic sense. They do not function to defer a constitutive lack in the subject. There is just not enough distance between information elements and users, and consequently no space for the articulation of an imaginary or for the intrusion of the symbolic. In this respect, Azuma appears to embrace technological determinism, for it is as if otaku activities entailed a behavioral materialization of computer processes that digitalize everything, transforming the world into equalized bytes of information. Complete technological determinism spells not only the end of the subject with an imaginary and symbolic, but also the end of narrative and of history.

At the same time, however, Azuma remarks that the database structure is not reducible to the Internet. And he sometimes speaks in terms of a postmodern condition, which is not simply a matter of technological or structural determinism. Although he never clarifies his thinking about technology, it would seem that he sees the database structure not as a deterministic structure but as an integral part of the postmodern technological condition. This implies that consumers are not merely programmed for automatic responses to *moe* elements, which they would, like the aphasiac evoked by Foucault, incessantly combine and recombine without arriving at a satisfactory ensemble.[19] Rather, the technological condition would determine, structure, or condition their actions, but not deterministically. The database structure would be integral to forming a field of possible actions, not determining outcomes.

Overall, however, when he speaks of the first tier of consumption, Azuma tends toward technological determinism. Even though he sometimes mentions the creativity of otaku, as if eager to step out of the determinism that he unwittingly stages, he tends to portray the database structure in terms of a behavioral materialization of computer processes of digitalization. This is the animalizing postmodern. It is only at the second tier that Azuma finds something other than deterministic animalization. He detects a sort of humanism, or at least something "humanesque" (*ningenteki*), which promises the emergence of a new sociality. He concludes with the coexistence of "two images of the consumer: that of the solitary animalesque consumer who withdraws into favorite 'small narratives,' cutting off communication with the outside world, and that of the humanesque consumer who actively intervenes in received commodities, constructing a flexible network of communication via the 'grand database.'"[20]

In sum, where Saitō posits the male otaku as an instance of constitutive lack striving successfully for ontological consistency (subjective unity), Azuma provides a dialectical image, in which the male otaku is at once technologically isolated/exposed and technologically connected/included. It is a variation on the otaku as a residence of one, and one of the residence, but at the level of communication technologies. The postmodern condition is one in which male otaku are simultaneously spun apart (atomized and dispersed) and spun together (coalesced). Azuma thus effectively challenges and dispenses with the unity-in-lack of the male subject that is so pronounced in Saitō's discussion. Yet something haunts Azuma's analysis, for even as he denies the unity of the human subject, he retains the unity of the human form.

While Azuma's emphasis is on animalization rather than humanization, the human form is a specter haunting his vision of the animalized postmodern. For instance, when Azuma discusses the male otaku's disassembly and reassembly of characters, it is the human form that underlies the process. Yet the persistence of human form, as a centripetal force, remains largely unexamined and unexplained. The human form is spectral in that it is always there and not there; even as the human appears to be coming apart and dispersing, it is also holding everything together. This is an exploded view of the human form, reminiscent of the anime cel bank and the transformation of the human into a standing reserve or human park in *Nadia*. In fact, I would go so far as to say that the underlying structure in Azuma, which he calls database structure, is actually exploded projection. And, to be more precise, in Azuma's account, it is above all the shojo form that is spectralized in accordance with structures of exploded projection.

One of Azuma's favorite examples is De Ji Kyaratto or Dejiko (Di Gi Charat in English), a girl character with *moe* elements (bell, cat ears, tail, maid uniform). Dejiko did not begin as an anime or manga character but as an "image character" or commercial mascot for a game and anime shop in the mid-1990s.[21] Dejiko caught the attention of otaku, who created a Web site, invented spin-off characters, and compiled background data on Dejiko. The result was the world of *De Ji Kyaratto* or *Di Gi Charat*, which generated a series of popular anime and games (Figure 39). For Azuma, *Di Gi Charat* is representative of a general trend

Figure 39. *Characters from the animated television series* De Ji Kyaratto *or* Di Gi Charat, *derived from the mascot character De Ji Kyarat or Dejiko, who appears here with two new character friends, Puchi Kyaratto and Ra Bi An Rōzu. The three characters display the characteristic* moe *elements of attraction taken up in Azuma Hiroki's account of postmodern otaku-related culture: removable cat or bunny ears, maid uniforms, and other accessories.*

in the otaku anime world toward the priority of character over narrative. Fans no longer feel a need for grand fictions or large narrative worlds; they prefer to construct personalized little narrative worlds by disassembling and reassembling characters.

It is, however, precisely a human form that allows the otaku to take apart and put together variations on Dejiko. The rabbit ears, the cat tails, the colored hair are attached to, or reassembled around, a girl form. This is essentially an exploded projection of shojo. In Azuma's account, there is also an exploded projection of male otaku consumers, at once atomized/dispersed and coalesced. Yet there appears to be an asymmetry between the exploded view of shojo characters and that of male otaku. The dispersion/cohesion of male otaku appears to be predicated on the dispersion/cohesion of shojo characters. In other words,

Azuma's account of male otaku seems to repeat, in an a-subjective material register, the fundamental male/female asymmetry of desire found in Saitō. The spectralization of the shojo echoes the hystericization of woman, and the animalization of the male otaku, which remains in tension with his rehumanization or socialization, resonates with the man's search for ontological consistency.

As if intent on bracketing such questions about gender and sexuality, Azuma also argues that, in the new mode of database disassembly and reassembly, male otaku users have moved beyond pornography.[22] His argument here centers on recent video games that present novelistic stories with multiple endings accompanied by illustrations of beautiful girls. Although such games initially entailed pornography, Azuma emphasizes that sexual elements have all but disappeared in favor of an experience of sheer affective response. In addition to the tears evoked by these stories, users are also invited to take apart character images and appropriate elements of them, allowing users to assemble their own characters and stories, and to share data elements and little stories. Thus male otaku oscillate between animalized responses and new sociality. With such examples, Azuma implies that analysis of the database structure is more important and fundamental than analysis of sexuality or subjectivity. But how are we to distinguish the allegedly new database sociality from the "old" homosociality (male sociality)? Is it enough to insist that male otaku have dispensed with ogling women in favor of weeping over them? As we saw with Murakami Takashi, "little boys" with "little narratives" do not necessarily signal a break with great men and grand narratives but mark a moment in which great men, the "Great War" and patriarchy are at once irrevocable and irredeemable.

A great deal depends, then, on whether we can differentiate spectrality and symptomacity, or specter and symptom. This can prove exceedingly difficult, and psychoanalytically informed feminism frequently calls attention to the ways in which the technological spectralization of woman is a symptom of male desire and even of patriarchal institutions. In her critique of technophilia in cinema, for instance, Mary Anne Doane shows how films that love technology (usually films with high-tech concepts and SFX) tend to dwell anxiously on the breakdown of the line between biological reproduction and mechanical reproduction.[23] Looking at films about female cyborgs and about machines that give birth, she notes how maternal functions become dispersed through the social rather than localizable in women's bodies. A society saturated with technology is also one in which Woman is highly dispersed, nonlocalizable. In other words, Doane draws attention to the overlap between spectralization and hystericization of woman. The specter becomes, in her account, a symptom of male desire for ontological consistency.

In response to such questions about male desire, at the conference that brought together Azuma, Saitō, and others to exchange ideas about otaku, feminist critic Kotani Mari presented a paper with a title that nicely sums up the situation: "I, Otakueen, Have Dreamed of Otakueers!" *(Otakuiin wa, otakuia no yume o mita wa)*. Kotani has written a number of books taking up feminist theory in the context of popular culture, notably *Seibō naru Evangerion* (Immaculate Mother Evangelion, 1997). In the context of *Chobits*, however, I would like to refer to her recent work, *Tekuno-goshikku* (Techno-Gothic, 2005), in which she considers the politics of girls dressing like baby dolls.[24]

Kotani is well aware that shojo is a fantasy that potentially sustains patriarchal attitudes toward young women. Indeed she traces shojo back to bourgeois family institutions that insisted on cultivation of its girls, showing how the system of masculine hegemony strove to preserve future femininity by handling girls like dolls before they reach sexual maturity. In other words, the cultivation of shojo constituted a preemptive strike on women, which was calculated to assure their future status as symptom of male desire. Yet, just as preemptive war may actually produce what it fears, so Kotani notes that the cultivation of shojo has historically resulted in an attitude of "aggressiveness" in the shojo, "which, while formed within the system, insofar as it was cultivated surreptitiously, ended up paradoxically possessing an aesthetic and sexual magic that shook the system."[25] Put another way, the struggle to assure the future symptomaticity of female desire transformed shojo into a specter, a kind of materiality haunting the received asymmetry of male and female desire, while suggesting other possibilities, not yet imagined or materialized.

For Kotani, then, the question is one of what happens when girls today dress in the most lavish and extravagant shojo costumes, baby doll or Gothic Lolita fashions. There is a risk, of course, that this "cosplay" or costume play will be taken as a simple capitulation to traditional notions of femininity. Yet, looking at the dynamics of cosplay in the film *Shimotsuma monogatari* (Tales of Shimotsuma, released in English as *Kamikaze Girls*, 2004), Kotani notes that dressing as a baby doll can also be read as a gothic technique whereby abandoned girls "regenerate" themselves.[26] In effect, although Kotani does not use these terms, such cosplay entails *preemptive capitulation*, which undermines the effectiveness of the preemptive strike on female desire, not by making the strike unnecessary but by creating confusion about where and what to strike. The symptom comes too early; it is already there.

Crucially, however, the future symptom now appears as an effect of outdated technology, of the technology of antique Rococo clothing. Shojo consistency is thus spectral consistency, an effect of materiality, of material conditions turned back on themselves. What is more, insofar as clothing is technology, cosplay affords another approach to the mecha shojo. What is the tactical armor or giant robot if not an antique or medieval fashion that has been reprised? This is how shojo cosplay undermines the emergence of Woman as symptom: the costume-mechanization of shojo transforms the symptom into a material artifact, which functions as a screen behind which the girl disappears, in an attempt to appear as something other than Woman, as spectralized shojo, as proto- and postmechanical woman.

Kotani reminds us that such a politics is always tenuous and tentative, because, as psychoanalytic theory attests, sexuality still tends to be constituted through the putative unity-in-lack of male desire. This means that shojo will continue to hover between symptom and specter. Chii, as gynoid computer or mechanical shojo of *Chobits*, exemplifies this oscillation between symptom and specter. *Chobits* echoes the sentiment expressed succinctly in Donna Haraway's declaration, "Though both are bound in the spiral dance, I would rather be a cyborg than a goddess."[27] I would add that the robot or cyborg is specter, and goddess is symptom. Chii is bound in the spiral dance of specter and symptom, of robot and goddess, of mecha and shojo, but there is no obvious way for her to step out of the dance or to unravel the spiral, even if, like Haraway, she would rather be a specter than a symptom.

On the one hand, in *Chobits*, we have an exceedingly traditional and conservative reckoning with the asymmetry of male and female desire, in which Chii functions as symptom of male desire. On the other hand, even though it is Hideki who insists on modestly veiling Chii in baby doll fashions, Chii's preemptive capitulation to her staging as symptom of male desire troubles the very temporal logic of symptomacity. The mechanically produced shojo becomes the symptom before the symptom, a specter that no one can grasp or possess. In this respect, to follow Kotani's lead, I think that, rather than fret that pop culture, as regulated difference, is fated to return us to the same old positions, we need to try to position ourselves differently. Thinking technology *and* sexuality potentially shifts our relation significantly. But in thinking technology in the context of anime, we need also to consider how anime thinks technology. And so, to rethink and challenge the psychoanalytic tendency to insist on the gynoid as symptom, we must reconsider two important contributions of psychoanalytic theory to the analysis of the moving image: positioning and suture.

CHAPTER 21

EMERGENT POSITIONS

I N HIS DISCUSSION of the asymmetry between male otaku desire and female otaku desire, Saitō Tamaki cites Enomoto Nariko who writes both *yaoi* manga (often under the name Nobi Nobita) and criticism. According to Enomoto, male fans cannot experience *moe* until they have fixed their own position.[1] If Saitō likes Enomoto's comment, it is because it agrees with psychoanalytic notions about how men establish their viewing position and thus their subject position. The man fears the dissolution of his subject position; he must define the position and orientation of the phallus; he must orientate himself in relation to symbolic castration, if he is to face the object of desire (Woman).

The psychoanalytic approach thus raises serious questions about how we talk about the materiality of anime and manga. Thus far I have consistently focused attention on the material orientations that unfold directly out of the animated moving image. But Saitō gives the impression that animation does not really matter. He implies that our tendency to position ourselves in relation to symbolic castration takes priority over other material orientations and configurations. Because he gives complete ontological priority to human desire, he focuses on how a man or woman will position themselves in a specifically male or female way vis-à-vis manga or anime, regardless of the material configurations of the manga or anime in question. In sum, the weird substance of human enjoyment always takes priority over the materiality of animation, analytically and ontologically. The danger of psychoanalytic theory, then, is that it will discover the same basic structures of the unity-in-lack of male desire everywhere. It risks losing all sense of material specificity and thus all sense of historical, cultural, or technological specificity.

In this chapter, I will nonetheless continue to explore the implications of psychoanalytic theory for reading animation. My aim is neither to dismiss nor to redeem such theories. Rather they are a springboard for thinking through the relation between technology and gender, or more specifically, the relation between the materiality of anime and the weird substance of enjoyment. The underlying question is very simple: does the anime image position its viewers, or rather its interactors, in specifically gendered ways, or do interactors bring those gender positions to anime from without? In other words, is the logic of gender external to anime? To what extent is the logic of gender internal to anime? The same question can be posed of my discussion of *Chobits* thus far. For instance, in the chapter on perversion, I detected a profound sexual asymmetry in the gynoid scenario of *Chobits*, reminiscent of Saitō-Lacan. Yet, in effect, I adopted Motosuwa Hideki's perspective. Did I do so because the material orientations of *Chobits* encouraged such an angle? Or did I begin with this perspective because I am a male interactor? Needless to say, I justified my reading of *Chobits* by reference to its seinen or male-directed mode of address, which is a sort of material orientation. Is there then a material limit to multiple orientations within the animation itself? Such questions naturally arise when gender comes into play, and thus it is crucial to ask whether there is a material horizon or limit with implications for gender that is internal to *Chobits*.

In this chapter, I will consider three different ways of dealing with such questions. First, I will look at the consequences of Saitō Tamaki's tendency to give complete priority to structures of desire above and beyond the materiality of anime and manga. The material horizon for him is human enjoyment (phallus). Second, I will contrast his thinking with that of Azuma Hiroki, who sees contemporary material conditions overriding and even dispensing with symbolic castration (and thus gendered positioning). Third, I will return to the distributive field associated with the flattening of layers in anime, which brings depth to the surface and dehierarchizes elements within the image. I will argue that the distributive field does generate material asymmetries, in the form of emergent positions (attractor/cooperator), which makes for an affective machine. This is where the anime image becomes amenable to gendered positioning, to subject structures.

This is also where I find *Chobits* of interest, not because it radically undermines received asymmetries of sexuality, but because, as I will discuss, it inscribes an encounter between an affective machine and a subjective structure. I have previously discussed this encounter at the level of the gynoid body in terms of a tension between specter and symptom. In this chapter and the next, I will discuss how *Chobits* sticks perversely close to emergent positions, which results in an exploded view or assembly diagram of the normative heterosexual household that Saitō takes for granted and embraces. In effect, to anticipate my subsequent discussion, the otaku situation, in which the otaku is one of a household and a household of one, allows *Chobits* to transform the Lacanian subject into a standing reserve, a sort of domestic park for female perversion. But let me begin with a return to Saitō.

Because it does not give ontological priority to materiality or to technological determinations, psychoanalytic theory can easily be sidetracked into a view of subject formation that presumes our transcendence of material conditions. This is the case with Saitō's insistence that otaku fictionalization (sexual fantasies) allow otaku to resist material conditions (data-ification). Saitō sees otaku overcoming or transcending the postmodern technological condition. Oddly, however, he anticipates and assures the transcendence of the subject by setting forth a theory of postmodern material conditions in which materiality does not actually matter.[2]

Building on Murakami Takashi's and Azuma Hiroki's characterizations of superflat, Saitō agrees that anime and manga are visual fields without depth. He also agrees with them that manga and anime do not entail fixed or stabilized viewing positions. This is why, in Saitō's opinion, otaku have multiple orientations vis-à-vis their manga and anime narratives. Otaku show a keen awareness of different contexts both within the text and around the production of the text. Such awareness encourages them to make it their own by producing their own amateur versions as part of the generalized, delocalized layers of context. At this level, Saitō's notion of multiple orientations and fictionalized contexts seems to follow from, or at least to be consonant with, the very postmodern condition that Azuma calls grand database or database structure.

Significantly, however, above and beyond these material conditions, Saitō insists on a male positioning vis-à-vis the distributive field, structured through the man's relation to symbolic castration. Suddenly, multiple orientations turn out to be organized around "having the phallus." Thus Saitō remains convinced that the ways in which men strive to make anime their own (male otaku creativity) proves entirely different from how women make anime their own (female otaku production). Even when men and women explore the same genre and character types (his example is *shōta* fiction), the crucial difference is the asymmetrical nature of sexual desire.[3] In sum, for Saitō, the dynamics of heterosexual desire transcend material conditions. He concludes, "It is interesting that even in seemingly structureless artistic expression by otaku, the asymmetry of male and female desire is maintained."[4] Yet such transcendence is a product of his approach: his theory assures that manga and anime structures do not matter, that they are effectively structureless, awaiting structuration. Saitō thus uses the idea of super-flat in order to confirm that material conditions or technological determinations do not have an impact on structures of desire. Ultimately, manga and anime do not, indeed cannot, perturb the unity-in-lack constitutive of male desire.

In keeping with his dematerialization of manga and anime, Saitō speaks of "drawn sexuality," which is his way of referring to the processes by which otaku write and draw their amateur productions.[5] In other words, to draw attention away from computers, he puts the emphasis on low tech over high tech, thus implying a divide between technique and technology, and between poiesis and technē. Yet, as we have seen, if there is anything that characterizes otaku production, it is the lack of interest in sustaining these questionable distinctions between low tech and high tech, or between technique and technology. Saitō evokes such distinctions in an effort to force multiplicity back into unity, to shore up the unity-in-lack of male desire. Anything that appears to afford material divergence ultimately proves for Saitō to be a symptom or supplement to the unity of male desire. In sum, in Saitō, the material horizon lies not in anime or manga but in the phallus, in the male drive for ontological consistency that comes of man's constitutive lack.

At the same time, as I suggested previously, Saitō seems as much Jungian as Lacanian, because his emphasis falls on fantasy as therapy and transcendence rather than "tarrying with the negative."[6] In other words, he does not linger over the difficulties of being or having the phallus but sees otaku fantasies as successfully overcoming material challenges to the normative heterosexual scenario. Nonetheless, whether we deem him Jungian or Lacanian, it is clear that for him technological determinations or material orientations have no material essence. Their essence is always relative to human enjoyment. As a consequence, his kind of psychoanalytic theory risks repeating what Heidegger calls technological behavior, for it gauges everything in terms of what it is for the human, albeit at the level of therapy rather than scientific reason.[7]

Azuma's treatment of Lacan deserves attention here, for he tries to dispense with psychoanalytic questions by attributing them to another time and place—Western modernity. This is Azuma's stance in his contribution to the superflat catalog in which he assesses the art of Murakami Takashi. Azuma contrasts Murakami's superflat with Lacan's discussion of a portrait by Hans Holbein called *The Ambassadors*.[8] In Holbein's portrait, the two ambassadors and their opulent surroundings are rendered in what we think of as perfect geometric or one-point perspective. Yet, in the low center of the portrait lies an oblong smear, which Lacan saw as the "embodiment of castration within the image."[9] When looked at from another angle, the smear turns out to be a skull. This is the artist Holbein's commentary on anamorphosis: although one-point perspective is often taken as a natural and scientifically accurate representation of the world, when you apply it consistently, things in the foreground around the edge of the "window on the world" tend to buckle and blur—a fishbowl effect, or anamorphosis. In fact, if you want to enhance effects of depth, a fishbowl effect around the edges is very effective, even though it is not the conventional one-point way of rendering depth.

Holbein's use of anamorphic blur in his painting is frequently read as a critical commentary on the tendency of classical representation to remove what did not suit its illusion of a perfectly ordered geometric world. The fishbowl effect clearly disturbed the classical grid of perfectly measured order, but Holbein puts it front and center in the painting. For Lacan, this is indicative of symbolic castration in the visual field: anamorphosis is where the imaginary perfection of geometric perspective breaks down. We have to abandon our sense of visual omnipotence, of seeing the world perfectly ordered, and confront our lack (in the form of death in Holbein's painting). Moreover, the painting forces us to change our viewing position to see what the blur really is. These features imply for Lacan a critique of the transcendent and rational Cartesian subject, which is consonant with Lacan's psychoanalytic critique based on symbolic castration.

Strangely enough, in his reading of Lacan on Holbein, Azuma equates castration with geometric perspective rather than with anamorphosis as Lacan does. In Holbein's smeared skull, Azuma sees evidence of another space invading that of geometric perspective castration—a space in which castration is suppressed, a space that allows for the possibility of a noncastrated gaze. In the distortion of characters swarming across Murakami's paintings (especially the distortion of D.O.B., who is one character in Murakami's repeating cast of animation-inspired characters), Azuma sees the triumph of anamorphosis and thus the liberation of seeing from symbolic castration. Generally speaking, in superflat and in anime, Azuma sees evidence of a postmodern condition that does not produce a space in which the spectator can look at the painting, and the painting cannot look back at the spectator. Central to this part of his theory are anime eyes.

As Azuma notes, so much attention goes into the production of different kinds of eyes in anime that the design and degree of elaboration of eyes often serve to define an artist's work. Sometimes eyes swell to overwhelm the face and body, sometimes there are eyes within eyes. In Azuma's opinion, such eyes are specters (*yūrei*). When you look at such eyes, they do not look back at you, as do the eyes of the ambassadors in Holbein's painting. Azuma insists that the spectral eyes of anime are lifeless eyes. They are signs of seeing but they do not see. They do not return our gaze. Consequently, with anime eyes, seeing is at once everywhere and nowhere. There are no fixed viewing positions.

In sum, in superflat and anime, Azuma submits that the combination of flatness, anamorphosis, and spectral eyes serve to generate a space entirely different from that of Western modernity (as exemplified by the Cartesian and/or Lacanian subject). In fact, Azuma claims that space and the eye no longer play a dominant role in Japanese postmodernity. He argues that there is no spatial continuity between viewer and viewed. While I find these comments somewhat obscure, it seems to me that, when Azuma speaks of the lack of spatial continuity, he means something like a lack of space or depth that would allow enough perceptual distance for an exchange of looks to take place between viewer and painting. This interpretation is born out in his discussion of *kyara-moe*, in which he underscores how otaku do not require or look for a narrative structure or world around a character. Otaku do not need that kind of space. Rather they respond affectively to *moe* elements that compose characters, which allows them to make little narratives or, if you will, mutable little nonspaces. There is no room for perception, only for affective response.

In effect, for Azuma, the dynamics of symbolic castration are part of a modern technological condition that structures spatial relations in specific way; the advent of a postmodern condition spells the end of castration. Postmodernity means the end of Cartesian technologies of depth, with their rectilinear order or universal grid. In the postmodern, there are no structures to fix the position of the observer and thus produce a stable rational subject. For Azuma, then, material conditions have conspired to erase the very structures of positioning that made symbolic castration thinkable and viable.

In contrast, Saitō Tamaki takes superflat as an invitation to ignore the material horizons of anime and manga. Paradoxically, in Saitō, the flatness and multiple orientations that initially appear to threaten the dynamics of symbolic castration with uncontrolled substitution, ultimately reconfirm the ascendancy of symbolic castration—of positioning. For Saitō, superflat means that information technologies have no material horizon or limit, and thus no significant impact. The fundamental determinant for Saitō remains the unity of male desire. For Saitō, gendered positioning is guaranteed by the very flatness of data, whereas for Azuma, gendered positioning has been dispersed and erased by flatness, by the advent of the grand database.

Since Azuma is clearly taking the materiality of anime seriously where Saitō does not, questions arise about the material limit or horizon for Azuma's postmodern-superflat-anime-character database structure.

In his discussion of Lacan and Western modernity, Azuma is so intent on establishing how Japanese postmodernity breaks with the material configurations of subjectivity characteristic of Western modernity that he tends to attribute material limitations to Western modernity, while Japanese postmodernity feels boundless, limitless, without material horizon. It is telling in this respect that Azuma collapses the Lacanian subject into the Cartesian subject, reading Lacan's critique of the Cartesian subject as an instance of the Cartesian subject. Azuma does not see anamorphosis as constitutive of the modern subject (as Lacan does) but as a sign of the postmodern (noncastration). Yet many of features of anime that Azuma presents as breaking with Western modernity can be read (and have been read) as generating modernity. Lack of depth, distortion, and hollow eyes—these may be easily read as a mutation of the classical that makes for modernity.

In making these points, I do not aim to correct Azuma, to say that what he calls postmodern is, in fact, modern. Nor do I care whether Azuma reads Lacan correctly. Rather I wish to call attention to the consequences of a manner of thinking that insists on total ruptures and absolute breaks. Much of the interest of Azuma's discussion of anime and otaku comes of his insistence on thinking the difference between different formations—in contrast to Saitō's insistent drive for unity. Yet Azuma thinks difference on the basis of rupture, which tends to homogenize and totalize formations, however unwittingly. Sometimes Azuma posits exceedingly grand historical and geopolitical ruptures (such as Japan versus the West), but generally his manner of thinking tends to settle on generational breaks, particularly on the differences among three generations of otaku.

Now, the logic of rupture is usually deemed characteristic of modern rather than postmodern thought. As Judith Butler succinctly notes in her early work on Hegel, modernity is defined as a break, and thus, the idea of a break with modernity implies a break with a break.[10] How do you break with a break? In effect, Azuma tries to overcome the modern logic of rupture by inscribing the break at smaller and smaller levels. He miniaturizes the logic of rupture, beginning with grand ruptures (modern/postmodern, prewar/postwar) and gradually establishing smaller breaks (three eras, the emergence of otaku, and three generations of otaku). In *Animalizing Postmodern* (aka *Otaku: Japan's Database Animals*), for instance, his focus is largely on the third generation of otaku, and it is with this generation that the break with modern forms feels complete for him. The breakdown of grand narratives (and of history and ideology) remained incomplete in the first period of the postmodern, because grand narratives lingered tenuously in the form of grand fictions, as in the vast fictional worlds of *Gundam* and *Macross* and *Brave Saga*. Finally, in the second period of the postmodern, which is also the third generation of otaku, male otaku consumers completely dispense with narrative in favor of character or character-centered activities.

Because Azuma frequently presents the postmodern break with grand narrative in highly sensational terms (namely, the end of narrative or the end of history), it is important to signal that, when he speaks of the end of narrative, he means something specific. He refers to a situation in which otaku consumers do not seek to access a vast fictional world or fantasy universe through narratives. What is more, Azuma construes narrative as a unified structuration of space that underlies, and guarantees the coherence of, consumer–character relations. With the third, fully postmodern generation of otaku, the emphasis on characters no longer implies such narrative worlds. As evidence, Azuma cites examples of characters (like Deijiko) that do not begin with any narrative support; rather their popularity as icons leads to the production of games, manga, anime, and other merchandise.

In effect, Azuma is referring to a transformation from a narrative-centered media mix to a character-centered media mix. Azuma sees a breakdown of the "classic" pattern of developing an animated series from a manga series and then generating related merchandise that refer consumers back to the anime-manga narrative. Today, he suggests, otaku consumers grasp the narratives on the same level as card games, video games, and other ways of interacting with the character. It is not that narratives or stories disappear.[11] If Azuma still speaks of little narratives at the same time that he announces the end of narrative, it is because little narrative is the form in which narrative persists, but narrative is now effectively subordinated to character and character-centered game-like activities. From the angle of video game theory, and in light of his intermittent emphasis on games, Azuma's distinction is reminiscent of the difference between narratology and ludology, or between a narrative-centered world and a play-centered "ludic" world.[12] But Azuma stresses the centrality of character, and of *kyara-moe*, or what we might call the elements of attraction of characters.

Does the character then operate as the material limit or horizon within this new ludic consumer regime?

In Azuma's account, character form does appear to function as the material limit for this new kind of production, distribution, and consumption, in the sense that the character retains some degree of unity and integrity across its different implementations. Yet, in keeping with his tendency to think on the basis of breaks and ruptures, Azuma also implies that this mode of consumption breaks with the unity and integrity of characters. He insists, for instance, that consumers are more interested in *moe* elements than in the character per se. Put another way, the character is not a personality or personage. As evidence, Azuma refers us to the repetition of *moe* elements across different female characters from very different worlds and with very different personalities.[13] This repetition is not due to influence; it is not a matter of conscious citation. Instead, in Azuma's opinion, such repetition is evidence that otaku consumers' interests are not centered on characters as such; their interests are centered on data and databases, from which they extract and recombine affective elements, unconsciously as it were. Ultimately, then, for Azuma, the database is what structures otaku consumption. Hence he insists on a two-tiered model in which, even as male otaku are thoroughly isolated and animalized (affectively programmed and prey to statistical control), they are simultaneously socialized and even humanized through database structuration.

Nonetheless, despite Azuma's movement from the character to its elements, the question of character form persists. After all, however anonymous, impersonal, and conventional the *moe* elements may be, they hang onto a character form—in all of Azuma's examples, a shojo form. It seems to me that Azuma avoids thinking of the character as a material limit precisely because he wishes to bracket the impasse of psychoanalytic theory and modernist theories, which tend to presume a fixed subject position in advance, even if that unity lies in lack. Yet Azuma's manner of thinking, with its insistence on total ruptures, rules out an important possibility: there can be *positionality*, that is, a quality of positioning, which is not the same as a fixed or stabilized viewing position (Cartesian subject) or a subject anxiously seeking consistency by disavowing its lack (Lacanian subject). There may be lines of sights, a subjectile, effects of subjectification. Is it not possible to acknowledge that all these *moe* elements somehow depend on shojo form, without concluding that shojo thus functions as the symptom of a male lack of ontological phallic consistency—without insisting that *moe* elements hang from her, phallus-like?

Previously I used the term *distributive field* to characterize the tendency toward a dehierarchization of elements within the anime image, to acknowledge a loss of the sense of center and periphery, which comes with the flattening of layers (especially prevalent in the male otaku anime lineage of limited animation). I prefer distributive field to database structure, not only because distributive field gives a better sense of the dynamics of the image but also because it avoids the impasse that attends Azuma's account of database structure. Azuma acknowledges that certain elements (*moe* elements of attraction) serve as attractors, and yet in his haste to establish absolute breaks between modern and postmodern, he denies all forms of asymmetry. He construes the database structure in terms of a total erasure or complete disappearance of all forms of asymmetry. Consequently, when he tries to explain the attraction of *moe* elements, he calls on conventions and control. Which is to say, he does not see the emergence of attractive elements in terms of the materiality of the database. Instead he leaps outside the database structure, and suddenly and arbitrarily posits forces of control and social conventions that program the male otaku consumers to focus attention on specific elements, whence his references to brainwashing and drugging. Needless to say, this is where Azuma, despite his evocation of postmodern thought, is crudely modern and deterministic in his manner of thinking.

While I agree with him that forms of control come with *moe* elements of attraction, I do not see these forms of control coming to the database consumers entirely from outside. Rather the controls are implicit in the distributive field, precisely because power demands material limits and horizons for its exercise. This is why I think that distributive field is a better concept than database structure. For, unlike database structure, which Azuma construes as an erasure of asymmetry, the distributive field implies emergence of asymmetry. There is constant symmetry breaking.[14] The distributive field is a dynamic field that generates asymmetries. It is not a static structure that makes everything perfectly symmetrical and equivalent.

We might think of the symmetry breaking within the distributive field in terms of *emergent patterns*. Theories of emergence look at the emergence of patterns from a simple, almost minimal network of elements interconnected in a distributive fashion, based on the self-organizing capacities implicit in the system.[15] While there is no unified formal theory of emergent properties, observation and experimentation suggest that it is difficult for any densely connected aggregate to escape emergent properties. Internal coherences arise that are not predictable on the basis of the elements. A pattern emerges. What happens is a function of what all the components are doing; yet the global coherence does not resemble the elements. This is a cooperative system insofar as all the elements interact, at once locally and globally.

In discussions of the emergence of patterns within dynamic systems, some theorists speak of pattern in terms of *attractor* and *cooperator*. The attractor is the set toward which a dynamic system evolves. It can be a point, curve, manifold, or a fractal structure (strange attractor). The cooperator is the function involved in the evolution toward the attractor. In the context of the distributive field associated with the flattening of the multiplanar anime image, *moe* elements function as attractors. Attractors are those *moe* elements that become salient on the field of dehierarchized distribution of elements. The otaku interactor, then, is a cooperator. An affective loop or circuit links cooperator and attractor, or the otaku and the *moe* elements of attraction. The cooperator (or interactor) is more than just another element in the field and less than a viewing position. It is not a stable viewing position or subject. The cooperator is a *function* that integrates and differentiates elements in relation to the attractor. The little worlds or little narratives of otaku cooperators are the complex patterns that emerge through the interaction of densely packed elements distributed in the field.

The distributive field is not an infinitely symmetrical material structure, without horizons or limits, which is how Azuma describes the database structure. Material limits emerge, in the form of attractors, and they emerge with affectively linked cooperators. Simply put, the distributive field generates affective asymmetries not subjective asymmetries (subject/object asymmetries). This is very much like what Félix Guattari calls a *machine* in contrast to *structure*. It is heterogenetic rather than autopoietic.[16] In sum, the distributive field implies a machine, affective asymmetries, and heteropoiesis, which are not in opposition to, but ontologically prior to, structure, subjective asymmetries, and autopoiesis. Structures and subjective asymmetries may come to inhabit this field. But they do not simply come from without; they are not merely imposed upon the field. Rather, to inhabit the field, structures must transform and mutate, in effect opening themselves to accommodate themselves to the field. Structures become, if only temporarily, machine-like, heteropoietic. This is why Guattari speaks of heterogenesis as folding other machines into it.

This is also the key to understanding how gendered positionalities can emerge between the affective asymmetries of the distributive field and the subjective structures of sexuality (Saitō-Lacan's fundamental asymmetry of male/female desire). It is not inevitable that the unity-in-lack characteristic of male desire will entirely overcode the distributive field or completely override its material orientations, as Saitō wishes. Azuma is correct to resist this approach. Nonetheless, the distributive field does not erase asymmetry, as Azuma wishes. Rather we have an encounter between a machine of emergent affective asymmetries (attractor/cooperator) and a structure of symbolically stabilized subjective asymmetries (symptomizing male and symptomaticized female). There is, of course, no guarantee that this encounter will turn out well, that it will change anything. Psychoanalytically inspired feminist theory tends to dwell on the "bad" outcome: it frequently stresses how new technologies, even when they appear to challenge and transform received structurations of gender, succeed only in entrenching them, in digging us deeper. Nonetheless, it is the task of the critics to inhabit the moment of encounter between machine and structure, not to foreclose it. Naturally, it will not do to open the encounter into utopianism, to boldly declare that technologies are changing everything, completely undermining all received sexual positions! But feminism needs a machine theory of technology if it is to challenge and transform the psychoanalytic theory of sexuality in the context of media and animation studies.

Again, this is where I find *Chobits* of interest, not because it thoroughly undermines received asymmetries of sexuality (it is, in many ways, highly conservative in its depictions of gender), but because it inscribes an encounter between affective machine and subjective structure. The tension between specter and symptom that I previously evoked at the level of the gynoid body is a manifestation of this encounter. This tension is equally manifested in the male character Motosuwa Hideki in the form of male perversion, which is gradually dispersed (or spectralized) across the series. Perversion, then, is where the encounter of machine with structure transforms into the gynoid spiral dance of specter and symptom.

CHAPTER 22

ANIME EYES MANGA

HIDEKI'S EYES SET HIM APART FROM THE WORLD. Like many anime and manga characters, his eyes appear preternaturally large. But, unlike the elaborate eyes commonly associated with anime, in which eyes are composed of orbs within orbs within orbs, with pupils and irises that appear inhabited by smaller eyes, Hideki's eyes are relatively simple. Two bold black lines define a large ovoid area (not entirely closed at the edges), with a small black oval within it. A smaller white dot inhabits the small black dot. The overall effect is of a highly contracted iris and pupil within a huge eye. This arrangement gives Hideki an aura of intense, almost maniacal focus. Even when relaxed, he looks wigged out. In contrast, the dark iris of Chii's eye expands to fill the entire eye, and the pupil appears as a sideways white oval, usually at the lower corner of the iris. This gives Chii an aura of concern and depth of reverie, of innocent openness and of withdrawal from the world.

Because persocoms are computers not humans, it may be misleading to speak of eyes, of irises and pupils. At times, the animated *Chobits* reminds us that persocom eyes are somehow not eyes: when persocoms process information, for instance, the whitish pupil-like ovals drift across the surface of the eyes, like lights circling an orb. Such moments remind us that Chii is definitely not human, and these eyes are not human eyes. They are humanoid eyes. But humanoid eyes are not uncommon in manga and anime. Of all the traits of characters, it is above all the eyes that are subject to intensive elaboration, and the eyes of persocoms in *Chobits* fit with the general manga and anime tendency to magnify, multiply, and distort elements of the human eye. In *Chobits*, Chii's humanoid eyes are dark, as if dilated, with pupil-like lights that traverse the orb.

In light of prior discussion of gender asymmetry, the asymmetry between Chii's eyes and Hideki's eyes is striking. Their eyes are almost diametrically opposed: Hideki's eyes, with their little black dot of a pupil in an expanse of white, appear almost maniacally active, which contrasts sharply with Chii's pensively dark eyes redolent of deep inner illumination. In the manga, for instance, right after Hideki has switched on Chii, and the wrappings billow away from her body, there is a split page of Chii and Hideki looking at each other. In the top half of the page is Chii, her eyes are large and dark, as if the iris had swollen to fill the eye, with a glimmer of white in the corner, as if a pupil or a reflection. In contrast, the reduced irises of Hideki's eyes give him an air of astonishment. For lack of better terms to describe this difference, let's just say that Hideki's eyes appear highly contracted, and Chii's eyes look highly dilated.

The contrast in eyes between Chii and Hideki is so pronounced that only gradually do we notice that the eyes of the other persocoms resemble Chii's eyes. In fact, even the eyes of the other female human characters are remarkably similar to Chii's—those of Ms. Shimizu, Ms. Hibiya, and Yumi. As for the men, Kokubunji's eyes are uncannily close to persocom eyes, while the eyes of Hideki's fellow student and boarder, Shinbo, appear poised between Hideki and Chii: he has large dark irises but with a greater expanse of white around them. The manga thus establishes a spectrum of eyes with Chii's at one pole and Hideki's at the other. Gradually, as new characters appear, they gravitate toward Chii's pole. Hideki is remarkably different from everyone else. The striking asymmetry in eyes between Chii and Hideki is gradually inscribed as an asymmetry between Hideki and the world, the world of Tokyo. Because the Tokyo of *Chobits* is above all a world of advanced persocom technologies, in which Hideki, a total rube, is always at a loss, this "eye asymmetry" also implicates a relation to technology. It potentially implies a way of looking at technology.

Because Hideki is the odd man out in this world, and the design of his eyes so plainly signals his exceptional status, he apparently functions as the focal point for readers-viewers to interact with the series. Apparently, we are supposed to interact with the gynoid persocom world from his angle. But does the character Hideki thus constitute a viewing position?

As the prior discussion of Saitō and Azuma has shown, when we ask whether Hideki constitutes a viewing position, we are also asking whether Hideki serves as *the* subject position that organizes the perceptual field of *Chobits*. Recall that, although Saitō acknowledges multiple orientations in and around manga and anime, he thinks that men and women will nonetheless establish a subject position in accordance to the fundamental asymmetry of desire, men striving for ontological consistency by hystericizing the woman, and women striving to inhabit hystericization. In contrast, Azuma argued that anime, like superflat, does not allow sufficient space or distance for a subject to position itself vis-à-vis an object or even a partial object. This is how Azuma establishes that the postmodern database structure does not allow for the emergence of a modern subject, Cartesian or Lacanian.

For my part, while I appreciate Azuma's challenge to the insistence in psychoanalytic theory on the unity-in-lack of the subject and on the castrated viewing position, his denial of asymmetry to the database is disturbing. In effect, like Saitō, he neutralizes the materiality of the database, and of information technologies and information-related modes of expression, even as he verges on technological determinism. This is because Azuma focuses almost exclusively on the leveling and flattening effects of new media, in which modes of fragmentation appear to equalize the field. In contrast, I offered a theory of emergence of asymmetries upon the distributive field: attractor and cooperator emerging together, held in conjunction within an affective loop. This is exactly how the asymmetry between Chii's eyes and Hideki's eyes functions, as an affective asymmetry. Even as the eye asymmetry gradually unfolds into an asymmetry between Hideki and the (technologized) world, its asymmetry is not that of a (male) subject or viewing position, not exactly. As if in agreement with Azuma's remarks about how the spectral eyes of anime are lifeless and do not look back at us, eye asymmetry in *Chobits* does not ineluctably structure the world around the unity-in-lack of the male position. Yet, contrary to Azuma's proclamations, it does not resolutely break with and thus bar such structures either.

If we take her computer eyes literally, when Chii looks at Hideki, she is not so much seeing him as processing him. This is borne out in her responses to him: some of the more touching and hilarious moments of the series are those in which Chii mimics Hideki's behavior (Figure 40). He rolls wildly on the floor, she rolls wildly on the floor. He pokes out an arm, she pokes out an arm. Such responses, almost purely mimetic, are not of the logic of symptom but of affect. Likewise, Hideki's responses to Chii are often affective, but of a different sort. Frequently when he sees her, it is as if he were struck. He jumps back, leaps about, gesticulates, or gets an erection, as if he had not so much looked at her but had been touched by her.

Hideki's responses recall Henri Bergson's remarks about perception and affection: "there is no perception without affection" and "[affection] is the impurity with which perception is alloyed."[1] Chii and Hideki are in a zone where seeing turns into touching, and perception into mimetic response. Consequently, at this level of Chii and Hideki "looking-feeling" at each other, there is an asymmetry, yet it is one that remains very close to an emergent asymmetry, which

Figure 40. *A series of images in which Chii mimics Hideki's behavior from the animated* Chobits.

forms a loop of affective response rather than viewing positions. She processes him, while he ogles, babbles, and gesticulates. The question then is: what would it take to transform the affective loop of emergent asymmetries into viewing positions that are structured in accordance with the unity-in-lack of male desire?

A well-known response to this question appears in Laura Mulvey's seminal essay, "Visual Pleasure and Narrative Cinema," in which she argues that classical cinema, that is, Hollywood narrative cinema, had a profound gender bias. In classical cinema, she claims, women are largely positioned as objects to be seen, while men are positioned as the subjects of that seeing. In effect, women appear as symptoms of male desire.

First, Mulvey writes, comes visual pleasure or scopophilia, a sheer delight in looking that implies a sense of mastery over the image. For men, images of women are especially likely to evoke scopophilia. In light of prior discussion, we might also gloss scopophilia as affective response or as *moe*, because it is a matter of the attractiveness of things prior to the formation of a distinct subject or viewing position.

Second, in keeping with Lacanian ideas about subject formation, Mulvey claims that this pleasure becomes a problem for men: they must stabilize their position vis-à-vis images of women; men strive to place themselves in the subject position, to assure that they are looking at the woman, rather than allow the woman to look at them. This idea of a male drive to stabilize his viewing position echoes Enomoto's point about male spectators being unable to experience *moe* without fixing their position. There is an unstated reversal implicit in such approaches: the affective responses that were prior to subject formation now seem to follow from the constitution of the male subject: men only feel turned on (affectively) when positioned (as subject).

Third, as a consequence of the male desire to fix its subject position, there are various cinematic procedures that work to attribute the viewing position to men. Mulvey calls attention to the fetishization of the woman's body, for instance, which recalls the hystericization of the phallic fighting girl in Saitō's analysis. In other words, in its drive for ontological consistency, male desire makes women into Woman, into a symptom of its desire. Mulvey's account here appears to dovetail with Saitō's stance, and yet Mulvey grapples seriously with the material structuration of the visual field in cinema, whereas Saitō largely bypasses consideration of the materiality of manga and anime, asserting that the otaku subject is structured in accordance with the Lacanian theory of desire. It is in the technologies and conventions of cinema that Mulvey detects a material instantiation of the operations of the unity-in-lack of male desire. She finds that cinematic conventions echo the formation of the male subject as Lacan described it.

A series of responses and objections to Mulvey's essay have appeared in the many years since its publication, running the gamut from a demand for statistical analysis to prove that Hollywood cinema truly produces such a visual bias, to reminders that cinema also has female spectators and offers other pleasures.[2] What interests me in this context is Mulvey's emphasis on the camera. While Mulvey's discussion also deals with clothing, mise-en-scène, and narrative structure, it is above all the monocular lens of the camera that structures the visual pleasures of cinema in accordance with male desire; narrative and other techniques seem to reinforce the effects of the monocular lens or to compensate for its momentary lapses. Not surprisingly, Mulvey associates the camera with Renaissance perspective. The implication is that the monocular lens brings with it structures of depth that stabilize or fix a viewing position. In this respect, her critique of the male structure of desire in classical cinema builds on the apparatus theory that was once central to the specificity thesis for cinema, as discussed in the Introduction, in which (to cite Comolli again), "the camera is what produces the 'visible' in accordance with the system of 'monocular' perspective governing the representation of space."[3]

Basically, Mulvey introduces a gender twist into the critique of the modern Cartesian subject: where other commentators associate geometric perspective with the construction of a modern rational subject (subjecting the object world by imposing a visual order and subject–object hierarchy), Mulvey shows how monocular perspective in cinema shores up the male subject, protecting its fragile consistency. In effect, for Mulvey, the male becomes the Cartesian subject by subjecting the woman, projecting anxieties onto her, and objectifying her in various ways. As such, the Cartesian subject is an imaginary generated by the male drive for ontological consistency. Ultimately, Mulvey wishes to destroy the male-centered viewing position in Hollywood cinema, calling for new practices that might disrupt or annihilate this regime. Her account thus stands in contrast to Martin Jay, for instance, who situates Cartesian perspectivalism as one modern visual regime among others, even expressing concern that we risk losing rationalism and modern science when we impute all the woes of modernity to it.

Given that Mulvey's critique of classical cinema blurs the distinction between the Cartesian subject and Lacanian subject (as does Azuma), it is hardly surprising that strict Lacanian theorists object to her account of the male gaze in cinema. Joan Copjec, for instance, shows how Mulvey's essay misrepresents the Lacanian theory of subject formation, insisting that the gaze is not a question of material determination. For Lacan, the gaze follows from constitutive lack. It is a matter of indetermination, not determination.[4] The gaze thus cannot be determined as male or female or as anything else. Psychoanalytic theory tends to treat the structuration of the visual field in terms of the unity-in-lack (gaze or phallus) at the heart of symbolization, and the ontology of human lack always takes precedence over material or technological determinations. The true substance of psychoanalytic theory is the weird substance of human enjoyment, not the materiality of such technologies as the movie camera or geometric perspective.

At this juncture, returning to *Chobits* in light of Mulvey's discussion of the male gaze, I have to agree with Azuma that the material determinations associated with the visual construction of the Cartesian-*cum*-Lacanian male subject are not at all in evidence in the manga or anime. As is typical of manga and limited animation, technologies of one-point perspective are not used to structure the visual field in accordance with a unified viewing position (or positions). When such perspective is used, it is used iconically and ornamentally, to establish or embellish a scene or place. What is more, as we have seen, although animation does typically use an actual or simulated camera, the camera in animation does not generally function as it does in cinema. Which is to say, the operations of the monocular lens, associated with the production of geometric depth and a viewing position, are not in evidence. Rather the camera, actual or digital, tends to slide over the image, becoming a layer among layers. As we have seen, compositing takes precedence over producing a sense of movement into depth or producing consistency in viewing position across images. As a consequence, as Azuma aptly insists, anime does not tend to produce a Cartesian subject—nor, I might add, a hyper-Cartesian subject (cinematism). This does not mean that limited animation absolutely cannot produce Cartesian or hyper-Cartesian modalities of perception. Yet, as Anno's hyperlimited animation attests, when anime aspires to such modalities, it tends to flatten and distribute them, which invites the production of distributive fields rather than coordinate spaces.

Nonetheless, for all that the manga version and anime adaptation of *Chobits* show none of the material determinations associated with the monocular lens of "classical" cinema (Cartesianism), *Chobits* sets up a very Lacanian game. As we have seen in chapters 18, 19, and 20, the series plays a game in which, contrary to all appearances, there is no woman, and there is no sexual relationship. Everything pivots on the secret between Chii's legs, and *Chobits* duly fetishizes her gynoid body, wrapping it in layers of mystery, which, like her flowing tresses and frilly or billowing costumes, generate a voluminous and shifting field of forces around her. Everything appears to assure and sustain male perversion and a fetishistic hystericization or symptomatization of the girl as shojo. In other words, in *Chobits*, it seems possible to arrive at an almost paradigmatically Lacanian scenario without any of the material determinations associated with the modern Cartesian subject. The flattening of the multiplanar image that serves to bring depth to the surface and embody the animetic interval in soulful bodies, while materially very different from classic cinema, seems in *Chobits* to conspire with male fetishism and perversion nonetheless. Is it possible that ultimately the material determinations of the animated moving image count for nothing, merely serving to incarnate the Lacanian subject in another body? Does *Chobits* confirm Saitō's and Copjec's insistence that the fundamental asymmetry of sexual desire will ultimately organize, underwrite, and overcode any material field? Does the weird substance of human desire truly take priority over technological or material determinations?

As I have already indicated in passing, what I find interesting about *Chobits* is how the series at once stages and transforms the fundamental asymmetry of sexual desire implicit in the seinen mode of address that the CLAMP studio takes as its point of departure. In this respect, I find that material determinations really do matter, and in *Chobits*, the material essence of animation—the force of the moving image—undermines the formation of the subject positions essential to the full-blown Lacanian scenario, by using the emergent asymmetries inherent in manga and anime in order to disperse the structure of sexual asymmetry implicit in the male fetishization and technologization of girls. This holds out the promise of liberating perversion from its male otaku enclave and domesticating it for girls. Put another way, the unity-in-lack of male desire loses its universality, becoming fodder for a divergent series of animation. But, to make this point, I must return to the question of how psychoanalytic theory thinks technology before continuing with a discussion of manga and anime.

I previously stressed that, in psychoanalytic theory, materiality, as material conditions or technological determinations, does not really *matter*.[5] This is not entirely true, however. Psychoanalytic theory tends to look for the sites of indeterminacy within particular material structures, but only to show that it is here that the Lacanian subject invariably plays out its universal drama of constitutive lack. In other words, in its sites of indeterminacy, every structure has the capacity to incarnate the universal subject in its highly particular way. This is what Žižek, following Hegel, calls "concrete universality."[6] As a result, when psychoanalytic theory does deal with materiality and thus with history, it tends toward a broadly Hegelian view of historical movement, in which universal spirit or *Geist* becomes incarnated in different formations. Because spirit initially comes to matter from without, subsequent history is that of the unfolding as spirit as it gradually transcends the bonds of material determinations and materialism.[7] In his evocation of animalization, which derives from Kojève's book on Hegel, Azuma endorses this broadly Hegelian view of history, for it allows him to situate male otaku beyond the fetters of materialism, within a materiality that no longer matters because it is boundless, horizonless, and infinitely symmetrical. In contrast, I have continually spoken of divergent series of animation, to highlight how technological determinations truly matter, yet their material and historical unfolding does not map onto a unitary history of progress. As such, they invite topological transfigurations of technological value rather than blueprints for technologized convergence or material solutions.

When it comes to how psychoanalytic theory thinks through specific material determinations relevant to the moving image, Žižek's recent summary of the logic of suture is useful. Drawing on the extensive literature about the suture in cinema, Žižek offers a pared-down and accessible summary of suture, breaking it down into three elementary steps.[8] First, the spectator, confronted with a shot, finds pleasure in it in an immediate, imaginary way. The shot absorbs the spectator's attention. This is comparable to Mulvey's ideas about scopophilia or Azuma's about *moe*. Second, an awareness of the frame undermines this full immersion. What you see is only a part, and you thus have a sense that you do not master what you see. Žižek stresses that, at this stage, you sense that you are in a passive position vis-à-vis the image; the Absent Other runs the show, manipulating the images behind your back. Third, a complementary shot follows, as if to reveal the place from which the Absent Other is looking. But you never see the Absent Other in the shot. Rather you see one of the protagonists, who thus appears to be the one looking. Žižek stresses, however, that the protagonist who seems to be the one looking is not the one who runs the show. The camera can pull back again, so to speak, to show someone looking at the looker. Clearly, this looking at looking can go on forever, and it is possible to imagine a film in which a new person or group of persons continually appears from behind the scenes, seemingly the one (or ones) running the show. It is also clear why this version of psychoanalytic theory likes film noir: these are films in which we are constantly looking for the one running the show. But it is not just film noir that uses suture. There are countless variations on the logic of suture.

To follow Žižek's account, even if we know that the protagonist-looker is not running the show, we gradually get a sense that he or she at least appears to own the place. We know very well, but all the same . . . As a consequence, the looker appears to have the phallus, to function as the site that accrues ontological consistency in the filmic field, thus launching viewers on a similar quest for ontological consistency.

In sum, the elementary logic of suture is that of a first shot that appears objective, yet, because it is materially incomplete or partial, it demands a subjective shot.[9] Regardless of the order in which they appear, the fundamental movement is from an objective shot to a subjective shot. Žižek stresses that this is also a movement from the imaginary to the symbolic, a movement to a sign; which is to say, it entails a drive for unity in lack. He does not immediately map the fundamental asymmetry of sexual desire onto suture, but clearly such concerns are in the offing.

Now, as we have seen, *Chobits* deploys a similar logic in its presentation of Chii. By dwelling on the mystery of what lies between Chii's legs, *Chobits* nudges us into a situation in which we want to see and know what she really is, and thus what we really are. The situation reinforces a sense of the partial nature of our seeing. Because we cannot see it all, we begin our search for that someone behind the scenes who must know what Chii really is. Thus begins our quest to place ourselves in a position from which we can see the truth. Since it is Hideki who finds Chii and wants to know what she is, we tend to follow him looking at and exploring Chii. In this respect, Hideki appears to be in the position of the subjective shot, and Chii in that of the objective shot.

In its material determinations, however, *Chobits* differs from cinema. Note that Žižek's discussion of suture posits the frame as the material limit of cinematic perception, and in his account, techniques of editing displace the frame. You can't see it all, but then, when images are edited into sequences, you have the impression that maybe you can see it all, or at least you can see a lot more of it. Yet ultimately, Žižek tells us, what you get is a *sign* of the underlying totality or truth, a symbolic expression that inevitably remains partial and incomplete. In this way, Žižek puts all the movement and indeterminacy of cinema into the interval between frames, which is expressed at the level of editing shots and takes. This cinematic field is structured by the material limit of the frame displaced into editing. Suture is basically the procedure of imparting subjective or immaterial consistency to material discontinuities or intervals.

In the case of animation, however, in contrast to cinema, I have emphasized that the material limit lies above all in the animetic interval, which means that internal editing or editing within the image (compositing) takes priority over what we usually think of as editing or montage. To further the contrast between cinema's montage and animation's compositing, I might add that cinema's "external editing" is postshoot editing or continuity editing (sequencing of shots, takes, sequences). This is not to say that continuity editing has no purchase in animation. Generally, however, unlike cinema in which extensive footage is shot then pared down through editing, animation tends to build the editing into the production process, rather than place emphasis on tweaking and refining the flow through editing after shooting footage.

When I say that compositing takes priority over continuity editing in defining the materiality of animation, I do not mean simply that compositing comes first in terms of workflow. I mean that compositing is of the material essence of animation. Thus we can return to the previous questions about viewing position in a different way. Does it make sense to speak of "subjective shots" and "objective shots" in the context of compositing, and if it does, how so? Here, because *Chobits* follows the classic pattern of adapting the anime series from the manga, another question quickly follows: what difference does manga make? Does manga matter here?

Let me first address manga, with the understanding that there is no way to do justice to manga in a couple paragraphs, and so my account will necessarily be cursory and slanted toward my primary concern with animation and technologies of the moving image.

Historically, at many key points in its development, manga intersects with cinema and animation, to the point that manga almost appears to be a variety of moving image. At the very least, although manga is not, technically speaking, a moving image, we can style it as an image-based (narrative) movement, which draws inspiration from cinema and animation as well as other kinds of spectacles, entertainments, and performances, and which in turn has profoundly affected cinema and animation. In this respect, in historical terms, I agree entirely with Ōtsuka Eiji's emphasis on manga as a modern form. He writes,

> It is not impossible to see manga in terms of a lineage that goes back to *ukiyoe* of the Edo period or comic animal art of the medieval period, but such a view of history ignores the "invented traditions" prevalent in so many of the introductory books on manga published in the late 1920s and early 1930s. With respect to stylistic innovations at that time, the reception of Disney [animation] is exceedingly important.[10]

As Ōtsuka Eiji insists, within a relatively short period of time, animators and manga illustrators in Japan had so thoroughly worked through and worked over Disney animations (and others such as *Popeye* and *Felix the Cat*) that the manga form is indelibly marked with the procedures of the animated moving image. In fact, manga and manga film became so inextricably intertwined by the 1930s that in a 1941 manga, when a manga artist boards a train and gives a boy and his father a demonstration of manga, he actually explains the production of animation or manga films.[11]

In sum, in its sources and in its formation, manga entails a series of direct and indirect intersections with the moving image. Indeed, if Tezuka Osamu's manga are frequently hailed as the moment or site of the coalescence and consolidation of manga itself (making him the god or father of the postwar story manga), it is in no small part because his manga used conventions associated with cinema to a greater degree than his predecessors. Particularly notable are his techniques for laying out manga frames on the page in a manner that expressly evokes cinematic sequences, emulating not only variations in distance of shots (analytic styles of editing) but also assembling what I previously called, after Deleuze, the action-images reminiscent of classical cinema. In effect, Tezuka's manga provide an exploded view of cinema. Or more precisely, since his sources of inspiration were often animated films, Tezuka's manga provide an exploded view of the classical movement-image, as it appears in both cinema and full animation. It is telling that Tezuka's writings include frequent comments about the various ways he learned about how films, especially animated films, were put together. He frequently dwells on the assembly of films. It is not surprising then that his manga likewise tend toward a presentation of the "classical" action-image in exploded projection.

Still, technically speaking, manga are not moving images in the manner of cinema or animation. Even if we can persuasively speak of a succession of images in accordance with what Deleuze calls "any-instant-whatever" in the context of manga, nonetheless manga differs substantially from cinema and animation. Manga offers something like an assembly diagram or layout of the overall action-image or movement-image, inviting the reader-viewer to read in the manner of a film projector, recomposing movement.[12]

The fascination of cinema with manga, evident in recent years in various locations, surely stems from this capacity of manga to present the movement-image in a sort of exploded projection. Manga's exploded projection of cinematic techniques promises an instantaneous expansion of the cinematic action-image, in which cinema retains its cinematic identity (albeit in iconic form) while folding other media and modes of expression into it. Likewise with the fascination with cartoons and comics among the high-budget, 3-D heirs to full animation: laying out the animated action-image promises to expand classic animation mediatically, while retaining its classic feel. Anime, especially those limited animations adapted from manga, have long grappled with such effects, which helps to explain some of the current impact of anime on transnational action cinema: following manga, limited animations in Japan have for many years "projectively" exploded the classical action-image in various ways. It is, however, difficult to gauge whether Japanese animations are today being folded into an expanded classical cinema à la Hollywood, or whether classical cinema has truly been subsumed by animation, or whether this is a mutually yet asymmetrically profitable embrace.

In any event, in light of manga's exploded view of the action-image, if we want to think the possibility of the Lacanian gaze in manga, we would first have to acknowledge that manga frames (*koma* or panels) differ from the frames of cinema. You might argue that manga is ideally suited to Žižek's discussion of suture insofar as the manga reader moves from one panel to the next in an attempt to compensate for, or grapple with, the incompleteness of the prior panel. Yet, because you see many panels at once on the page, even if your attention moves from panel to panel, there is a sense in which the panel is not the material limit or horizon in manga. The "frame" in manga is the page or pages. But pages are not like the frame of a painting or even that of the movie screen or moving image, especially because manga includes multiple panels within its paper expanse. The page does not insist on a gap between shots, which in Žižek's account serves to transform shots into frames. The manga page always presents its reader-viewers with multiple panels.

What is more, it is not unusual for your line of sight to vary wildly from panel to panel on the page, and when a sort of viewing position arises, it appears as an exploded projection across the page and panels. There occur affective fo-calizations and lines of sight that generate mood-enhanced potential depths, but a fixed subject position does not really cohere in the classical Cartesian sense.[13]

The manga page tends toward a distributive field, on which panels and their accompanying hints of subjective positions are dispersed and dehierarchized. It is not surprising then that, at moments of great affective importance, some shojo manga tend to dispense with panels altogether, in favor of sparkling collages and temporal whirlpools, while some shonen manga draw lines of force and splatter ink across the pages as their combat scenes sprawl over and finally destroy the frames of action. The material limit of manga is the force of black ink across white paper, and the reveries of love and the lusts of battle tend toward a complete dispersal of panels and of forms, into swirls, splashes, splotches, and dashes of ink. Like the canvas edge of a Jackson Pollock painting, the edge of the manga page does not really frame things in the manner of a camera shot or window.

Unlike a Pollock canvas, however, narrative manga inscribe stories or story-like continuities. As a result, a function appears upon the distributive field, which builds on the emergence of attractor–cooperator asymmetries and tends to settle on characters. Rather than dwell on character form or character design, however, I wish here to stress the character as function. I do not mean function in the sense of "how character is used"—such a functionalist approach usually presumes that characters are used as forms, thus placing form prior to function. I mean func-tion in the mathematical sense: characters sustain a continuous function of dif-ferentiation/integration across the page and pages. Panels begin to float upon a sea of bubbles or wisps of smoke, while the ovoid traits of characters drift in and out of geometric patterns that hover around them half-tangible like unspoken and ungraspable thoughts. Or, amid bursting stars and glittering sparkles, or amid the rustling draperies, scattering flowers, or streaming lace, a girl appears at the threshold of exquisite patterning, poised between dissolving and coalescing, sometimes drawing the entire cosmos into play and into crisis, as order emerges from chaos. This is what occurs at crucial junctures in certain shojo modes of ad-dress, for instance, in Ikeda Riyoko, Hagio Moto, or Takemiya Keiko, in *Orufeusu no mado* (Window of Orpheus), *Pō no ichizoku* (The Family Poe), or *Natsu e no tobira* (Door into summer).

The character function plays a "chaosmotic" role at the level of form, nei-ther bringing order (cosmos) to the page nor scrambling all into disorder (chaos). Characters' eyes come to stage a chaosmotic *mise-en-abîme* of perception and affection, staging eyes within eyes to infinity, or eyes brimming over and cloud-ing over with otherworldly glints, hints, and gleams. The character function (not the shot-frame as in Žižek's cinema) becomes the material limit for the story manga, embodying the edge of the page in the form of a bleed between ordered geometries (because the rectilinear page implies Euclidean geometries and cosmos) and nonlinear or non-Euclidean fuzziness (because the page is, after all, a meshing of wood fibers, or a perceptual blurring of orderly flashing cathode rays if you read on a computer screen). This is also where asymmetries emerge.

Asymmetry works in an affective register where everything depends on what floats your boat (what elements are *moe* for you). In another register, however, asymmetry begins to implicate perception, to imply emergent positions, which hover at the threshold between a viewing position (subject) and sheer delight, disgust, lust, or terror (affect). This shift toward positionality happens because the character function that differentiates and integrates across the manga's geometry/fuzziness is so closely associated with form, specifically with a character form, that the reader-viewer begins to invest in formal asymmetries. Form brings with it a shift from emergent asymmetries toward formal asymmetries, which is where received wisdom or social injunctions become folded into the heteropoietic machine. This is also where many commentators on manga betray a strange desire to capitulate to marketing categories such as shonen and shojo, to act as if fundamental differences between boys and girls organized the entire field of manga, and could thus serve as a satisfactory framework for understanding manga. This is about as interesting as saying, "it's a boy!" or "it's a girl!"[14] It is a matter of using commercial categories in order to impose form upon function, and consequently, of avoiding the questions of value associated with material limits or affective horizons. But the "boyness" or "girlness" of shonen and shojo manga is exceedingly fuzzy: even though many manga fans become obsessed with girl forms and boy forms in a manner that suggests a brutal reterritorialization of gender divisions, they often gravitate at the same time toward manga that deterritorialize the same divisions, at the bleed between form and fuzziness, devoting themselves to characters who literally change gender, adopt the trappings of another gender, or somehow recombine or reinvent gender conventions.

In any event, in the context of this analysis of gender asymmetry in anime and manga, I wish to highlight two things. First, I want to underscore that manga frequently present an exploded view of the classical movement-image, that is, the overall coordinating action-image associated with classical cinema and full animation. I am not saying that this is all manga ever does; rather this is the relevance of manga in this context. Second, because manga allows for multiple panels on a page, and for the fragmenting, angling, contracting, dilating, warping, and blurring of panels, manga implies a distributive field whose physical limits are white paper and black ink. Yet, as ink traces lines across the page, lines generate functions for integrating and differentiating across the page. Building on the attractiveness of lines, the material limit of the story manga gravitates toward the character as function. It is the character function that enables or abets a controlled or structured explosion of the action-image.

Now, as I mentioned in chapter 15, for Deleuze, who introduces these terms in his *Cinema* books, the movement-image of classic cinema is actually a coordination of a variety of movement-images, such as the perception-image, affection-image, action-image, impulse-image, and a number of others. He argues, however, that, among the varieties of movement-image coordinated within classic cinema, the action-image is the one that effectively came to differentiate and integrate the relations between the other kinds of images. Insofar as the action-image for Deleuze entails a subordination of time to space as well as an emphasis on goal-orientated or motivated action, his discussion is not entirely at odds with the characterizations of classical cinema that have appeared elsewhere in film theory.[15] It is the crisis in the ability of the action-image to sustain an overall coordination, that is, an overall integration and differentiation, of cinema that spurs the emergence of the time-image from within classic cinema. Previously I argued for an analogous transformation in animation: a crisis in the ability of the action-image to sustain its overall coordination of full or classic animation spurred the emergence of limited animation. The allegedly still images of limited animation are analogous to what Deleuze calls the time-image. I indicated that the time-image of limited animation becomes manifest in the tendency in character design to inscribe the soul onto the surface of bodies. This was also my way of stressing the affinity of the animated time-image with the emergence of corporations with souls (and even soulful corporatism). My goal was a theory of *moe* elements of attraction (souls) that takes into account the material emergence of asymmetries.

In light of my overall approach to limited animation, the importance of manga lies in its exploded view of the classic cinematic action-image. As manga arrays the action-image across its pages, it simultaneously produces a crisis in the action-image: the affection-images and perception-images, previously coordinated by the action-image as the overall movement-image, are equally "exploded" across pages. But is this truly a crisis in the action-image? Or is it a simulation of the crisis of classic "full" cinema and animation?

Such a question begs a fuller discussion of transformations in manga and their divergent series, which it is not possible to provide in this context. What matters here is how the animated moving image (animation and cinema) encounters manga. The animated moving image can build on manga as if manga were *a crisis* in the classic coordinating action-image (movement-image). Or the animated moving image can address manga as if manga were *a new way* of coordinating a variety of images within the movement-image. In either case, considered from the angle of the moving image, manga presents a "post-action-image." The prefix "post-" refers here, as elsewhere, to a situation in which the coordinating action-image is inhabited at its site of crisis. The movement-image feels somehow intractable and irrevocable, as if we still must have it or as if we have it by default. Yet it is not entirely redeemable, as if we sense that that sort of relation to the world is utterly outmoded and indefensible—rather like the excessive girliness of young women dressed as baby dolls, which, as Kotani Mari has it, presents us with an indefensible yet fundamental girliness.

When the moving image makes its encounter with manga, as in the adaptation of manga into animated film and television series, or into live-action cinema and television series, there are a number of considerations that come into play. Small screen and big screen, animation and live-action cinema, have very different parameters and long-established conventions related to production, distribution, and reception. When we look at the manga/anime encounter from the angle of the animation "machine," the problem of the moving image becomes crucial. While not technically a moving image, manga presents an exploded view of the coordinating action-image of classic cinema and animation, which makes for a sort of stabilized crisis generating the post-action-image. As such, when anime encounters manga, it may simply seize the post-action-image as an action-image. Which is to say, the anime can simply take the manga as a blueprint for an action-image to be rendered in animation. This process of adaptation is not merely a matter of shuffling the order of story elements in order to produce a classic television series story arc.[16] It is also a matter of using the action-image for an overall coordination of other kinds of images, such as the perception-image and affection-image. Recall that this use of the action-image to coordinate other kinds of images is what Deleuze calls the movement-image.

Anime adaptations of manga thus run the risk of getting the subjective register of manga entirely wrong, not least because animation introduces the perceptual dynamics of shot and reverse shot at a very different level than manga does. In manga, with the use of multiple frames, the logic of shot and reverse shot (when used) is projected across the page or pages. In animation, procedures for editing shots come into play, and they echo the basic conventions of cinema and television. Deploying such basic or "classic" procedures of editing tends to make for suture as Žižek describes it. An asymmetry develops at the level of the editing shots, between the objective shot and subjective shot. In other words, even though, as Žižek argues, a definitive and complete viewing position never coheres (the Cartesian subject remains in the Lacanian imaginary), there is a tendency toward such a viewing position. The "unity" of such a viewing position coheres in its impossibility, or due to its impossibility. Or at least this is what Lacan, Saitō, and Žižek tell us. Looked at another way, the logic of suture entails an emphasis on the perception-image. Yet the perception-image relies on the movement-image to assure its suture; the movement-image coordinates the dynamics of perception. For instance, the perception-image may become coordinated within an emotional or psychological story of symbolic intrusions and narrative reversals, as in *Chobits*.

Something like suture does happen in the animated *Chobits*. Early in the opening episode is a shot of a store window with female persocoms prettily lined up, for "our" viewing pleasure—an objective shot. A shot of Hideki looking immediately follows—a subjective shot that makes Hideki the subject (Figure 41, panel 1) who is looking at these "objects," which reappear in objectified form in the following image (Figure 41, panel 2), before returning us to a broader shot of Hideki's maniac pleasure (Figure 41, panel 3).

The *Chobits* anime generally follows this pattern of editing, providing a subjective shot that explains who is looking at the objective shots. Usually the anime associates the subjective shot with Hideki. Thus, as Žižek says, even though we know that Motosuwa Hideki is not the one who runs the show, we get a sense that he owns the place. Which is to say, we have the impression that it is Hideki's viewing position that is striving to find its place in this world. The anime thus gives a sense of Hideki as the subject striving for ontological consistency, which is the place from which we are encouraged to watch or interact with the unfolding story. But this is only half of it. As soon as it establishes Hideki in the place of the subjective shot, the *Chobits* anime immediately turns the tables on him. For instance, the sequence of Hideki looking at persocoms in the store window initially posits him as the viewing position, but then as Hideki goes into spasms of delight (Figure 41, panel 3), the subjective shot suddenly shifts from Hideki to the eyes of the crowd (Figure 41, panel 4). We see every eye turned on him (Figure 41, panel 5). Hideki is caught in their eyes (Figure 41, panel 6), suddenly placed in the objective shot, together with his would-be "symptoms," the female persocoms. The general idea is that he is caught in the act, so to speak. He is caught in an embarrassing moment, posture, or action.

The anime borrows these moments of Hideki caught in the act directly from the manga. As a moving image, however, the anime lays them out differently than the manga does.

The *Chobits* manga localizes perception in panels (panels are the locus of perception-images), while arraying the twists and turns of perception in panels across pages. Moments of affect tend to contract, expand, tilt, or split the panels, making it impossible for perception to coalesce around the unity-in-lack of a

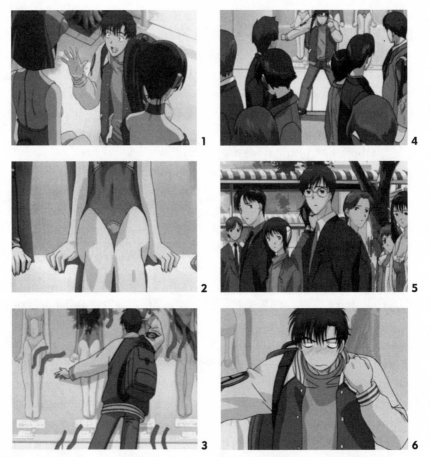

Figure 41. *In this sequence from the animated* Chobits, *Motosuwa Hideki, beguiled by the female persocoms in the store window, ogles them and responds enthusiastically, only to find that the crowd is watching him. In terms of the logic of suture, the first two panels present a subjective shot and an objective shot, which transforms in the third panel into a objective shot of Hideki's affective response, followed by shots that confer subjectivity on the crowd. Ultimately, the crowd does not constitute a site of otherness or authority; everyone becomes an accomplice, and the logic of suture unravels.*

viewing position. This is an exploded view of perception and affection (or affect). Action, too, is arrayed across pages, such that we have a sense of its general orientations and directions (where characters are going, who does what to whom). There is a general sense that looking and feeling, perception and mood, are as important as action, and maybe more important. Yet, as I mentioned above, this is not exactly the crisis of the movement-image (of the overall coordination of the action-image) of which Deleuze speaks. It is a post-action-image in which looks, moods, and acts appear in exploded view across pages.

In the manga, the character function serves as an internal limit to this exploded projection, or post-action-image. The form of characters also becomes important. It is primarily girl characters that are shown head to toe, and among them, Chii appears with the greatest frequency, in different costumes. As a matter of form, such a use of characters allows for a direct presentation of soulful bodies. Yet the character *function* of differentiating and integrating within the structure of exploded projection settles on the eyes, on eyes that do not so much see as feel, and on the asymmetry between Hideki's manic eyes and Chii's withdrawn eyes. The character function is an emergent affective asymmetry that does not coalesce structurally into subjective/objective shots, because the perception-image is already projected across the page. Thus, in the manga, in the scenes in which Hideki feels caught in the act, we do not have a play on a sudden reversal or inversion of the subjective shot as in the anime. The manga offers a moment of tonal variation.

In contrast, the anime plays out the scenes of Hideki caught in the act with an emphasis on a sudden reversal of the place of the subjective shot, as if pumping him up as a subject and instantly deflating him. In the moment of deflation, an affection-image or affect-image appears—an image of Hideki cut off from the world, caught up in his own affective loop of fantasy—Hideki snapped in a bold pose upon a brilliant abstract backdrop of undulating stripes or spirals or circles (see chapter 19, Figure 38). Then, just as suddenly, he is snapped out of his affective loop, thrown back into the everyday world by a simple remark or look from someone nearby.

Episode 13 provides a prime example. When Hideki learns that he must rub lotion on Chii, we see him in shock (Figure 42, panel 1), and then predictably, he goes into his familiar spasms of embarrassment and excitement (Figure 42, panel 2). A word from Kokubunji suffices to break his moment of solitary asocial rapture. Hideki is caught in the eyes of the world (Figure 42, panel 3), and the affective bubble bursts (Figure 42, panel 4), only to be followed by new bursts of affect (such as humiliation). Thus a rhythm develops, with affective outbursts undermining the build-up of subjective positioning.

What is striking about these sudden shifts of the subjective shot from Hideki to the eyes of others out in the world (to the social) is the absence of authority in the look of others. Even though Hideki orientates himself toward others as if they were passing judgment on him, it is only Hideki who thinks his behavior abnormal. Each time he feels caught in the act, he frets that people will think him a pervert, and yet those who see him apparently find his behavior normal. Shimbo does not think it odd that Hideki would have sex with a persocom. Nor does anyone think that his porn collection signals perversion. The women remark on

Figure 42. *When his friend tells him he must put lotion all over Chii's body, Hideki's surprise turns to affective outburst as he imagines rubbing his hands over her body: "I can't do something like that!" His friend calmly replies that he can order Chii to do it herself, and Hideki turns to his "normal" state. Note in the first panel the "eye asymmetry" between Chii and Hideki.*

his array of pornography as typical for a young man. In other words, Hideki is embarrassed by his use of pornography, but no one else is. As a consequence, the look of others carries no weight of prohibition or authority. Others aid and abet his fantasy. Hideki orientates himself toward them as toward the law, but they turn out to be accomplices not Others. This transformation of Others into accomplices is, needless to say, one of the characteristic features of perversion. The world of perversion is one in which the entire world plays along with the fantasy. Consequently, in the anime, although the subjective shot shifts onto the eyes of the world, the world does not function as the Absent Other, as the big Other who runs the show, to evoke Žižek's turn of phrase.

In light of prior discussion, it now seems fair to say that when Žižek (and psychoanalytic theory) refers to the Absent Other, he refers to a situation in which the god-like omniscient Cartesian subject remains operative in its absence, because of its absence. In different ways and for different reasons, Azuma and Mulvey also make this equation between the Lacanian subject and the Cartesian subject. The logic of suture, then, is that of a perverse desire on the part of viewers to achieve an omniscient viewing position that escapes them. *Chobits* further perverts the perversion implicit in the Lacanian take on the Cartesian subject by flattening the Absent Other, making prohibition into an accomplice of fantasy.

If the animated *Chobits* is able to pervert the "classic" logic of cinematic suture, it is because it builds on the tendency of animation to harness a different potential of the moving image than cinema, and the tendency of limited animation to inhabit a crisis in the movement-image of classic cinema and classic full animation. In the course of this book, I have stressed that, where cinema tends to unfold the potential of the moving image into camera work and editing (montage), animation tends to explore the potential of the moving image in compositing and character animation. The emergence of the animation stand makes clear this divergence. Broadly speaking, full animation tends to eliminate a sense of the animetic interval between planes of the image by using compositing techniques to close or mask the gap. This does not force a convergence of animation and cinema (although some full animations deliberately try to reproduce cinematic movement). But it did put animation and cinema on parallel tracks in the age of classic full animation, making for an overall coordinating action-image (or movement-image) in both. Limited animation marks a crisis in the movement-image by simultaneously flattening the relation between planes of the image and opening the animetic interval (moving the drawings, with sliding across and between layers of the image). Depth (the animetic interval) comes to the surface. There are, however, different ways of working with limited animation, and thus divergent series.

I used the example of Gainax Studios and especially Anno Hideaki's animations in order to speak of a "lineage" (I used this term rather than *series* in order to avoid confusion with the word as commonly used for animated television series), in which flattening is optimized. In this optimized or hyperlimited animation, the story spirals into multiple frames of reference, and character animation gives way to character designs. Yet underlying structures of exploded projection serve to keep the animation elements and layers from utter dispersal or sheer difference. The problem of structural stability settles on assembly and disassembly of characters (cel bank, garage kits, character franchise, video games), as a formal limit to the apparently continuous and boundless field of animation. Likewise, the central question of Anno's animations becomes that of the human park, of the transformation of humans into a standing reserve for engineering the lifeworld.

I discussed exploded projection in terms of *structure* as a challenge to Azuma's insistence that the world of manga, anime, and games is a world without subjectivity and beyond modernity, simply because the Cartesian or Lacanian subject does not cohere. My point is not that analysis should begin and end with structure and the subject, as Saitō does. On the contrary, I wish to indicate that there are other ways of thinking modernity and subjectivity than Cartesianism or Lacanianism. I argued that Miyazaki's way of thinking modernity is rather Heideggerian, and Anno's post-Heideggerian. CLAMP's view might be styled as post-Lacanian, because, as *Chobits* demonstrates so beautifully, the unity-in-lack of the male subject, typical of the Lacanian scenario, comes into play at the level of fantasy. It is a perversion of male perversion.

To return to what matters in limited animation: even as the animated *Chobits* plays with editing in accordance with shot and reverse shot, which establishes objective and subjective shots, the flattening of planes brings the animetic interval to the surface of the image. This undermines the sense of a frame, at least in the usual cinematic sense. The movement of the simulated camera, as it slides over sliding planes, does not rely on structures of depth related to geometric perspective. Such movement does not rely on a sense of the bounded camera (echoed in perspectival depth) or of the bounded image. The animetic interval is dispersed into the play of elements upon the surface of the image. This is a variation on the distributive field, which is unbounded and continuous like Azuma's database structure; but it is not a structure and not infinitely symmetrical. It generates emergent asymmetries.

An affective asymmetry coalesces around the "eye asymmetry" between Hideki and Chii. At the same time, as is typical of limited animation, the animetic interval becomes embodied in character design, where the movement that might be shunted into full animation of characters appears instead in the design of characters. When it introduces shot and reverse shot, the *Chobits* anime tends to subjectify this situation. In fact, the animated *Chobits* continually verges on adopting Hideki's position, on making this story subject to his viewing position. The added modesty of the animated series vis-à-vis Chii's reset button furthers this tendency, adding a different layer of secrecy not operative in the manga. In this respect, in its presentation of gender asymmetry, the manga is more challenging than the anime. Nonetheless, even in the animation, techniques of limited animation tend to undermine a subjective localization of the series around the unity-in-lack of Hideki. Even as the simulated camera tries to subjectivize an objective shot—of Chii seen by Hideki, or of Chii and Hideki seen by others, it cannot frame characters within the superplanar image. It confronts characters that, as material limits upon the flattened and dehierarchized field, organize the field yet defy framing.

This is where it becomes obvious that the editing of shots in *Chobits* does not really follow from cinema or television; even though it recalls them, the cinematic conventions for editing have already passed through manga and limited animation. The layout of shots in *Chobits*, with its perversion of suture, follows from the encounter of limited animation with the post-action-image of manga. The anime/manga encounter is a meeting of different responses to the crisis of the movement-image. The two responses intersect at a structure of exploded projection, where they may also become superimposed. It is where the manga post-action-image meets the anime embodiment of the crisis in the movement-image (superplanar image and soulful body).

Exploded projections are structures crisscrossed with lines of sight, in which our eyes and ears only afford a fantastical coherence, generating affective depths that afford fleeting inhabitation by a series of modern specters, by Cartesian, Lacanian, and Heideggerian ghosts. In the specific instance of *Chobits*, as we read between manga and anime, we traverse a distinctively post-Lacanian world that dances in circles between specters and symptoms, a world in which the coordination of perception into emotional movement (suture) feels entirely possible yet thoroughly untenable, unsustainable. We inhabit a world in which romance is everything and nothing, an indefensible ground for coordinating action or emotion, which leaves us with an utterly perverse sexual asymmetry in which girliness swirls with mechanical delicacy of line around computers, while the last man babbles and gesticulates frantically, overcome by the surge of strobe-like layers that he radiates.

PATTERNS OF SERIALIZATION

A S AZUMA REMINDS US, television anime narratives like *Chobits* or *Evangelion* may no longer be *the* pivotal form in the contemporary otaku multimedia world. Character now plays that role. The emphasis on character is not entirely new, of course. Character merchandising, character licensing, and character franchises have long been important in generating and sustaining connections across media, in form of media mixes or image alliances. In the context of anime, the emphasis on character can be traced back to Tezuka Osamu's animated version of *Tetsuwan Atomu* (aka *Astro Boy*). *Astro Boy* is frequently cited as the beginning of limited animation in Japan, and character-related merchandising and advertising proved crucial to the economic viability of the series.[1] *Macross* is frequently cited as the subsequent moment when the "classic" pattern of developing animated series from manga began to give way to development of animated series using toys as the point of departure. Later, with Okada's General Products and Gainax Studios, the serialization of merchandise associated with anime series, especially games and garage kits, reinforced the narrative–character connections, gradually giving character priority over narrative.

In Azuma's opinion, it is today the character—or more precisely, *kyara-moe*, the affective elements of characters—that plays the pivotal role in organizing and holding together media franchises or media mixes. Azuma sees, in effect, a break between an animation-narrative-centered multimedia industry and a character-driven multimedia industry, which implies a new emphasis on games and online activities rather than on animation or animated series. Animated series are still produced, of course. Yet, Azuma notes, they are consumed within a thoroughly dehierarchized array of products, as one interface with character among others. Animation, he concludes, has lost its privilege.

While my discussion of animation intersects and agrees with Azuma's account on many points, I have nonetheless made animation central to analysis, even to the analysis of character. In this respect, my point of departure and emphasis is very different from Azuma's. This book has centered on the anime image as a moving image, on the force that comes of the mechanical succession of images. I have thus insisted on sticking to the facts of animation, on looking at the material essence of animation, or animation as such.

To stick to the facts of anime requires some manner of specificity thesis for animation. Sticking to the facts of anime thus runs the risk of falling into material or technological determinism, as happens with the apparatus theory of cinema with its insistence on the monocular lens. To counter such determinism, even while placing emphasis on the invention of the animation stand, I have insistently differentiated determination from determinism. Similarly, I have stressed machine over structure. To speak of an animetic machine is to think in terms of an interval, gap, or spacing; in terms of a materially specific indetermination at the heart of a material apparatus. This is why I have sometimes described it in terms of underdetermination or passive determination. The animetic interval unfolds into divergent series, in an ongoing exfoliation or explication that is powered (so to speak) by the mechanical succession of images. At the same time, the animetic interval folds into it, in an ongoing process of implication, various modes of expression and other operative functions. This combination of folding-out and folding-in is what Guattari calls heterogenesis. This makes for a "thinking and feeling machine." Consonant with Guattari's move to strip the word "machine" of its mechanistic connotations, when I call animation a thinking machine, I do not mean a mechanical device that thinks and feels independently of humans. A thinking machine is a heteropoietic process in which human thinking happens differently than it would otherwise, in another flow of material forms and immaterial fields. It is in this sense that I have stressed how anime thinks technology "animetically," calling attention to an "animetic manner of thinking technology."

In keeping with this approach, I see recent developments in transmedial serialization not in terms of a break with animation but in terms of divergent series of animation unfolding from the animetic machine. Instead of breaks between eras or generations, I see divergent series that entail mutations and transformations, transitions and passages, in which different series remain on stage. Divergent series today crowd the scene. Indeed, even if they are somehow outdated or passé, the animations associated with Ghibli, Gainax, and CLAMP remain an important force, alongside a wide variety of anime-game series and other serial franchises.

At a historical level, this book has tracked transformations in the animated moving image from the early 1980s to the early 2000s, from *Castle in the Sky* (1985), to *Nadia* (1989–90) and *Evangelion* (1995–96), and to *Chobits* (2001–2), that is, across the twenty-year period when animation was becoming ever more intimately entwined with information technologies. Yet, to avoid a simple linear history of Japanese animations, I have pursued divergent series, with these particular animations as nodal points, with an emphasis on how different manners of working through the force of the moving image in animation tended to spur certain ways of thinking technology, of imparting technological value.

The question then is, how does a particular divergent series come to dominate other series, or fold them into itself, or force them to converge, at particular historical moments?

I have frequently made reference to studio organization, marketing, and consumer activities. At the same time, however, I have given precedence to questions of technical determination and technology over questions about economic determination and economy. My intention is not to dispense with questions about economic determination, any more than I wish to dispense with questions about social or cultural determinations. Instead I have shown how thinking through technological determination opens into questions about material conditions or structures, which in turn imply a confrontation with technological *value*. Questions of technological value frequently take center stage in Japanese animations (and not only animations that are overtly SF). This is partly because thinking with/through technologies of the moving image forces a consideration of technological value, brings value to the surface, as it were. Thus, my emphasis on technical determination and the transfiguration of technological value is not calculated to dispense with questions about social, cultural, or economic determination but, on the contrary, to lay the ground for approaching such questions in the world of animation. Naturally, because animations are, after all, commodities, the question of economic determination nonetheless feels urgent. And so, by way of conclusion, as I summarize and strive to clarify the major points of this book, I will consider, somewhat schematically, how an emphasis on technology might enable us to take a new look at economic determinations.

First and foremost, looking at technological determination reminds us that media convergence or product alliances are not inherent in the animetic interval or in the media associated with animation. We might use the term *media mix*, because "mix" feels decidedly more neutral than "convergence" or "alliance."[2] Yet I think it necessary to back up another step and consider, however schematically, what is at stake in starting with the divergent series that follow from the moving image. It is on the basis of divergent series that we can begin to look at how modes of production and distribution intersect with, and strive to capture, the animetic machine.

Isabelle Stengers sums up the situation nicely when she comments, "only what diverges communicates, and communication here relies on the fact that, for diverging reasons, both experimental science and technology need to address things not from the point of view of their submission, but in terms of what can generically be called their force, what they are able to do in particular well-defined circumstances. When a scientific statement is stabilised, or when a technology works, it may well look like some kind of submission has been achieved, but it is a force which has been both unfolded and re-folded."[3]

In this book, I have adopted something of the attitude of experimental science and technology studies in my approach to animation. In effect, such an approach presumes some degree of free relation to technology. The use of the term *machine*—in the manner of Guattari, without its usual mechanistic associations—also presumes that there can be a freer relation to technology, something other than structural capture, technological determinism, or operative submission. As Stengers so neatly puts it, this implies looking at a technology not from the point of view of its inevitable submission but in terms of its force. Thus, when I approached animation in terms of a technical determination, it was not from the angle of its inevitable submission to the logic of the market, or national identity, or media convergence. Instead, I began with the gaps or intervals that become prevalent when the mechanical succession of images encounters the layers of drawings used in animation. Thus I could look at animation techniques and technologies in terms of their force (a term which I have used rather generically, as Stengers does). Whence my emphasis on the animation stand: it channeled the force implicit in the succession of moving images into the gap between planes of the image—through the animetic interval.

By allowing animators to work with the relation between layers, the animation stand at once highlighted the animetic interval and promised to control, contain, or harness it. From the earliest days of animation, procedures of "editing within the image" came to the fore, especially in the context of working with the relation between planes of the image or "compositing." Otherwise, the image, under conditions of movement, would appear to fall apart, because the force of the moving image would not be orientated or coordinated. In other words, the animation stand can be seen as an apparatus or technology that invites the production of a sensorimotor schema, a body, or an overall movement-image. Yet this apparatus does not constitute a thoroughly instrumental capture of the force of the moving image. This is not because animation is art not technology, or more art than technology. It is because animation technology implies an underlying machine, which means that the machine comes both before and after the apparatus.

The machine comes before: the fundamental problem addressed by the animation stand is already apparent in the layering of celluloid sheets and even in the use of tracing paper—multiplanarity. The machine comes after: procedures of compositing are as important in digital animation as in cel animation, and not only in digital animation that reprises the look and feel of cel animation but also in so-called 3-D digital animation and CGI in live-action cinema. This is because both streams of digital animation face a similar problematic: how to make the layers of the image appear to hold together under conditions of movement, due to the mechanical succession of images.

There is a machine before and after the apparatus or technology of the animation stand, a machine underlying and prolonging the force that arises where multiple planes of the image meet with movement. I initially referred to this machine as the multiplanar machine. Subsequently, I also qualified it as an animetic machine to account for this encounter of multiple planes with the mechanical succession of images, the moving image. Thus animation—the multiplanar animetic machine—unfolds into divergent series as it starts to fold other machines into it.

Looking at the technical determination of animation from the angle of its force and thus its divergence, I parsed some of different tendencies in compositing. I spoke of a sort of "closed" compositing that allowed for a sense of movement into depth, which, following Virilio, I associated with cinematism. Cinematism is not merely cinema. If Virilio reads cinematism out of cinema, it is on the basis of what he sees as an inherent tendency of cinema toward a ballistic logistics of perception, which for him is yet another brick in the wall of our unredeemable technological condition. In contrast to Virilio, who sees technology from the angle of an inherent submission to a massive modern or postmodern condition of logistic instrumentalization, I feel it important to grasp technology from the angle of its force, not in order to redeem technology but in the interest of better understanding the forces that make possible media convergence and communication networks in our daily multimedia animetic environments.

Virilio's cinematism is nevertheless a useful point of departure for a consideration of compositing, because it reminds us that a specific way of channeling or harnessing the force of the animetic machine will bring with it a specific set of values. Cinematism, for instance, implies an acceleration and intensification of Cartesian perspectivalism and of the Cartesian subject, which in turn implies a set of relations to the modern technological condition and the natural world. Techniques of closed compositing that channel the force of the moving image into cinematism allow techno-scientific rationalism to mesh seamlessly with the thrills and exhilaration of ballistic optics. Acceleration promises to abolish our sense of material limitations and to erase the tedious labor of rationalizing the space of the image, both of which are integral to the production of exhilarating movement into depth. Acceleration affords a glimpse of liberation from material conditions, but only as the viewing position literally abolishes the human body in speed, in a technologically driven elimination of the human. This is what truly worries Virilio: the rational "gridding" or striation of the world proves thrilling when perceived at speed, yet it is a suicidal trajectory for individuals and for the species.

To counter cinematism, the animations of Miyazaki Hayao resort to procedures of open compositing at crucial moments of technological interface, which promises a different relation to technologies and to the natural world. Like Virilio, Miyazaki associates ballistic perception and action genres with a technological drive toward global annihilation and elimination of the human lifeworld. Yet, unlike Virilio, Miyazaki's animations strive to actualize a different relation to technology through a different use of the animated moving image. In effect, Miyazaki sees glimmers of a different world of technology, which spark from the capacity for animation techniques to diverge, to open the force of animation prior to its submission to cinematism. Above all, it is in the sliding planes of the moving image that Miyazaki's animations try to open the force inherent in animation technologies, to divert it from the channels of cinematism into new flows. The sliding planes offer hope that the force of animation can be diverted from high-speed, hyper-Cartesian optical regimes—diverted into "animetism."

Because Miyazaki's animations do not (cannot) dispense with animation technologies but strive to inhabit the animetic interval in a different way, they resonate with Heidegger's ideas about gaining a free relation to technology. They do not imagine the technological condition in terms of problems with solutions. Instead they seek the moments of indetermination within technology that might open it into the world, which promises salvation from the modern technological condition. Miyazaki's animations falter, however, at the very moment when their sliding planes appear to inhabit modernity differently, with minimal technologies (windmill, glider) based on apparently inexhaustible and untamable natural energy sources (wind). There is, in Miyazaki as in Heidegger, the problem of how to prolong this event, this new way of dwelling.

Miyazaki's animations adopt two tacks. On the one hand, there are, as in Heidegger, rumors and glimpses of a new god to afford minimal consistency to the vision of salvation. In Miyazaki the god is Shojo. On the other hand, the sliding planes of Miyazaki's animations present a new set of relations between movement and depth. Yet this new set of movement/depth relations ultimately seems to minimalize rather than challenge the Cartesianism implicit in the ballistics of cinematism. Even as Miyazaki's animations open the animetic interval, revealing the gaps between planes of the image, they strive for a panoramic vision of the world of Nature. Classic panoramic vision opens a divide between the subject and the object world that affords a sense of the subject standing over and above nature, able to control and order it. Miyazaki's multiplanar version of panoramic vision imparts the sense of a more dynamic, less controllable nature, but nonetheless insists on an absolute frame of reference: Nature. This is especially evident when painterly backgrounds serve to ground panoramic vision and to structure depth. In sum, the Miyazaki response to hyper-Cartesianism is a mitigated and minimalized hypo-Cartesianism.

These two factors surely account for the "universal" appeal of his girl animations. But they also present troubling echoes of "giving up the gun" and "overcoming modernity," moments of an authoritarian rejection of technologies that haunt Miyazaki's animetistic, movementful worlds of minimalized technological impact that offer a vision of salvation from the technological condition, coalescing around the little savior girl.

In contrast, limited animation tends to flatten the animetic interval, bringing its forces to the surface. It does not get rid of the animetic interval; it still uses sliding planes and tends to move drawings. But it diverts its force. Where Miyazaki's open compositing makes for a sense of an underlying and abiding depth (reinforced with painterly backgrounds), the tendency of limited animation to flatten the relation between planes of the image makes for depth spread across a surface. This also relativizes movement, opening the image to multiple frames of reference. Drawing on various discussions of otaku perception and theories of superflat art, I proposed thinking of this flattening and dehierarchizing of the planes of the image in terms of the production of a superplanar image, that is, an image in which all the planes appear on the surface. I also introduced the concepts of the distributive field and exploded projection, in order to avoid some of the pitfalls that I detected in superflat theories and otaku discourses.

What especially concerned me was how superflat theories and otaku discourses tend to fall back on a simple divide between depth and flatness, between geometric perspective and superflat, which gradually escalates into a divide between Western modernity and Japanese postmodernity. Western modernity is defined in terms of Cartesian perspectivalism, and superflat Japanese postmodernity by a break with Cartesian perspectivalism. The result is an exceedingly simple and not especially productive way of thinking modernity and postmodernity. I thus felt it important to challenge the superflat theory of modernity.

There are many more visual regimes of modernity than superflat acknowledges. For many commentators, a break with or inversion of the Cartesian subject is indicative of modernity; it is not indicative of breaking with, moving beyond, or otherwise overcoming modernity. What is more, it is possible to think in terms of qualities of Cartesianism: there is the hyper-Cartesianism lambasted by Virilio, or the hypo-Cartesianism persisting in Miyazaki. Superflat theories and otaku discourses betray their indebtedness to modernization theory and articulations of national identity in their reliance and insistence on the logic of historical breaks and ruptures, usually based on a break with Cartesianism writ large. As a consequence, when such theories and discourses confront the boundless, unfixed, and horizonless materiality allegedly characteristic of Japanese postmodernity, they prove unwilling or unable to think material limits, as if the immaterial nature of information signaled a complete absence of materiality or an actual break with materiality.

To avoid such impasses, sticking to the facts of animation, I stressed how the superplanar image tends toward a distributive field, on which elements are at once densely packed and dehierarchized. Here, in keeping in my overall emphasis on compositing, I first considered the compositional side of things. Yet, in order to avoid the tendency of superflat theories to take the absence of geometric perspective as an absence of structure, of materiality, and even of modernity, I also wished to deal with questions about structure. Although for empirical reasons I see machines as prior to structures, this does not mean that there are no such things as structures, that we can merely sweep them away.

Looked at in terms of composition, the distributive field favors structures of exploded projection or an exploded view. Unlike geometric perspective and Cartesian perspectivalism, the structure of exploded projection does not posit a fixed viewing position. It implies lines of sight across the projection. Exploded projection tends to dispense with the logic of the frame in favor of attractor and cooperator. Because attractor and cooperator have materiality, the exploded view implies some degree of rationalization and instrumentalization. If one wishes to give exploded projection a genealogy, one might think of it in terms of a modernization of orthogonal perspective used in Edo art and other traditional forms of sketching and painting. Nonetheless, I would insist that exploded projection is not a direct inheritor or embodiment of traditional or Edo art. The intercession of scientific modernity is crucial. Moroever, we must recall that Cartesianism is not the one and only mode of rationalization of imaging, however large its legacy, and other modes can interact with Cartesianism. In fact, depending on how you look at it, exploded projection can implicate a greater degree of instrumentalization and rationalization than Cartesian perspectivalism, because it operates well under conditions of movement, and it proves amenable to temporary inhabitation by a variety of modern subject effects.

To trace some of the implications of structures of exploded projection, I looked at Daicon and Gainax animations, with an emphasis on Anno Hideaki and *Nadia*. The flattening of the animetic interval in *Nadia* had a pronounced impact on panoramic vision. On the one hand, the frame of reference for the perception of actions, conflicts, and histories exploded into multiple relative frames of reference, as if there was no position from which to view the series itself panoramically, and no way to watch the series as an ordered whole seen via a fixed point of reference or fixed set of points of reference. *Evangelion* goes further than *Nadia* in this respect, but *Nadia* clearly starts the ball rolling.

On the other hand, moments of panoramic vision were consistently enclosed, at once evoking and imprisoning the Cartesian impulse toward technoscientific rationality. In sum, the viewing position was at once exploded into lines of sight (exploded projection) and enclosed into reserves (encompassed sites of rationality and instrumentality). The site of intersection of these two impulses was the little worlds of characters, with their bid for personalized lifestyles in a world in which human nature and history had already been thoroughly engineered. The result is an ambivalent optimization of human engineering, in which the transformation of humans into a standing reserve or human park allows for humans to engineer themselves. *Nadia* thus resonates with Azuma's evocation of Kojève to define otaku activities in terms of a posthistorical snobbishness. The technological animalization or domestication (engineering) of humans unfurls into little worlds articulated in terms of personal preferences and self-stylization. This is a movement of deterritorialization and reterritorialization of the human, a movement in which the limits of the human are at once shattered and regrouped differently.[4]

Because Azuma tends to emphasize a break with Cartesian structuration, he tends to dwell on deterritorialization and to ignore material limits and immaterial structures. Reterritorialization is where those limits appear. If we look at exploded projection in *Nadia* from the angle of reterritorialization, we get a better sense of what kinds of subjectification or subjective effects might accompany and reinforce structures of exploded projection. In effect, structures of exploded projection promise (or threaten) to turn any modern subject formation into a standing reserve. They provide an assembly diagram of the modern subject, of any modern subjectivity, dispersing it and holding it together, showing how to take it apart and put it back together. *Nadia* explodes the Cartesian subject, but, just when you think that the consequent enclosure of panorama might offer a solid variation on what Foucault calls the subject of disciplinization or a self-governing, post-Enlightenment modern subject, it becomes clear that this modern subject too is exploded into personalized lifestyles. Likewise with the Heideggerian attempt to gain a free relation to technology: we already have it in exploded projection. If such a world is postmodern, it is postmodern in the sense that the modern regimes or modern formations are exploded across its surface, where they genuinely function as material limits. But this does not imply that modernity is an incomplete project demanding greater efforts. Modernity here is like the shojo garage kit or girl game *(gyaru geemu)* taken up by the male otaku now past redemption: accessible, attractive, entirely legitimate, yet somehow debased, childish, vaguely criminal, and somehow indefensible.

With this evocation of the garage kit and girl game, let me return to the facts of animation. Because limited animation builds on technologies of the moving image, the distributive field generated by the superplanar image finds its material limits under conditions of movement. Compositing is not merely a matter of composition (and thus structure) but of an encounter between structure and the machine that comes prior to it. Structures of exploded projection, for instance, encounter the animetic machine powered by the moving image. We have seen how, in animation, the mechanical succession of images becomes sensible where there is the movement between planes, in the animetic interval, which is addressed, managed, or harnessed in compositing. When flat compositing brings the animetic interval to the surface in limited animation, the force of the animetic interval becomes distributed across the perceptual field. Two things follow from this distribution of the force of the moving image.

On the one hand, in limited animation, structures of exploded projection step in to manage this flattened and dehierarchized distribution of force. Much as camera work in classical cinema tends to rely on structures of geometric perspective (viewing position) and of suture (objective shot and subjective shot), so animation gravitates toward structures of compositing and of exploded projection. In effect, compositing is to animation what camera movement is to cinema. In the instance of classical or full animation, animation tends to follow cinema, emphasizing the necessity to produce movement into depth by isolating and moving the viewing position. Yet, because compositing pushes animation toward exploded projection, when full animation strives toward the classical cinematic ideal of movement into depth, it easily turns into a hyper-Cartesianism, exploding and expanding the parameters of coordinate space across the screen. Special effects animation and digital animation are particularly well suited to this impulse.

On the other hand, as the animetic interval comes to the surface, character animation also comes under pressure to negotiate the spread of force across the image. Much as montage in classical cinema tends to dwell on movement of the human body in order to coordinate various kinds of images across the mechanical succession of images, so character animation promises to step in to coordinate the movement across images. With limited animation, however, the flattening of multiplanarity into superplanarity produces a crisis in the ability of character animation to coordinate movement across images. Or, to put it another way, as animation discovers its capacity to generate a distributive field, it finds that it can readily summon and blast past the conventions of classical cinema that tended to rely on the logic of the frame, montage, and suture. The character, suddenly unframed and uninterested in conventional procedures of montage or suture, is nonetheless full of the energies of the moving image that are channeled through the animetic interval onto the image surface. Now, rather than move calmly and fluidly across frames and shots, the uncoordinated body of the character leaps arhythmically across media in an erratic montage. Animation explodes across media, striving to summon a range of additional abstract and expressive machines into its multiplanar animetic machine, while exfoliating divergent series. The character appears in toys and accessories, on the bookshelf in manga or light novels, on the television screen as animation or video game, or on the big screen at the multiplex, or all these.

The jumping of characters across media supports and platforms happens as television saturates society, first the television set and then a succession of plug-ins such as the VCR, DVD player, DivX player, PlayStation, and Wii, which expand the purview and intensify the experience of television. Yet, as noted by Stengers, "only what diverges communicates," which means that, even when the saturation, expansion, and intensification of television-screen communication networks may work to capture or stabilize the leaps and bounds of characters across media, underlying these communication networks is the force of the moving image channeled through the animetic machine. It is here that commerce enters the picture too.

The leaping of characters across media is precisely where the studio or corporation or some combination thereof strives to exercise some degree of control over how the character leaps and how much, at the same time that they must actively spur its leaping. The market and corporate interests tend to act at the level of the communication technologies, primarily the disk player or game box or computer, addressing the disks or games or software that go in them, as well as the movement between media, between cinema and disk player, or between bookshelf and game box. They act here because it is here that the divergent series of the animated moving image intersect with media platforms. There is techno-logical *confluence* inherent in the communications network of television with plug-ins, and for the corporate interests, technological confluence appears to afford opportunities for economic *convergence*, provided it is enforced with such axiomatic codes as author's rights or copyright law, or buttressed with strategies based on brand or signature features, or both. In addition, in the new millen-nium, the Japanese government has joined the act, elevating manga and anime to national cultural status and seeking to identify those features that make for their global appeal and future profitability.

In sum, at sites of technological confluence (say, television with VCR or DVD or game box or all of these), the corporate entities struggle to unfold and refold the divergent series of animation, for profit. Ideally, each jump of a character would produce a return—mandated by government fiat if necessary. Between economic convergence and media divergence, then, arises a stunning array of patterns of se-rialization, which are designed to build controls onto divergence, to encourage the divergent paths of animetic force into those patterns that allow for greater returns. Genre is one familiar pattern, which allows studios to build on already successful forms and to churn out manga or animations or films in greater numbers. There are also various patterns of adaptation, from novel to film, from manga to animated se-ries, manga to television drama, or manga to feature film, to name just a few. Here it is in the interest of the corporation to own the different versions, the light novel, the manga, the film, the video game, the soundtrack, and so on. But it is equally common for different interests to work together across companies and studios.

In addition to serialization based on genre or adaptation, some animation studios in Japan deliberately experiment with other kinds of serialization. Some of these patterns of serialization arise from those mentioned above. There is the *Gundam* world or the "Leiji-verse" (the Matsumoto Leiji universe), both grounded in a seemingly endless narrative serialization, with sequels, prequels, side stories, retellings, and new story worlds. But there are more recent efforts to use the stu-dios' control over different media installations to alter the expressive dynamics of serialization. Around *Blood: The Last Vampire*, IG Productions has serialized chapters of a quasi-historical narrative dwelling on sites and moments of political emergency, across an animated film, a series of novels, a video game, an animated television series, and manga. In contrast, with sensations such as *Densha otoko*, there is a seemingly instantaneous proliferation of versions across media platforms. *Pokémon* and *Suzumiya Haruhi* present yet other patterns of serialization, all of which merit attention in assessing how the force implicit in divergent series of animation is unfolded and refolded in patterns of serialization through the appli-cation of capital onto communication networks (technological confluence).

When Azuma stresses the priority of character in organizing the activities of third-generation male otaku, he is, in effect, signaling a transformation in patterns of serialization. Where he sees this transformation in terms of historical rupture, however, I have strived to grasp it in terms of technical and historical transformation, at the level of the force of animation, in terms of material essence of animation across divergent series. Hence my insistence that, even if animated television narratives (that is, the classic pattern of serialization in which manga is adapted into anime) are not as fundamental as they once were, nonetheless the anime *moving image* is the key to understanding mutations in serialization patterns, historically and ethically, in terms of a transfiguration of values. Hence, too, my emphasis on how the animetic interval affects thinking technology, with divergent series unfurling different assessments of the technological condition.

Still, I should reiterate that, in looking at animation from the angle of divergent series, in terms of the unfolding and refolding of the animetic interval, I do not wish to imply that divergence is tantamount to resistance or subversion vis-à-vis convergence and by extension vis-à-vis capital. But it does afford a point of entry into questions about the modern or postmodern technological condition, ever more closely associated with the confluence of information and communication technologies within networks, and with the contribution of fans to the production of knowledge. Actually, I might put it more strongly: because only what diverges communicates, if we do not consider the material essence of animation (the animetic interval) in its divergent series, we have no way to think about the relation between animation and communication networks; we risk doing no more than endlessly amassing anecdotes about studios and commodities, producers and fans.

As specific procedures of limited animation shift the force of the animetic interval onto characters, character design starts to take priority over character animation, as if only certain kinds of bodies could endure the glacial pauses between phases of corporeal movement or muster the energy to leap successfully onto other platforms without suffering complete deformation. The result is a soulful body, in which movements of heart, soul, and mind are inscribed onto the surface of the character, flickering over its contours or winding restlessly through its interstices. The soulful body is analogous to Deleuze's concept of the time-image, which emerges from the crisis in the movement-image, from the impossibility of producing a movement-image capable of an overall coordination of movement-images (affection-image, perception-image, action-image, for instance) based on the action-image.

In classical cinema, in Deleuze's reading, the action-image came to function as a "third," as an overall coordinator or mediator, differentiating and integrating cinematic movement into a coherent sensorimotor schema. As I mentioned previously, where in cinema the interval (or force) that arises from the mechanical succession of images tends to shift onto camera movement, in animation it shifts into the animetic interval between planes of the image and thus into compositing. In classic animation, character animation functions like the movement-image of which Deleuze writes, providing an overall coordination by differentiating and integrating perception, affect, and action within a movement-image that also serves to mask the gap between layers by shifting it into "full" character movement. In contrast, the soulful body finds itself unable to act, unable to coordinate its feelings and thoughts into a coherent or consistent course of action or purpose, as with Nadia in *Nadia* or Shinji in *Evangelion*. Its actions are continually sidetracked into musings, recriminations, uncertainty, and insecurity, which are inscribed in advance into the character's design as potential depths.

If I hedged somewhat in my discussion of the soulful body and the Deleuzian time-image, it is because the effects of commercialization become acute in the context of character design in ways that they do not in Deleuze's account of the time-image. Deleuze nonetheless presents the problem succinctly when he comments, "if all images have become clichés, internally as well as externally, how can an Image be extracted from all these clichés, 'just an image,' an autonomous mental image?"[5] In the context of corporate-driven media convergence built upon sites of technological confluence, the time-image risks becoming a cliché. It is a risk that has always been there; it is a risk in cinema, too. The risk is different today than in the moment of Deleuze's *Cinema* books, which were largely written prior to and without the VCR. But it is difficult to say how today's risk differs if we do not first consider how Deleuze sees the risk that the cliché poses to the time-image.

The time-image is a doubling of the movement-image (a fold of a fold) that generates an autonomous mental image, much as the brain, in course of embryonic development, is folded to the outer surface, only to be folded inward again. Similarly, in the course of the "development" of animation into different bodies (sensorimotor schema), the construction of an overall action-image pushes what will be later be the soul and brain to the outside. The overall action-image forces the animetic interval outside the image, by using compositing and full character animation (and then in montage) to keep the gap out of the picture, as it were. With limited animation, however, the interval rises to the surface of the image and spreads across it, disabling the movement-image of full character animation. The gap is always in the picture. This makes for a fold of a fold, a doubling back of coordinated movement on itself, to produce an image of thought, a thinking image, an image whose force of indeterminacy results in a shock to thought, moving us to think and feel animetically. This is the time-image, a fold of a fold, a folding back into the image of a gap that was initially pushed (folded) toward the exterior.

In contrast, a cliché is but a fold. Or, more precisely, a cliché is a force unfolded and refolded, to borrow Stengers's turn of phrase. The force of the animetic interval, for instance, might be unfolded, only to be refolded at a site of technological confluence and fed into market-driven convergence. It is then a cliché, without autonomy. If today we run the risk of mistaking the cliché for a thinking image, and vice versa, it is because it is difficult to tell the difference between a genuine fold of a fold, and a re-fold. We might say that this is, at another level, a crisis in distinguishing between invention and reproduction, at a historical moment where it is difficult to tell them apart. This is what concerns Deleuze when he later comments that it is truly frightening to think that corporations may have souls.[6] Invention itself may be subsumed by production and reproduction. Deleuze calls this *modulation*.[7] Rather than expunging or isolating difference, modulation subsumes difference within repetition. Instead of an autonomous time-image, there is a commercially modulated time-image, that is, a cliché that appears to have a soul. Simply put, modulation signals a new moment of crisis, which also amounts to a crisis in the time-image.[8]

The crisis of the time-image and the emergence of modulation are commonly associated with the rise of the information society, which, roughly speaking, begins in the mid- to late 1960s and gathers momentum in the 1980s, emerging as a cultural dominant in the 1990s. Limited animation follows a similar arc from the early 1960s, and the transnational boom in anime in the 1990s made Japanese animations inseparable from new information and communications technologies. The very idea of animation subsuming cinema, or of animation becoming the dominant logic of the moving image, comes from this apparent merger of animation with information, by way of digital technologies and communication networks.

The ubiquity, centrality, and popularity of animation today spur commentators to evoke animation in a unitary manner. But, if we are to address modulation, that is, the crisis in the time-image, we need to look at animation not as a unitary entity but from the angle of the force of the moving image and the generation of divergent series with different manners of thinking technology and technological value. Again, the question is, what happens when divergent series encounter economic and social determinants that strive to capture, or encourage the submission of, technological innovation and inventiveness vis-à-vis the force of the moving image? This is (again) where patterns of serialization are important.

Schematically speaking, three manners of thinking technology animetically have appeared in this book: minimization (Miyazaki), optimization (Anno), and perversion (CLAMP). There is, potentially, a critical force in each of these approaches.

In Miyazaki, we see a *critical minimization* of animation technologies, which goes hand in hand with a strategic reprisal of the classic body of full animation in a world of open compositing. This is, in effect, neo-classicism: the idea is to produce a body coordinated to the slow human-scaled world in which the dynamism of Nature promises to deflate and minimize hyper-Cartesianism. As I discussed in chapter 8, Miyazaki and Ghibli try to extend critical minimization to the market, but with mixed results. The idea is to prevent the unfolding and refolding of animation implicit in communication networks and media convergence. Yet, as Oshii Mamoru insistently points out, this strategy threatens to erase the very inventiveness that it claims to value. The result is an insistence on authority and the brand. In effect, Ghibli uses the forces of convergence implicit in the market to fold the force of the animetic interval around the film, which makes everything depend on seeing a film with an *auteur*. Ghibli serializes *auteurs*. As Oshii indicates, the emphasis thus falls on artful patterns of distribution and commercialization rather than on genuine invention or experimentation. There is more of the same beautiful brand, waiting for new *auteurs* to make it. This is the current impasse of Ghibli.

In Anno, we see a *critical optimization* of animation technologies, which builds on the crisis of the classic body of full animation already implicit in a certain lineage of limited animation. Flat compositing promises the advent of a boundless and horizonless world, a distributive field, in which anyone might now participate, becoming producers in their own right. Yet the distributive field, for all its aura of flat, boundless dehierarchization, implies material limits. As the distributive field encounters the force of the moving image, flat compositing brings that force to the surface as potential depth or potentiality, which becomes inscribed onto characters. Thus characters become the site of serialization. As Azuma notes, *Evangelion* entailed a new pattern of serialization, based not on the expansion of its narrative world but on character play (RPG games).

Clearly, however, Anno has doubts about how the force of the moving image can be channeled into characters, about how characters become available for personalized otaku-like serialization. Indeed there is a paradox, for the inventiveness and innovation of these new otaku "coproducers" does not only address series (based on divergence) but also serialization (orientated toward convergence). As such, media convergence threatens to subsume divergent series. The cliché does not appear as a negative condition for the generation of the time-image. Instead, the time-image, in the form of the soulful body, appears as the negative condition for the reproduction of clichés. In response, Anno sadistically pushes the unfolding of the time-image to its limit, in a manner calculated to foreclose its submissive refolding in convergence, to challenge or to put an end to the activities of fans that apparently reproduce the character everywhere, indiscriminately, as if he wished to say: "If invention is never genuine, then reproduction itself may be discredited." With the intensive serialization of characters appears the cruel *auteur* who strives to produce a shock of enlightenment.

The approach, too, reaches an impasse: animation cannot be imagined to enable thought or theory, because the force of the animetic interval, its divergence into series, is not addressed as such. Convergence thus appears to precede divergence, albeit in the postmodern manner of Anno's bravura FX film reboot of the *Cutie Honey* serialization for Gainax, or in the afterlife of narrative within the contents industry addressed in Azuma's sequel to *Animalizing Postmodern*.[9]

In CLAMP, we see a *critical perversion* of information technologies (computers), wherein computerization and hystericization seem to go hand in glove. Because *Chobits* follows the classic pattern of anime adaptation from manga, it takes up the crisis of the movement-image in a very different way from, say, *Nadia* or *Evangelion*. *Chobits* begins with the post-action-image characteristic of story manga.

When commentators speak disparagingly of limited animation in Japan, they frequently conjure up the deleterious effects of the story manga, signaling that anime is full of still images and awkward voice-overs because it follows manga. This is not entirely untrue, especially if we consider the precedent of *Astro Boy*. There is no need to rue or regret the impact of manga on anime, however. The so-called still images of limited animation are not truly static; they entail a different way of directing the force of the moving image. In the adaptation of anime from manga, I see the impact of manga's reworking of the movement-image derived from classical cinemas and animations. Manga thus tends toward the post-action-image, in which the subjective structures and viewing positions associated with cinema and full animation are presented in exploded projection.

With various kinds of movement-image (affection-image, perception-image, and action-image) sprawling across its pages, the *Chobits* manga is able to reconfigure the seinen mode of address. The seinen mode of address implies, of course, a viewing position. Which to say, it implies an overall coordinating movement-image that gives priority to perception—in this case, to how young men look at girls. At the level of the seinen mode of address, however, CLAMP inscribes a very Lacanian scenario into their manga, drawing an equation between computerization and the hystericization of the girl's body, showing the information-driven transformation of girl into shojo. Girl computerized is girl hystericized. In this register (of the perception-image coordinated into the overall movement of the story manga), *Chobits* appears perfectly content to replicate the fundamental asymmetry of sexual desire in the classic Saitō-Lacan fashion. Yet this is not all there is to *Chobits*, to the manga or the anime.

Because manga presents an exploded projection of the overall coordination of movement, it gives freer reign to the other kinds of movement-image, and in particular to the affection-image, to affect. Affect does not entirely free itself of the overall coordination, however. Nor does it produce the sort of crisis that Deleuze detects in cinema with the time-image. Manga entails a post-action-image rather than a time-image. Nonetheless, the freer reign given to affect allows *Chobits* to stick close to emergent positions, and to inscribe an encounter between subjective structure (male viewing position) and the character function that trembles eternally on the edge of formal dissolution and consolidation. This is also why I find *Chobits* of interest, not because it radically undermines received asymmetries of sexuality (viewing positions), but because it inscribes an encounter between affective machine (character function) and subjective structure (suture). The encounter is inscribed in the gynoid body of Chii as a tension between specter and symptom. The encounter is actualized between Chii and Hideki in their "eye asymmetry." This is where the manga oscillates between the Lacanian scenario implicit in seinen viewing positions (male perversion) and their deconstruction (perversion of perversion).

Now, the *Chobits* anime adaptation runs the risk of tipping the scales toward the subjective structure and the Lacanian scenario, because there are conventions for editing in television animation, especially shot and reverse shot, that are much like the objective shot and subjective shot that make for suture, that is, for an overall coordination within the movement-image that gives priority to perception-images as movement-images. Yet, in animation, and especially in limited animation, compositing and character animation take priority over editing and montage (which are literally *drawn* into the animetic machine). In *Chobits*, which is digitally produced limited animation, there is an overall tendency toward the flat compositing characteristic of limited cel animation, which gives priority to the rhythms of appearance and disappearance of relatively immobile characters. Rhythms of characters take precedence over, and even dictate, patterns of editing. Thus, the would-be viewing position of Hideki is continually caught in the act, trapped in a moment of sheer affect.

This is also where the male anime producers become stuck, as if caught in their own attempt to overcode the manga with the male viewing position. This is also where the crisis of the movement-image appears as perversion, and perversion starts to inhabit the crisis of the time-image as well.

Although the anime version of *Chobits* is not as subjectifying as cinematic suture, it does subjectify more than the manga does. The anime plays with the emergence of a subjective shot. The anime makes a running joke of the moments when Hideki is caught in the act, and these rhythms, based on Hideki frozen in poses upon strobe-like backgrounds, begin to structure the series. The hilariously maniac responses of Hideki propel the anime. At the same time, for a number of reasons, the anime avoids direct reference to Chii's reset button, which adds a layer of modesty and uncertainty about what it means for a man to live with a gynoid. In the combination of reticence vis-à-vis Chii and the investment in Hideki's antics, I see a different orientation vis-à-vis the movement-image, which is not only due to procedures of animation but also to the gender dynamics associated with the classic pattern of serialization of anime from manga.

The world of shojo manga is today one of the most significant cultural industries in terms of the number of women producing image-based narratives largely about women and largely for women. It is an industry that builds directly on amateur productions. CLAMP, for instance, first won audiences through *dōjinshi* or amateur manga circuits. Manga production also provides a constant stream of new stories for the television anime and manga film industries. Indeed, from the 1980s, the creativity of women manga writers, illustrators, and producers became one of the most important forces in the anime industry, and many of the sexy girl figures associated with shonen modes of address are riffs on figures first produced by women manga artists.

This does not mean that women creators are treated particularly well in the manga industry, where male editors still dominate. More importantly, while women's manga remain a major source for anime production (and more recently for television dramas), the anime industry rarely has women in positions of authority. As anyone who watches the special features on anime DVDs has probably noted, women mostly labor at the lowest levels of production in terms of prestige, cleaning up sketches, applying color, and probably pouring tea. Moreover, as the industry produces animation digitally on computers, it is precisely such jobs that disappear. Rumi in *Chobits*, for instance, worries that she cannot compete with a computer in terms of looks or labor. In fact, in anime production, the woman's job might actually go to a computer. In this sense, the gynoid scenario in *Chobits* evokes an asymmetry in labor and prestige between men and women, and between animation and manga. And it recalls the highly repetitive, tedious, "automated" work required in manga and anime, which frequently falls to women.

The importance of softcore pornography in the film and anime industries in Japan also deserves mention. About a third of the films produced in Japan are so-called pink films, largely softcore porn, and it is not unusual for film directors, male and female, to begin their careers in pink film (and many end there). Similarly, a significant portion of anime production is male-targeted pornography. And you need only Google *hentai anime* to see what inroads the sex anime industry has made outside Japan via the Web. This softcore makes an appearance in *Chobits* in the form of Hideki's infatuation with skin books.

In sum, in manga and anime production, women often become a source of inexpensive creativity that feeds into male-dominated sectors of production, and the same industries churn out quantities of softcore, frequently blurring the boundaries between pornography and nonpornography in the domain of mass-targeted entertainment. It is into this world that CLAMP ventured with their first foray into manga that specifically addresses young men—the seinen mode of address.

This pattern of serialization, from manga to anime, is unlike that of Miyazaki-Ghibli's animations or Anno-Gainax's animations, where so much prestige and authority is accorded to the male director as *auteur*, whether as benevolent patron or cruel taskmaster. As a four-woman team whose members sometimes take on new names, CLAMP presents a very different structure of authority. Its spokeswoman, Ohkawa Ageha (not so long ago Ohkawa Nanase), also styles herself as the producer, serving as the liaison with the anime production, frequently receiving credit as a writer on the anime series. In sum, in the adaptation of CLAMP manga to anime, there is frequently a sort of liaison officer who acts for the ensemble of the four-woman team, like an author or creator but whose impact is as hard to gauge as that of the different women within the CLAMP team.

When the male-directed anime version of *Chobits* gets stuck on Hideki caught in the act to propel the comedy of the series, it is as if there is something about the manga that the anime cannot digest, a form of creativity and authority in the manga that puzzles the anime. It is not merely a matter of the general difficulty of adapting manga to anime, of the formal surplus that the adaptation cannot manage. It is equally a matter of gender asymmetry. This is where the CLAMP entity exerts its cloud-like effect, as if encrypting itself across media with its earnest yet subtle realignments of genre expectations. For instance, the seinen mode of address does not entirely cohere in *Chobits*. There is just too much shojo in *Chobits*. In fact, it is easy to read *Chobits* as a shojo series. Yet this shojo quality of *Chobits* is not merely a matter of multiple orientations, as Saitō suggests, which allow men and women to inhabit the same text differently, men hystericizing women, and women coming to terms with their hystericization. If this were the case, the anime would not get stuck alongside Hideki or obscure Chii's reset button.

The anime's trouble with the reset button suggests that the indigestible shojo quality is somehow localized in Chii's reset button. The reset button is supposed to function as the crypt of Hideki's desire and thus to stabilize the sexuality in the absence of the sexual relation—again, the classic Lacanian scenario. Yet, once the button is an open secret, it opens the possibility that, with each reset, there might be new Chii adventures with men other than Hideki. Of course Chii would no longer be Chii, but someone else. Yet Chii is already playing at being someone else. Chii is constantly changing clothes, taking on different looks and poses, to the point that we are not sure who or what Chii is. She has already been reset.

Psychoanalysis has a way of writing such behavior back into the unity-in-lack of male desire. Žižek, for instance, sees the sex fantasy in which the woman imagines herself as someone else as the essence of hystericization. Yet the situation in *Chobits* is clearly more perverse than this classic psychoanalytic situation. Perversion does not confirm the unity-in-lack of Hideki or that of the movement-image (via suture). It is as if female mutability, which is also the mutability of CLAMP in serialization, becomes localized in the reset button, and is just too much. Likewise, the combination of computerization and hystericization becomes too much. It recalls Foucault's view of female hysterical simulation as a counter-maneuver in which the patient gets the better of the neurologist, insisting: "if you want to use me to denounce the simulators, well then, you really will have to hear what I want to say and see what I want to do!"[10] With Chii in *Chobits*, CLAMP issues this cry: "if you guys really want to play with the perversion implicit in the male gaze, then you'll have to see what I want to wear and read what I want to read! You'll have to deal with a lot of frills!"

Perversion, then, need not be thought on the model of lack—for instance, a lack of coordination in the body that makes it fail and yearn for supplementation. It can be thought on the model of "encephalization" of the body, on the liberation of Images and Elements from apparently useless dead ends and "spandrels" of evolution, in divergent series.[11] It is part of the conceit of *Chobits* that there is an "evolution" in romance, or an adaptation of romance to the computer era. Of course, in many respects, this new romance looks pretty much like the old ones. Yet there is an important gap between the advance of romance and the advance of technology, which destroys what Heidegger calls "merely technological behavior," but not by gathering and focusing attention on the technological conditions. On the one hand, in *Chobits*, romance is a matter of fetishizing new technologies, of looking at them awry. On the other hand, romance becomes a way of settling on apparently useless or redundant features, on dead ends, spandrels, and useless frills of our technological advances, which serve as a reminder that genuine transformation happens not in linear progress but in divagation and divergence.

In sum, in *Chobits*, when the post-action-image of manga meets the force of the moving image, it affects how that force is shunted into the potential depths of soulful bodies, encouraging it to gather perversely in seemingly redundant lines of force, in the delicate yet implacable lines of hair and clothes that stream around Chii's body; in the lines that bend perceptual space into the impurity of affect, with pools of eyes within eyes; and in the story lines that conspire to incite a steady movement into inaction, in an exploded projection of action. Such lines conspire to open the male otaku perversion to engineering, to disassembly and reassembly. Such lines delineate an otaku park, a reserve of perversion, a technologized stocking of potential labor to be perversely and generically folded into the service of gynoid surfaces. The male otaku, the proto-Lacanian subject, is transformed into a standing reserve, a domesticated viewer for female perversion. This is a perversion of perversion, a serialization of serialization that potentially reopens divergent series.

In an age of modulation in which technical confluence (communications networks) begin to allow capital to enter more profoundly into divergent series of animation, the risk is that the divergence inherent in the force of the moving image, because caught between manga and anime, between the post-action-image and the crisis of the time-image, can become so technologized that thought and feeling remain paralyzed in a series of shocks and crises that go nowhere. The response of *Chobits* to this postmodern technological condition is as ingeniously and cryptically simple as the most basic intervention into the computer network: not retreat (like Miyazaki), not rebuild (like Anno), but reset.

NOTES

Introduction

Note on Romanization and Translation: The romanization of Japanese in this book follows the Hepburn system, with one exception in the instance of proper names beginning with "oo." Commonly macrons are used to indicate the long o "ou" but not the long o "oo." With proper names beginning with "oo," however, I have used a macron—for instance, Ōtomo rather than Ootomo, and Ōtsuka rather than Ootsuka. Although these names frequently appear without a macron or as "oh," they rarely appear in searches in the latter form, and I have made this exception to avoid confusing readers.

In addition, I have provided translations for the titles of Japanese publications in the bibliography and occasionally within the text. Sometimes the title translations are not mine: many books published in Japanese provide an English version of the title, and as a courtesy, if an English version is provided, I have generally used it, as with *Otakugaku nyūmon* (Introduction to otakuology) and *Dōbutsu ka suru posutomodan* (Animalizing postmodern).

1. See, for instance, Kirby, *Parallel Tracks*, and Aumont, "The Variable Eye, or the Mobilization of the Gaze."

2. In a series of dialogues gathered in *Nihon fūkei ron*, Kiridooshi Risaku and Maruta Shōzō use the motif of the train, especially the emergence of the bullet train, to trace connections across their experience of postwar Japan. While their associations are largely geared toward the symbolism of trains (as harbingers of speed or modernity), the ease with which they make the train into a postwar landscape dialogue speaks to the centrality and ubiquity of trains in everyday life in Japan. Here, in contrast, I begin with the train not to underscore the Japaneseness of anime but to highlight how the "spacing" or "animetic interval" of Japanese animations meshes with the technicity or technological spacing integral to the spacings of everyday life, which accounts not only for their current ubiquity on a variety of media platforms in the Japanese commuter system but

also for their resonance with other intervals prevalent in the technological mobilization of everyday life in other global urban environments. In the initial draft of this book, I concluded with a chapter on anime and commuting time, based on two prior presentations: "Commuting Time" (paper presented at Cultural Typhoon, Tokyo, June 29, 2006) and "Mobile Imaging and Commuting in Tokyo" (paper presented at Visualizing Knowledge, Stanford Humanities Center, May 22, 2007). Although the chapter itself will have to wait for another publication opportunity, I would like to thank participants for their comments, which surely have had an impact on this introduction.

3. Schivelbusch, *The Railway Journey*, 54.

4. Ibid., 64.

5. Ibid.

6. Ibid.

7. Comolli, "Technique and Ideology," 44. See, too, Baudry, "Ideological Effects."

8. Comolli, "Technique and Ideology," 55.

9. In the case of Japan, the specificity thesis appears under the aegis of the "pure film movement" *(junsui eigageki undō)*. For accounts to the pure film movement, see Bernardi, *Writing in Light*; Gerow, *Visions of Japanese Modernity*; and Lamarre, *Shadows on the Screen*. Daisuke Miyao rethinks the implications of Gerow's discussion of the pure film movement for the history of Japanese animation in, "Before *Anime*."

10. Carroll, "The Specificity Thesis," 334.

11. Ibid.

12. Ibid., 336.

13. David Bordwell proposes to group these efforts under the rubric of a "modernity thesis" in *On the History of Film Style*, and Ben Singer elaborates on his idea in *Melodrama and Modernity*.

14. Hansen, "The Mass Production of the Senses."

15. Alan Cholodenko, in his introduction to *The Illusion of Life II: More Essays on Animation* (27–33), provides a nice overview of some of the seminal works on animation.

16. When editing a collection of essays on anime, "Between Cinema and Anime," as a special issue of *Japan Forum*, I vacillated on the merits of using the term "animetic" or "anime-ic" to refer to a quality of animation, which would roughly correspond with the use of *animeteki* in the final chapter of Ueno Toshiya's book *Kurenai no metaru suutsu: anime to iu senjō*. At that time, we opted generally to use "anime-ic," following the usage in Thomas Looser's essay in the issue, "From Edogawa to Miyazaki: Cinematic and *Anime*-ic Architectures of Early and Late Twentieth Century Japan." Here, however, precisely to avoid particularizing anime in advance, I prefer the term "animetic," which refers to qualities of the animated moving image more generally, of which the anime-ic might apply to one variety or, more probably, a series of varieties.

17. See, too, Lamarre, "Animation Studies."

18. Cited in Furniss, *Art in Motion*, 5.

19. See Thain, "Wandering Stars," for a brilliant analysis of how the animetic machine implicates and explicates moving bodies, especially of dancers but also between media.

20. I adopt the term "underdetermination" from Paul Dumouchel's discussion of Gilbert Simondon, in "Simondon's Plea for a Philosophy of Technology."

21. Guattari, *Chaosmosis*, 33–35.

22. Ibid., 33.

23. Baudry, "Ideological Effects," 355.

24. Ibid., 356.

25. I draw here on Tsugata Nobuyuki's account in his book on Kitayama Seitarō, *Nihon hajime no animeeshon sakka Kitayama Seitarō*, 6–12. I am also indebted to the recent retrospective of prewar Japanese animation in Montreal, held February 27 to April 6, and to the lectures of Tochigi Akira from the National Film Center in Tokyo on that occasion.

26. Tsugata, *Nihon hajime no animeeshon*, 57–59.

27. I am drawing here on Henri Bergson's introduction to *Matter and Memory*, as well as Ronald Bogue's presentation in *Deleuze on Cinema*.

28. Bogue, *Deleuze on Cinema*, 30.

29. I am drawing here on Gilbert Simondon, *Du mode d'existence des objects techniques*, as well as an excellent introduction to Simondon by Muriel Combes, *Simondon, Individu et collectivité*.

30. Naoki Sakai provides one of the most succinct and insightful accounts of this problem in "Modernity and Its Critique."

31. On micromasses, see Marilyn Ivy, "Formations of Mass Culture."

32. Borthwick et al., "Meiji," 126.

33. This bid for nonmetaphysical spirit–matter continuity takes a number of guises, as different as Nishida Kitarō's *mu* (nothingness or full void), Watsuji Tetsurō's *fūdo* (climate), or Kuki Shūzō's *iki* (spirit, style, panache), but in this instance, given the constant references to Edo culture in anime commentary and anime, Leslie Pincus's *Authenticating Culture*, an account of Kuki Shūzō and *iki*, is a good point of reference.

34. For an introduction to "overcoming modernity," see Sun Ge's essay, "In Search of the Modern: Tracing Japanese Thought on 'Overcoming Modernity.'" See, too, Richard Calichman's translation of the debates, *Overcoming Modernity*.

35. Naoki Sakai's discussion of Heidegger and Watsuji Tetsurō is exemplary here. See *Translation and Subjectivity*, 76–86.

36. See H. D. Harootunian's extended discussion of the political stakes of overcoming modernity in prewar Japan in *Overcome by Modernity*.

37. On the black ships and giant robots, see Tanizaki, "Anime mekanikku hensenshi," 158–59. On otaku and the atomic bomb, see Murakami, "Earth in my Window," 117–18.

1. Cinematism and Animetism

1. Schivelbusch, *The Railway Journey*, 64.

2. See Kirby, *Parallel Tracks*.

3. Virilio, "Cyberwar, God, and Television."

4. Virilio, *Pure War*, 85.

5. In *The Age of the World Target* (2006), Rey Chow argues that what Heidegger called the "world picture" or "world image" implies the transformation of the world into a target, which she then dubs the age of the world target.

2. Animation Stand

1. Rutsky, *High Technē*, 4.

2. Zielinski, *Deep Time of the Media*.

3. Scott McCloud, *Understanding Comics: The Invisible Art* (New York: Harper Collins, 1993). In keeping with this primitivism, in a provocative series of Orientalist generalizations, he also draws a wholesale equation between the visual conventions of manga and Zen thinking.

4. Santorii Bijutsukan, ed., *Chōjūgiga ga yatte kita!*

5. See Shimamoto, ed., *Anime no hajimari Chōjūgiga*, and the interview with Takahata Isao in a special issue of *Bijutsu techō* dedicated to *Chōjūgiga*.

6. See Sawaragi, *Nihon—Gendai—Bijutsu*, chapter 10, note 9.

7. Gunning, "An Aesthetic of Astonishment."

8. See Introduction, note 9.

9. Needless to say, one can also seek the origins of the movie camera in the camera obscura or other devices, looking at the apparatus in "deeper" time.

10. See Takeda Yasuhiro's account of paper animation in *Nootenki tsūshin*, 9. The book has recently appeared in English translation as *Notenki Memoirs: Studio Gainax and the Men Who Created Evangelion*; see page 48, as well as the discussion in chapter 11.

11. This account derives in part from the discussion entitled "The Multiplane Camera" at the Golden Gate Disneyana Club's 100 Years of Magic, http://www.ggdc .org/mp-100multiplane.htm.

12. Burch, *Life to Those Shadows*, 59. Jacques Aumont, in "The Variable Eye, or the Mobilization of the Gaze," also talks about the problem of motion in cinema in relation to panoramas and trains.

13. Yamaguchi and Watanabe, *Nihon animeeshon eiga shi*, 33. Kimura began work in animation with Asahi Kinema Studio, which was an independent producer of educational films.

14. James Utterbeck, cited in Nye, *Technology Matters*, 33.

15. Yamaguchi and Watanabe, *Nihon animeeshon eiga shi*, 63.

3. Compositing

1. Jay, "Scopic Regimes of Modernity," 6.

2. Ibid., 4.

3. Recollections of the film tend to dwell on its lyricism. Tsuji Masaki recalls crying in amazement over it, in *Bokutachi no anime shi*, 5. Ōtsuka Eiji takes up the question

of such animated war films that were remembered not for their violence or warlike quality but as visions of peace, akin to "culture films." See Ōtsuka, "'Bunka eiga' to shite no *Momotarō umi no shinpei.*"

4. See Anne Friedberg's chapter on Alberti's windows in *The Virtual Window: From Alberti to Microsoft.* While I build on her discussion implicitly here, because I am looking at animation, I tend to see the movement from Alberti's windows to the multiple windows of Microsoft through the "lens" of compositing. Which is to say, multiple windows also read as divergent series of animation based on technologies of the moving image.

5. Guattari, *Chaosmosis,* 43.

6. Ibid.

7. Cited in Virilio, *War and Cinema.*

8. Manovich, *The Language of New Media,* 302.

9. Oshii, "Zenryaku Miyazaki Hayao-sama," 14.

10. See especially the dialogue titled "'Jissha' to 'dōga' no shinjitsu." For a discussion of the term *actuality* in Japanese film theory, see Furuhata, "Return to Actuality."

11. There are a number of ways of taking into account the tendency of Miyazaki to avoid horizontal and vertical orientations as part of his effort to impart a sense of dynamism to the image without resorting to geometric perspective. In "'Guchoku na kororozashi' e no kussetsu shita sanji: 'Mirai shōnen Konan' kara 'Mononoke-hime' made no kiseki," Mori Takuya cites Miyazaki's complaint about Disney placing the entrance and exit at the same level, for instance. There is also the angling of characters, a legacy of Ōtsuka Yasuo, to which Gotō Tsuyoshi and Kuroda Mitsuhiro call attention in *Mononoke-hime kenkyū josetsu,* 108.

12. As early as 1982, in a piece published in *Shuppatsuten* called "Animeeshon to manga eiga," Miyazaki contrasts animation and the manga film with a running analog to the jumbo jet versus the earlier years of flight. The earlier years of flight are associated with manga films, while the jumbo jet is associated with animation and anime. It is not hard to read the jumbo jet as the very essence of postwar ballistic technologies. Miyazaki's increased insistence over the years that he does manga films and not anime is part of his resistance to jumbo-jet optical logistics.

13. Rutsky, *High Technē,* 4.

14. Hughes, *Human-Built World,* 4.

15. Jay, "Scopic Regimes of Modernity," 3.

4. Merely Technological Behavior

1. Takahata Isao, who served as producer for the film, recalls that part of the conception of *Castle in the Sky* was to have machines and locations that looked Western, but without any sense of a specific location. In *Eiga o tsukurinagara kangaeta koto,* 296.

2. Commentators on Miyazaki's films generally call attention to their critique of techno-scientific modernity. In *Miyazaki Hayao wa sayoku nan darō,* Inoue Shizuka refers us specifically to a critique of scientific enlightenment and progress in Miyazaki

(64). Inoue suggests that what distinguishes Miyazaki's leftist critique of scientific progress is that, unlike the more right-wing critique in which technological forces self-destruct (which is the easy way out), Miyazaki allows the ecological faction to score a victory. Similarly, in an essay on *Princess Mononoke*, Susan Napier calls attention to how Miyazaki's film forces viewers to address myths about progress. If *Princess Mononoke* tends to come to mind in the context of *Castle of the Sky*, it is because, as Sasakibara Gō notes, there is a sense of a return to Miyzaki's earlier preoccupations with the impact of technologies in *Princess Mononoke*. See "Kantoku izen no Miyazaki Hayo."

3. McCarthy, *Hayao Miyazaki*, 97.

4. Ibid., 98.

5. Dreyfus, "Heidegger on Gaining a Free Relation to Technology."

6. Heidegger, "The Question Concerning Technology."

7. Dreyfus, "Heidegger on Gaining a Free Relation to Technology," 54.

8. In his reading of *Nausicaä* and *Castle in the Sky*, in "Kantoku izen no Miyazaki Hayao," Sasakibara Gō suggests that there is a sense of absolutism in the heroics of the children when they opt for self-sacrifice. This is a sign that Miyazaki thinks technology in terms of a condition and salvation rather than problem and solution.

9. Miyazaki Hayao and Murakami Ryū, "Misshitsu kara no dasshutsu," 363–64. There are, of course, other commentators who insist that Miyazaki's films are profoundly humanist, such as Ishiko Jun in "Hyuumanizumu ni taisuru yasashisa to kibishisa." Needless to say, there are many ways of thinking humanism, but I agree with Murakami Ryū that, even if Miyazaki is to some degree humanist, Miyazaki does not embrace a human-centered worldview in the manner of High Humanism.

10. As Takahata notes in *Eiga o tsukurinagara kangaeta koto*, the very idea of *Castle in the Sky* was to make an "amusing and rousing classic action adventure" (296), but it seems that Miyazaki was not only plagued with doubts about the genre but also continued to fret about the constraints implicit in it.

11. Miyazaki, "*Tenkū no shiro Rapyuta* kikaku gen'an," 394.

12. Sharff, "Introduction: Heidegger on Technology," in *Philosophy of Technology: The Technological Condition*, ed. Sharff and Dusek, 247.

13. Dreyfus, "Heidegger on Gaining a Free Relation to Technology," 56.

14. Ibid.

15. Ibid., 58.

16. Talbot, "The Auteur of Anime."

5. Flying Machines

1. In "Yutakana shizen, dōji ni kyōbō na shizen nan desu," Miyazaki refers to *Nausicaä* in terms of living in a nature that is at once fecund and brutal. It is a commonplace of Miyazaki criticism that the crueler twists of nature are muted in later works; even in *Princess Mononoke*, in which the *shishigami*, a sort of nature god, threatens to pollute the land, the threat of pollution follows from human actions. Nature in itself is not cruel.

2. I rely here on the chronology in the September 2, 1997, special issue of *Kinema junpō* on Miyazaki and Studio Ghibli, "Miyazaki Hayao to Mononoke-hime to Sutajio Jiburi."

3. The term *dōga*, originally coined by Masaoka Kenzō in the prewar era and subsequently deployed with a variety of connotations from animation in general to animated experiments in movement, becomes roughly equivalent to animated films in Tōei's usage, analogous to Disney's animated films and distinct from primarily cartoonish cartoon films.

4. In "Miyazaki anime no hiroin no keifu," Okada Emiko traces the connections between Hilda and Luna. My account overlaps more with that of Shimizu Tomoko, who sees in such girl characters an allegory of modern communications. See "'Jiburi monsutaazu' to kankaku no toporojii." Shimizu aptly calls attention to Ghibli monsters, in which modern communications (as in the pendant) function as a gift of labor, and as a curse.

5. In praise of *Castle in the Sky*, in "Ano kumo no mine no mukō ni," fantasy writer Itō Hidehiko dwells on the resemblance of Pazu and Conan, which serves as a reminder not only of the inspiration that Miyazaki drew from Key in making *Nausicaä* and *Castle in the Sky* but also (and more importantly) of how closely Miyazaki associated the boy's adventure story with questions of the modern technological condition.

6. Yonezawa Yoshihiro, who writes primarily about manga, provides an interesting approach to Miyazaki's animations by stressing their origins in manga, in "Manga to anime to Miyazaki Hayao."

7. In "Kantoku izen no Miyazaki Hayao," Sasakibara Gō makes a similar point in his overview of Miyazaki's earlier works, suggesting that *Nausicaä* and *Castle in the Sky* were rather despairing works, whence Miyazaki's turn to everyday realities in *Totoro* and *Kiki*. While I agree with him, I don't see *Castle in the Sky* so much as a dead end. Instead I think Miyazaki begins to inhabit the posttechnological world of crisis implied in the prior films, and the crisis of *Castle in the Sky* reappears in *Princess Mononoke*, and the crisis implicit in *Kiki* reappears in *Howl's Moving Castle*.

8. A review of *Castle in the Sky* from 1986 by Honda Yūkichi is included in the special issue of *Kinema junpō* on Miyazaki and Studio Ghibli. In it Honda sees a mismatch between the scenes with a fairytale quality and the comic scenes, suggesting that the mismatch came of a desire to mix foreign and Japanese styles. While I do not agree with this characterization of the comic scenes as foreign, I think that the point is important in a different register: in the comic scenes, Miyazaki was still working with the action-adventure mode of address that he later disavowed. In *Castle in the Sky*, he negotiates the ballistic optics implicit in action-adventure with comic deflation, which makes for a film with a genuine sense of humor, as Tsuneishi Fumiko notes in "Tenkū no shiro Rapyuta."

9. Miyazaki's characterization of manga film in terms of earlier days of flight in contrast to the jumbo jet comes to mind here again. Above all, he wishes to avoid or deflate the jumbo jet mode of perception. See his "Animeeshon to manga eiga," 154–55.

10. It is telling that when Miyazaki speaks of flying, he not only claims that he is a glider type not a plane type, but also speaks of his preference of clouds and light over Landsat images. In other words, his world of flight is designed to avoid the Landsat view in favor of the wonder of sliding through clouds as on the sliding planes of celluloid.

6. Full Animation

1. See Jasper Sharp's discussion of digital imaging and *Tachiguchishi retsuden* in "Between Dimensions."

2. There is a lineage of commentary on Miyazaki Hayao that builds on Miyazaki's comments about how the Japanese were happier in the Jōmon age due to their sense of the vitality and animism of the natural world. See Miyazaki, "Nihonjin ga ichiban shiawase datta no wa Jōmon jidai." In "*Mononoke-hime* no kiso chishiki," Kanō Seiji follows a chart of the work flow for the animation of *Princess Mononoke* with a discussion of nature related to Miyazaki's remarks on Jōmon animism. In "Miyazaki anime no kanōsei," Masaki Akira stresses the animism of the ancient Japanese in understanding Miyazaki's animation (117–19). Yet, as Ueno Toshiya reminds us, this is animism in an age of technology. See Ueno Toshiya, "Majo ni sayonara o iu no wa muzukashii," 24. The most direct critique of Miyazaki's image of nature and his Jōmon conceit appears in Nagase Tadashi, *Yokubō no mirai*, 235–56.

3. Kanō Seiji makes this claim in "Miyazaki sakuhin no animeeshon gijutsukō," 93–94.

4. Yamaguchi and Watanabe, *Nihon animeeshon eiga shi*, 64–65.

5. Yamaguchi and Watanabe mention this ambition to become the Disney of the East, ibid., 66.

6. Ibid., 64–65.

7. Daisuke, "Before *Anime*," 207.

8. Yamaguchi and Watanabe, *Nihon animeeshon eiga shi*, 65.

9. Frank and Johnson include "squash and stretch" among the twelve basic principles of animation in *The Illusion of Life: Disney Animation*.

10. Miyazaki, "Excerpts: Miyazaki on Heroines."

11. Klein, "Animation and Animorphs," 23.

12. See, for instance, Jensen and Daly, "High Toon."

13. In *Mononoke-hime kenkyū josetsu*, Gotō Tsuyoshi and Kuroda Mitsuhiro call attention to the tendency of Miyazaki's characters to act on the diagonal or incline rather than the horizontal (108). They tend, however, to read this movement in archetypal terms.

7. Only a Girl Can Save Us Now

1. See Miyazaki, "Animeeshon to manga eiga" and "Kojinteki ni wa *Naushika* kara no renzokusei ga arundesu."

2. In a book of interviews of Ōtsuka Yasuo with Mori Yūki entitled *Ōtsuka Yasuo intabyuu: animeeshon jūō mujin,* Mori begins with the characterization of Ōtsuka's style as masculine dynamic movement (54).

3. In her discussion of *Castle in the Sky* in *The Anime Art of Miyazaki Hayao,* Dana Cavallaro calls attention to the problems of weight and exertion, yet oddly does not address the specifics of character animation and angling in Miyazaki and Ghibli; she gives no account of Japanese animators or animation such as Ōtsuka and Tōei *dōga,* but refers largely to former Disney animator Frank Thomas. Nor does she note the gender differential implicit in character animation in this film.

4. Miyazaki and Murakami, "Misshitsu kara no dasshutsu," 363–64.

5. Miyazaki, "Excerpts: Miyazaki on Heroines."

6. See chapter 5, note 7.

7. Kotani Mari, in "Nanoteku-hime," notes the tendency in certain Miyazaki films to develop a contrast between technophilia and technophobia as embodied in contrasting girl types. In effect, it is a question of ability or competency vis-à-vis technologies coded as masculine, and also of a gender differential.

8. Shizimu Tomoko notes something analogous when she writes of the gift of labor and the gift of communication in Miyazaki, aptly stressing the importance of a distance from sexuality, with monstrous implications for girls in the topology of perception. See Shimizu, "'Jiburi monsutaazu' to kankaku no toporojii."

9. Okada Emiko, "Miyazaki anime no hiroin no keifu."

10. Napier, "Confronting Master Narratives," 480.

11. Dreyfus, "Heidegger on Gaining a Free Relation to Technology," 58.

12. Ibid., 59.

13. Here, despite my reservations about his bid to impart humanism to Miyazaki, I agree with Ishiko Jun that depicting the past in Miyazaki is here depicting the future. See Ishiko, "Hyuumanizumu ni taisuru yasashisa to kibishisa," 70.

8. Giving Up the Gun

1. Takeda, *Nootenki tsūshin,* 51–53, and *Notenki Memoirs,* 50–52.

2. The work of Shinkai Makoto is frequently cited as the exception, and the release of his first full-length animation, *Hoshi no koe* (*The Voices of a Distant Star,* 2002) was met with great enthusiasm for its technical finesse and artistic quality, and critics alternatively characterized him as the new Miyazaki or, because he produced the film alone on his computer, as the "one-man Gainax." See Ōtsuka Eiji's introduction to *"Hoshi no koe" o kike,* 14. See, too, Akita Takahiro. *"Koma" kara "firumu" e,* 199. *Tamala 2010* (2004), a full-length animation produced by a three-person team called toL or trees of Life, also deserves mention.

3. I draw here on Samuel Weber's argument in *Theatricality as Medium,* which also presents a shift away from representation theory toward an analysis of the operative quality of images, how they operate to deterritorialize and reterritorialize, that

is, how they work to break down and relocate boundaries, perimeters, or theaters of operations.

4. See, for instance, Befu, *Hegemony of Homogenity.*

5. Napier, "Confronting Master Narratives."

6. Actually Ōtsuka Eiji put this question quite directly to Ueno Toshiya, Thomas Looser, and myself in a dialogue called "Sekai no naka no, senjika no otaku."

7. Ueno, "Japanimation and Techno-Orientalism."

8. Nye, *Technology Matters,* 21.

9. Ibid., 25.

10. Inoue Shizuka explicitly situates Miyazaki on the left in *Miyazaki Hayao wa sayoku nan darō,* in contrast with the world of Matsumoto Leiji and other space-opera future-war anime. What is more, in keeping with Nye's characterization, Inoue stresses how Miyazaki's leftism entails a critique of scientific progress and enlightenment.

11. Nye, *Technology Matters,* 17, emphasis mine. The same argument appears in Noel Perrin, *Giving Up the Gun,* and in Basalla, *The Evolution of Technology.*

12. In a defense of the Ghibli film *Gedo senki* by Miyazaki Hayao's son Miyazaki Gōrō, released as a free publication to promote sales of the DVD, Nakazawa Shin'ichi argues that the image of the shojo as a wind girl is characteristically Japanese (he cites Hayao's *Nausicaä*), and is fundamentally different from the fire girl of Ursula K. LeGuin (who spoke openly of her disappointment with the film, which was Gōrō's adapation of her *Tales of Earthsea*), with its critique of white patriarchy wherein knowledge equals power. In sum, in a tour de force of suggestive generalization, Nakazawa detects behind the film adaptation a current of Japaneseness in the wind girl. See Nakazawa, "'Gedo senki' no tanoshimikata."

13. I am thinking here of David Couzens Hoy's account of power in Michel Foucault, which offers a fine response to the stranglehold of structure versus agency that reigns in Nye's book. See Hoy, "Power, Repression, Progress."

14. Examples of Iwai Toshio's experiments with early moving image technologies appear in *Iwai Toshio no shigoto to shūhen.* This is in keeping with Miyazaki's emphasis on the relation between manga film and earlier technologies and experiences of flight. Hikawa Ryūsuke, in "Genjitsu no sokubaku o koeru," even suggests that Miyazaki's films recall the films of the silent era.

15. See Talbot, "The Auteur of Anime," 70.

16. A range of commentators has noted the appeal of Miyazaki's earlier film heroines for male otaku. In "Kumorinaki sunda me de mitsumeru 'sei no yami'" (57–60), Murase Hiromi addresses the male otaku interest in Clarisse and Nausicaä. In "Miyazaki anime to 'otaku anime,'" Itoyama Toshikazu sees *Nausicaä* as the turning point toward general audiences, which introduced a gradual shift from male otaku audiences (187). He also notes how Miyazaki's transformation from anime maker to film director affected his otaku appeal (192). In "'Otaku' to iu gainen," Morikawa Kaichirō includes Sheeta with Clarisse and Nausicaä as early Miyazaki bishōjo who appealed to male otaku. Once again, together with *Nausicaä, Castle in the Sky* appears

as a summation of Miyazaki's anime-related endeavors and as a transition to general animated films.

17. In a dialogue with Ueno Toshiya, "Miyazaki Hayao no kōzai, aruiwa, Sutajio Jiburi to iu 'tetsu no tō' ni tsuite" Oshii Mamoru discusses the rigidity and hierarchy of Studio Ghibli and how it strangles creativity; Oshii sees in this a certain kind of totalitarian politics of the left (89–92). There is an English translation of an interview with Oshii Mamoru that iterates some of the same points. See "Interview."

9. Relative Movement

1. Fujimori, "Miyazaki anime no kotsu," 59.
2. Miyazaki and Satō, "Miyazaki Hayao—Satō Tadao taidan," 35.
3. In his writings on Disney, Sergei Eisenstein detects a similar problem emerging as early as *Bambi*. See *Eisenstein on Disney*, 99, n. 70. See too chapter 6, note 2, in this volume for a critique of Miyazaki's reliance on Jōmon primitivism.
4. I draw here on Livia Monnet's account of Tabaimo in "Such Is the Contrivance of the Cinematograph."
5. Ibid., 217.
6. Azuma, *Dōbutsuka suru posutomodan*, 13. Azuma's book is published in English as *Otaku: Japan's Database Animals*.

10. Structures of Depth

1. Sometimes the term *superflat* is written as two words "super flat" or "Super Flat," or with other variations in typeface.
2. For further engagement with Tsuji, see Monnet, "Such Is the Contrivance of the Cinematograph," especially 214–15. The term *kisō* could be rendered as "extraordinary," and the emphasis on using Western perspective to generate odd or eccentric view points or lines of sight in Edo art might be seen as analogous to what scholars in other areas have referred to as "cultures of curiosity."
3. See Murakami, "Suupaafuratto Nihon bijutsu ron" and "A Theory of Super Flat Japanese Art."
4. Jay, "Scopic Regimes of Modernity," 4.
5. Foucault, *The Order of Things*.
6. Crary, "Modernizing Vision," 31.
7. Ibid., 40.
8. Kittler, *Gramophone, Film, Typewriter*. See especially his chapter "Film."
9. In *Nihon—Gendai—Bijutsu*, Sawaragi Noi takes up precisely this question of how the impact of modernity and then of the influence of American pop was eliminated from the reception and exhibition of Japanese art in the 1990s. In effect, the idea of "modern Japanese art" results in a closed circle, which will eventually become a "bad place," that is, a site removed from history, and in a sense, an inauthentic site. Interestingly

enough, Azuma Hiroki, who develops an opposition between Western modernity as Cartesianism and Japanese postmodernity as superflat in his contribution to the *Super Flat* catalog ("Suupaafuratto de shiben suru" and "Super Flat Speculation"), presents an argument more in keeping with Sawaragi in the first part of *Dōbutsuka suru posutomodan*, namely, that one cannot isolate anime from the impact of American entertainment and pop art. For a fine critique of Murakami's relation to Warhol, see Holmes, "Warhol au Soleil levant."

10. See Steinberg, "Otaku Consumption, Superflat Art and the Return to Edo."

11. In *Dōbutsuka suru posutomodan*, Azuma presents the outlines of this idea, as it travels from Ōtsuka Eiji to Okada Toshio, which Azuma disputes (35–36).

12. An animated short by Kitakubo Hiroyuki, *Meiji karakuri bunmei kitan* (A strange tale of Meiji karakuri), in the *Robot Carnival* omnibus (1987) would make an interesting point of departure for such a discussion, for it offers a mecha battle between Japan's nineteenth-century "robots" and those of nineteenth-century Western Europe.

13. Edgerton, *The Heritage of Giotto's Geometry*, 289.

14. Ibid., 287.

15. Ibid., 289.

16. Jay, "Scopic Regimes of Modernity," 19.

17. Murakami, "Suupaafuratto Nihon bijutsu ron" and "A Theory of Super Flat Japanese Art," 114–15.

18. Murakami, "Earth in My Window." While I refer readers here to his essay, I am also thinking of the layout and comments on the exhibit in New York in spring 2005.

19. Chow, *The Age of the World Target*, 34.

20. Murakami, "Superflat Trilogy," 161.

21. Lisa Yoneyama, for instance, writes of how in Japan "a global narrative of the universal history of humanity" has helped to sustain "a national victimology and phantasm of innocence throughout most of the postwar years." Yoneyama, *Hiroshima Traces*, 13.

22. Looser, "Superflat and the Layers of Image and History in 1990s Japan," 101.

23. Ibid., 107.

24. Nye, *Technology Matters*, 52–56.

25. Damisch, *The Origin of Perspective*, 173–74.

11. The Distributive Field

1. See, too, Lev Manovich's discussion of "compositing and new types of montage" in *The Language of New Media*, 155–60.

2. In the *Little Boy* catalog, Murakami Takashi provides glossy images and a succinct overview of the *Daicon III* and *IV Opening Animations*, 6–11.

3. Takeda, *Nootenki tsūshin*, 48–53, 69–72. See, too, Takeda, *Notenki Memoirs*, 47–52, 68–71.

4. Ibid., 49. See, too, Takeda, *Notenki Memoirs*, 48.

5. Ibid., 52. See, too, Takeda, *Notenki Memoirs*, 51.

6. Murakami, ed., *Little Boy*, 10–11.

7. Morris-Suzuki, *Beyond Computopia*.

8. "By demonstrating that they would not recoil from a civilian holocaust, the Americans triggered in the minds of the enemy that *information explosion* which Einstein, towards the end of his life, thought to be as formidable as the atomic blast itself." Virilio, *War and Cinema*, 6.

9. As Thomas Friedman's *The World Is Flat: A Brief History of the World in the Twenty-First Century* suggests, with its breathless embrace of flatness, that the dehierarchization or flattening of the world due to globalization and communication networks is very much a part of neoliberal accumulation. A comparable but less utopian analysis, centered more on media, appears in Sasaki, *Furatto kakumei*.

10. In *Komyunikeeshon fuzenshōkōgun*, Nakajima Azusa hints at something like this when, contrary to the definition of otaku as someone who cannot relate to others, she builds on the implications of the term "otaku" (residence) to suggest that otaku can only affirm himself via a relation with his territory. See Azuma Hiroki's explanation in *Dōbutsu ka suru posuto modan*, 42–43. In a similar way, the anonymous writer of the novel based on Internet exchanges, *Densha otoko*, styles "himself" as *Nakano Hitori*, that is, "one of the crowd" or "one of the them." Building on these suggestions, I will read the otaku in terms of this oscillation between one of the household and a household of one. In effect, to adopt the view of Gabriel Tarde's microsociology, the otaku is an infinitesimal of the household, a differential of domesticity. On Tarde's infinitesimals, see Dean and Lamarre, "Microsociology and the Ritual Event."

12. Otaku Imaging

1. Okada Toshio, *Otakugaku nyūmon*, 14. Okada provides the English translation "Introduction to Otakuology" on the title page of the book.

2. Ibid., 16–17.

3. On his summary chart on page 363, Okada inserts a definitive rupture between Edo culture and postwar children's culture (anime, toys, manga), with a tiny image of a mushroom cloud and defeat written under it marking this rupture. Yet he refers us to a culture of connoisseurship and patronage with characteristics like that of Edo culture (359). It is at this level of commodity appreciation that otaku provide the direct connection to Edo Japan that is apparently barred to other manifestations of consumer culture. Okada seems to draw here on Ōtsuka Eiji's use of concepts related to Edo theater (Kabuki and Bunraku) in his analysis of subculture narrative consumption. See the 1989 essay by Ōtsuka, "Sekai to shukō," in the "standard text" paperback edition of *Teihon Monogatari shōhiron*. In *Dōbutsuka suru posutomodan*, Azuma Hiroki argues against Ōtsuka, Okada, and Murakami, showing that the evocation of Edo in anime is a fantasy of Edo townspeople culture *(chōnin bunka)* whose very artificiality and phantasmatic quality betrays Japan's historical passage through Americanization (35–37). His example is *Seibaa marionetto J (Saber Marionette J)*.

4. In *Otakugaku nyūmon*, Okada discusses how Tezuka had no choice but to enter into limited animation and then cites Miyazaki's lack of appreciation for Tezuka's animation (325). Clearly Miyazaki's remarks had a great impact, reinforcing the sense of a divide between full and limited animation, because, in *Nihon animeeshon no chikara: hachijūgo nen no rekishi o tsuranuku futatsu no jiku*, Tsugata Nobuyuki uses the same quote and argument (30–31). Okada's account also bears comparison with Ōtsuka Eiji's account of Miyazaki and Tezuka in *Teihon Monogatari shōhiron*, 249–54.

5. Murakami Takashi, *Super Flat*.

6. Wikipedia mentions that the first use of the term *shinjinrui* was in 1984 in a marketing publication called *akurosu* (published by Paruko), also noting the transformation into first-generation otaku.

7. Cédric Littardi, "An Interview with Isao Takahata." Takahata has recently published a book in praise of the work of Paul Grimault, which begins with the release of his unfinished film *La Bergère et le ramoneur* (*Yabunirami no bōkun* in Japanese). Grimault later procured the rights and completed the film under a new title *Le Roi et l'oiseau* (*Ō to tori* in Japanese). See Takahata Isao, *Animeeshon no kokorozashi*. Interestingly enough, Takahata sees this film, with a script by Jacques Prévert, as a major influence on his film *Prince of the Sun* (discussed in chapter 5).

8. Okada, *Otakugaku nyūmon*, 55–62.

9. Ibid., 358. See note 3 for this chapter.

10. Okada, *Otaku no mayoi-michi*, 11. For a fuller interpretation of Okada's evocation of American otaku, see LaMarre, "Otaku Movement."

11. The liner notes to the English video release (available online) do a fine job tracing the references, imparting a good sense of this information-dense field.

12. Kinsella, *Adult Manga*, 126–28. See, too, the Wikipedia entry on Miyazaki Tsutomu. Miyazaki Tsutomu was executed by hanging on June 17, 2008.

13. In *Shakai teki hikikomori: owaranai shishunki*, Saitō Tamaki used the term *shakai teki hikikomori* as a translation for the English *social withdrawal* in order to address what he saw as a widespread tendency toward acute social withdrawal in Japan. Étienne Barral, in *Otaku: Les enfants du virtuel*, provides a provocative and sometimes sensational report on otaku in Japan, which gradually dwells on the male otaku's pathological mother complex.

14. Nakano Hitori, *Densha otoko*.

15. Murakami, *Ai to gensō no fashizumu*.

13. Multiple Frames of Reference

1. The Hayao Miyazaki Web site: http://www.nausicaa.net/miyazaki/nonmiyazaki/ #nadia. Accessed July 9, 2007. The source of this information is an article "The Secret of Blue Water: Nadia Arrives (Finally) in the US" by Marc Hairston, initially written for *Animerica* in 1995 and later posted on his Web site. Hairston builds on an interview with Okada Toshio in *Animerica* 4, no. 3 (March 1996) in which Okada confirms that

Nadia was a Miyazaki project. Hairston also addresses the resemblance of Disney's *Atlantis: The Lost Empire* (2001) to both *Castle in the Sky* and *Nadia*, which also became something of an issue among North American anime fans. See, too, Lee Zion, "*Nadia* vs. *Atlantis*, Revisited!" Needless to say, such comparisons tend to dwell on categorizing story elements and references rather than looking at animation or at ideology (at which levels the three animations are profoundly different). In his discussion of the fan controversy surrounding Disney's alleged use of Tezuka's *Jyanguru tatei* (Jungle Emperor, aka *Kimba the White Lion*) in making *The Lion King*, Fred Patten aptly concludes that the real scandal is not that Disney borrowed from Tezuka but that Disney refused to admit that its animators knew of Tezuka. See Patten, "Simba versus Kimba: Pride of Lions." 311. With *Atlantis* too, the scandal is not that of borrowing. After all, *Nadia* and *Castle in the Sky* borrow extensively from other films and books. The scandal lies in Disney's refusal to acknowledge the work of other animators and animations.

2. In addition to the sources mentioned in the previous note, I would like to acknowledge two Web sites that I found particularly useful. *Fushigi no umi no Nadia Rifarensu* at http://chara.s17.xrera.com/ (Accessed July 9, 2007) and *Tamarro Forever presents . . . The Secret of Blue Water* at http://www.thesecretofbluewater.com/.

3. Recall how Ōtsuka and Miyazaki tend to angle character movement to impart dynamism without going to the lengths of the full animation of Disney. Seen from the angle of Anno's limited animation, theirs is an effort to prevent the sliding of planes of the image from undermining the dynamism of characters, yet it can also be construed as an adaptation of the diagonals and rhythms of television animation to the big screen, which is precisely what they wish to deny.

4. See Hairston's "The Secret of Blue Water" for details on the gradual whitening and de-Africanizing of Nadia.

5. For a broader account of the impact of 1960s design on Anno, see Yoshimura Yasutaka, "Rokujū nendai no mochiifu: Evangerion-pop no tame no sonata." Although his account is based on *Evangelion*, the overlaps with *Nadia* are evident, especially in the Neo-Atlantean designs. Needless to say, the *Nadia* animators also draw on famous anime series in their character and vehicle designs: the Grandis Gang recalls *Time Bokan*, and Nemo recalls Captain Grobal of *Macross* as well as Captain Harlock. See Hairston and the two Web sites listed in note 2 for this chapter.

14. Inner Natures

1. Bruno Latour suggests this terminology in *We Have Never Been Modern*. Although I borrow his turn of phrase, I am in effect using his terms against the grain. Latour sees modernity as an effect of a modern constitution, which insists on separating nature and culture only to mix the two more thoroughly and effectively; in effect, modernity does more thoroughly and secretly what "nonmodern" cultures always did openly. Once the operations of modernity are unveiled, he implies, they will vanish. Here, however, I see the emergence of nature-cultures as an effect of technology to

some extent, and as indicative of a postmodernity that does not break with modernity but signals it as indefensible yet irrevocable (rather than immediately revocable as in Latour).

2. Heidegger, "The Age of the World Picture." See, too, Chow, *The Age of the World Target.*

3. I am drawing here on Yves Michaud's account of Peter Sloterdjik's discussion in *Regeln für den Menschenpark: Ein Antwortschreiben zu Heideggers "Brief über den Humanismus."* See Michaud, *Humain, Inhumain, Trop Humain.*

4. Lyotard, *The Postmodern Condition.*

5. Ōtsuka, *Teihon Monogatari shōhiron,* 267–70. As remarked previously, Ōtsuka here links the consumption of small narratives to Edo-era forms of discernment that emphasize the production of worlds.

6. Azuma, *Dōbutsu ka suru posutomodan,* 54–58. See, too, Azuma Hiroki, "The Animalization of Otaku Culture."

7. Oettermann, *Panorama,* 21.

8. Oettermann draws on Michel Foucault's account of the panopticon in *Discipline and Punish,* 195–228.

9. Otaku-gaku or otakuology repeats the double bind of humanism. With the modern collapse of universal knowledge and universal truth guaranteed by God or some other absolute, knowledge tried to ground itself by centering on the human. Thus the human is situated as both the subject and object of knowledge. Similarly, the structure of otaku knowledge is one in which otaku is both subject and object. Otaku comes to function as what Foucault dubs the transcendental-empirical doublet.

10. Interview cited in Samuels, "Let's Die Together," 5.

15. Full Limited Animation

1. In *Art in Motion,* Furniss provides a brief overview of full and limited animation in the American context (135–53). In the context of Japanese animation, the distinction between full and limited animation has gradually settled on a distinction between Tōei *dōga* and Ghibli manga films on the one hand, and Mushi Pro and Tezuka Osamu's *Tetsuwan Atomu* on the other. Discussion often hinges on establishing the importance of the one over the other. For an account that leans toward Miyazaki's virtues, see Kanō, "Miyazaki sakuhin no animeeshon gijutsu-kō," 90–91. Scriptwriter Tsuji Masaki, lays out the biases against television animation in *Bokutachi no anime shi,* 161–63. Accounts of Japanese animation that dwell on otaku and subculture tend to look more favorably on Tezuka and developments in limited animation, as we have seen. In *Nihon animeeshon no chikara,* Tsugata Nobuyuki organizes his account around two axes, which reprises the contrast between Miyazaki and Tezuka, with Miyazaki's statements about the lack of value of Tezuka's animation playing a crucial role (30–31).

2. There was indeed dialogue and interaction between full and limited animation. In his chapter on the prehistory of television animation, "Terebi anime zenshi,"

Sugiyama Taku traces the movement of animators from Tōei to Mushi Pro, and later other television animation studios, which led to the image of Tōei Animation as Tōei University, as a training site for animators (115–16, 119). He also reminds us that the success of Mushi Pro spurred Tōei into the television animation industry, where they too had to make adjustments toward limited animation (134–36).

3. Ōtsuka provides one of the clearest statements of this distinction in a book of interviews with Mori Yūki entitled *Ōtsuka Yasuo intabyuu: animeeshon jūō mujin*, in the second chapter, especially pages 54–55. See, too, Kanō, "Miyazaki sakuhin no animeeshon gijutsu-kō," 50–58. Even psychoanalytic commentator Saitō Tamaki tries to build on the idea that Miyazaki does not use *tome-e*, but oddly enough, in order to ground an emphasis on context over materiality, which recalls the logic of suture. See Saitō, "'Undō' no rinri," 77–85.

4. In *Anime ga sekai o tsunagu*, artist, animator, and director Suzuki Shin'ichi speaks of his interest in design in a positive way (106–7), without insisting on a divide between design and animation, in a manner that contrasts sharply with that of Ghibli researcher Kanō Seiji in "Miyazaki sakuhin no animeeshon gijutsu-kō."

5. Mori, *Animeeshon nyūmon*, especially 41–45.

6. The exhibition originally ran from July 15 to August 31, 2004, but subsequently moved to Kobe December 12, 2004, to January 15, 2005. The full title of the exhibit and catalog was *Nihon manga eiga no zenbō: sono tanjō kara Sen to Chiro no kamikakushi, soshite . . .* The official English title omits reference to manga films, styling the title *Japanese Animated Films*. Ōtsuka Yasuo is credited as editorial supervisor.

7. *Ōtsuka Yasuo no ugokasu yorokobi* (Studio Ghibli telebi-man-yunion, 2004).

8. Miyazaki insisted on calling his films *manga eiga* as early as the first Ghibli production *Castle in the Sky* in 1985. His miscellaneous writings show that he was conscious of the distinctiveness of manga films even earlier: "Animeeshon to manga eiga," from 1982, makes this clear. In a 1988 essay, "Nihon animeeshon ni tsuite," Miyazaki gives a nice account of the emphasis on anime adaptation of manga and the resulting techniques that meant that "movement itself could not help to change" (106–7). He thus parses two streams of animation, styling anime as *hyōgenshugi*, a manner of "representationalism," which led in limited animation to an emphasis on *tome-e* (107). Despite Miyazaki's long emphasis on this distinction, it is only in recent years that Studio Ghibli has become insistent on developing and promoting their manga film lineage, and was even responsible for the republication of Imamura Taihei's *Manga eiga ron*, originally published in 1941 and reprinted in an expanded edition in 1965, and often touted as the first book-length study of animation. This is odd in the sense that Imamura Taihei evokes very different terms for the analysis of anime, which are more in keeping with Oshii Mamoru's discussion of actuality. See my discussion in chapter 3 and note 9 to that chapter. See, too, Driscoll, "From Kino-eye to *Anime*-eye/*ai*."

9. Especially in the first chapter of his book *Sakuga asemamire*, Ōtsuka Yasuo provides an introduction to movement in animation, using many of the examples that

appear in the documentary film and stressing the Tōei Dōga and Studio Ghibli lineage. See too his discussion of *ugoki-e* in *Ōtsuka Yasuo intabyuu*.

10. In the Ghibli documentary, Takahata and Miyazaki credit Ōtsuka with introducing radical new artistic possibilities into television animation, which sparked their enthusiasm for this medium. Even in the context of television, they strive to differentiate their work from anime. Ghibli researcher Kanō Seiji, in "Miyazaki sakuhin no animeeshon gijutsu-kō," points out that the number of sheets used in Miyazaki's television animations (often Takahata and Ōtsuka Yasuo collaborations) was steadily rising, and stresses that they were using full animation techniques in their television productions (93–94).

11. Tsugata, *Nihon animeeshon no chikara*, 32.

12. Akitauki, *"Koma" kara "firumu" e*, 153.

13. Mori Takuya, *Animeeshon nyūmon*, 29. See, too, the entry on "limited animation" at Wikipedia as well as Furniss, *Art in Motion*, 135–53.

14. Ibid., 33.

15. Ban Toshio and Tezuka Purodakushon, *Tezuka Osamu monogatari*, 43–45. Insofar as this is a manga biography endorsed by Tezuka Production, there is a tendency to stress Tezuka's aspirations as an artist, whence the mention of his experimental animation. But the point about mass culture versus avant-garde experimentation holds.

16. Misono, "Terebi anime reimeiki no paionia-tachi," 134.

17. Ibid., 136.

18. Kanō, "Miyazaki sakuhin no animeeshon gijutsu-kō," 93–94.

19. Miyazaki's use of the term *hyōgenshugi* to describe limited animation is interesting here if read against the grain, for it could be read less in terms of static representation and in terms of a dynamic art of describing. I have deliberately avoided characterizing the effect of moving the drawing or viewing position in terms of parallax or parallax scrolling, because such discussions frequently strive to sustain the centrality of one-point perspective and Cartesianism, implying that, even as the viewing position moves along the image, the stability of certain layers of the image follows from Cartesian perspective. This is entirely misleading, and a more productive way of thinking about such effects would be the sort of distinction that Martin Jay draws between perspectivalism and describing as different modern regimes of visuality in "Scopic Regimes of Modernity."

20. Tsugata, *Nihon animeeshon no chikara*, 140–42.

21. Ibid., 32–33, and note 4 on page 32.

22. Ishiyama Yukihiro, in *Kamishibai bunkashi*, provides a thorough overview of the chronology of kamishibai, while Kang Jun, in *Kamishibai to "Bukimi na mono" tachi no kindai*, gives an analysis of the relation between sound and voice, with an emphasis on the strangeness or the uncanny quality that this lent to paper theater. See, too, the photos on 42–43 of Kan Jun's book. I am especially grateful to Yacchan at the Kyoto Manga Museum for his demonstrations and explanations, long after hours.

23. Akita, *"Koma" kara "firumu" e*, 153.

24. An exhibit on Yamakawa Sōji, held at Yayoi Bijutsukan in Tokyo from April 3 to June 29, 2008, included examples of kamishibai-like paperboard illustrations based on his experience in silent film production. While those examples did not make it into the exhibit-related book, it is easy enough to see the impact of film and animation in the examples used in the presentations of his prewar kamishibai. See Mitani and Nakamura, *Yamakawa Sōji*.

25. Tsukihashi, "Eizō gihō to sakuhin no kōzō," 40–53.

26. Azuma Hiroki discusses how Anno's style of editing elicits comparisons with avant-garde filmmakers such as Okamoto Kihachi and Jean-Luc Godard, in Azuma and Woznicki, "Toward a Cartography of Japanese Anime." Here, in keeping with my general emphasis on compositing, I tend to see Anno's editing following from his compositing.

27. Akita Takahiro approaches a similar understanding when he suggests that animation must follow Newton's three laws: inertia, resultant force, and reciprocal action, in *"Koma" kara "firumu" e*, 123. But if animation sets up such a schema of motion, it eventually will find it uninhabitable, or rather, that "body" will need to "evolve" beyond the Newtonian world, which is Deleuze's point.

28. This view of Hollywood cinema has become so common that the references are too numerous to cite. Miriam Hansen provides a nice summary of the argument and its implications in her essay "The Mass Production of the Senses," 336. For an explanation of the emergence of a continuity style in Japan, see LaMarre, *Shadows on the Screen*, 237–42.

29. I draw here on Ronald Bogue's overview in *Deleuze on Cinema*, especially chapter 3.

30. Deleuze, *Cinema I*, 205.

31. Stuart Hall, in *Modernity: An Introduction to Modern Societies*, 3–18, provides a very useful introduction to thinking Western modernity in terms of formations rather than as a monolithic totality or modern/postmodern ruptures.

32. See Deleuze, "The Brain Is the Screen."

33. I continue to put evolution in scare quotes to avoid the misreading of Simondon's notion of individuation, Deleuze's time-image, and my account in terms of an adaptationist paradigm. For a critique of adaptationism consonant with my account here, see Gould and Lewotin, "The Spandrels of San Marco and the Panglossian Paradigm: A Critique of the Adaptationist Programme."

34. I am deliberating evoking some of the language of Max Horkeimer and Theodor Adorno's notion of a "shock of enlightenment" in *Dialectics of Enlightenment*, not merely to layer it suggestively onto Deleuze's notion of the time-image but to suggest that we might read these two different dialectics (one leading to the time-image, and the other to the shock of enlightenment) polyphonically, even though such a project extends well beyond the scope of this book.

35. This is, of course, a different aspect of Cartesianism, the mind–body dualism that is generally albeit loosely attributed to Cartesianism in the form of so-called Cartesian dualism. Channeling the animetic interval into character animation creates

a sense of a gap within character action, which can be stabilized in Cartesian dualism or opened as a crisis in Cartesian dualism. Although, due to considerations of length, I excised material related to this aspect of how anime thinks technology, I should mention, parenthetically, because it bears on my discussion here, that such a line of inquiry passed through Oshii Mamoru's neo-Platonic take on the cyborg, which reprises the problems of Cartesian dualism that both Merleau-Ponty and Yuasa Yasuo strived to overcome phenomenologically, and which Vicki Kirby has recently deconstructed in preparation for a feminist critique of the dualisms that still attend thinking about the body. See Vicki Kirby, "Culpability and the Double-Cross."

36. Deleuze, *Cinema I*, 215.

37. Deleuze, "Postscript on Control Societies," 181.

38. In one of his discussions of limited animation and anime, "Nihon animeeshon ni tsuite," Miyazaki stresses the emphasis on manga sources in limited animation. This may appear ironic in the light of his own adaptation of his manga *Nausicaä* into an animated film, but in fact, Miyazaki not only opposed adapting the manga but also felt he had written a manga that resisted adaptation. Indeed his animated version significantly changes the manga.

39. Marc Steinberg also takes up the question of the relation between limited animation and the serialization of anime characters across media, but with a different emphasis and in the specific context of *Astro Boy*. See Steinberg, "Immobile Sections and Trans-series Movement."

40. These comments originally appeared in an interview with Sadamoto Yoshiyuki included in the 1999 deluxe edition of *Der Mond*, a book on Sadamoto's art. I am citing from a "fanlation" and commentary on Sadamoto, accessed July 18, 2007, at http://eva .onegeek.org/pipermail/evangelion.2006-November.

41. Morikawa Kaichirō, in "Evangerion no dezain riron," puts the bandages of Ayanami Rei in a broader context of the art historical unconscious, and in *Dōbutsuka suru posutomodan*, Azuma Hiroki sees in this character image a turning point in the history of animation toward otaku assemblage and thus database.

16. A Face on the Train

1. Yokokawa, *Shochō to iu kirifuda*. Yonezawa Yoshihiro, in his overview of postwar shojo manga, *Sengo shōjo manga*, continually indicates the operations of fantasy, implying a divide between girls and shojo images. See, too, Murase Hiromi's overview of the term *shōjo* in "Kumorinaki sunda me de mitsumeru 'sei no yami,'" 54–55.

2. The one exception may be Fio Pikkoro (Piccolo), the young woman aircraft designer and mechanic in *Porco Rosso*, but she is already seventeen, old enough to fall in love with Marco. Yet, insofar as she is still on the model of what Murase calls the healthy girl, we would have to question how truly different this depiction is. Kotani Mari argues, for instance, that Miyazaki's films inscribe a tension between technophobia and technophilia onto different feminine types within the film, which asks us to look not simply at

a character like Fio Piccolo as an isolated type but as part of a dialectics of technology inscribed across feminine bodies. See Kotani Mari, "Nanoteku-hime," 119–20.

3. Murase, "Kumorinaki yasunda me de mitsumeru 'sei no yami,'" 56.

4. Ōtsuka Eiji, "Disarming Atom," 119–20.

5. Ibid., 120.

6. On squash and stretch, see note 9, chapter 6 of this book.

7. Ōtsuka, "Disarming Atom," 161. A number of commentators have signaled the male otaku fascination with Miyazaki's earlier heroines, such as Clarisse, Nausicaä, and Sheeta. See Murase, "Kumorinaki yasunda me de mitsumeru 'sei no yami,'" 59–60; Itoyama, "Miyazaki anime to 'otaku anime,'" 187; and Morikawa, "'Otaku' to iu gainen," 67.

8. In an overview of manga parsing eighty-three genres, the genre of *dotō no ren'ai*, which I render here as "angry love," makes an appearance among the romance genres. See Tokusatsu Takarajima henshūbu and "Kono manga ga sugoi" sentei kaiinkai, eds., *Kono manga ga sugoi*, 132–33. Simply put, this is the genre in which the guy that the girl hates at first sight turns out to be the one for her, or vice versa.

9. Interestingly enough, Oshii Mamoru characterizes Anno as exceedingly Oedipal. See Oshii and Ueno, "Miyazaki Hayao no kōzai, aruiwa, Sutajio Jiburi to iu 'tetsu no tō' ni tsuite," 101–3.

10. For a definition and introduction of gynoid, see Tatsumi, *Full Metal Apache*, 97.

11. Tanizaki Akira gives a succinct overview of the shift from the remote-control giant robot to the piloted robot of *Mazinger Z*, in "Anime mekanikku: henyōshi," 159–60.

12. Haraway, "The Cyborg Manifesto," 181.

13. In *Seibō Evangerion*, Kotani Mari provides the outlines for such a reading of *Evangelion* in terms of a mecha-ification rather than shojo-ification of the daughters of Eve.

14. CLAMP, "Chobits Interviews."

15. Murakami, ed., *Super Flat*, 89 and 132–33. Takekuma has also written a manga using Thomas the Tank Engine, designed to discourage train suicides.

16. In *Full Metal Apache*, Tatsumi Takayuki addresses a similar dynamics in the context of J. G. Ballard's techno-erotics (88–89), associating it with a queer fascination for kamikaze pilots as well.

17. The Absence of Sex

1. In the manga, he exclaims, "Ore wa yarashii koto kangaeteru n ja nai zo!" See CLAMP, *Chobits*, 1:19. As mentioned previously, *Chobits* was initially serialized in Young Magazine Comics from February 2001 to November 2002.

2. Lacan, "Dieu et la jouissance de la femme," 65; and in English: Lacan, "God and the Jouissance of the Woman," 141.

3. Žižek, *Looking Awry*, 136.

4. CLAMP, "Chobits Interviews," 2003.

5. Motosuwa Hideki is nineteen years old in the manga but eighteen in the anime.

6. Freud, "Fetishism."

7. See the catalog for the CLAMP exhibit held January 22 to April 10, 2005, at the Kawasaki City Museum: CLAMP, *CLAMP-su: MANGA aato ha toki o koeru*. See, too, Solomon, "Four Mothers of Manga Gain American Fans."

8. The "I" (Atashi) of Hibiya's illustrated books is Chii, and Atashi's companion stands in for Chii's lost sister Freya.

18. Platonic Sex

1. Lacan, "Dieu et la jouissance de la femme," 68; Lacan, "God and the Jouissance of the Woman," 144

2. Žižek, *Looking Awry*, 65.

3. Irigaray, *This Sex Which Is Not One*.

4. Žižek, "Eastern Europe's Republics of Gilead."

5. Žižek, *Enjoy Your Symptom!* 155; emphasis his.

6. Psychoanalytic theory merits attention because, although frequently debunked and discredited, it remains a stable fallback position in gender-based analyses of popular culture, partly due to the profound renewal of the Lacanian mirror in Judith Butler's theories of performance and subjectivity. On the persistence of Lacan in Butler's conceptualization of performance, see Pheng Cheah, "Mattering," and Vicki Kirby's "Poststructuralist Feminisms Pt 2—Substance Abuse: Judith Butler," in her *Telling Flesh*, 101–28.

7. McClintock, *Imperial Leather*, 200.

8. Yokokawa Sumiko explores the gap between "girl" and "shojo," and the suspension of female maturation implicit in shojo, in *Shochō to iu kirifuda*. Drawing on her work, Murase Hiromi reminds us of the literary and distanced quality of the term *shojo*, in "Kumorinaki sunda me de mitsumeru 'sei no yami,'" 54–55.

9. In the anime version, Hideki discovers Chii upon his arrival in Tokyo (in the manga he is already working part-time, and discovers Chii on his way home from work), which underscores the importance of Chii in allowing Hideki to take on consistency where previously it had proved impossible for him.

10. Žižek, *Looking Awry*, 65.

11. French philosophers, for instance, make a distinction between *amour platonique* (Platonic love) and *amour platonicien* (love according to Plato).

12. See Tanizaki Jun'ichirō, "Love and Sexual Desire," trans. Thomas LaMarre, in Lamarre, *Shadows on the Screen*, 319–55.

13. Williams, "Film Bodies," 732.

19. Perversion

1. Žižek, "Eastern Europe's Republics of Gilead."

2. Žižek, *On Belief*.

3. Rothenberg and Foster, "Introduction. Beneath the Skin: Perversion and Social Analysis," 3.

4. Fink, "Perversion."

5. Mannoni, "I Know Well, but All the Same . . ."

6. Nagasawa, *AV joyū*. Nagasawa compiles interviews with adult video actresses done between 1991 and 1996.

7. McGray, "Japan's Gross National Cool."

8. Frederick, "What's Right with Japan."

9. I should add that, in psychoanalytic theory, full substitution is not inherently full, normal, or adequate; it only appears full, normal, or adequate from the angle of social expectations and prohibitions. Full substitution affords just enough ontological consistency to allow us to function within a chaotic and potentially distressing state of affairs. As feminist theory in particular has insisted, the gist of psychoanalysis is that perversion is the normal state of affairs. In other words, full substitution and full ontological consistency are social fictions, but for psychoanalytic theory, necessary ones.

20. The Spiral Dance of Symptom and Specter

1. See, too, William Gardner's review, "Attack of the Phallic Girls."

2. Saitō, "Otaku sekushuaritii ni tsuite." I am deeply indebted here to the precise rendering of the Lacanian terminology in Christopher Bolton's flawless translation of this essay. See Saitō, "Otaku Sexuality." I will subsequently refer to Bolton's translation, with reference to the Japanese version in parentheses.

3. Saitō, "Otaku Sexuality," 234 (36).

4. Rose, cited in McClintock, *Imperial Leather*, 200.

5. Saitō, "Otaku Sexuality," 234 (36).

6. Ibid.

7. Ibid., 233 (34).

8. McClintock, *Imperial Leather*, 202–3.

9. Butler, *Gender Trouble*, 72–78.

10. Saitō, "Otaku sekushuaritii ni tsuite," 24 and 44–45. Bolton translates *tōsaku* as "odd sexuality" to convey the sense of abhorrence associated with the term (228) and later as "perversion" (236).

11. Saitō uses the term *egakareta sekushuaritei*; Saitō, "Otaku Sexuality," 239 (48).

12. Saitō uses the term *jōhōka*, which might also be rendered "informatization" or "informationalization." Saitō, "Otaku Sexuality," 241 (52).

13. Žižek, "Eastern Europe's Republics of Gilead."

14. McClintock, *Imperial Leather*, 202.

15. See chapter 11, note 10.

16. The English translation was not available at the time when I was writing this account, and so I provide references to the Japanese edition in my subsequent discussion.

17. Azuma Hiroki, "Dōbutsuka suru otaku-kei bunka," published in *Mōjō genron*

F-kai. The "net-state" project that provided the occasion for this paper began as a discussion hosted on Azuma's Web site to which various contributors would present their opinions of a recent book. Gradually, as contributions increased, the "net-state book review" expanded into "net-state discourse." Discussion of Saitō Tamaki's *Sentō bishōjo no seishin bunseki* provided the occasion for the volume *Mōjō genron F-kai*. See, too, the translation of this essay: Azuma, "The Animalization of Otaku Culture."

18. Azuma discusses *kyara-moe* and two-tiered consumption in *Dōbutsuka suru posutomodan*, 75–76. See, too, Morikawa Kaichirō's introduction in *Moeru toshi Akihabara: shuto no tanjō*, 27–32.

19. Foucault, *The Order of Things*, xviii.

20. Azuma, "The Animalization of Otaku Culture," 187. Azuma uses the term *ningenteki shōhisha-zō* or "humanized consumer figure," which he contrasts to "animalized consumer figure." See, too, "Dōbutsuka suru otaku-kei bunka," 38.

21. Azuma, "The Animalization of Otaku Culture," 183. See, too, Azuma, *Dōbutsu ka suru posutomodan*, 62–64.

22. Azuma, "The Animalization of Otaku Culture," 185.

23. Doane, "Technophilia."

24. I cite here from the translation of chapter 16 of *Tekuno-goshikku* (2005), Kotani "Bishōjo ningyō/cosupurei," which appears as "Doll Beauties and Cosplay," trans. Thomas LaMarre, in *Mechademia* 2.

25. Ibid., 87.

26. Ibid., 93.

27. Haraway, "The Cyborg Manifesto," 181.

21. Emergent Positions

1. Saitō, "Otaku Sexuality," 231 (28).

2. In an essay on Miyazaki, "'Undō' no rinri," (1997), written before the publication of *Sentō bishōjo no seishin bunseki* (2000), Saitō had begun to work through his ideas on the importance of context and contextualization on which his later theories of fictionalization and multiple orientations are based. In this essay, Saitō basically argues that anime has very high context, which means that it tends to impart a strong sense of orientation to readers or viewers, and yet it fails to work as well as Miyazaki's manga films, because anime does not coordinate the overall movement from context to context (because of its "still images"). In effect, he sees anime pushing its viewers in discordant directions, while Miyazaki coordinates movement, rather like the overall action-image. Saitō is close to the logic of suture here, aptly enough situating it in animation at the level of character animation rather than montage as in cinema. While I don't agree with his preference for suture-like movement, it is interesting, in light of later discussion (chapter 22), that he locates suture in full animation. Oddly enough, however, in his subsequent writings about manga and anime, such as "Otaku Sexuality," he seems to presume that suture happens regardless of the image. The idea of multiple orientations

(a variation on high context) simply signals a delight in fictionalization, and it is the unity-in-lack of male desire that holds everything together.

3. Saitō, "Otaku Sexuality," 236–37 (39–40).

4. Ibid., 244 (54).

5. Ibid., 239 (48).

6. Žižek makes this a hallmark of his thinking. See Žižek, *Tarrying with the Negative*.

7. There is an analogous moment in Lacan, in his interest in cybernetics, when his notion of the calculable subject seems to carry him into Jungian territory.

8. Azuma, "Suupaafuratto de shiben suru."

9. See Lacan, "Of the Gaze as *Objet petit a*."

10. Vicki Kirby, *Judith Butler: Live Theory*, 3. See, too, Peter Osborne, *The Politics of Time: Modernity and the Avant-Garde*.

11. Indeed, in his sequel to *Dōbutsu ka suru posutomodan*, Azuma's basic question is, what procedures are needed for animals without narrative to go on making narratives? See Azuma and Ōtsuka, "'Kōkyōsei' no kōgakuka' wa kanō ka," 82; and Azuma, *Geemu teki riarizumu no tanjō: dōbutsuka suru posutomodan 2*.

12. See Frasca, "Simulation versus Narrative: Introduction to Ludology."

13. Azuma, *Dōbutsu ka suru posutomodan*, 74.

14. On symmetry breaking, see Stewart, *Nature's Numbers*, 73–91.

15. See Francisco Varela, Evan Thompson, and Eleanor Rosch, *The Embodied Mind: Cognitive Science and Human Experience*. Varela et al. wish to present an alternative way of thinking the self, as an emergent property, and in relation to Buddhism; and their account of emergence is germane here. Insofar as they insist on autopoiesis and the self, however, their account runs counter to my emphasis on machine and heterogenesis.

16. It is telling that Azuma characterizes the database as autopoietic, which is consonant on his emphasis on database *structure*.

22. Anime Eyes Manga

1. Bergson, *Matter and Memory*, 58.

2. In *Theorizing the Moving Image*, especially in the chapter "The Image of Women in Film," Noël Carroll calls for something like statistical analysis to parse the association of the camera with the male protagonist and spectator responses to it. In "Masochism and the Perverse Pleasures of Cinema," Gaylyn Studlar points out that spectators may not identify with the sadistic treatment of women but adopt a more masochist stance. David Rodowick, in "The Difficulty of Difference," suggests that the fundamental idea of the structuration of the visual field is an important one, even if the specifics of Mulvey's analysis do not hold.

3. Comolli, "Technique and Ideology," 44.

4. Copjec, *Read My Desire*.

5. My emphasis on mattering is inspired by Cheah and Kirby; see chapter 18, note 6.

6. Žižek, *The Fright of Real Tears*, 33. For Žižek, suture concerns the gap between Universal and Particular, which might well be critiqued from Naoki Sakai's direction as well. See Sakai, "Modernity and Its Critique."

7. Matt Matsuda also provides a good angle on this question of Hegelianism, which is particularly relevant here. See Matsuda, "EAST OF NO WEST."

8. Žižek, *The Fright of Real Tears*, 32.

9. Although one might think of this in terms of an image or an object (or objective reality) followed by an image of the person who sees that object, Žižek insists the subjective shot does not simply follow the objective shot. Which is to say, the objective shot may not even come first; the spectator might see the subjective shot first. Or, there might be long sequences of objective shots, implying but not giving a subjective shot. In other words, this is a logic or logical structure with a range of empirical variations. Ultimately, Žižek's point is that classical cinema hates point-of-view shots that do not return to a character in diegetic space, in the space of the story.

10. Ōtsuka, "Disarming Atom," 152.

11. Ōshiro, *Kisha ryokō*, 37–55.

12. In his recollections of his formation in art design and animation, Suzuki Shin'ichi provides a perfect example of this exploded projection of cinema. He describes how he would go to the movie theater and make people angry by snapping pictures at various angles. Suzuki Shin'ichi, *Anime ga sekai o tsunagu*, 121.

13. For this reason, manga that explore the implications of the monocular lens of the camera are particularly interesting. In an essay in which I first explored these issues, I turned to Okazaki Mari's *Shataa rabu*, discussing how her use of manga conventions allows her to flatten and defang the camera, which is initially coded as male and phallic. See Lamarre, "Platonic Sex." This manga bears comparison with *Nozokiya* (translated as *Voyeurs, Inc.*), which plays the game from the male side of voyeurism.

14. See Brian Massumi's account of the order word in *A User's Guide to Capitalism and Schizophrenia: Deviations from Deleuze and Guattari*, 31–33.

15. See chapter 15, note 27.

16. A good example would be the detailed presentation of the brothers' backstory in the first episode of the animated adaptation of *Full Metal Alchemist* (*Hagane no renkinjutsushi*).

Conclusion

1. Steinberg, "Immobile Sections and Trans-series Movement," 190–206.

2. While I use some of the same terms (particulary convergence) as Henry Jenkins in *Convergence Culture*, my point of departure is very different in that I begin with material divergence and strive to differentiate material or media divergence, technical or technological confluence, and economic convergence, in order to provide a more

layered account of what appears today as an almost ineluctable media convergence, an account that respects the materials in question and the interplay of materiality and immateriality.

3. Stengers, "Introductory Notes on an Ecology of Practices," 190.

4. For a handy overview of the implications of different ways of articulating the limits of the humans, see Christopher Bolton's "Introduction: The Limits of 'The Limits of the Human.'"

5. Deleuze, *Cinema I*, 214.

6. Deleuze, "Postscript on Control Societies," 181.

7. Ibid., 178–79.

8. As Deleuze's books on cinema become more influential in North America, there is a constant discovery or rediscovery of the time-image everywhere. But it seems to me that, if we wish to think with and through Deleuze, we need to address the crisis of the time-image, which begins precisely when the time-image appears everywhere, making its difference from the cliché hard to discern. The point is not to get back to the good old days when we had the time-image, but to work through and past the crisis in the time-image.

9. Azuma, *Geemu teki riarizumu no tanjō*.

10. Foucault, *Psychiatric Power*, 322–23.

11. I draw here on Deleuze's account of perversion in *The Logic of Sense*. For Deleuze, whose analysis departs from the psychoanalytic insistence on the unity-in-lack of male desire, with the phallus and the Other, the world of perversion is one in which "we are tempted to conclude that bodies are but detours to the attainment of Images, and that sexuality reaches its goal much better and much more promptly to the extent that it economizes the detour and addresses itself directly to Images and to the Elements freed from bodies" (313). In other words, he sees in perversion a liberation of doubles, of doubles without resemblance. In other words, perversion turns into a delirious Platonism, in which bodies liberate Images and Elements. This is the world of Platonic sex, in which Chii and Hideki can reach their goal much more effectively by addressing themselves directly to images and the elements freed from bodies—doubles of bodies without resemblance to them, much as the time-image doubles the movement-image. This is not, of course, traditional Platonism. It is not a movement from the lower realm of body with its sensations and pleasures to the higher realm of the mind or spirit with its intellectual purity. Rather Deleuze detects the emergence of thought from within bodies, rising to their surfaces, as with the emergence of the time-image.

BIBLIOGRAPHY

Akita Takahiro. *"Koma" kara "firumu" e: manga to manga eiga* (From "panel" to "film": manga and manga films). Tokyo: NTT shuppan, 2005.

Aumont, Jacques. "The Variable Eye, or the Mobilization of the Gaze." In *The Image in Dispute*. Austin: University of Texas Press, 1997.

Azuma Hiroki. "The Animalization of Otaku Culture." Trans. Yuriko Furuhata and Marc Steinberg. In *Mechademia 2: Networks of Desire*, ed. Frenchy Lunning, 175–88.

———. *Dōbutsu ka suru posutomodan: otaku kara mita Nihon shakai* (Animalizing postmodern: Japanese society as seen from otaku). Kōdansha gendai shinsho 1575. Tokyo: Kōdansha, 2001. Published in English as *Otaku: Japan's Database Animals*. Minneapolis: University of Minnesota Press, 2009.

———. "Dōbutsuka suru otaku-kei bunka" (Animalization of otaku-type culture). In *Mōjō genron F-kai* (Net-state discourses, F-sessions), 19–38. Tokyo: Seidosha, 2003.

———. *Fukashina mono no sekai* (Overvisualized world). Tokyo: Asahi shinbunsha, 2000.

———. *Geemu teki riarizumu no tanjō: dōbutsuka suru posutomodan 2* (The birth of game-ic realism: animalizing postmodern 2). Kōdansha gendai shinsho 1883. Tokyo: Kōdansha, 2007.

———. *Sonzaiteki, yūbinteki: Jacques Derrida ni tsuite* (Existential, postal: on Jacques Derrida). Tokyo: Shinchōsha, 1998.

———. "Suupaafuratto de shiben suru" and "Super Flat Speculation." In *SUPER FLAT*, 138–151. Tokyo: Madras, 2000.

———. *Yūbinteki fuantachi* (The postally anxious). Tokyo: Asahi shinbunsha, 1999.

Azuma Hiroki and Ōtsuka Eiji. "'Kōkyōsei' no 'kōgakuka' wa kanō ka" (Is the "technologization" of the "communal" possible?). In *Shingenjitsu 5*, 80–146. Tokyo: Ōta shuppan, 2008.

Azuma Hiroki and Krystian Woznicki. "Toward a Cartography of Japanese Anime: Anno's Hideaki's *Evangelion*, Interview with Azuma Hiroki." www.nettime.org/ Lists-Archives/.

Ban Toshio and Tezuka Purodakushon. *Tezuka Osamu monogatari: manga no yume, anime no yume 1960–1989* (The Tezuka Osamu story: dreams of manga, dreams of anime, 1960–1989). Tokyo: Asahi shinbunsha, 1992.

Barral, Étienne. *Otaku: Les enfants du virtuel* (Otaku: children of the virtual). Paris: Éditions Denoël, 1999.

Bassala, George. *The Evolution of Technology*. Cambridge: Cambridge University Press, 1988.

Baudry, Jean. "Ideological Effects of the Basic Cinematographic Apparatus." In *Film Theory and Criticism*, 6th ed., ed. Leo Braudy and Marshall Cohen, 355–65.

Befu Harumi. *Hegemony of Homogenity: An Anthropological Analysis of Nihonjinron*. Melbourne, Australia: Trans Pacific Press, 2001.

Bergson, Henri. *Matter and Memory*. Trans. N. M. Paul and W. S. Palmer. New York: Zone Books, 1988.

Bernardi, Joanne R. *Writing in Light: The Silent Scenario and the Japanese Pure Film Movement*. Detroit, Mich.: Wayne State University Press, 2001.

Bogue, Ronald. *Deleuze on Cinema*. London: Routledge, 2003.

Bolton, Christopher. "Introduction: The Limits of 'The Limits of the Human.'" In *Mechademia 3: The Limits of the Human*, ed. Frenchy Lunning, xi–xvi.

Bordwell, David. *On the History of Film Style*. Cambridge, Mass.: Harvard University Press, 1997.

Bordwell, David, and Kristin Thompson. *Film Art: An Introduction*, 5th ed. New York: McGraw-Hill, 1997.

Borthwick, Mark, et al. "Meiji: Japan in the Age of Imperialism." In *The Pacific Century: The Emergence of Modern Pacific Asia*, 119–60. Boulder, Colo.: Westview Press, 1992.

Braudy, Leo, and Marshall Cohen, eds. *Film Theory and Criticism*, 6th ed. Oxford: Oxford University Press, 2004.

Burch, Noel. *Life to Those Shadows*. Chicago: University of Chicago Press, 1990.

Butler, Judith. *Gender Trouble: Feminism and the Subversion of Identity*. New York: Routledge, 1990.

Calichman, Richard, ed. and trans. *Overcoming Modernity*. New York: Columbia University Press, 2008.

Carroll, Noël. "The Specificity Thesis." In *Film Theory and Criticism*, 6th ed., ed. Leo Braudy and Marshall Cohen, 332–38.

———. *Theorizing the Moving Image*. Cambridge: Cambridge University Press, 1996.

Cavallaro, Dana. *The Anime Art of Miyazaki Hayao*. Jefferson, N.C.: McFarland and Company, 2006.

Cheah, Pheng. "Mattering." *Diacritics* 26, no. 1 (Spring 1996): 108–39.

Cholodenko, Alan, ed. *The Illusion of Life II: More Essays on Animation.* Sydney: Power Publications, 2007.

Chow, Rey. *The Age of the World Target: Self-Referentiality in War, Theory, and Comparative Work.* Durham, N.C.: Duke University Press, 2006.

CLAMP. *Chobits.* 8 volumes. Young Magazine Comics. Tokyo: Kōdansha, 2001–2002.

———. "Chobits Interviews." *Newtype USA* 2, no. 3 (March 2003).

———. *CLAMP-su: MANGA aato wa toki o koeru* (The CLAMP-4: manga art transcends time). Kanagawa: Kanagawa-shi shimin myuujiamu and Pairotekunisuto, 2005.

Combes, Muriel. *Simondon, Individu et collectivité* (Simondon: individual and collectivity). Philosophes 117. Paris: Presses Universitaires de France, 1999.

Comolli, Jean-Louis. "Technique and Ideology: Camera, Perspective, Depth of Field." In *Movies and Methods: An Anthology Volume II,* ed. Bill Nichols, 40–57.

Copjec, Joan. *Read My Desire: Lacan against the Historicists.* Cambridge, Mass.: MIT Press, 1994.

Crary, Jonathan. "Modernizing Vision." In *Vision and Visuality,* ed. Hal Foster, 29–44. Seattle, Wash.: Bay Press, 1988.

Daisuke Miyao. "Before *Anime*: Animation and the Pure Film Movement in Pre-War Japan." In "Between Cinema and Anime," ed. Thomas Lamarre, 191–209.

Damisch, Hubert. *The Origin of Perspective.* Trans. John Goodman. Cambridge, Mass.: MIT Press, 1994.

Dean, Kenneth, and Thomas Lamarre. "Microsociology and the Ritual Event." In *Deleuzian Encounters: Studies in Contemporary Social Issues,* ed. Anna Hickey-Moody and Peta Malins, 181–94. New York: Palgrave Macmillan, 2007.

Deleuze, Gilles. "The Brain Is the Screen: An Interview with Gilles Deleuze." In *The Brain is the Screen,* ed. Gregory Flaxman, 365–73. Minneapolis: University of Minnesota Press, 2000.

———. *Cinema I: The Movement-Image.* Minneapolis: University of Minnesota Press, 1986.

———. *Cinema II: The Time-Image.* Minneapolis: University of Minnesota Press, 1989.

———. *The Logic of Sense.* Trans. Mark Lester. New York: Columbia University Press, 1990.

———. "Postscript on Control Societies." In *Negotiations: 1972–1990,* 177–82. New York: Columbia University Press, 1995.

Doane, Mary Anne. "Technophilia: Technology, Representation, and the Feminine." In *Cybersexualites: A Reader on Feminist Theory, Cyborgs, and Cyberspace,* ed. Jenny Wolmark, 20–33. Edinburgh: Edinburgh University Press, 1999.

Dreyfus, Hubert L. "Heidegger on Gaining a Free Relation to Technology." In *Readings in the Philosophy of Technology,* ed. David M. Kaplan, 53–62. Oxford: Rowman and Littlefield, 2004.

Driscoll, Mark. "From Kino-eye to *Anime*-eye/*ai*: The Filmed and the Animated in

Imamura Taihei's Media Theory." In "Between Cinema and Anime," ed. Thomas Lamarre, 269–96.

Dumouchel, Paul. "Simondon's Plea for a Philosophy of Technology." In *Technology and the Politics of Knowledge*, ed. Andrew Feenberg and Alastair Hannay, 225–71. Indianapolis: Indiana University Press, 1995.

Edgerton, Samuel. *The Heritage of Giotto's Geometry: Art and Science on the Eve of the Scientific Revolution*. Ithaca, N.Y.: Cornell University Press, 1991.

Eisenstein, Sergei. *Eisenstein on Disney*. Ed. Jay Leyda. Trans. Alan Upchurch. London: Methuen, 1988.

Fink, Bruce. "Perversion." In *Perversion and the Social Relation*, ed. Molly Anne Rothenberg et al., 38–67.

Foucault, Michel. *Discipline and Punish: The Birth of the Prison*. New York: Vintage Books, 1995.

———. *The Order of Things: An Archaeology of the Human Sciences*. New York: Random House, 1970.

———. *Psychiatric Power: Lectures at the Collège de France 1973–1974*. Trans. Graham Burchell. New York: Picador, 2006.

Frank, Thomas, and Ollie Johnson. *The Illusion of Life: Disney Animation*. New York: Abbeville Press, 1981.

Frasca, Gonzalo. "Simulation versus Narrative: Introduction to Ludology." In *The Video Game Theory Reader*, ed. Mark J. P. Wolf and Bernard Perron, 221–36. London: Routledge, 2003.

Frederick, Jim. "What's Right with Japan." *Time Asia*. August 11, 2003.

Freud, Sigmund. "Fetishism." In *The Standard Edition of the Complete Psychological Works of Sigmund Freud*, 24 volumes, ed. James Strachey, 21:152–57. London: Hogarth, 1953–74.

Friedberg, Anne. *The Virtual Window: From Alberti to Microsoft*. Cambridge, Mass.: MIT Press, 2006.

Friedman, Thomas. *The World Is Flat: A Brief History of the World in the Twenty-first Century*. New York: Farrar, Straus and Giroux, 2007.

Fujimori Terunobu. "Miyazaki anime no kotsu" (The knack of Miyazaki anime). In "Miyazaki Hayao to Sutajio Jiburi," ed. Koori Jun'ichirō, 57–59.

Furniss, Maureen. *Art in Motion: Animation Aesthetics*. Bloomington: Indiana University Press, 1988.

Furuhata, Yuriko. "Return to Actuality: *Fūkeiron* and the Landscape Film." *Screen* 49, no. 3 (Autumn 2007): 345–62.

Gardner, William. "Attack of the Phallic Girls." *Science Fiction Studies* 29, no. 3 (November 2003): 485–88.

Gerow, Aaron. *Visions of Japanese Modernity: Articulations of Cinema, Nation, and Spectatorship 1895–1925*. Berkeley and Los Angeles: University of California Press, forthcoming.

Gotō Tsuyoshi and Kuroda Mitsuhiro. *Mononoke-hime kenkyū josetsu: "Anime" de wa naku "animeeshon" to shite* (An introduction to the study of *Princess Mononoke,* not as "anime" but as "animation"). Tokyo: KK besutoseraazu, 1998.

Gould, Stephen Jay, and Richard C. Lewotin. "The Spandrels of San Marco and the Panglossian Paradigm: A Critique of the Adaptationist Programme." *Proceedings of the Royal Society of London B* 205 (1979): 581–98.

Guattari, Félix. *Chaosmosis: An Ethico-Aesthetic Paradigm.* Trans. Paul Bains and Julian Pefanis. Indianapolis: University of Indiana Press, 1995.

Gunning, Tom. "An Aesthetic of Astonishment: Early Film and the (In)Credulous Spectator." In *Viewing Positions: Ways of Seeing Film,* ed. Linda Williams, 114–33. Piscataway, N.J.: Rutgers University Press, 1995.

Hairston, Marc. "The Secret of Blue Water: Nadia Arrives (Finally) in the US." http://utd500.utdallas.edu/~hairston.mainnadia.html.

Hall, Stuart, et al. *Modernity: An Introduction to Modern Societies.* Cambridge: Polity Press, 1995.

Hansen, Miriam. "The Mass Production of the Senses: Classical Cinema as Vernacular Modernism." In *Reinventing Film Studies,* ed. Christine Gledhill and Linda Williams, 332–50. London: Arnold, 2000.

Haraway, Donna. "The Cyborg Manifesto: Science, Technology, and Socialist-Feminism in the Late Twentieth Century." In *Simians, Cyborgs, and Women: The Reinvention of Nature,* 149–81. London: Routledge, 1991.

Harootunian, H. D. *Overcome by Modernity: History, Culture, and Community in Interwar Japan.* Princeton, N.J.: Princeton University Press, 2000.

Heidegger, Martin. "The Age of the World Picture." In *The Question Concerning Technology and Other Essays,* 115–54. Trans. William Lovitt. New York: Harper and Row, 1977.

———. "The Question Concerning Technology." In *The Question Concerning Technology and Other Essays,* 3–35. Trans. William Lovitt. New York: Harper and Row, 1977.

Hikawa Ryūsuke. "Genjitsu no sokubaku o koeru: Miyazaki-shiki 'animeeshon' no chikara" (Going beyond the constraints of reality: the power of Miyazaki-style "animation"). In *Miyazaki Hayao no sekai,* ed. Umigishi Hirobumi, 78–86.

Holmes, Brian. "Warhol au Soleil levant" (Warhol of the rising sun). *Multitudes* 13 (Summer 2003): http://multitudes.samizdat.net/spip.php?.article1098.

Honda Yūkichi. "Tenkū no shiro Rapyuta" (*Castle in the Sky,* 1986). In "Miyazaki Hayao to Mononoke-hime to Sutajio Jiburi," ed. Uekusa Nobukazu, 126–27.

Horkeimer, Max, and Theodor Adorno. *Dialectics of Enlightenment.* Trans. Joan Cumming. New York: Continuum, 1982.

Hoy, David Couzens. "Power, Repression, Progress." In *Foucault: A Critical Reader,* ed. David Couzens Hoy, 123–47. Oxford: Basil Blackwell, 1986.

Hughes, Thomas P. *Human-Built World: How to Think about Technology and Culture.* Chicago: University of Chicago Press, 2004.

Imamura Taihei. *Manga eiga ron* (On cartoon films). 1941; repr. Tokyo: Tokuma shoten, 2005.

Inoue Shizuka. *Miyazaki Hayao wa sayoku nan darō* (Miyazaki Hayao is to the left). Tokyo: Yoron jihōsha, 1998.

Irigaray, Luce. *This Sex Which Is Not One.* Trans. Catherine Porter with Carolyn Burke. Ithaca, N.Y.: Cornell University Press, 1985.

Ishiko Jun. "Hyuumanizumu ni taisuru yasashisa to kibishisa: Kono futari no meta-morufoozee" (Lenience and severity vis-à-vis humanism: the metamorphosis of these two). In "Miyazaki Hayao to Mononoke-hime to Sutajio Jiburi," ed. Uekusa Nobukazu, 66–70.

Ishiyama Yukihiro. *Kamishibai bunkashi: shiryō de yomitoku kamishibai no rekishi* (A cultural history of kamishibai: reading the history of kamishibai through the material record). Tokyo: Hōbun shorin, 2008.

Itō Hidehiko. "Ano kumo no mine no mukō ni" (Beyond the peak in the clouds). In *Miyazaki Hayao no sekai*, ed. Umigishi Hirobumi, 185–89.

Itoyama Toshikazu. "Miyazaki anime to 'otaku anime': 'bishōjo' ni narenakatta bishōjo-tachi no tame ni" (Miyazaki anime and "otaku anime": for those beautiful girls who did not become "beautiful girls"). In "Miyazaki Hayao no sekai," ed. Sugawa Yoshiyuki, 186–92.

Ivy, Marilyn. "Formations of Mass Culture." In *Postwar Japan as History*, ed. Andrew Gordon, 239–58. Berkeley and Los Angeles: University of California Press, 1993.

Iwai Toshio. *Iwai Toshio no shigoto to shūhen* (Iwai Toshio's works and surroundings). Tokyo: Rikuyosha, 2000.

Jay, Martin. "Scopic Regimes of Modernity." In *Vision and Visuality*, ed. Hal Foster, 3–23. Seattle: Bay Press, 1988.

Jenkins, Henry. *Convergence Culture: Where Old and New Media Collide.* New York: New York University Press, 2006.

Jensen, Jeff, and Steve Daly. "High Toon." *Entertainment Weekly,* June 22, 2001, pp. 50–54.

Kang Jun. *Kamishibai to "Bukimi na mono" tachi no kindai* (Kamishibai and the modernity of those deemed "uncanny"). Tokyo: Seikyūsha, 2007.

Kanō Seiji. "Miyazaki sakuhin no animeeshon gijutsu-kō" (A study of animation techniques in Miyazaki's works). In *Miyazaki Hayao*, ed. Yōrō Takeshi, 90–104.

———. "*Mononoke-hime* no kiso chishiki" (The basic knowledge about *Princess Mononoke*). In "Miyazaki Hayao to Mononoke-hime to Sutajio Jiburi," ed. Uekusa Nobukazu, 50–58.

Kinsella, Sharon. *Adult Manga: Culture and Power in Contemporary Japanese Society.* Honolulu: University of Hawaii Press, 2000.

Kirby, Lynne. *Parallel Tracks: The Railroad and Silent Cinema.* Durham, N.C.: Duke University Press, 1997.

Kirby, Vicki. "Culpability and the Double-Cross: Irigaray with Merleau-Ponty." In *Feminist Interpretations of Maurice Merleau-Ponty*, ed. Dorothy Olkowski and Gail Weiss, 127–146. University Park: Pennsylvania State University Press, 2006.

———. *Judith Butler: Live Theory.* New York: Continuum, 2006.

———. *Telling Flesh: The Substance of the Corporeal.* London: Routledge, 1997.

Kiridooshi Risaku and Maruta Shōzō. *Nihon fūkei ron* (On Japanese landscape). Tokyo: Shunjūsha, 2000.

Kitano Taiitsu. *Nihon anime shigaku kenkyū josetsu* (Introduction to the historical study of Japanese anime). Tokyo: Hachiman shoten, 1998.

Kittler, Friedrich. *Gramophone, Film, Typewriter*. Stanford, Calif.: Stanford University Press, 1999.

Klein, Norman M. "Animation and Animorphs: A Brief Disappearing Act." In *Meta-Morphing: Visual Transformation and the Culture of Quick Change*, ed. Vivian Sobchak, 20–40. Minneapolis: University of Minnesota Press, 2000.

Koori Jun'ichirō, ed. "Miyazaki Hayao to Sutajio Jiburi" (Miyazaki Hayao and Studio Ghibli), special issue, *Eureka* 36, no. 13 (December 2004).

Kotani Mari. "Doll Beauties and Cosplay." Trans. Thomas LaMarre. In *Mechademia 2: Networks of Desire*, ed. Frenchy Lunning, 49–62.

———. "Nanoteku-hime" (Princess nanotech). In "Miyazaki Hayao no sekai," ed. Sugawa Yoshiyuki, 117–23.

———. "Otakuiin wa, otakuia no yume o mita wa" (I Otaqueen have dreamed of otaqueers). In *Mōjō genron F-kai* (Net-state discourses, F-sessions), 115–27. Tokyo: Seidosha, 2003.

———. *Seibō Evangerion* (Immaculate Mother Evangelion). Tokyo: Magazine House, 1997.

———. *Tekuno-goshikku* (Techno-gothic). Tokyo: Hoomu-sha, 2005.

Lacan, Jacques. "Dieu et la jouissance de la femme." In *Le Séminaire de Jacques Lacan. Livre XX. Encore, 1972–1973*, ed. Jacques-Alain Miller, 61–71. Paris: Seuil, 1975.

———. "Du regard comme objet petit a." In *Le Séminaire de Jacques Lacan. Livre XI: Les quatre concepts fondamentaux de la psychanalyse*, ed. Jacques-Alain Miller, 65–109. Paris: Seuil, 1973.

———. "God and the Jouissance of the Woman." Trans. Jacqueline Rose. In *Feminine Sexuality: Jacques Lacan and the École freudienne*, eds. Juliet Mitchell and Jacqueline Rose, 137–48. London: Macmillan, 1982.

———. "Of the Gaze as *Objet petit a*." Trans. Alan Sheridan. In *The Four Fundamental Concepts of Psycho-analysis*, 67–119. New York: Norton, 1978.

Lamarre, Thomas. "Animation Studies." *The Semiotic Review of Books* 17, no. 3 (2008): 1–6.

———. "From Animation to Anime: Drawing Movements and Moving Drawings." In "Between Cinema and Anime," ed. Thomas Lamarre, 329–67.

———. "The Multiplanar Image." In *Mechademia 1: Emerging Worlds of Anime and Manga*, ed. Frenchy Lunning, 120–44.

———. "Otaku Movement." In *Japan after Japan: Rethinking the Nation in an Age of Recession*, ed. Tomiko Yoda and H. D. Harootunian, 358–94. Durham, N.C.: Duke University Press, 2006.

———. "Platonic Sex." *animation: an interdisciplinary journal* 1, no. 1 (2006): 45–60; and 2, no. 1 (2007): 9–25.

————. *Shadows on the Screen: Tanizaki Jun'ichirō on Cinema and "Oriental" Aesthetics.* Center for Japanese Studies. Ann Arbor: University of Michigan Press, 2005.

————, ed. "Between Cinema and Anime," special issue, *Japan Forum* 14, no. 2 (2002).

Latour, Bruno. *We Have Never Been Modern.* Trans. Catherine Porter. Cambridge, Mass.: Harvard University Press, 1993.

Littardi, Cédric. "An Interview with Isao Takahata." Trans. Ken Elescor. *Animeland* 6 (July/August 1992): 27–29; www.nausicaa.net.

Looser, Thomas. "From Edogawa to Miyazaki: Cinematic and *Anime*-ic Architectures of Early and Late Twentieth Century Japan." In "Between Cinema and Anime," ed. Thomas Lamarre, 297–327.

————. "Superflat and the Layers of Image and History in 1990s Japan." In *Mechademia 1: Emerging Worlds of Anime and Manga*, ed. Frenchy Lunning, 92–111.

Lunning, Frenchy, ed. *Mechademia 1: Emerging Worlds of Anime and Manga*. Minneapolis: University of Minnesota Press, 2006.

————, ed. *Mechademia 2: Networks of Desire*. Minneapolis: University of Minnesota Press, 2007.

————, ed. *Mechademia 3: The Limits of the Human.* Minneapolis: University of Minnesota Press, 2008.

Lyotard, Jean-François. *The Postmodern Condition: A Report on Knowledge.* Trans. Geoff Bennington and Brian Massumi. Minneapolis: University of Minnesota Press, 1984.

Mannoni, Octave. "I Know Well, but All the Same . . ." In *Perversion and the Social Relation*, eds. Molly Anne Rothenberg et al., 68–92.

Manovich, Lev. *The Language of New Media.* Cambridge, Mass.: MIT Press, 2001.

Masaki Akira. "Miyazaki anime no kanōsei" (The potentiality of Miyazaki anime). In *Miyazaki Hayao no sekai*, ed. Umigishi Hirobumi, 116–20.

Massumi, Brian. *A User's Guide to Capitalism and Schizophrenia: Deviations from Deleuze and Guattari.* Cambridge, Mass.: MIT Press, 1992.

Matsuda, Matt. "EAST OF NO WEST: The Posthistoire of Postwar France and Japan." In *Confluences: Postwar Japan and France*, ed. Doug Slaymaker, 15–33. Ann Arbor: University of Michigan Press, 2002.

McCarthy, Helen. *Hayao Miyazaki, Master of Japanese Animation: Films, Themes, Artistry.* Berkeley, Calif.: Stone Bridge Press, 1999.

McClintock, Anne. *Imperial Leather: Race, Gender, Sexuality in the Colonial Contest.* New York: Routledge, 1995.

McCloud, Scott. *Understanding Comics: The Invisible Art.* New York: Harper Collins, 1993.

McGray, Douglas. "Japan's Gross National Cool." *Foreign Policy* 130 (May–June 2002): 44–54.

Michaud, Yves. *Humain, Inhumain, Trop Humain: Réflexions philosophiques sur les biotechnologies, la vie et la conservation de soi à partir de l'oeuvre de Peter Sloterdijk* (Human, inhuman, too human: philosophical reflections on biotechnologies, life, and the preservation of self based on the work of Peter Sloterdijk). Paris: Climats, 2002.

Misono Makoto. "Terebi anime reimeiki no paionia-tachi" (The pioneers at the dawn of television animation). In *Zusetsu terebi anime zensho*, ed Misono Makoto, 121–54.

———, ed. *Zusetsu terebi anime zensho* (The complete book of television anime, illustrated). Tokyo: Hara shobō, 1999.

Mitani Kaoru and Nakamura Keiko. *Yamakawa Sōji: "Shōnen ōja" "Shōnen Keniya" no e-monogatari sakka* (Yamakawa Sōji: the artist of such image-stories as *Shōnen ōja* and *Shōnen Keniya*). Tokyo: Kawade shobō, 2008.

Miyazaki Hayao. "Animeeshon to manga eiga" (Animation and manga films, 1982). In *Shuppatsuten: 1979–1996*, ed. Studio Ghibli, 151–58.

———. "Excerpts: Miyazaki on Heroines" (1984–94). http://www.nausicaa.net/miyazaki/interviews/heroines.html (accessed March 15, 2001).

———. "Kojinteki ni wa *Naushika* kara no renzokusei ga arundesu" (Personally, there is continuity with *Nausicaä*, 1986). In *Shuppatsuten 1979–1996*, ed. Studio Ghibli, 477–85.

———. "Nihon animeeshon ni tsuite" (On Japanese animation, 1988). In *Shuppatsuten 1979–1996*, ed. Studio Ghibli, 100–115.

———. "Nihonjin ga ichiban shiawase datta no wa Jōmon jidai" (The Jōmon period was when the Japanese were happiest, 1984). In *Shuppatsuten 1979–1996*, ed. Studio Ghibli, 260–62.

———. "*Tenkū no shiro Rapyuta* kikaku gen'an" (The original plans and ideas for *Castle in the Sky*, 1984). In *Shuppatsuten 1979–1996*, ed. Studio Ghibli, 394–97.

———. "Yutakana shizen, dōji ni kyōbō na shizen nan desu" (A nature at once bountiful and fierce, 1984). In *Shuppatsuten 1979–1996*, ed. Studio Ghibli, 472–76.

Miyazaki Hayao and Murakami Ryū. "Misshitsu kara no dasshutsu" (Escape from the locked room, 1989). In *Shuppatsuten 1979–1996*, ed. Studio Ghibli, 353–65.

Miyazaki Hayao and Satō Tadao. "Miyazaki Hayao—Satō Tadao taidan" (A dialogue between Miyazaki Hayao and Satō Tadao). In "Miyazaki Hayao to Mononoke-hime to Sutajio Jiburi," ed. Uekusa Nobukazu, 32–44.

Monnet, Livia. "'Such Is the Contrivance of the Cinematograph': Dur(anim)ation, Modernity, and Edo Culture in Tabaimo's Animated Installations." In *Cinema Anime*, ed. Steven Brown, 189–225. New York: Palgrave Macmillan, 2006.

Mori Takuya. *Animeeshon nyūmon* (Introduction to animation). Tokyo: Bijutsu shuppansha, 1966.

———. "'Guchoku na kororozashi' e no kussetsu shita sanji: 'Mirai shōnen Konan, kara 'Mononoke-hime' made no kiseki." (A tribute turned toward "sheer honesty:" the trail from *Future Boy Conan* to *Princess Mononoke*). In *Miyazaki Hayao*, ed. Yōrō Takeshi, 59–65.

Morikawa Kaichirō. "Evangerion no dezain riron" (Design theory of *Evangelion*). In *Evangerion sutairu*, ed. Morikawa Kaichirō, 18–31.

———. *Moeru toshi Akihabara: shuto no tanjō* (Learning from Akihabara: the birth of a personapolis). Tokyo: Gentōsha, 2003.

———. "'Otaku' to iu gainen" (The concept of "otaku"). In *Miyazaki Hayao no sekai*, ed. Umigishi Hirobumi, 66–72.

———, ed. *Evangerion sutairu* (The Evangelion Style). Tokyo: Daisan shokan, 1997.

Morris-Suzuki, Tessa. *Beyond Computopia: Information, Automation, and Democracy in Japan*. London: Kegan Paul, 1988.

Mulvey, Laura. "Visual Pleasure and Narrative Cinema." In *Movies and Methods: An Anthology Volume II*, ed. Bill Nichols, 303–14.

Murakami Ryū. *Ai to gensō no fashizumu* (Love and fantasy fascism). 2 vols. Kōdansha bunko 733. Tokyo: Kōdansha, 1990.

Murakami Takashi. "Earth in My Window." In *Little Boy: The Arts of Japan's Exploding Subculture*, ed. Murakami Takashi. New York: Japan Society, 2005.

———. "Superflat Trilogy: Greetings You Are Alive." In *Little Boy: The Arts of Japan's Exploding Subculture*, ed. Murakami Takashi. New York: Japan Society, 2005.

———. "Suupaafuratto Nihon bijutsu ron" and "A Theory of Super Flat Japanese Art." In *Super Flat*, ed. Murakami Takashi, 8–25. Tokyo: MADRA Publishing, 2000.

———, ed. *Super Flat*. Tokyo: MADRA Publishing, 2000.

Murase Hiromi. "Kumorinaki sunda me de mitsumeru 'sei no yami': Miyazaki anime no josei-zō" (The "darkness of sex" viewed with clear cloudless eyes: the image of woman in Miyazaki anime). In *Pop Culture Critique 1: Miyazaki Hayao no chakuchiten o saguru* (Pop Culture Critique 1: investigating sites where Miyazaki Hayao touches down), 53–66. Tokyo: Seikyūsha, 1997.

Nagasawa Mitsuo. *AV joyū* (Adult video actresses). Tokyo: Birejji sentaa, 1996.

Nagase Tadashi. *Yokubō no mirai: kikaijikake no yume no bunkashi* (The futures of desire: a cultural treatise on mechanical dreams). Tokyo: Suiseisha, 1999.

Nakajima Azusa. *Komyunikeeshon fuzenshōkōgun* (Communication insufficiency syndrome). Tokyo: Chikuma shobō, 1995.

Nakano Hitori. *Densha otoko (Train Man)*. Tokyo: Shinchōsha, 2004.

Nakazawa Shin'ichi. "'Gedo senki' no tanoshimikata" (How to enjoy *Tales of Earthsea*). In *Gedo wo yomu* (Reading Earthsea), prod. Itoi Shigesato, 11–60. Tokyo: Iwanami shoten and Studio Ghibli, 2007.

Napier, Susan. "Confronting Master Narratives: History as Vision in Miyazaki Hayao's Cinema of De-assurance." *Positions* 9, no. 2 (Fall 2001): 467–93.

Nichols, Bill, ed. *Movies and Methods: An Anthology Volume II*. Berkeley and Los Angeles: University of California Press, 1985.

Nye, David. *Technology Matters: Questions to Live With*. Cambridge, Mass.: MIT Press, 2006.

Oettermann, Stephan. *Panorama: History of a Mass Medium*. Trans. Deborah Lucas Schneider. New York: Zone Books, 1997.

Okada Emiko. "Miyazaki anime no hiroin no keifu: Hiruda to Runa kara, San, Eboshi-gozen made" (A geneaology of Miyazaki's animation heroines: from

Hilda and Luna, to San and Eboshi-gozen). In "Miyazaki Hayao to Mononoke-hime to Sutajio Jiburi," ed. Uekusa Nobukazu, 45–49.

Okada Toshio. "Interview." *Animerica* 4, no. 3 (March 1996).

———. *Otaku no mayoi-michi* (The labyrinth of otaku). Bunshun bunko 29. Tokyo: Bungei shunshū, 2003.

———. *Otakugaku nyūmon: tōdai "otaku bunkaron zemi" kōnin tekisuto* (Introduction to otakuology: the official text of the "seminar on otaku culture" at Tokyo University). Shinchō OH! bunkō 019. Tokyo: Shinchōsha, 1996.

Okazaki Mari. *Shattaa rabu* (Shutter Love). Margaret Comics 2842. Tokyo: Shūeisha, 1998.

Osborne, Peter. *The Politics of Time: Modernity and the Avant-Garde.* London: Verso, 1995.

Oshii Mamoru. "Interview." In *Miyazaki Hayao, Takahata Isao, Sutajio Jiburi no animeeshon* (Miyazaki Hayao, Takahata Isao, Studio Ghibli animation). Special issue, *KineJunpō* 1166 (July 16, 1995). www.nausicaa.net/miyazaki/interviews/oshii_on_mt.html (accessed May 29, 2006).

———. "'Jissha' to 'dōga' no shinjitsu" (The truth about "live action" and "animation"). In *Subete no eiga wa anime ni naru* (All films are becoming anime), 286–322. 1998; repr. Tokyo: Tokuma shoten, 2004.

———. "Zenryaku Miyazaki Hayao-sama: 'Manga-eiga ni tsuite'" (Dear Miyazaki Hayao: on manga films). In *Subete no eiga wa anime ni naru* (All films are becoming anime), 6–17. 1984; repr. Tokyo: Tokuma shoten, 2004.

Oshii Mamoru and Ueno Toshiya. "Miyazaki Hayao no kōzai, aruiwa, Sutajio Jiburi to iu 'tetsu no tō' ni tsuite" (The merits and demerits of Miyazaki Hayao, or, concerning the "iron party" of Studio Ghibli). In *Miyazaki Hayao no sekai*, ed. Umigishi Hirobumi, 87–106.

Ōshiro Noboru. *Kisha ryokō* (Travel by Rail). 1941; repr. Tokyo: Shōgakukan, 2005.

Ōtsuka Eiji. "'Bunka eiga' to shite no *Momotarō umi no shinpei*" (*Momotarō umi no shinpei* as a "culture film"). In *Shingenjitsu* 4 (April 2007): 115–39.

———. "Disarming Atom: Tezuka Osamu's Manga at War and Peace." Trans. Thomas Lamarre. In *Mechademia 3: The Limits of the Human*, ed. Frenchy Lunning, 111–126.

———. "Nichi-bei kōwa to 'Tetsuwan Atomu': Tezuka Osamu wa naze 'Atomu' wo busō kaijo shita ka" (The U.S.–Japan Peace Treaty and *Tetsuwan Atomu*: why did Tezuka disarm 'Atom'?). *Kan* 22 (Summer 2005): 178–89.

———. *Teihon Monogatari shōhiron* (On narrative consumption, standard text). Kadokawa bunko 39–2. Tokyo: Kadokawa, 2001.

Ōtsuka Eiji et al. "*Hoshi no koe* o kike" (Listen to *Voices of a Distant Star*). Tokyo: Tokuma shoten, 2002.

———. "Sekai no naka no, senjika no otaku" (Otaku in a time of war, in the world). In *Shingenjitsu* 4 (April 2007): 16–28.

Ōtsuka Yasuo, ed. *Nihon manga eiga no zenbō: sono tanjō kara "Sen to Chiro no kami-kakushi," soshite . . .* (A complete view of Japanese manga films: from their birth until *Spirited Away,* and onward . . .). Tokyo: Tōkyō-to gendai bijutsukan, 2004.

———. *Sakuga asemamire* (The blood, sweat, and tears of making pictures). Tokyo: Tokuma shoten, 2001.

Ōtsuka Yasuo and Mori Yūki. *Ōtsuka Yasuo intabyuu: animeeshon jūō mujin* (Ōtsuka Yasuo interviews: animation every which way). Tokyo: Jitsugyō no Nihonsha, 2006.

Patten, Fred. "Simba versus Kimba: Pride of Lions." In *The Illusion of Life II: More Essays on Animation*, ed. Alan Cholodenko, 275–311. Sydney: Power Publications, 2007.

Perrin, Noel. *Giving Up the Gun: Japan's Reversion to the Sword, 1543–1879*. Boulder, Colo.: Shambala Publications, 1979.

Pincus, Leslie. *Authenticating Culture: Kuki Shūzō and the Rise of National Aesthetics*. Berkeley and Los Angeles: University of California Press, 1996.

Rodowick, D. N. "The Difficulty of Difference." In *The Difficulty of Difference*. London: Routledge, 1995.

Rose, Jacqueline. "Introduction—II." In *Feminine Sexuality: Jacques Lacan and the école freudienne*, ed. Juliet Mitchell and Jacqueline Rose, 27–57. New York: Pantheon Books, 1982.

Rothenberg, Molly Anne, and Dennis Foster. "Introduction. Beneath the Skin: Perversion and Social Analysis." In *Perversion and the Social Relation*, ed. Molly Anne Rothenberg et al., 1–14.

Rothenberg, Molly Anne, Dennis Foster, and Slavoj Žižek. *Perversion and the Social Relation*. Durham, N.C.: Duke University Press, 2003.

Rutsky, R. L. *High Technē: Art and Technology from the Machine Aesthetic to the Posthuman*. Minneapolis: University of Minnesota Press, 1999.

Sadamoto Yoshiyuki. *Der Mond*. Tokyo: Kadokawa shoten, 2000.

Sakai, Naoki. "Modernity and Its Critique: The Problem of Universalism and Particularism." In *Postmodernism and Japan*, ed. H. D. Harootunian and Masao Miyoshi, 93–122. Durham, N.C.: Duke University Press, 1989.

———. *Translation and Subjectivity: On "Japan" and Cultural Nationalism*. Minneapolis: University of Minnesota Press, 1997.

Saitō Tamaki. "Otaku sekushuaritii ni tsuite" (On otaku sexuality). In *Hakase no kimyō na shishunki* (The doctor's strange adolescence), 17–56. Tokyo: Nihon hyōronsha, 2003.

———. "Otaku Sexuality." Trans. Christopher Bolton. In *Robot Ghosts and Wired Dreams: Japanese Science Fiction from Origins to Anime*, ed. Christopher Bolton, Istvan Csicsery-Ronay Jr., and Takayuki Tatsumi, 224–49. Minneapolis: University of Minnesota Press, 2007.

———. *Sentō bishōjo no seishin bunseki* (Psychoanalysis of beautiful warrior girls). Tokyo: Ōta shuppan, 2000.

———. *Shakai teki hikikomori: owaranai shishunki* (Social withdrawal: endless adolescence). Tokyo: PHP kenkyūsho, 1998.

———. "'Undō' no ronri, aruiwa hyōshō kontekusuto shiron" (Logic of "movement,"

or a preliminary account of symbolic context). In "Miyazaki Hayao no sekai,"
ed. Sugawa Yoshiyuki, 77–85.

Samuels, David. "Let's Die Together." *Atlantic Monthly,* May 2007.

Santorii Bijutsukan, ed. *Chōjūgiga ga yatte kita! Kokuhō "Chōjūgiga jinbutsu giga emaki"
no zenbō* (The animal caricatures have arrived! A comprehensive view of the
national treasure, *Chōjūgiga jinbutsu giga emaki*). Tokyo: Yomiura shinbunsha,
2007.

Sasaki Toshinao. *Furatto kakumei* (Flat revolution). Tokyo: Kōdansha, 2007.

Sasakibara Gō. "Kantoku izen no Miyazaki Hayo: Miyazaki sakuhin sai'nyūmon no
tame ni" (Miyazaki before he was a director: for a new introduction to the works
of Miyazaki Hayao). In *Miyazaki Hayao no sekai,* ed. Umigishi Hirobumi, 128–32.

Sawaragi Noi. *Nihon—Gendai—Bijutsu* (Japan, Modern, Art). Tokyo: Shinchōsha, 1998.

Schaffer, William. "Animation I: Control Image." In *The Illusion of Life 2: More
Essays on Animation,* ed. Alan Cholodenko, 456–85. Sydney: Power Publications,
2007.

Schivelbusch, Wolfgang. *The Railway Journey: The Industrialization of Time and Space
in the 19th Century.* Berkeley and Los Angeles: University of California Press,
1986.

Sharff, Robert C., and Val Dusek, ed. *Philosophy of Technology: The Technological
Condition.* London: Blackwell, 2003.

Sharp, Jasper. "Between Dimensions: 3D Computer-Generated Animation in Anime."
In *Ga-Netchū: The Manga-Anime Syndrome,* 120–33. Frankfurt am Main:
Deutsches Filminstitut, 2008.

Shimamoto Shūji, ed. *Anime no hajimari Chōjūgiga* (*Chōjūgiga,* the beginning of
anime). Nihon no bi o meguru 15. Tokyo: Shōgakukan, 2002.

Shimizu Tomoko. "'Jiburi monsutaazu' to kankaku no toporojii" ("Ghibli monsters"
and the topology of sensation). In *Miyazaki Hayao no sekai,* ed. Umigishi
Hirobumi, 107–15.

Simondon, Gilbert. *Du mode d'existence des objects techniques* (On the mode of existence of technical objects). Paris: Éditions Aubier, 1958.

Singer, Ben. *Melodrama and Modernity: Early Sensational Cinema and Its Contexts.*
New York: Columbia University Press, 2001.

Sloterdjik, Peter. *Regeln für den Menschenpark: Ein Antwortschreiben zu Heideggers
"Brief über den Humanismus."* (Rules for the human park: a reply to Heidegger's
"Letter on Humanism"). Frankfurt am Main: Suhrkamp, 1999.

Solomon, Charles. "Four Mothers of Manga Gain American Fans with Expertise in a
Variety of Visual Styles." *New York Times,* November 28, 2006.

Steinberg, Marc. "Immobile Sections and Trans-series Movement: *Astro Boy* and the
Emergence of Anime." *Animation: An Interdiscipinary Journal* 1, no. 2 (2006):
190–206.

———. "Otaku Consumption, Superflat Art, and the Return to Edo." *Japan Forum* 16,
no. 3 (November 2004): 449–71.

Stengers, Isabelle. "Introductory Notes on an Ecology of Practices." *Cultural Studies Review* 11, no. 1 (2005): 183–96.

Stewart, Ian. *Nature's Numbers: The Unreal Reality of Mathematics.* Boston: Basic Books, 1995.

Studio Ghibli, ed. *Shuppatsuten: 1979–1996* (Point of departure, 1979–1996). Tokyo: Tokuma shoten, 1996.

Studlar, Gaylyn. "Masochism and the Perverse Pleasures of Cinema." In *Movies and Methods: An Anthology Volume II*, ed. Bill Nichols, 602–21.

Sugawa Yoshiyuki, ed. "Miyazaki Hayao no sekai," special issue, *Eureka* 29, no. 11 (August 1997).

Sugiyama Taku. "Terebi anime zenshi: Tōei chōhen anime no jidai" (Prehistory of television anime: the age of Tōei's feature-length anime). In *Zusetsu terebi anime zensho*, ed. Misono Makoto, 91–120.

Sun Ge. "In Search of the Modern: Tracing Japanese Thought on 'Overcoming Modernity.'" Trans. Peter Button. In "Impacts of Modernity," ed. Thomas Lamarre and Kang Nae-hui. Special issue, *Traces* 3 (2004): 53–76.

Suzuki Shin'ichi. *Anime ga sekai o tsunagu* (Anime connects the world). Iwanami junia shinsho 591. Tokyo: Iwanami shoten, 2008.

Takahata Isao. *Animeeshon no kokorozashi: "Yabunirami no bōkun" to "Ō to tori"* (The ambition of animation: *La Bergère et le ramoneur* and *Le Roi et l'oiseau*). Tokyo: Iwanami shoten, 2007.

———. *Eiga o tsukurinagara kangaeta koto* (My thoughts while making films). Tokyo: Tokuma shoten, 1991.

———. *Jūni seiki no animeeshon: kokuhō emakimono ni miru eigateki—animeteki naru mono* (Twelfth-century animation: cinematic and animetic effects seen in our national treasure picture scrolls). Tokyo: Tokuma shoten, 1999.

———. "Kessaku emaki wa ika ni shite umareta no ka" (How were the masterpieces of illustrated scrolls born?). *Bijutsu techō* 59: 901 (November 2007): 82–88.

Takayuki Tatsumi. *Full Metal Apache: Transactions between Cyberpunk Japan and Avant-Pop America.* Durham, N.C.: Duke University Press, 2007.

Takeda Yasuhiro. *Nootenki tsūshin: Evangelion o tsukutta otoko-tachi* (Nootenki memoirs: the men who created Evangelion). Tokyo: Wani bukkusu, 2002.

———. *Notenki Memoirs: Studio Gainax and the Men Who Created Evangelion.* Houston, Tex.: ADV Manga, 2005.

Talbot, Margot. "The Auteur of Anime." *New Yorker*, January 17, 2005.

Tanizaki Akira. "Anime mekanikku hensenshi" (A history of transformations in anime mecha). In *Zusetsu terebi anime zensho*, ed. Misono Makoto, 155–82.

Thain, Alanna. "Wandering Stars: William Kentridge's Err(ant) Choreographies." *parallax* 14, no. 1 (2008): 68–81.

Tokusatsu Takarajima henshūbu and "Kono manga ga sugoi" sentei kaiinkai, eds. *Kono manga ga sugoi* (These manga are awesome). Tokusatsu Takarajima 257. Tokyo: Takarajima-sha, 1996.

Tsugata Nobuyuki. *Nihon animeeshon no chikara: hachijūgo nen no rekishi o tsuranuku futatsu no jiku* (The power of Japanese animation: two axes running through an eighty-five year history). Tokyo: NTT shuppan, 2004.

———. *Nihon hajime no animeeshon sakka Kitayama Seitarō* (Kitayama Seitarō, Japan's first animation artist). Tokyo: Rinsen shoten, 2007.

Tsuji Masaki. *Bokutachi no anime shi* (Our anime history). Iwanami junia shinsho 587. Tokyo: Iwanami shoten, 2008.

Tsuji Nobuo. *Kisō no keifu* (The geneaology of eccentricity). Tokyo: Chikuma shobō, 2004.

Tsukihashi Osamu. "Eizō gihō to sakuhin no kōzō: Eva sutorakuchaa" (Image techniques and the structure of the work: the structure of *Evangelion*). In *Evangerion sutairu*, ed. Morikawa Kaichirō, 40–53.

Tsuneishi Fumiko. "Tenkū no shiro Rapyuta: tenkū no nokosarejima." (*Castle in the Sky*: the abandoned island in the sky). In *Miyazaki Hayao*, ed. Yōrō Takeshi, 126–29.

Uekusa Nobukazu, ed. "Miyazaki Hayao to Mononoke-hime to Sutajio Jiburi" (Miyazaki Hayao, *Princess Mononoke*, and Studio Ghibli), special issue, *Kinema junpō* 1233 (September 2, 1997).

Ueno Toshiya. "Japanimation and Techno-Orientalism." http://www.t0.or.at/ueno/japan.htm (Accessed September 10, 2008).

———. *Kurenai no metaru suutsu: anime to iu senjō* (Blood-red metal suits: the battlefield called anime). Tokyo: Kinokuniya shoten, 1998.

———. "Majo ni sayonara o iu no wa muzukashii" (It's hard to say goodbye to the magical girl). In *Miyazaki Hayao no sekai*, ed. Umigishi Hirobumi, 24–32.

Umigishi Hirobumi, ed. *Miyazaki Hayao no sekai* (The world of Miyazaki Hayao). Tokyo: Takeshobō, 2005.

Varela, Francisco, Evan Thompson, and Eleanor Rosch. *The Embodied Mind: Cognitive Science and Human Experience*. Cambridge, Mass.: MIT Press, 1993.

Virilio, Paul. "Cyberwar, God, and Television: Interview with Louise Wilson." In *Digital Delirium*, ed. Arthur Kroker and Marilouise Kroker, 41–48. Montréal: New World Perspectives, 1997.

———. *Pure War*. 2nd ed. New York: Semiotext(e), 1997.

———. *War and Cinema: The Logistics of Perception*. London: Verso, 1989.

Weber, Samuel. *Theatricality as Medium*. New York: Fordham University Press, 2004.

Williams, Linda. "Film Bodies: Gender, Genre, and Excess." In *Film Theory and Criticism*, 6th Edition, ed. Leo Braudy and Marshall Cohen, 727–41.

Yamaguchi Katsunori and Watanabe Yasushi. *Nihon animeeshon eiga shi* (A history of Japanese animation films). Osaka: Yūbunsha, 1978.

Yokokawa Sumiko. *Shochō to iu kirifuda: "shōjo" hihanjosetsu* (Menarchy as trump card: a critical introduction to "shojo"). Tokyo: JICC shuppan, 1991.

Yoneyama, Lisa. *Hiroshima Traces: Time, Space, and the Dialectics of Memory*. Berkeley and Los Angeles: University of California Press, 1999.

Yonezawa Yoshihiro. "Manga to anime to Miyazaki Hayao" (Manga, anime, and Miyazaki Hayao). In *Miyazaki Hayao no sekai*, ed. Umigishi Hirobumi, 156–64.

———. *Sengo shōjo manga* (Postwar shojo manga). Chikuma bunko 19. Tokyo: Chikuma, 2007.

Yōrō Takeshi, ed. *Miyazaki Hayao*. Firumumeekaazu 6. Tokyo: Kinema junpō sha, 1994.

Yoshimura Yasutaka. "Rokujū nendai no mochiifu: Evangerion-pop no tame no sonata" (Sonata for Evangelion-pop: a compilation of 1960s motifs). In *Evangerion sutairu*, ed. Morikawa Kaichirō, 32–39.

Zielinski, Siegfried. *Deep Time of the Media: Toward an Archaeology of Hearing and Seeing by Technical Means*. Trans. Gloria Custance. Cambridge, Mass.: MIT Press, 2006.

Zion, Lee. "*Nadia* vs. *Atlantis*, Revisited!" *AnimeNewsNetwork*, http://www.animenewsnetwork.com/feature/2001-07-19.

Žižek, Slavoj. "Eastern Europe's Republics of Gilead." *New Left Review* 183 (September/October 1990): 50–62.

———. *Enjoy Your Symptom! Jacques Lacan in Hollywood and Out*. New York: Routledge, 1992.

———. *The Fright of Real Tears: Krzysztof Kieslowski between Theory and Post-theory*. London: BFI, 2001.

———. *Looking Awry: An Introduction to Jacques Lacan through Popular Culture*. Cambridge, Mass.: MIT Press, 1991.

———. *On Belief*. New York: Routledge, 2001.

———. *Tarrying with the Negative: Kant, Hegel, and the Critique of Ideology*. Durham, N.C.: Duke University Press, 1993.

postmodern, 170; public policy, 249, 311; rhetoric of, 161, 194; superflat, 111–13, 116, 145–46; time-image, 185–86; VCR, 145

Animeland, 147

animetic interval, 10, 23, 201, 210, 298, 316; character animation, 73, 195–96, 201, 283, 297, 298, 310, 312, 341n35; commerce, 96, 314–15; compositing, 32, 162, 191, 286, 309, 313; definition, xxx, 7; digital animation, 22; editing and, 196; full animation, 73, 76, 190, 297; instrumentalization, 9; limited animation, 196, 199–200, 297, 306; media mix, 302–3; Miyazaki, 74, 76, 85, 104, 305; movement, 8, 301, 313; *Nadia,* 308; techniques, 18–19, 23, 303; technology and, xxxvi, 25, 312. *See also* animetic machine; indetermination; spacing

animetic machine, xxvii, 18, 76, 86, 191, 309; Anno and, 200; apparatus and, xxxiii, 25, 317; cinematism and, 7, 10, 37, 43, 62, 77, 133; compositing, 36–37; cultural determination, 89; Daicon animation, 133; definition, xxvi, xxxi, 33, 38, 44, 134, 159, 301; depth, 7, 38; divergent series, xxxiv, 301, 303–4, 310; flying, 61–62, 95; Miyazaki and, 38, 42–43, 61–62, 77, 100, 133, 305; Tabaimo and, 105; thinking and feeling, xxviii, xxx, xxxvi. *See also* animetic interval; machine; multiplanar machine

aminetism, 9, 36; anime and, 10; definition, 9; Ōtomo and, 7; potential of moving image, 7, 9–10, 44; technological condition, 6–7, 54, 94, 98

animism, 66, 78, 330n2

Anne of Green Gables, 58, 59

annihilation, xxxvii, 156, 169, 179, 214, 219–20, 231, 305. *See also* destruction

Anno Hideaki, xxxvi; anime-media networks, 186, 316; auteur, 319; background, 129, 146–47; critique of otaku, 149, 151, 154, 173, 179–80, 315–16; editing, 183, 196; exploded view, 185; Gainax and, 129, 147, 186, 190; gender, 215; hyperlimited animation, 193–96, 203, 283, 297; Hayao Miyazaki and, 156, 151, 154, 173, 179–80, 315–16; multiplication of frames, 165, 308; Murakami Takashi and, 146, 180, 214; as Oedipal, 343n9; Okada Toshio and, 129, 146, 149, 151; post-Heideggerian, xxxvi, 298; salvation, 170; sketches, 129–30, 135; Tabaimo and, 162; thinking technology, 156, 162, 170, 183, 200, 203, 213–14, 215, 225, 298, 315, 321. *See also Nadia; Neon Genesis Evangelion*

antiquity (ancient), 13–14, 66, 78, 96, 114, 155, 165, 172, 330n2

Anzu to Zushiomaru, 58

apocalyptic imagery, xxxi, 51, 119, 137, 139, 231–2. *See also* postapocalyptic

apparatus theory, x, 4–5, 17, 26, 282, 301; determinism, xix–xx, xxv–xxvi, xxxii, 33–34, 44; film history, 14, 25, 90

A Pro, 58

Ari-chan. See Little Ant

Armitage III, 216, 235

art. *See* hand, (art)work of the

art history, x, 12–13, 104, 114

Aru machikado no monogatari (Tezuka), 188

Arumiteeji za saado. See Armitage III

Arupusu no shōjo Haiji, 40, 58, 59

assembly diagram, 120–21, 132, 142, 148, 174, 192, 196, 203, 260, 262, 267, 288, 298, 308, 321

Astro Boy (Tezuka), 145–46, 186–88, 202, 204, 300, 316, 338n1

atomic bombs, xxxvi, 6, 117, 139, 142, 163–64

attractor, 266, 273–75, 279, 289, 307

auteur, xxxiii, 87, 315–19

autopoiesis, xxxi, xxxiii, 88, 111, 275, 347n15, 347n16

Avalon, 35, 125

Avatar: The Last Airbender, 36

Azuma Hiroki, xi, xxxvii, 213, 266, 274, 298, 316, 353n3; background, 257–58; Cartesian, 279, 282–83, 297, 308; character, 260–61, 272, 300–301, 312, 315; database, 245, 252, 256, 257, 259–60, 267, 273, 279; gender, 262–63; Hegel (Kojève), 284, 308; human, 260; Lacan, 268–71, 279, 282, 284, 297; logic of rupture, 272–73; *moe*, 259–60, 272–73, 285; narrative, 170, 271–72, 300–301, 315; otaku, 109, 258–60, 263, 272; postmodern, 170, 260, 267, 270, 279; Saitō Tamaki and, 258, 262; superflat, 267–70; technological condition, 259

Baburugamu kuraishisu TOKYO 2040. *See* Bubble Gum Crisis

Back, Frédéric, 147

background, xxiii, 9, 16, 21, 74, 112, 204; art, xxvii, 20, 65, 104, 110, 126, 159–60, 189, 245–46, 318; depth, 17–18, 30, 105, 110, 125, 130, 133, 192; frame of reference, 133, 306; reuse, 17, 64; rotoscoping, 65–66; weightlessness, 72. *See also* landscape

ballistics: cinematism, 6, 11, 30, 43, 54, 60, 77, 92, 138; definition, xvi; hyper-Cartesian, 11, 31, 125, 128, 130, 219, 306; information, 136; movement into depth, 20, 27, 105, 133, 136, 147, 175, 177; one-point perspective, 5, 27–28, 131, 135; perception, 46, 127, 131–32, 304–5; technological condition, 5, 42, 60–61, 63, 116–17, 139, 148, 156, 169, 171

Bambi, 73

Baudry, Jean, xix, xxvi–xxvii

Beauty and the Beast, 72

benshi, 14, 193

Bergson, Henri, xxxii–xxxiii, xxxv, 279

Bishōjo senshi Seeraa Muun. See Sailor Moon

Blue Sky Studios, 73

body, 46, 81, 94, 219, 269, 276, 299; animation of, 70–71, 73–74, 79, 183, 192–93; engineering and enclosing, 168, 172, 174, 305; fetishism, 227–31, 233, 278, 281, 283, 316, 321; gender, 82–83, 93, 220, 221, 223, 227, 238, 246; human dimension, 42, 60–61, 67; mecha and, 129–30, 212; mind and, x, xxxv, xxvii; sensorimotor schema (movement-image), 124, 198–200, 202, 203, 303, 310, 312, 315, 320; spectralized, 234, 266, 279, 317. *See also* embodiment of movement in character; encephalization; gynoid; soulful bodies

Bogue, Ronald, xxxii

Bordwell, David, x, xxi

boys: address to, 216–18, 252, 290; adventure genre, 51–52, 60, 79, 81; energies and roles, 78–83, 213; mecha and, 215–16; Murakami Takashi and, 117–18, 128, 137, 262; otaku, 108–9, 128, 150, 152, 250; technophilia, 156, 179, 209–10, 212–13, 219. *See also* gender; girls; shojo

brand, 87, 97–99, 190, 227, 311, 315

Brave Saga, 271

Bray, John, 16

Bubble Gum Crisis, 216

bunmei kaika, xxxv

Burch, Noel, 21

Butler, Judith, 213, 255, 271

camera: animation and, xxiv–xxv, xxix–xxx, 9, 16, 19, 20, 22, 23, 30–33, 37–38, 73, 124, 126–27, 157, 162, 189, 191, 283, 298; animetism and, 37; apparatus theory and, xix, xxvi–xxvii,

design, 229–30, 282; costume, 229, 263; crisis of movement-image, 316–18; eyes, 277–78; family drama, 233, 253–54; fetishism, 231, 233, 242–43, 257, 283; noir, 238–39; otaku, 248–51, 257; perversion, 246–47, 250–51, 276, 297–98, 320; pornography, 240–41, 318–19; sexuality, 222–25, 235–37, 239–40, 257; story, 221–25, 232; structure of shots, 285–86, 293–95, 318–19; thinking technology, 219–20, 225, 231–33, 241, 255, 320–21

Chōjū jinbutsu giga emaki, 13

Chōjuku yōsai Macross. See Macross

Chōjuku yōsai Macross: Ai oboete imasu ka. See Superdimensional Fortress Macross: Do You Remember Love?

Chow, Rei, 117, 168, 213

cinema: animation and, xix, xxi–xxiii, xxviii, xxx, 7–9, 12, 14, 21–22, 34–37, 86, 89, 114, 124–25, 191, 286–87, 292, 297, 299, 309, 313–14; apparatus theory and, xix, xxvii, 5, 17, 26–27, 34, 301; character animation and, 64, 67–68, 72–73; classical, 197–98, 280–83, 287–88, 290–92, 309–10, 312, 316; deep time, 13; Deleuze and, ix, 196–99, 201, 291, 312–13; early, xiii, xx–xxi, xxiii, 14, 21, 31, 72; live action, 19, 31, 33, 65, 72, 124, 292, 304; manga and, 288–92, 317–18; mobile camera, xxiv, xxv, xxx, 32, 34–35, 124, 127, 191; modernity, xiii–xix, 138, 197–98, 262; modernity thesis, xxi; specificity thesis, xx–xix, xxxi, 14–15; trains and, xiii–xiv, 3–5; Žižek and, 284–86

cinematism: action film and, 34, 43, 54; animation, 9, 34, 35, 73; animetism and, 6–7, 10, 36, 133; Daicon animations and, 128, 133, 138; definition, 5–6, 304; digital animation, 34–35; hyper-Cartesianism, 11, 35, 126, 282; Miyazaki's resistance to, 38–42, 60, 62, 77, 92, 305–6; movement into depth, 31, 34, 77; multiplane camera and, 25, 30; one-point perspective and, 26–28; technological condition, 11, 43, 60, 200, 305; tendency, 10, 34, 37, 44. *See also* animetism; open compositing

CLAMP: address to girls, 222–23, 229–30; address to young men, 231, 283, 319–20; background, 218, 228, 233, 318–19; character design, 229–30; thinking technology, xxxvi, 225, 298, 315–17

classical film style. *See* cinema: classical

clean-up, 9, 70–71, 74, 86

closed compositing, xxiv, 32, 37, 40, 65, 73, 132–33, 200, 304–5. *See also* compositing

Cohl, Émile, xxix

comics, 13, 218, 288. *See also* manga

commodity, xxviii, xxxv, 96–97, 99, 153, 170, 202, 260, 302, 312, 335n3

communication networks and technologies, xvi, xxxvi, 81–82, 116, 139, 143, 225, 241, 260, 304, 310–12, 314–15, 321

Comolli, Jean-Louis, xix, xxv–xxvi, 282

compositing: artwork and, xxix; character animation and, 72, 130, 192, 200, 203, 217, 297, 313; composition and, 30, 32, 307, 309; definition, xxiv, 31, 125; depth, 32, 37–38, 73, 130, 304; digital animation and, 33, 36, 41, 65, 124, 200, 304; editing, 162, 191, 286; machine, 33; priority in animation, xxiv–xv, xxvii–xxiv, xxx, 9, 36, 124–25, 159, 191, 283, 286, 303, 317, 327n4; technological condition and, 44, 54. *See also* closed compositing; flat compositing; open compositing; volumetric compositing

computer, 16, 200, 218, 257, 277, 279,

320; animation, xxv; animation production, 12, 31, 36, 41, 65, 70, 87, 318; animation reception, xiv, xvi, 148, 259, 290, 310; fetishism, 231, 251, 256–57; gender and, 218, 221–24, 226, 235, 264, 299, 318; hystericization and, 316, 320; imagery, ix, xiii, xxii; perversion and, 243–44, 247, 251, 316; screen, xvii, 137, 290; technological condition, 225, 241, 242, 250, 258–59, 268, 321

Conan, 40, 42, 55, 58–59, 67, 74–76, 78, 95, 156, 329n5

convergence, xviii, 34, 96, 284, 294, 302–3, 311–16, 348n2; visual, 131, 141

cooperator. *See* attractor

Copjec, Joan, 213, 282–83

cosplay, xiv, 151, 185, 220, 263–64

Crary, Jonathan, 114, 198, 213

cultural choice, 91–95

cultural determinism. *See* determinism: cultural; Japaneseness

culturalism. *See* determinism: cultural; Japaneseness

cultural nationalism. *See* Japaneseness

Cutie Honey (Anno), 316

cut-paper animation, 16, 23–24

cyborg, 215–18, 262, 264, 341–42n35

Daicon (Osaka Science Fiction Convention), 129, 130, 146, 150

Daicon III Opening Animation, 87, 129–34. *See also* Daicon animations; Daicon Studios

Daicon IV Opening Animation, 87, 134–43. *See also* Daicon animations; Daicon Studios

Daicon animations, 147, 151, 154, 194, 203, 308

Daicon Studios, 134, 143, 146. *See also* Gainax Studios

Daikubara Akira, 67–68, 71

Damisch, Hubert, 120

database structure. *See* structure: database

dehierarchizing, 108, 110–11, 118–19, 122–23, 126, 134, 145, 149, 161, 183, 200, 204, 266, 273–74, 289, 299, 301, 306–7, 309, 315. *See also* distributive field

De Ji Kyaratto. See Di Gi Charat

Deleuze, Gilles, xxix, 185, 196–99, 201–2, 213, 287–88, 291–92, 294, 312–14, 317, 341n27, 341n33, 349n8, 349n11

Den'ei shōjo Video Girl Ai. See Video Girl Ai

Densha otoko. See Train Man

depth: affective, 299; effects of, 17–19, 32, 42, 45, 46, 62, 103–4, 119–20, 125–26, 192; of field, xxv, 17, 19, 30, 125–26, 129, 133; iconic, 126, 192; implied, 204; movement between layers and, 7, 18, 60, 62, 77, 191; movement into, xxv, 7, 9, 19–23, 25, 30–32, 34, 37–38, 72–73, 77, 105, 124–25, 129, 283, 304–5, 309; movement over or across, 38–41, 104, 110, 130, 214, 306; panoramic, 104, 110; perceptual, 270; perspective and, 269–70, 283, 298, 306; potential, 133–34, 136–37, 153, 173, 176–77, 185, 298, 313, 315, 321; preexisting, 105, 130, 133, 143, 160, 166; psychological, 177, 206; relative, 147, 166, 171; structures of, 113–14, 122, 130, 134, 147, 281, 298; surface, 107, 110, 126–27, 131–33, 136–37, 147, 172, 191, 193, 203, 266, 269, 277, 283, 297; volumetric, 40, 73, 105, 126, 133. *See also* background; Cartesianism; superflat; superplanarity

Derrida, Jacques, xxxvi, 213, 257

destruction, xxxv–xxxvi, 42, 45, 47–51, 53, 58, 82–84, 91–92, 117–18, 134, 137, 139, 142, 147, 155, 157, 162, 167, 179, 211, 215, 217, 232–33. *See also* annihilation

determination: authorial, 88, 91; cultural,

xxvii, 15, 88, 90, 91, 302; determinism and, xxiii, xxxi, 88, 119, 301; economic, xxxviii, 302; machine and, xxiii–xxiv, 34, 88, 119, 303–4; material, x, xxxi, 33, 99, 282–84, 286; social, xxxviii, 302; socioeconomic, xi; sociohistorical, 89; technical, x–xi, xxvii–xxviii, xxx, 15, 88–90, 94, 302–4; technological, xxvii, 89, 92, 119, 267–68, 282, 284, 302. *See also* determinism; indetermination; machine; underdetermination

determinism: apparatus theory and, x, xix–xx, xxi, xxv–xxvi, xxxii, 14, 44, 88; cultural, xxviii, 15, 89, 92, 95; determination and, xxiii, xxxi, 88, 119, 301; modernity theory and, 116–117, 119, 122, 137; specificity thesis and, x, xx–xxii; structures of perspective and, 26, 44, 116, 119, 122, 259, 303; technological, x, xix–xx, xxii, xxv–xxvii, xxxii, 14, 26, 42, 44, 49–50, 85, 88, 90–91, 96, 116–17, 118, 137, 259, 279, 301–3. *See also* determination; technological condition

diagram: abstract, 33–34, 38, 70–71; assembly, 132, 140, 148, 174, 177, 192, 203, 267, 288, 308; scientific, 121–22, 131, 160, 211

Di Gi Charat, 260–61

digital animation, ix, xxiii, xxv, xxx, 17, 22–23, 31, 33–35, 41, 65, 70, 72–73, 87, 125–26, 128, 200, 283, 304, 309, 317, 318

digital film, 31, 35, 65, 124

digitalization, xv, 150, 153, 257, 259, 314

diorama, 3–4, 6–7

Disney, Walt, xxv, 19, 21–24, 30, 66, 73, 147, 204

Disney animations, xxix, 10, 19, 25, 64, 66–68, 73–74, 86, 90, 186–88, 212, 287, 327n11, 337n1

distributive field, 110, 122, 133, 137, 139, 141, 143–45, 148, 160, 168, 175,

183, 192, 266–67, 293–75, 279, 283, 289–90, 298, 306–7, 309–10, 315. *See also* dehierarchizing

divergence: animation, 304, 316; convergence and, 311, 316; machinic, xxxiv, 122; material, 268, 311, 320, 348n2; moving image and, 36, 297, 321; visual field, 131, 135, 141

divergent series, xxvi–xxvii, xxx, xxxii–xxxiv, 10, 15, 34, 36–37, 96, 120, 122, 143, 171, 284, 291, 297, 301–4, 310–12, 314–15, 320–21

division of labor. *See* workflow

Doane, Mary Anne, 262

dōga, 35–36, 42, 58, 59, 60, 74, 77

dōjinshi, xii–xiv, 151, 185, 204, 218, 318

Doraemon, 136

Dreyfus, Hubert, 50, 53, 83–84, 95

dubbing, 56, 89

early cinema. *See* cinema: early

Edgerton, Samuel, 115–16, 120–21, 136, 211

editing, x, 20, 132, 162, 196, 286–87, 292–93, 297–99, 317, 341n26; continuity editing, 196, 286; internal, xxiv, xxviii, 9, 125, 191, 286, 303; superplanar, 196

Edo, 13, 17, 111, 113–16, 119–20, 145, 149, 173, 287, 307, 335n3. *See also* Tokugawa

Eien kazoku. See Eternal Family

Eitoman. See Tobor the Eighth Man

emaki, 13

embodiment of movement in character, 73, 129–30, 168, 195, 199, 202, 283, 298–99

emergence: theories of, 273–74, 289, 291. *See also* distributive field

encephalization, 199, 320

enframing, 62–63, 162, 166, 168–69, 171, 174, 188, 192, 196, 200, 203

enjoyment, 242, 265–66, 268, 282

machine, xi, xxiii–xxix, xxxi–xxxiv, 15,
23, 25, 33–34, 88–89, 111, 119–20, 143,
275, 301, 303–4, 309–10. *See also* animetic machine; multiplanar machine

Macross, 146–47, 150, 194, 202, 211,
271, 300

Magic Boy. See Shōnen Sarutobi Sasuke

Magic Knight Rayearth, 218

Mahha Go Go Go. See Speed Racer

*Mahō kishi majikku naito reiaasu. See
Magic Knight Rayearth*

Majingaa Z. See Mazinger Z

*Majo no takkyūbin. See Kiki's Delivery
Service*

manga: adaptations, 58, 153, 187, 202,
217–18, 222, 272, 292, 300, 311,
316–18; circulation, xvii–xviii, 108–9,
170, 180, 185, 211–12, 228, 267, 318;
eyes, 277–78; moving image and,
286–92, 310, 312, 317; otaku and, 117,
150–52, 185, 249, 254–55, 258; production, 318–19; style, 13–14, 105

manga-eiga. See manga film

manga film, 35, 42–43, 56–57, 60, 98, 145,
159, 184, 186–91, 287, 318

Mannoni, Octave, 247

Manovich, Lev, xxviii, 35

Marx, xxi, 91

masculinity, 60–61, 78, 83, 210–12, 216,
233, 257. *See also* boys; father

mass destruction. *See* destruction

material essence. *See* essence: material

Mazinger Z, 202, 211, 343n11

McClintock, Anne, 213, 237, 256–57

McCloud, Scott, 13

McGray, Douglas, 249

McLaren, Norman, xxiv, xxix, 66

McLuhan, Marshall, 91

mecha, 129–30, 145, 147, 165, 173, 194,
200, 211–12, 215–16; shojo and, 217–20,
232–35, 264. *See also* mechaphilia

mechaphilia, 212, 214–15, 217, 219,
225–26. *See also* technophilia

media, xxx, 275, 288, 302; across, xiv,
xvi, 97, 150, 203, 300, 310–11, 319;
art, 105–7, 111, 162; categories, 10;
condition, xxi, xxii; convergence, xviii,
302–4, 313, 315; fields, 203; flows, 109;
franchises, 300; global, xxii; interactions, xxi; mass, 108, 153; mix, xvi,
xxii, 186, 272, 303; networks, 114, 128,
179; new, 35–36, 97, 279; platforms,
35, 156, 310–11; practices, xx, 109;
storage, 148; structures, 258; types,
108; worlds, xiv, 108

Memories, 7

Metropolis (Lang), 136

micromasses, xxxiv. *See also* subculture

military, xxxvi, 6, 28, 47–48, 90, 117–19,
122, 125, 128, 137, 139, 142, 153, 175,
210–12

Mind Game, 7

Mirai shōnen Konan. See Conan

Miyaji Mariko, 67

Miyazaki, Hayao: animetism, 42–43;
auteur, 87–88; background, 59–66,
155–56, 189; commerce, 97–100;
depth, 20–21, 103–5, 110, 147; gender,
70, 78–85, 169, 210–14; Heidegger
and, xxxvi, 44, 50–52, 83–84, 225;
humanism, 51–52; lineage, 42–43,
74, 145, 184, 186–87; open compositing, 25, 38–42, 54, 132–33, 305;
techniques, 71, 74–76, 160, 189–90;
thinking technology, 42–44, 47–50,
52–54, 59–63, 77–78, 91–96, 138, 170,
188, 198, 217, 305–7, 315; Paul Virilio
and, 42, 116–28

Miyazaki Tsutomu, 151, 179, 248, 255

modernity thesis, xxi–xxiii, 5

modernization theory, xxi, xxxiv–xxxvi,
115–18, 121–22, 137, 211, 307

moe, 258–61, 265, 270, 272–74, 281, 285,
290–91, 300

Mokona Apapa, 218

Momotarō no umiwashi, 28–29